Chinese Communication
Theory and Research

Chinese Communication Theory and Research

Reflections, New Frontiers, and New Directions

Edited by
Wenshan Jia, Xing Lu, and D. Ray Heisey

Advances in Communication and Culture

Ablex Publishing
Westport, Connecticut • London

Library of Congress Cataloging-in-Publication Data

Chinese communication theory and research : reflections, new frontiers, and new
directions / edited by Wenshan Jia, Xing Lu, and D. Ray Heisey.
    p. cm.—(Advances in communication and culture)
    Includes index.
    ISBN 1-56750-655-0 (alk. paper)
    1. Communication—China. I. Jia, Wenshan, 1961– II. Lu, Xing. III. Heisey,
D. Ray. IV. Series.
P92.C5 c514 2002
302.2′0951—dc21   2001053834

British Library Cataloguing in Publication Data is available.

Library of Congress Catalog Card Number: 2001053834
ISBN: 1-56750-655-0

First published in 2002

Ablex Publishing, 88 Post Road West, Westport, CT 06881
An imprint of Greenwood Publishing Group, Inc.
www.ablexbooks.com

Printed in the United States of America

The paper used in this book complies with the
Permanent Paper Standard issued by the National
Information Standards Organization (Z39.48-1984).

10 9 8 7 6 5 4 3 2 1

This book is dedicated to my father, Xukang Chen, who passed away in China due to a heart attack, whom I had not seen for almost a decade and will no longer have a chance to see again but who will live in my heart forever; to my mother, Congying Jia, who has been one of my most important teachers of communication; to my wife, Jianyun Ren, my daughter, Xuanzi Jia, and my son Jishuai Jia, who have provided me strong support during my two years' coediting process.

Contents

Acknowledgments

This project is partially funded by a small creative and research project award granted by SUNY at New Paltz. I wish to thank D. Ray Heisey whose strong commitment and contributions to the advancement of (inter)cultural communication through Chinese communication studies have been a constant inspiration to me. I thank Xing Lu and D. Ray Heisey, who provided valuable reviews of the chapters and the book manuscript. Furthermore, I thank the Association for Chinese Communication Studies and many other colleagues from various disciplines such as communication and Asian studies with an interest in Chinese communication for their encouragement. Finally, my heartfelt thanks go to Eric Levy, Acquisitions Editor at Greenwood Publishing Group, and all other personnel who have contributed to the production of this book.

Introduction: The Significance of Chinese Communication Theory and Research in a Glocalizing World

Wenshan Jia

ORIGIN

Having finished my book chapter "Chinese Communication Scholarship as an Expansion of the Communication and Culture Paradigm" (Jia, 2000), which was first presented at a panel on "Chinese Communication Research: Lessons Learned, New Directions" at the NCA 1998 Annual Convention in New York City, I realized this: If the field of communication in the United States had included other cultural views of communication and if scholars and students of Chinese communication studies had been more critical of the concepts, theories, and methods they used in their studies of Chinese communication, the field of Chinese communication could have advanced significantly and made a larger contribution to the general field of communication. I also realized that one book chapter is not sufficient to review and critique a large body of scholarship called Chinese communication studies. I thought of editing a volume such as the present one and told D. Ray Heisey about it, knowing that he was editing a communication series titled *Advances in Communication and Culture*. Prof. Heisey lauded the idea, which was later supported by Xing Lu, my second editor. During the past two years, we received twenty-five submissions, out of which we chose sixteen chapters.

The contributors are mostly Chinese or Chinese Americans, with a significant number of Caucasian Americans, who are mostly seasoned scholars of Chinese communication with a publication record in each of their special research concentrations. The literature reviewed and/or critiqued is published in either English or Chinese.

RATIONALE

In "Communication Theory for a Globalizing World," Peter Monge laments the fact that while many publications exist on culture-specific communication practices, very few attempts are made to approach them from a theoretical perspective (1998, p. 4). Monge's discovery applies to the field of Chinese communication studies. The present volume is an attempt to bring Chinese communication studies closer to an explicitly theoretical level. It constitutes the first systematic critical review of Chinese communication studies in the history of the field of communications. Its major focus is on studies situated in Mainland China, but includes studies based in other Chinese societies and communities around the world. The volume also places a major emphasis on Chinese speech communication scholarship. It includes a few chapters on mass communication as well.

Previously published literature (Kincaid, 1987; Dissanayake, 1988) related to the topic of this volume does not center on Chinese communication, particularly Chinese speech communication, whose research has made strides in the past two decades but without a systematic review and critique. While Kincaid's volume is speech communication-centered, it attempts to provide comparative Eastern-Western perspectives to communication theory without a grounding in in-depth critiques of the relevant literature, let alone empirical research. Such an approach to theory building seems premature. For a young field such as Chinese communication studies to contribute to theory building, I believe, it should start from critique; guided by critique, culture-centered, well-conceptualized and designed, grounded and self-reflective research could produce defensible findings that form a basis for theory building. Dissanayake's volume centers on Asian mass communication, which omits Asian speech communication. In addition, chapters on Chinese communication in both volumes cover literature only up to the 1980s. However, the 1990s witnessed growth in various aspects of Chinese communication studies that remains unevaluated at the systematic level. The present volume is another major evaluative effort to continue and advance communication theory from an Eastern cultural perspective, as initiated by Robert Oliver (1971), carried on by D. L. Kincaid and his associates (1987), Dissanayake and his associates (1988), and many others. It is not only a step toward a revolution in Chinese communication studies in the twenty-first century, but also a remedy for Eurocentrism in the field of communication theory and research in general.

The volume also attempts to contribute to the development of an explicitly culture-centered theory of communication. Specifically, it functions as a critique of and a significant complement to the book *Communication: Views from the Helm for the 21st Century* (Trent, 1998) and the theories reviewed by Craig (1997a, 1997b). The field of communication is still entrenched in Eurocentrism or Americanism (Monge, 1998; Heisey, 2000). Heisey reflects upon communication research in the West, "For too long we in the West have been satisfied to settle for our own interpretation of rhetorical and communication reality" (2000, p. xix). Similarly, Monge concludes, "There is little doubt that the preponderance of contemporary communication theory has been developed from the singular perspective of the United States" (1998, p. 4). Ironically, Trent's volume, in which Monge's remarks appear, and Craig's papers exactly reflect what Monge laments. In these writings, culture is largely treated as a mere component of communication rather than a central construct. The "views from the helm" remain largely American views, but without adding the adjective "American" before "views of communication," they misleadingly suggest that these views are universal, applicable to all cultures. Virtually excluding culture-centered views of communication embedded in cultures outside the United States and the West, these writings, instead of explicating globally diverse views from the helm for the twenty-first century, confine themselves within this American view of the twentieth century. As a consequence, they submerge culture-centered views of communication while promoting the globalization of the American agenda for communication research in the twenty-first century. Our volume exemplifies resistance to such submergence and points to a set of more heuristic alternative views about communication in the twenty-first century, rooted in a significant non-Western culture, the Chinese culture. We hope that these views will engage the authors in Trent's volume and other scholars of a Western orientation in an intellectual dialogue, to create a significant potential for enriching human understanding of communication.

CONCLUSION

This volume does not intend to suggest that native perspectives are the only correct ones and that nonnative or foreign perspectives are biased. That depends on how the perspectives are used and for what purposes. The practical theory I used in my book on the transformation of Chinese face practices and Chinese identity (Jia, 2001) offers not only a different interpretation of Chinese face practices from that of Geertz's anthropological/ethnographic inquiry (1974), which seems to rigidify the native views, but also offers a way to facilitate change to better Chinese life. This theory is developed by Vernon Cronen and his associates, who have incorporated American pragmatism, Wittgenstein's philosophical ideas on everyday language, systems theory, and British social constructionism (Cronen & Lang, 1994, 1995, 1996).

Is there bias in this approach? Yes. But it is intended. The issue is not whether a certain perspective is biased or not. It is whether or not one perspective, believed to be the only correct one by the majority, dominates, and whether or not researchers are aware of and self-critical of their own biases and respectful of and curious about other legitimate perspectives. The truth seems to be that it is most beneficial for us to keep multiple perspectives alive, to retain "skeptical pluralism" (Smith, 1998, p. 38) or, to use Penman's words (1992), to recognize "diversity" (p. 245) and "incompleteness" (p. 246) in every perspective.

The purpose of critiquing Western biases in the present chapters is not only to reduce such biases but also to appeal for active inclusion of the views expressed in these chapters as an enrichment to the current dominant perspectives. Hopefully, this will contribute to explicit communication theory building, which can "accommodate multiple forms of knowledge" (Monge, 1998, p. 4) and which will help make constructive East-West mutual critique, mutual learning, mutual enlightenment, and mutual transformation possible, an idea repeatedly suggested by far-sighted scholars from both the East (Chang, C., Tang, C., Mou, T., & Hsu, F., 1957; Cheng, 1988; Tu, 1994, pp. 1140-1141) and the West (Fingarette, 1972, p.vii; De Bary, 1988; Ames & Hall, 1987, 1995, 1998; Clarke, 1997). I hope each reader will make his or her own judgment on the value of each chapter in promoting such intercultural communication.

REFERENCES

Chang, C., Tang, C., Mou, T., & Hsu, F. (1957). A manifesto for re-appraisal of Sinology and reconstruction of Chinese culture. In C. Chang (Ed.), *The development of neo-Confucian thought* (pp. 455-483). New York: Bookman Associates.

Cheng, C. Y. (1988). *Xian dai hua yu zhong guo wen hua shi jie hua (Modernization and globalization of Chinese culture).* Beijing, China: China Peace Press.

Clarke, J. J. (1997). *Oriental enlightenment: The encounter between Asian and Western thought.* New York: Routledge.

Craig, R. T. (1997a). Communication theory as a field, Part I. Paper presented at the annual convention of the International Communication Association, Montreal, May 24, 1997.

Craig, R. T. (1997b). Communication theory as a field, Part II. Paper presented at the annual convention of the National Communication Association, Chicago, November 1997.

Cronen, V. E. (1996). Practical theory and the logic of inquiry. Paper presented at the Speech Communication Association Convention, San Diego, November 25, 1996.

Cronen, V. E. (1995). Practical theory and the tasks ahead for social approaches to communication. In W. Leeds-Hurwitz (Ed.), *Social approaches to communication* (pp. 217-242). New York: The Guilford Press.

Cronen, V. E. (1994). Coordinated management of meaning: Practical theory for the complexities and contradictions of everyday life. In J. Sigfried (Ed.), *The status of common sense in psychology* (pp. 183-207). Stamford, CT: Ablex.

Cronen, V. E., & Lang, P. (1994). Language and action: Wittgenstein and Dewey in the practice of therapy and consultation. *Human Systems, 5*, 5-43.

De Bary, W. T. (1988). *East Asian civilizations: A dialogue in five stages.* Cambridge, MA: Harvard University Press.

Dissanayake, W. (1988). *Communication theory: The Asian perspective.* Singapore: Asian Mass Communication Research and Information Center.

Fingarette, H. (1972). Preface. In H. Fingarette, *Confucius: The secular as sacred.* New York: Harper & Row.

Geertz, C. (1974). "From the native's point of view": On the nature of anthropological understanding. *Bulletin of the American Academy of Arts and Sciences, 28* (1), 221-237.

Hall, D. L., & Ames, R. T. (1987). *Thinking through Confucius.* Albany: State University of New York Press.

Hall, D. L., & Ames, R. T. (1995). *Anticipating China.* Albany: State University of New York Press.

Hall, D. L., & Ames, R. T. (1998). *Thinking from the Han.* Albany: State University of New York Press.

Heisey, D. R. (2000). Introduction: Chinese perspectives coming of age in the West and serving as a balance in theory and practice. In D. R. Heisey (Ed.), *Chinese perspectives in rhetoric and communication.* Stamford, CT: Ablex.

Jia, W. (2001). *The Remaking of the Chinese character and identity in the 21st century: The Chinese face practices.* Westport, CT: Greenwood Publishing Group, Inc.

Jia, W. (2000). Chinese communication scholarship as an expansion of the communication and culture paradigm. In D. R. Heisey (Ed.), *Chinese perspectives in rhetoric and communication.* Stamford, CT: Ablex.

Kincaid, D. L. (1987). *Communication theory: Eastern and Western perspectives.* San Diego: Academic Press.

Monge, P. R. (1998). Communication theory for a globalizing world. In J. S. Trent (Ed.), *Communication: Views from the helm for the 21st century.* Boston: Allyn & Bacon.

Oliver, R. T. (1971). Communication and culture in ancient India and China. Syracuse, NY: Syracuse University Press.

Penman, R. (1992). Good theory and good practice: An argument in progress. *Communication Theory, 2* (3), 234-250.

Smith III, T. J. (1988). Diversity and order in communication theory: The uses of philosophical analysis. *Communication Quarterly, 36* (1), 28-40.

Trent, J. S. (Ed.). (1998). *Communication: Views from the helm for the 21st century.* Boston: Allyn & Bacon.

Tu, W. (1994). The historical significance of the Confucian discourse. *The China Quarterly, 140*, 1131-1141.

State of the Field

Communication Studies in China: State of the Art

Zhenbin Sun

As a study area, Chinese communications has a history of about twenty-three years. It is initially based on the importation of Western, mainly American, communications. Western communications provides Chinese scholars with a new paradigm and freedom from the restraints of official and rigid doctrines of journalism. It offers a series of concepts that help promote the industrial-ization, commercialization, and globalization of Chinese mass media. It emphasizes the notion and importance of the audience, benefiting democra-tization and popular culture. It introduces a set of research methods, resulting in the regular use of the nationwide polls, surveys, and media ratings. How-ever, many Chinese researchers do not want to limit themselves to Western theories of communication; instead, they claim that although the discipline is established in the West, China has accumulated throughout its history rich experience and ideas about communication. Thus, these researchers set out to advance a theory that features a critical review of Chinese practices and views of communication and call it "the nativization of communications" (Xiao, 1995, pp. 34–36). To a large extent, the state of communication studies in China can be characterized as "a duet of importation and nativization of communications." A resulting tension has produced not only the achieve-ments of Chinese communications, but its problems.

This chapter explores the state of this study area by (1) reviewing its origin and development, (2) examining its themes and achievements, and (3) analyzing its characteristics and problems. I find that, although communication studies in China are enlightened by Western communications, their characteristics are indelibly Chinese: researchers consider solving media-related sociopolitical problems as their basic objective; Western concepts of communication are interpreted, evaluated, and used in relation to Chinese conditions; and theory construction is based on traditional Chinese resources and contemporary Chinese experience. While the state of Chinese communications reflects the orientation of modern Chinese scholarship and displays basic characteristics of Chinese culture, it also demonstrates how a culture influences communication and the way a communication theory is constructed. (Please note, (1) throughout this chapter I use "communication studies in China" and "Chinese communications" interchangeably, (2) while "communication" refers to human interaction, "communications" refers to studies of human interaction; and (3) by "China" I refer to the Mainland only.)

ORIGIN AND DEVELOPMENT

Even though communications is a new area of inquiry in China, several researchers have made efforts during the last ten years to review its history (Liu, 1991; Sun, 1994a; Huang & Han, 1997; Han, 1998; Xu, 1998; Liao, 1998; Han, 2000). Based on their investigations, I divide the history of Chinese communications into five stages: inception, introduction, inflection, integration, and intensification.

The Stage of Inception (1978–1981)

Initially identified as essentially journalism and mass communication, Chinese communications was first promoted by professors of journalism. Professor Zheng of Fudan University's Department of Journalism published a paper in 1978 to introduce American scholars' ideas on mass communication. This paper is recognized as the starting point of Chinese communications and has been followed by similar contributions from other scholars (Liao, 1998, pp. 24-25). In February 1980, this department offered an undergraduate course in Western communications (Liu, 1991, p. 9), which made communication part of the curriculum of higher education for the first time in China. This course helped move the academic discussion of Western theories of communication beyond a small number of scholars in China, making it fashionable among college students and providing them with a new perspective on the nature and function of mass media. In January 1981, five undergraduate students from the same department did a quantitative analysis of survey results on the news about the judgment of Lin Biao and the Gang of Four (Liu, 1991, p. 10), which is now known as the first quantitative study of Chinese communications.

The Stage of Introduction (1982–1985)

If Fudan University sowed the seeds of Chinese communications, then Wilbur Schramm definitely nurtured it. In May 1982, Schramm delivered a landmark lecture series in Beijing, Shanghai, and Guangzhou. He discussed the inherent relationship among communications, mass communication, and journalism (Shao, 1999a, p. 224) and inspired great interest among Chinese researchers and professors of journalism, leading them to go beyond journalism and step into mass communication. His lectures and Chinese translation of *Men, Women, Messages, and Media: Understanding Human Communication* (Shramm & Porter, 1984) amounted to a "standard history" of what became the Chinese understanding of communications (Wang, 1998, p. 28).

The First National Convention on Communications, held six months after Schramm left China, reached consensus on three issues. First, communications should be understood as a new discipline, an outcome of frequent exchange of information among human beings, reflecting social and technological developments. Second, the guiding principles for China's approach to this new discipline should include "systematic understanding," "analytical investigation," "critical learning," and "independent creation." Third, authoritative and representative Western works of communications should be translated and published; newspapers and journals should carry articles analyzing communications; and courses in communications should be offered at institutions of higher education (Xu, 1998, p. 3). This convention is popularly recognized as a groundbreaker for the development of Chinese communications. It created and promoted a nationwide program to import Western communications and to guide communication studies in China for many subsequent years.

The Stage of Inflection (1986–1991)

At the Second National Convention on Communications in 1986, participants reviewed the state of communication studies after the first convention, compared American with European communications, and projected plans for furthering the field. It called for (1) establishing a theory of communication with Chinese character and (2) setting journalism/mass communication as the focus of Chinese communications (Liao, 1998, p. 27). As a result, the first wave of Chinese books on communication appeared during 1988-1991. While these books use Western categories and frameworks, they all make arguments or analyses by drawing on Chinese culture. For example, after introducing Western theories of the relationship between culture and communication, Sha, Chen, and Zheng (1990) analyze how Chinese media of communication (written language and carved stone) influence Chinese culture (pp. 85-97).

Although researchers intentionally adapted communications to Chinese situations and tried to advance a Chinese theory, they failed to overcome the

Chinese Communist Party's leftist officials' and scholars' ideological screening of Western ideas on Chinese journalism. These leftists fought against any position or action that might weaken the CCP's control over mass media or undermine the official ideology. They believed that Western communications contributed to the Tiananman student protest in the summer of 1989. Thus, starting from Fall 1989, communications was officially criticized nationwide as bourgeois scholarship; courses and meetings on communications were canceled; and universities no longer enrolled graduate students in communications (Xu, 1998, p. 4).

The Stage of Integration (1992–1996)

In 1992 a dramatic shift took place with the publication of Deng Xiaoping's speech delivered during his inspection of Southern China. Chinese communications reached its fourth stage, marked by the opening of a national conference on the audience of mass media and by the publication of eight books aimed at contributing to a communications with Chinese characteristics.

At the Third National Convention on Communications in 1993, participants suggested that researchers should (1) systematically study the main schools of Western communications, appropriating what is useful and discarding the rest; (2) review the long history of Chinese communication, its rich ideas and experience; (3) investigate the problems of Chinese mass media; and (4) conduct research to fulfill social needs (Liao, 1998, pp. 29-30). From then on, the national convention was held every other year. Furthermore, in 1993, scholars from the Mainland, Hong Kong, and Taiwan gathered at Xiamen University for the first time and discussed Chinese communication as manifested in Chinese history, language, literature, philosophy, folkways, cross-cultural contacts, economy, public relations, and advertising. This meeting intentionally treated Chinese communication as a subject of interdisciplinary studies and deliberately brought together scholars with expertise in humanities and social sciences. The book *Cong Ling Kaishi* [Starting from the Very Beginning] (Yu & Zheng, eds., 1994) represents the achievement of the conference and a new trend: the connection of communication with culture in communication studies.

The Stage of Intensification (1997–2000)

Though the Fifth National Convention on Communication of 1997 adopted the convention theme "Communication and Economic Development," many attendees examined basic issues and problems in communication scholarship, inquiring into the standards, criteria, methodologies, and future directions of communication studies (Liao, 1998, p. 30).

In 1998 the Chinese government authorized some colleges/universities to offer M.A. and Ph.D. degrees in communications. Thus communications officially settled in China. In contrast to 1978, with only four journalism departments in the whole country, 1999 saw more than one hundred (about one tenth of the national total) colleges/universities with a journalism/communications school, department, or program (Zhang, 1999, p. 137). Journals and newspapers carried more and more articles on communications and four series of books on communications (two series of translations of English works and two series of original research) came out in 1999 alone.

THEMES AND ACHIEVEMENTS

In reviewing the origin and development of Chinese communications, I observe that early researchers focused on the discussion of basic concepts, theories, and methods of communication studies; they then paid more attention to history, inquiring into how this discipline developed in the West and how it was understood in Chinese tradition; from the middle 1980s, many applied theories and methods to the practices and problems of communication in Chinese life. Associated with this trajectory were the four themes that dominated Chinese communications: understanding communications, the issue of audience and effect, media reform, and the relationship between communication and culture. By quantitatively reviewing articles published in four influential journals of journalism/communications from 1981 to 1996, Huang and Han (1997) draw a conclusion similar to my observation. With a close look at these themes, therefore, we can grasp the main achievements of Chinese communications.

Understanding Communications

Since communications is a body of knowledge imported from the West, the first task Chinese scholars face is to define its nature, scope, and areas. While their understanding is deeply influenced by Western scholars, their focus is Chinese oriented.

In discussing the fundamentals of communications, Chinese scholars present various proposals or models, which, although varying from one to another in detail, are almost all derived from Lasswell's (1948) model of the five Ws (who says what to whom, through what channel and with what effect). Moreover, this model has become the framework that scholars employ to direct their research and structure their work. For example, Shao's (1997) "holistic and interactive model" is clearly an elaboration of the models introduced by McQuail and Windahl (1987). Dong's (1995) classification of human communication is also based on the Western model of communication.

However, when dealing with the concept "communication," Chinese scholars take a different approach. First of all, they adopt the Chinese translation of the English term "communication," "*chuanbo*," suggested by scholars in

Hong Kong and Taiwan. Then, they interpret *"chuanbo"* by tracing its etymological root. Yuan (1986) argues that in a passage from Confucius' *Analects*, the term *"chuan"* implied the meaning of "transmitting knowledge and information." Fang (1994) claims that *"chuanbo"* as a Chinese term has been used for at least 1,400 years. Huang (1994) suggests that a group of ancient Chinese terms is closely related to communication and that *"chuan"* stands for the most general Chinese conception of communication. The five basic types of communication practice and media in Chinese history include education, writings, speech, official post, and historical legends and biography; all are expressed through the word *"chuan."*

It is significant to realize that although researchers know the etymological relation of "community" to "communication" as well as the social implications of "communication" in Western culture, few of them pay enough attention to the semantic and cultural differences between *"chuanbo"* and "communication." They examine the Chinese history and practice of communication in light of *"chuanbo"* instead of "communication." This reflects the traditional orientation and emphasis of Chinese communication, that is, the flow of information from a center to margins rather than the sharing of information within a community.

Audience and Effect

By 1999 more than 20 books and 2,000 articles analyzing the content and audience of the mass media were published in China (Chen, 1999, pp. 187-188). These studies are based on Western theories of communication and apply quantitative methods. They demonstrate the most significant development in Chinese communications (Shen, 1999, p. 61).

Notice that audience analysis had never been an issue of journalistic theory and practice in Mao's era. Instead, disseminating the Party's doctrines, explaining its policies, and serving its interests were the ultimate objectives of mass media. The principle of the unity of theory and practice until the 1980s had held that since ordinary people's interests were represented by and realized through the Party, the focus of mass media should be the Party's, not the audience's, needs and wants. Chinese professionals of mass media did not ignore the importance of audience or the difference, even opposition, between the Party's and the people's interests. Though they were quite aware of all the theoretical and practical problems in this area, they had no theory capable of powerfully refuting Party-centered journalism and conceptually establishing the position of the audience and no methods capable of accurately measuring the real effect of mass media on the audience.

This situation was quickly changed with the importation of Western communications. On the one hand, the concept of "message," accompanied by information theory, broadens the content of mass media; the concept of "audience" identifies the people as a crucial factor of mass communication.

These concepts help professionals to accomplish a revolution in press and broadcast enterprise, i.e., the "Party-standard" is replaced by the "audience-standard" (Chen, 1993), and the audience's needs and wants are recognized as a legitimate right (Song, 1992). On the other hand, public surveys are used regularly and popularly; for example, from 1983 to 1998, 131 local, regional, or nationwide surveys were conducted (Chen, 1999, p. 187). Many academic and professional organizations have been established on public opinion, surveys, and rating. Among them, the People's University of China Institute of Public Opinion (Yu, 1999, pp. 169-170) and the CCTV-SOFRES Media Inc. (Chen, 1999, pp. 188-189) are the most influential ones. The findings of surveys reveal the effect of mass communication and push the reform of the mass media. Not only do professional communicators come to adjust strategies and contents of reports and programs in light of the findings, but media administrations and the local, regional, and even central governments take these findings into account when making policies and decisions.

Media Reform

Being aware of the importance of the communication media and their relation to sociopolitical and economic development, researchers pay great attention to the institutional and management reform of mass media.

Recall that the mass media in Mao's era were treated as tools of propaganda and class struggle to help maintain the government's control over society. While media guaranteed all information would accord with the government's position and policy, the government guaranteed media financial support. This situation began to encounter serious challenges in the late 1970s and early 1980s. As mass media disappointed the audience, who did not believe what they were fed by the media, the government could no longer provide the media sufficient financial support, since the country's economic system was facing an institutional transition from the planned economy to the market economy. Reform of mass media was pressing. Researchers discussed the rationale and ways of reform, arguing that (1) besides disseminating the Party's voice, mass media should also communicate information, knowledge, public opinion, and entertainment; (2) mass media should relate to both the society's superstructure and the information industry and thus necessitate involvement in economic activity; (3) since mass media have industrial characteristics, they should employ rules of the free market; and (4) industrialization and commercialization are the correct direction for media reform and a necessary outcome of the country's economic situation (Huang & Ding, 1997, pp. 10-12).

In developing these points, Huang and Ding (1997) propose a model of "the balance between social control and the media's interests," claiming that the reform of mass media is in essence a process of changing ideological media into industrialized media; this process lies in the interaction between social control over mass media and mass media's own interests. The weaker the social control, the more commercialized mass media become, and the stronger media's interests grow. Because social control varies from time to time and from medium to medium, there are different balance points and different types of media: some are more ideologically oriented, and others are more commercialized. Yet, along with the powerful growth of the market economy and the unavoidable dominance of popular culture, the commercialization of mass media is unstoppable and will continue to develop (pp. 12-19).

Huang and Ding's model comprehensively reflects the real situation and character of mass media in today's China and thus can be used to explain why media management is drawing more and more researchers' attention. Since the mass media have become a kind of industry, their regulation cannot be based on simple administrative orders; instead, a set of principles, strategies, and procedures is absolutely necessary, which is actually the topic of a number of publications (Zhou, 1994, Shao & Liu, 1998; Tang, 1999).

Communication and Culture

After Wu's *Wuxing de Wangluo [The Invisible Net]* (1988), the first book in China to study Chinese culture from the viewpoint of communication, more works of this sort have appeared. While sharing a common point, they take different approaches, such as communicative, cultural, folk, and philosophical.

The *communicative* approach is characterized by treating communication as a field and culture as a focus and investigating how Chinese communication shapes the features and history of Chinese culture. Wu's book stands for this approach. Based on his analysis of interpersonal, family, group, organizational, and political communication, Wu argues that there are three communicative structures in Chinese history, including the structure of life-communication, social communication, and historical communication; each reflects certain cultural characteristics. For example, life-communication is depicted as a structure of four concentric circles: "body," "family," "state," and "universe." This structure indicates that the closer to the center ("body") a circle is, the richer the information becomes, the more diverse the communication mode is, and the less dependent the circle is on a given communication channel. Accordingly, this structure explains three cultural characteristics associated with this sort of communication: cohesive collectivity, closed mentality, and flexible personality (pp. 213-215).

The cultural approach is characterized by treating culture as a field and communication as a focus and exploring how Chinese culture influenced the manner and content of Chinese communication. As an example, Li's *Tangdai Wenming yu Xinwen Chuanbo [The Culture of Tang Dynasty and News Communication]* (1999) claims that Chinese communication can be divided into three stages corresponding to specific social/political/economic institutions: information communication (before the seventh century), news communication (the seventh century to the ninetieth century), and mass communication (since the nineteenth century) (p. 358). The so-called news is publicly disseminated information about current and novel things (p. 105). It relies on (1) a developed social division of labor and mutually dependent professions; (2) the separation of sociocultural activities from work for survival; and (3) machine-interposed media and their operators, who link the seller/sender and the buyer/receiver (p. 370). Li suggests it was the Tang Dynasty that provided all these factors and thus underwent the great sociocultural change from information communication to news communication (p. 359).

The folk approach is characterized by its review of Chinese thought on communication as embedded in everyday sayings. Sun's (1994b) study is an example of this approach. In Sun's view, proverbs, maxims, and idioms display conventional principles and rules of communication that powerfully influence people's daily interaction; and in turn, these principles and rules reflect, in one way or another, the characteristics of Chinese culture. For example, a proverb reads: "Good things cannot go across the door of one's home; bad things can be talked about by people one thousand miles away." This rule holds that unusual things are much more attractive than usual things (p. 31). Another maxim suggests: "Don't expose others' weakness; don't talk about others' private matters." This does not mean Chinese people share with Western people the idea of privacy; instead, it warns one of the trouble or even danger one will get into if one violates the rule (p. 34). An idiom from Lao Zi claims that "Truthful words are not beautiful; beautiful words are not truthful." This shows that the speaker's moving speech may not benefit the listener (p. 34).

The philosophical approach is characterized by its examination of Chinese thought on communication as expressed in ancient Chinese scholarship. He's research (1995) demonstrates this approach. According to He, the function of communication on human survival and social development is a crucial subject of communication studies; schools of thoughts in pre-Qin times (551–221 B.C.E.) present many propositions on this subject. He analyzes the ideas of the Confucians, the Moists, the Daoists, the Legalists, and the Strategists, arguing that each school focuses on one dimension of communication function. For example, the Confucians draw attention mainly to the political cultivating function of communication; they treat education and persuasion as means of realizing the politics of "ren" (humanity) (p. 10). The Moists stress the social utilitarian function of communication; they insist that speeches and writings have to serve or tally with actions that benefit mutual "li" (interests) (p. 13). Finally, the Legalists suggest the ideological identification function of communication; they seek to change communication into a process of regulating people's thought and behavior with "fa" (laws) (p. 15).

CHARACTERISTICS AND PROBLEMS

After examining the history and major themes of Chinese communications, I discuss the characteristics that make Chinese communications different from Western communications and the problems that influence its direction in the early twenty-first century. These characteristics and problems are interrelated, displaying not only the trend of contemporary Chinese scholarship but the nature of traditional Chinese culture.

Sociopolitical Orientation and Practical *Zhi*

Among the characteristics of Chinese communications, two are of special significance: One is that issues of mass media dominate the area of inquiry; most publications deal with mass communication. The other is that American theories of communication are far more influential than European theories; few works of European scholars are translated into Chinese.

I believe that the key to understanding the prominence of mass media in Chinese communications lies in the close relationship between mass media/mass communication research and sociopolitics. Because mass media are directly involved in urgent and sensitive sociopolitical issues such as democratization, industrialization, commercialization, and globalization, communication studies have to provide people with insightful paradigms, convincing strategies, and feasible methods to predict, explain, and solve various problems that administrators, professionals, and consumers of mass media encounter. The truth-value and attractiveness of a particular kind of research or theory mainly depend on how clearly the research or theory is related to realistic problems and their solutions.

Certainly, scholars know that interpersonal, group, and organizational communication are significant areas of communication studies; some of them have published works in these areas. Yet, the history of Chinese communications parallels the process of crucial sociopolitical reform occurring in a vital period of Chinese history. It is impossible for researchers not to focus communication studies on sociopolitical issues such as audience rights and needs, mass media and public opinion, the Party's leadership and the reform of mass media, and competition and the commercialization of mass media. In this sense, it is not communications that chooses China; instead, it is China that chooses communications in terms of its own needs, purposes, and tradition.

The path Chinese communications has followed is an example of the specific character of Chinese scholarship as a whole. Throughout the history of Chinese scholarship, a purely intellectual investigation has never been the ultimate objective of theorizing activity; to separate the search for knowledge from realistic problem-solving goes against the basic characteristic of Chinese culture, which I call "practical *zhi*." As a Chinese concept, *zhi* (knowledge, intelligence, and wisdom) "consists of three dimensions and each of them has a theme, that is, (1) knowledge: knowing that and knowing how as a polarity; (2) intelligence: reasoning and discursive practice as a continuum; and (3) wisdom: antitheses as a synthesis" (Sun, 1997, p. 8). By practical *zhi* I mean that Chinese culture understands and treats knowledge, reason, and wisdom as inseparable from praxis in the lifeworld; while knowledge originates from and serves practices and reason lies in the process of choosing a right means, wisdom is manifested in combining theories and actions. Once the nature of practical *zhi* is grasped, one can easily appreciate its connection to and influence on Chinese scholarship and understand why Chinese communications concentrates on mass media and sociopolitical issues.

Interestingly enough, practical *zhi* has some similarities and even shares some essence with pragmatism, the native philosophy of America. Though pragmatists vary from one another in specific respects, we can still find among them some common points; that is, they believe philosophy should take real life as its basis, actions as its means, and effects as its aim. James (1960) describes a pragmatist's position as such: "He turns away from abstraction and insufficiency, from verbal solutions, from bad *a priori* reasons, from fixed principles, closed systems, and pretended absolutes and origins. He turns towards concreteness and adequacy, towards facts, towards action and towards power" (pp. 31-32). Both practical *zhi* and pragmatism, at least the Jamesian form of pragmatism, stress the lifeworld as the starting point and ultimate home of philosophy; both insist on practical effects and efficiency as the criteria of all theories; and both consider concrete issues the basis of abstract thinking. Rorty's (1982) distinction between real theories and philosophical theories and Hall and Ames's (1987) comparison between Confucian philosophy and pragmatism shed light on these similarities.

As pragmatism is sharply different from continental philosophy, the mainstream of American communications maintains a significant distance from European communications, including British cultural studies as a kind of mass communication research. To comprehend the nature and influence of pragmatism, one can simply glance at American communications. In most cases, it focuses on a particular issue raised from everyday communicative life rather than an abstract concept addressed in a theory; it unfolds argument inductively instead of deductively; and it presents findings that are measurable or solutions that are practicable. Because American communications embodies the spirit of pragmatism and because pragmatism is similar, in some respects, to practical *zhi*, Chinese researchers feel comfortable reading American works on communications. This is, to my understanding, the primary reason American communications is much more influential in China than European communications.

Nativization and Importation

As mentioned earlier, communications as a study area in China is imported from the West, but from the very beginning Chinese communications has focused on how to "nativize" communications and eventually to build a communication theory with Chinese character (Xu & Huang, 1982; Ming, 1994; Sun, ed., 1997; Shao, 1999b). This trend dominates the history of Chinese communications and generates several paradoxes.

First, while communications is an imported discipline, only about twenty Western books on communications had been translated into Chinese before 1999. Second, while few researchers have a clear understanding of all areas of communications and main theories or schools within each area, many writers like to draw a whole picture of communications, including its universal history, structure, realms, and methods. Third, while Western theories are almost the exclusive framework used to analyze and conceptualize Chinese practices of communication, nativization, rather than importation, of communications is recognized as the only way to develop Chinese communications. Associated with these paradoxes are some problems popularly identified by many scholars. For example, there has been a lack of effort to systematically introduce classical and new Western communication works in the past twenty years (Zhang, 1999, p. 136); and researchers' understanding of Western communications has been limited to isolated subjects and a few theorists (Dai, 1999, p. 22). Among the journalism and communication works written by Chinese scholars, most of them are introductory instead of original (Guo, 1999, p. 83); and these works usually repeat similar ideas (Xu, 1999, p. 250).

To be sure, the notion of "nativization of communications" is deeply rooted in modern Chinese intellectual history. It is an indirect response to the argument on the relationship between Chinese and Western scholarship starting in the late ninetieth century as well as a direct echo of the "cultural fever" and the "fever of traditional Chinese scholarship" prevailing in late 1980s and early 1990s. Although the backgrounds of the argument and of the two "fevers" are different (the political and military invasion of the West in the former and the economic and cultural dominance of the West in the latter), both the argument and the two "fevers" share the same beliefs, that is, China has a valuable cultural tradition and rich spiritual resources; this tradition and these resources enable China to answer all challenges it faces; and Western theories should be used to improve but not replace Chinese culture.

By applying these beliefs to the notion of "nativization of communications," one can generalize its primary position as follows: The essence of Chinese communications consists in Chinese principles, modes, ideas, and practices of communication. Western concepts and methods of communication studies are meaningful when they can be used as tools to solve theoretical and practical problems of Chinese communication. In the postcolonial and postmodern time, it is extremely important to build a theoretical system of communications with national character; and in this sense, nativization is primary, central, and permanent, while importation is secondary, marginal, and temporary. With this position in mind, one can now understand the paradoxes and problems and realize that as the practical importance and methodological value of nativization increase, the theoretical significance and epistemological meaning of importation decrease.

But, can nativization separate the East from the West and necessarily lead to the development of a Chinese theory of communication? Does importation only mean introducing Western thought to China and hence inevitably excluding the Chinese horizon? My answer to these questions is "No." In my view, the phrase "nativization of communications" implies the dependence of nativization on communications. In fact, here "communications" as a language (i.e., concepts) and grammar (i.e., the rule of using concepts to designate communicative behaviors) has established a *way of thinking* (in Wittgenstein's sense) for nativization. Thus, nativization is first of all a sort of application of the (Western) language and grammar in a specific discourse on Chinese practices of communication.

Under this condition, it is impossible for nativization to separate the East from the West. While there is no logical connection between nativization and a sound theory, reinforcing importation is a crucial way to develop Chinese communications. I believe that importation does not mean an orthodox and faithful repetition of Western ideas, but *the fusing of* the Eastern and Western *horizons* (in Gadamer's [1985] sense). Seen from the viewpoint of philosophical hermeneutics, the historical prejudice enables the Chinese interpreter not only to keep his/her cultural identity but also to engage in a dialogue with the Western author; when the author's and the interpreter's horizons become fused, a new communication theory may emerge. Since it is created by both parties, this new theory is neither purely Western nor entirely Chinese, but a manifestation of a "third" culture.

Communication Studies and Cultural Studies

When one looks closely at Chinese communications, there seems to be no clear dividing line between the "transmission perspective" and the "ritual perspective," since many researchers spontaneously and deliberately investigate communication in light of its relation to culture. Consequently, combining communication studies with cultural studies stands out as another characteristic.

The combination of communication studies and cultural studies or, better, the cultural studies of communication covers both traditional/high culture and contemporary/popular culture. While Sun's (1997) and Zhou's books (1994; 2000) represent works focusing on traditional/high culture, Yang's (1993) and Gao's (1996) essays are examples of works focusing on contemporary/popular culture. In the former case, scholars examine how Chinese practices and channels of communication shape and develop Chinese culture (beliefs, values, and norms) and, in turn, how Chinese culture guides and characterizes communicative acts in different walks of Chinese life. In the latter case, researchers explore how mass media reflect and promote popular culture, as well as how popular culture influences the reform of mass media and the development of media industry. Although the focus of the two types differ, they do not reject each other in their deep structure; instead, they take each other as a necessary reference and draw solutions in light of each other. As studies of traditional communication and high culture aim at enhancing an understanding of contemporary communication and popular culture, research in contemporary communication and popular culture takes lessons from traditional communication and high culture.

The cultural study of communication, although not yet the mainstream, seems to be the most likely direction of Chinese communications in the early twenty-first century. This is true, first, because it both enables Chinese communications to maintain its focus on present sociopolitical issues and also broadly and deeply involves interpersonal, group, and organizational communication; as sociopolitical issues and their studies go beyond the scope of mass media, themes of Chinese communications will become much more diverse. Second, it deepens empirical studies of communication by enhancing critical reason, which could balance the instrumental reason and quantitative studies that tend to dominate Chinese communications; in doing so, it may remedy possible biases of American communications in the Chinese context. Third, it breaks the boundaries between disciplines by applying various theories of humanities and social sciences; more and more scholars from other study areas participate in communications or take the communication perspective on their own subjects; the achievements of intercultural communication research are one example. Fourth, it illuminates the history, context, and characteristics of Chinese practices and ideas of communication and the interaction between the practices and ideas; thus, it indicates not only the relationship between intellectual tradition and contemporary life but also the differences between Chinese and non-Chinese cultures and communications.

As communication cannot be separated from culture, communication studies (including its history, achievements, problems, and attributes) cannot be separated from its native society (including its social/political/economic/cultural dimensions). The development of Chinese communications closely follows sociopolitical changes in the post-Mao era and vividly reflects the character of modern Chinese scholarship. While its primary concerns are centered on urgent practical issues, the way it deals with these issues displays practical *zhi* and implies theoretical significance. Its future direction depends not only on what sociopolitical conditions the society will provide but also more important on the extent of its ability to solve the problems mentioned here. Although until now it has not made any conceptual or grammatical breakthroughs, there remains the possibility that cultural studies of communication will yield a fundamental cultural turn, enhancing its position in the intellectual dialogue with the West and eventually enabling it to make a significant contribution toward a universal theory of human communication.

NOTE

I would like to thank the following professors for discussing Chinese communications with me and helping me to collect data: Lu Ye, Ning Shufan, and Zhang Guoliang of Fudan University; Huang Dan of Zhejiang University; Song Xiaowei and Chen Lidan of the Chinese Academy of Social Sciences; Hu Zhengrong and Huang Shengmin of Beijing Broadcasting Institute; and Ji Huaqiang of Xiamen University. Dr. James Morriss and Dr. Joan Boyle of Dowling College read this chapter; I appreciate their valuable suggestions and help.

REFERENCES

Chen, C. (1993). *Shouzhong benwei lun qian xi* [An analysis of the audience-standard]. *Xinwen Zongheng (On Journalism)*, 2, 3-5.

Chen, C. (1999). *Jiannan de qifei* [A hard taking-off]. In J. Yun, Y. Long, & Y. Han (Eds.), *Chunbaoxue zai Zhongguo [Communications in China]* (pp. 180-190). Beijing: Beijing Broadcasting Institute Press.

Dai, Y. (1999). *Chuanboxue yanjiu de shidai beijing he xianshi jichu* [The background and basis of communication studies]. In J. Yun, Y. Long, & Y. Han (Eds.), *Chunbaoxue zai Zhongguo [Communications in China]* (pp. 18-27). Beijing: Beijing Broadcasting Institute Press.

Dong, T. (1995). *Chuanboxue daolun (Introduction to communication)*. Chengdu: Sichuan University Publishing House.

Fang, H. (1994). *Zhongguo jindai chuanbo sixiang de yianbian* [The development of modern Chinese thought on communication]. *Xinwen yu Chuanbo Yanjiu (Journalism and Communication Research)*, 1, 79-87.

Gadamer, H. G. (1985). *Truth and Method*. New York: Crossroads. (Originally published 1960).

Gao, Q. (1996). *Dazhong chuanbo meijie yu dangdai wenhua zhenghe* [An integration of mass media and contemporary popular culture]. In Zhongguo Shehui Kexue Yuan Xinwen Yanjiu Suo (Journalism Institute of China Academy of Social Sciences), Sichuan Sheng Guangbo Dianshi Ting (Ministry of Culture of Sichuan Province), Sichuan Sheng Shehui Kexue Yuan (Sichuan Social Science Academy)(Eds.), *Chuanbo, shehui, fazhan [Communication, society, and development]* (pp. 480-486). Chengdu: Chengdue Science and Technology Publishing House.

Guo, Z. (1999). *Lijie Xifang chuanboxue* [Understanding Western communications]. In J. Yun, Y. Long, & Y. Han (Eds.), *Chunbaoxue zai Zhongguo [Communications in China]* (pp. 77-86). Beijing: Beijing Broadcasting Institute Press.

Hall, D., & Ames, R. (1987). *Thinking through Confucius*. Albany: State University of New York Press.

Han, G. (1998). *1990-1997 Sisuo gaoxiao xinwenxue yu chuanboxue de huigu he fenxi* [A review and analysis of journalism and communications in four universities from 1990 to 1997]. *Xinwen Daxue (Journalism University)*, Autumn, 21-26.

Han, Y. (2000). *Xifang chuanboxue yinru licheng ji qi qishi* [The process of importing Western communications and its enlightenment]. Unpublished M.A. thesis, Beijing Broadcasting Institute, Beijing.

He, Q. (1995). *Xianqin zhuzi dui chuanbo gongneng de renshi yu yingyong* [Pre-Qin scholars' understanding and application of communication functions]. *Xinwen yu Chuanbo Yanjiu (Journalism and Communication Research)*, 1, 10-16.

Huang, D., & Han, G. (1997). *1981-1996: Woguo chuanboxue yanjiu de lishi he xianzhuang* [1981-1996: The history and state of Chinese communications]. *Xinwen Daxue (Journalism University)*, Spring, 20-26.

Huang, J. (1994). *Cong chuan tansuo gudai Zhongguo chuanbo de leibie yu tezheng* ["*Chuan*": Its classifications and characteristics in ancient China]. In Y. Yu & X. Zheng (Eds.), *Cong ling kaishi [Starting from the very beginning]* (pp. 69-96). Xiamen: Xiamen University Press.

Huang, S., & Ding, J. (1997). *Meijie jingying yu chanyehua yanjiu* [A study of media management and industrialization]. Beijing: Beijing Broadcasting Institute Press.

James, W. (1960). What pragmatism means. In M. Konvitz & G. Kennedy (Eds.), *The American pragmatists* (pp. 28-43). New York: Meridian Books.

Lasswell, H. (1948). The structure and function of communication in society. In L. Bryson (Ed.), *The communication of ideas* (pp. 32-51). New York: Harper.

Li, B. (1999). *Tangdai wenming yu xinwen chuanbo [The culture of Tang Dynasty and journalistic communication]*. Beijing: Xinhua Publishing House.

Liao, S. (1998). *Wuoguo ershi nian lai chuanboxue yanjiu de huigu* [A review of twenty years of communication studies in China]. *Xinwen Daxue (Journalism University),* Winter, 24-30.

Liu, H. (1991). *Chuanboxue zai Zhongguo dalu de lishi yange yu zouxiang* [Communication studies in China: Its history and directions]. *Xinwen Daxue (Journalism University),* Autumn, 9-11.

McQuail, D., & Windahl, S. (1987). *Dazhong chuanbo moshi lun [Communication models for the study of mass communication].* (J. Zhu & W. Wu, Trans.). Shanghai: Shanghai Yiwen Publishing House.

Ming, A. (1994). *Disanci quanguo chuanboxue yantao hui xueshu guandian zongshu* [A report on the third national convention on communications]. In *Zhongguo Xinwen Nianjian Bianji Weiyuanhui* (Ed.), *Zhongguo xinwen nianjian [Yearbook of Chinese journalism]* (pp. 141-143). Beijing: Zhongguo Xinwen Nianjian She (Chinese Press of Yearbook on Journalism).

Rorty, R. (1982). *Consequences of pragmatism.* Minneapolis: University of Minnesota Press.

Schramm, W., & Porter, W. (1984). *Chuanbo xue gailun [Men, women, messages, and media: Understanding human communication]* (L. Chen, L. Zhou, & Q. Li, Trans.). Beijing: Xinhua Publishing House.

Sha, L., Chen, Y., & Zheng, W. (1990). *Chuanboxue: Yi ren wei zhuti de tuxiang shijie zhi mi [Communications: A puzzle of the human-centered symbolic world].* Beijing: The People's University of China Publishing House.

Shao, P. (1997). *Chuanboxue daolun [An introduction to communication].* Hangzhou: Zhejiang University Press.

Shao, P. (1999a). *Fangkuan chunbaoxue yanjiu de shiye* [Broadening the vision of communication studies]. In J. Yun, Y. Long, & Y. Han (Eds.), *Chunbaoxue zai Zhongguo [Communications in China]* (pp. 218-233). Hangzhou: Zhejiang University Press.

Shao, P. (1999b). *Chuanboxue bentuhua yanjiu de huigu yu qianzhan* [Native studies of communication: Review and perspective]. *Hangzhou Normal University Academic Journal, 4,* 36-41.

Shao, P., & Liu, Q. (1998). *Meijie jingying guanli xue* [A study of media management]. Hongzhou: Zhejiang University Press.

Shen, L. (1999). *Cong chuanboxue de yinru kan Zhongguo xinwen xueke de lilun jianshe* [The importation of communications and the theoretical construction of Chinese journalism]. In J. Yun, Y. Long, & Y. Han (Eds.), *Chunbaoxue zai Zhongguo [Communications in China]* (pp. 60-69). Beijing: Beijing Broadcasting Institute Press.

Song, X. (1992). *Shouzhong quanyi yanjiu daolun* [On the audience's rights and interests]. *Journalism Research Documents, 1,* 28-45.

Sun, X. (1994a). *Zhongguo dalu chuanbo yanjiu de huigu yu qianzhan* [Communication studies in China: Review and prospect]. *Xinwen yu Chuanbo Yanjiu, 1*, 2-9.

Sun, X. (1994b). *Yanyu geyan yu chuan de yuanli* [Proverbs, maxims, and the principles of communication]. In Y. Yu & X. Zheng. (Eds.), *Cong ling kaishi [Start from the very beginning]* (pp. 25-37). Xiamen: Xiamen University Press.

Sun, X. (Ed.). (1997). *Huaxia chuanbo lun* [On Chinese communication]. Beijing: The People's Press.

Sun, Z. (1997). *The discourse on ming-shi and practical zhi in ancient China.* Unpublished Ph.D. dissertation, New York University, New York.

Tang, X. (1999). *Baoyi jingji yu baoyi guanli [Newspaper industry and management].* Beijing: Xinhua Publishing House.

Xiao, X. (1995). Chuanboxue bentuhue de xuanze, xianzhuangji weilai fazhan [The nativization of communications: Its choice, state and future]. *Xinwen yu Yiangu, 4*, 34–39.

Wang, Y. (1998). *Jianghua yu duanlie* [Rigidity and fault]. *Xinwen yu Chuanbo Yanjiu, 4*, 24-30.

Wu, Y. (1988). *Wuxing de wangluo [The invisible net].* Beijing: China International Culture Publishing Company.

Xu, Y. (1998). *Wuoguo chuanboxue yanjiu de de yu shi* [Chinese communications: Achievements and weaknesses]. *Xinwen yu Chuanbo Yianjiu, 4*, 2-8.

Xu, Y. (1999). *Chuanboxue yanjiu yao jiehe Zhonguo shiji* [Adapting communication studies to Chinese realities]. In J. Yun, Y. Long, & Y. Han (Eds.), *Chunbaoxue zai Zhongguo [Communications in China]* (pp. 246-257). Beijing: Beijing Broadcasting Institute Press.

Xu, Y., & Huang L. (1982). *Xifang chuanboxue yanjiu zuotanhui zong*shu [The seminar on Western communications: A report]. *Guoji Xinwen Jie, 4*, 18-20.

Yang, R. (1993). *Lun dangdai Zhongguo dazhong wenhua langchao zhong de dazhong meijie* [Mass media and the waves of popular culture in contemporary China]. *Xinwen Daxue,* Winter, 21-24.

Yu, G. (1999). *Xunzhao yu meijie he shichang de zuijia Jiehe dian* [Looking for the best integrating point between media and market]. In J. Yun, Y. Long, & Y. Han (Eds.), *Chunbaoxue zai Zhongguo [Communications in China]* (pp. 169-179). Beijing: Beijing Broadcasting Institute Press.

Yu, Y., & Zheng, X. (Eds.). (1994). *Cong ling kaishi [Starting from the very beginning].* Xiamen: Xiamen University Press.

Yuan, Z. (1986). *Woguo chuanboxue yanjiu qingkuang* [The situations of communication studies in China]. *Newsletter of the Journalism Association, 3*, 12-15.

Yuan, J., Long, Y., & Han, Y. (Eds.). (1999). *Chunbaoxue zai Zhongguo*_[Communications in China]. Beijing: Beijing Broadcasting Institute Press.

Zhang, G. (1999). *Fudan chuanboxue yanjiu de guoqu, xianzai he weilai* [The past, present and future of communication studies at Fudan University]. In J. Yun, Y. Long, & Y. Han (Eds.), *Chunbaoxue zai Zhongguo [Communications in China]* (pp. 133-140). Beijing: Beijing Broadcasting Institute Press.

Zheng, B. (1978). *Meiguo zichan jieji xiwenxue: Gongzhong chuanbo* [Bourgeois journalism in American mass communication]. *Weiguo Xinwen Shiye Ziliao, 1* 10-16.

Zhou, H. (1994). *Zhongguo guangbo dianshi jingji guanli gailun [Introduction to the management of the Chinese broadcast industry].* Beijing: China International Culture's Publishing Company.

Zhou, Y. (2000). *Zhongguo gudai wenhua chuanbo shi [A history of Chinese cultural communication].* Beijing: Beijing Broadcasting Institute Publishing House.

2

Intercultural/Interpersonal Communication Research in China: A Preliminary Review

Ge Gao and Xiaosui Xiao

The study of human communication has a short history in China. For the past few years, the scope of human communication in China has been broadened to include not only intercultural communication (e.g., Guan, 1995; Jia, 1997), but also nonverbal communication (e.g., Yang & Bao, 1998) and, most recently, business communication/organizational communication (e.g., He & Li, 1998). *Kua wen hua jiao ji* ("intercultural communication") has continued to be the focus of the study of Chinese human communication since its first introduction in the early 1980s.

In the current literature published in English, research and theorizing on intercultural communication published in China in Chinese is not adequately reviewed or evaluated. This lack of representation can be attributed to the language barrier and the inaccessibility of published works. Moreover, given that communication is not yet an established field of study in China, communication research tends to be scattered in various journals. It is a task of paramount difficulty to gather all publications related to human communication in the absence of an indexing system.

In this chapter, we provide a selective review of research articles and book chapters published in Chinese, which we believe both represent the current status of the study of intercultural communication in China and are significant in bringing Chinese native perspectives to the study of intercultural communication. Nevertheless, the scope of our review is limited to research that has been conducted in mainland China and what were made available to us at the time of writing this chapter. In this chapter, the term "Chinese" refers to Han Chinese, who constitute the vast majority of the population in China. For the flow of the text, "Han" will be omitted from the text. In the following pages, we first present a brief review of the historical development of intercultural communication in China. Then, we summarize research relating to intercultural communication and provide a synopsis of communication research on Chinese native concepts. We conclude this chapter by presenting our suggestions for future intercultural communication research in China.

A BRIEF HISTORY

The study of intercultural communication was first introduced to China in the early 1980s. There were several translations of the term "intercultural communication" at the beginning stage (Lin, 1999). Lin notes that there are now widely accepted Chinese terms for both the study of intercultural or cross-cultural communication (*kua wen hua jiao ji xue* or *kua wen hua jiao ji yan jiu*) and the concept of intercultural or cross-cultural communication (*kua wen hua jiao ji*).

The development of intercultural communication in China can be divided into three phases: 1978–1987, 1988–1994, and 1995–present (Hu, 2000). The first phase reflects the attention given to culture in foreign language teaching in China. Many language-related topics were explored during this period by instructors of foreign languages. The relation between culture and language, the importance of cultural customs in language instruction, the embedded cultural meanings in words, and cultural misunderstanding were incorporated either in foreign language teaching or in textbooks (Hu, 2000).

The second phase (1988–1994) marks the emergence of the identity of Chinese intercultural communication as a discipline and a more systematic introduction of the study of intercultural communication in Western cultures. Hu (2000) has documented several areas of development in this endeavor. A handful of major Chinese universities started to offer a course in intercultural communication at both the undergraduate and the graduate level (e.g., Beijing Foreign Languages University, Peking University, Harbin Polytechnic, Shanghai Foreign Languages University, Fujian Normal University). A number of books on language and culture were published. In 1988, Samovar and Porter's *Intercultural Communication: A Reader* was translated into Chinese, followed by the publication of Hall's *Silent Language* in Chinese in 1991. Furthermore, new Chinese communication frontiers such as nonverbal communication and communication/conflicts in joint ventures were examined and analyzed in publications.

The third phase (1995–present) symbolizes the establishment of the discipline of Chinese intercultural communication. He (1999) notes that the year

1995 marks a turning point in communication research in China. Since 1995, a number of notable books on communication have been published in Chinese by Chinese scholars (e.g., Guan, 1995; Hu & Gao, 1997; Jia, 1997; Lin, 1996; Wang, 1996). Among them, three have paved the way for the establishment of the discipline of Chinese intercultural communication (He, 1999). Guan's book on intercultural communication (1995) has been used as a textbook for majors in the International Politics Department of Beijing University. Wang's book on intercultural communication and relating with foreigners (1996) popularizes the study of intercultural communication. Lin's book (1996) presents another systematic coverage of the study of intercultural communication. He (1999) contends that the advent of dedicated volumes in intercultural communication signifies the end of the import phase and the beginning of the creativity phase and suggests that intercultural communication as an imported discipline is undergoing the process of localization. In addition, the first Chinese intercultural communication conference convened in Harbin in 1995. The biannual conference has since provided a forum for organized exchanges of scholarship in intercultural communication in China.

INTRODUCTION AND CRITIQUE OF RESEARCH IN WESTERN TRADITIONS

A vast majority of the communication research published in Chinese academic journals appears to serve two primary purposes: to review research conducted outside China and to critique existing research from a Chinese cultural perspective. Data-based studies of human communication are still difficult to find. The state of research in Chinese communication reflects a healthy transformation from uncritical presentations of research in Western traditions to reflective applications of such research to the Chinese cultural context. The reflective turn is critical for Chinese communication research, as Jia (2000) aptly stated: "By analyzing the Western biases, Chinese communication research can be more productive and more useful to East-West intercultural communication" (p. 140). In our subsequent review of recent Chinese communication research, we focus on studies that exemplify the reflective turn. Those studies involve comparative analyses of culture and communication and applications of theories in Western traditions to the Chinese cultural context.

Culture and Communication

By engaging in comparative analyses of culture and communication, Chinese scholars have contributed to our understanding of various forms of communication in the Chinese cultural context. Several recent studies exemplify this contribution. Zou (1997) investigated the prominent influence of culture in word choices. In Chinese, for example, *ge ge* ("older brother"), *jie*

jie ("older sister"), *di di* ("younger brother"), and *mei mei* ("younger sister") represent sibling relationships, while in English, there are only two terms: "brother" and "sister." *Tang ge* ("older cousin on the paternal side") and *biao mei* ("younger cousin on the maternal side") in Chinese are replaced by "cousin" in English. Zou (1997) argues that the Chinese terms of address are more sophisticated. They serve to differentiate among young and old as well as close and distant, and they are influenced by kinship relationships in the Chinese culture.

First naming also bears cultural variations. Du (1999) notes that the Chinese language has a lot more variety of first-naming address forms than the American English language. The three most commonly used first-naming address forms include: (1) one-character first name, (2) two-character first-name, and (3) two-character first name made by the reduplication of a one-character first name. Du's (1999) research and observation reveal that the use of the first name in Chinese everyday interactions can be both symmetrical and asymmetrical. In families where members share a sense of solidarity, the symmetrical use of the first name is encouraged. That is, husband and wife, brothers, and cousins reciprocate in using each other's first name. The asymmetrical use of the first name applies to relationships defined as deferential. For example, grandparents, parents, and aunts can use first names of the younger generation, but the latter cannot reciprocate. An older sister or brother can use the first name of a younger sister or brother, but the latter cannot reciprocate. Chinese are culturally conditioned to be deferential, and Chinese speech often is characterized by its deferential features (Du, 1999).

Moreover, Du (1999) explains that one-character first names are seldom reciprocated in the Chinese culture because they are only used by the elder addressing the young or by intimate couples (e.g., husband and wife, boyfriend and girlfriend). When one-character first names are used, they are seldom exchanged in the presence of others. In general, first naming is most common among family members. Among friends and colleagues, first naming implies a close and intimate relationship. Thus it can be used as a rhetorical strategy to build solidarity and intimacy in a relationship. Given the implication of intimacy in first naming in Chinese culture, to address a person of the opposite sex by his or her first name signifies a special relationship (Du, 1999).

Comparative analyses of culture and communication have also enabled Chinese scholars to identify concepts indigenous to the culture being studied. One notable example is the concept of "rhetoric," which does not convey the same meaning across languages. Gu (1999) indicated that the English word "rhetoric" and the Chinese translation "*xiu ci xue*" are not equivalent. *Xiu ci xue* exemplifies the equivalent of the Western stylistic tradition, focusing on figures of speech and style, while the study of the Western humanistic tradition of rhetoric is close to the Chinese "*shui*." According to Gu, the study of *shui* was long lost in China, until very recently. The recent revival of this tradition is found in the business world, focusing on strategies for sales and marketing. In Chinese culture, three aspects of meanings are derived from the term *xiu ci xue*: (1) of the theorization of *xiu ci*, (2) of the theory of *xiu ci*, and (3) of an independent academic discipline. Peng (cited in Gu, 1999) is the first mainland Chinese scholar who, in 1996, elevated the status of the ancient traveling rhetors to scholars and presented their ten persuasive strategies, which include speaking, listening, and assessment. The English term "rhetoric" encompasses much broader meanings than the terms/expressions used in Chinese.

Applications of Theories

Chinese scholars have also engaged in critical evaluations and analyses of theories in the Western tradition. These efforts are indicative of the reflective turn in Chinese communication research. Politeness theories (e.g., Brown and Levinson, 1987; Grice, 1975; Leech, 1983) and an intercultural communication competence model (e.g., Dodd, 1995; Kim, 1991) are prominent examples under such scrutiny. Bi (1996), for example, argues that politeness is a culture-specific phenomenon. Politeness theories such as Brown and Levinson's (1987) face-saving theory and face-threatening acts, Leech's (1983) politeness principle, and Grice's (1975) cooperative principle cannot be directly applied to Chinese politeness. Bi maintains that, in Chinese culture, politeness is concerned with one's ethical self-cultivation, not the cost and the benefit of the self and the other in an interaction. Chinese personal relationships are based on *qing* ("human feeling"), not truthfulness, and moral constraints rather than the cooperative principle dictate the relationships. To illustrate, when Chinese use apologies to express their gratitude, they seek human feeling instead of truth. Showing warmth, expressing concern, and displaying modesty are polite ways to establish harmonious relationships (Bi, 1996).

Bi (1999) contends that in face-threatening-acts theory (Brown & Levinson, 1987), to respect individual autonomy is viewed as politeness, but in Chinese culture, mutual concern, modesty, and respect for others are signs of politeness. To Chinese, suggestions, reminders, advice, promises, and expressions of envy and admiration indicate a caring, helpful, and friendly attitude, but they are construed as threats to personal autonomy and constitute face-threatening acts in Western cultures. Bi (1999) offers four guiding principles that help explain Chinese polite communication. They include: (1) allowances for unforeseen circumstances (e.g., I think, probably), (2) denigrating self and respecting others (e.g., I'm a terrible cook; Chinese modesty is a virtue of self-cultivation), (3) mutual care (e.g., making comments about a person's welfare or giving direct advice to show concern), and (4) fulfillment of moral obligations (e.g., indirectness for harmony).

In a comparative study of politeness, Liu (1999) analyzed twenty Chinese letters and sixteen English letters written between the mid 1980s and the early 1990s by potential contributors to the editors. She found indirectness in

Chinese letters at the discourse level, but not at the sentence level. Chinese contributors described their work as clumsy, awkward, and poor and themselves as having limited capacity and having put in little effort, which was typical of Chinese politeness. Specifically, differences emerged in four areas between Chinese and English letters. In inside addressing, Chinese used many complicated honorifics and paid more attention to politeness, while English were more concerned with the level of formality. With regard to opening, Chinese letters began with either a greeting or phatic talk, while English letters got right down to business. In self-referring and other-referring, Chinese denigrated themselves and elevated the letter receivers, while no difference was present in English letters (Liu, 1999).

Gao (1998) challenged the conceptualization of intercultural communication competence (ICC; Dodd, 1995; Kim, 1991), raising concerns in four specific areas. First, defining ICC as "effective outcomes" is inherently illogical because competence refers to a person's internal ability, while outcome is external to a person. Second, there is a lack of an integrated system of clearly defined interrelationships among various components and predictors. The components of effectiveness and its predictors tend to be rather fragmented and atomistic. Third, as there is no clear rationale for including or excluding certain factors, the list can be expanded indefinitely. Finally, confusion arises when a predictor is also treated as an outcome. Gao contends that the assumptions of rationalism and individualism that underlie ICC are not shared in all cultures.

To address the concerns raised in ICC research, Gao claims that one needs to assume that ICC resides within a person and involves a person's internal potential, which is developed in communication with others. Gao proposes the adoption of *dao* and *qi*, two concepts present in major Chinese traditional philosophies, in conceptualizing ICC. The literal meanings of *dao* and *qi* are respectively "way" and "container," but their extended meanings imply "guiding principle" and "tool" or "instrument." *Dao* is the most fundamental element of ICC, which is holistic, nonquantifiable, and to be *wu*ed ("to awaken"). To the contrary, *qi*, similar to the present conceptualization of ICC, can be segmented, measured, and learned/trained. Current research, teaching, and training in ICC have limited its focus to *qi*, but "what one is and what one becomes is far more significant than what one knows and what one does" (Gao, 1998, p. 49). Gao calls for the development of *dao*, the cultivation of personality orientation, in ICC.

NATIVE CONCEPTS IN CHINESE CULTURE AND COMMUNICATION

A systematic study of native Chinese concepts in China is a rather recent phenomenon. Even though native Chinese concepts such as *mian zi* and *bao* are not new to Western literature, the vast majority of such research has been conducted by scholars outside China. In this section, we will review research by scholars inside China on several core concepts of Chinese interpersonal relationships. These concepts include *yuan*, *mian zi*, *bao*, and *ren qing*. Research in this endeavor has been grounded in Chinese philosophical traditions and has signified a move away from the reflective phase to the creative phase. We believe this move is promising for the study of communication in China. It marks a concrete step towards breaking patterns of Orientalism in the study of Chinese communication (Jia, 2000).

Yuan

Do Chinese have a sentiment of discontent toward others? If they do, how do they express it? These two questions are addressed in Peng's (1993) analysis of the native concept of *yuan*. According to Peng, *yuan* refers to behavior that expresses discontent. It is also the state of mind of a person who experiences discontent but issues no counterattack. Throughout Chinese history, millions of poems were written about *yuan*; thousands of Chinese phrases contain the word *yuan*, such as *yuan yan* ("words of complaint"), *yuan hen* ("resentment"), and *yuan qi* ("grievance"). Peng has identified four characteristics of *yuan* in Chinese culture: (1) it expresses discontent, unhappiness, a feeling of powerlessness, and helplessness; (2) its expression and dissemination are indirect; (3) it is cumulative; and (4) it can be sudden, full-scale, and destructive when it erupts.

As a key concept in Chinese interpersonal sentiment, *yuan* plays a pivotal role in a person's interpersonal exchanges and pursuit of life and happiness (Peng, 1993). When Chinese experience discontent toward others but feel that it is difficult to communicate, they bear a sentiment of *yuan*. Even though *yuan* enables Chinese to avoid face-to-face conflict with others, given its self-protective function, its cumulative effect can cause a heavy psychological burden for a person (Peng, 1993). Thus, *yuan* management becomes a critical issue. Peng points out that Chinese social norms restrain persons from engaging in behaviors that are impolite and rude and may hurt others' feelings. Expressions of interpersonal discontented sentiment, therefore, must adhere to the following principles: (1) *he li* ("conforming to rites"): if it doesn't conform, don't express it; (2) *zhong he* ("to value harmony"): expressions of discontented sentiment cannot disrupt harmonious interpersonal relationships; and (3) *you jie* ("to exercise moderation/control"): words should be gentle and measured.

In everyday interpersonal interactions, Chinese utilize multiple methods to manage *yuan* (Peng, 1993). Those methods are categorized into two approaches: positive and negative. The positive approach seeks an active and rational way to alleviate or resolve *yuan qi* ("grievance"). Some of the methods involve (1) getting a mediator, (2) self-adjustment (e.g., telling oneself not to take things to heart), and (3) the instigator's admitting the mistake and offering an apology. This last method is the best way to end the vicious cycle of *yuan*. The negative approach, on the contrary, serves to deepen one's discontent and form a vicious cycle. Several methods succeed in producing such outcomes: (1) to distance oneself from the other, (2) to attack by innuendo, (3) to fabricate rumors, (4) to vent *yuan qi* upon unrelated others, (5) to seek opportunities to retaliate, (6) to blame heaven and fate, (7) to engage in self-torment, and (8) to become self-intoxicated (Peng, 1993).

A survey study of 39 participants in 1990 found that three types of methods were used to express discontented: (1) direct, (2) tactful, and (3) "say nothing." A large percentage of the participants employed either the tactful or the "say nothing" method. Among close friends and members of the family, discontent was expressed directly. Several factors influenced the expression of discontent. One's relation with others was the most influential factor. In addition, the level of the intensity of the sentiment and personality were important. Participants gave four reasons for using an indirect method of expression: (1) concern for ethics (e.g., to show respect to others), (2) concern for strategy (e.g., an indirect method is believed to achieve a better result), (3) concern for *mian zi* (i.e., to not let others lose face), and (4) concern for self-interest (i.e., fear of revenge) (Peng, 1993). It appears that the majority of the Chinese elect to employ a constrained and tactful method to manage their discontent.

Furthermore, Peng proposes that a Chinese person's sentiment often is shared in a relational circle rather than experienced by himself or herself. Making distinctions between insiders and outsiders is very important in managing Chinese interpersonal relationships, as in expressing and disseminating sentiment. Chinese differentiate between insiders and outsiders, especially with negative sentiment. Within the relational circle, a person tends to express discontent directly, but the opposite holds true outside the circle. Within the circle, because there is trust, a person is not concerned with face, secrecy, or fear of revenge, but outside the circle, direct expressions of negative sentiment and different interests are most likely to cause retaliation. To maintain harmony, a person needs to exercise forbearance. Nevertheless, Peng puts strangers in a special category. Strangers can express their feelings directly because they carry no previous associations and the likelihood of future interaction is very slim. Peng concludes that a more appropriate unit of analysis of sentiment study is the sentiment circle.

Mian Zi

Zuo (1993) conducted a survey research on the notions of *lian* and *mian* among 107 college students in Wuhan, China. Respondents were asked to evaluate among a list of 30 events that involved (1) a loss of *lian*, (2) a loss of *mian zi*, (3) a loss of both *lian* and *mian*, and (4) no loss of *lian* or *mian*.

They were able to differentiate between *lian* loss and *mian* loss events and judged the former as more severe. Breaking the law and violating ethical and moral principles were perceived as *lian* loss. Some of the examples include an exposed extramarital affair, stealing, committing a crime, bullying elders and the young, and exposed corruption. *Lian* loss creates a long-term and psychological effect. *Mian* loss, on the other hand, is mostly concerned with improper manner in public or a lack of ability. Twenty out of 30 events were judged as *mian* loss events. Being drunk at a banquet, not being able to keep a promise, and public embarrassment such as loosening one's belt while eating are examples. *Mian* loss is situational and temporary. In the meantime, respondents evaluated conspiring, premarital pregnancy, and loss of chastity as cases of losing both *lian* and *mian*, because they felt the underlying motives were either unclear or difficult to judge.

In this study, women respondents differed significantly from their male counterparts (Zuo, 1993). Women attached more importance to the concepts of both *lian* and *mian*. They demonstrated more sensitivity to them and gave them a higher overall ranking. For example, women viewed events such as bullying elders and the young, exposed extramarital affairs, loss of chastity, and premarital pregnancy as a much more severe loss of *lian* or *mian* than did men. Even though divorce was not perceived as a *lian* or *mian* loss event, the endorsement from women was significantly stronger than that from men. Zuo argues that the gender role differences, different life paths, and different career goals for women and men in China and women's desire to receive a positive evaluation from others all contribute to the differences.

Another significant finding of the study reflects the changing values and the influence of education in shaping persons' perceptions. Inconsistent with traditional ways of thinking, respondents in this study did not perceive "divorce" and "infertility" as either *lian* loss or *mian* loss events.

Bao

Yang (1993) notes that *bao* is a very complex concept in Chinese interpersonal exchanges. *Bao* involves not only the exchange of social resources but also intricate interpersonal relationships and various regulations in force. Favor, *ren qing*, and ethics are all an integral part of *bao*.

There are eight attributes of *bao* in Chinese culture (Yang, 1993). First, *bao* is exchangeable. Unlike Western social exchange theory, the Chinese *bao* emphasizes the implicit nature of exchange in interpersonal relationships. Exchange is not only a social behavior but also one dictated by the rules of propriety. Both parties in a relationship initiate the exchange as stated in the following expression: *you en bu bao fei jun zi* ("He who does not pay a debt of gratitude is not a gentleman"). Second, *bao* is affective. Both the positive (e.g., to repay) and the negative (e.g., to retaliate) dimensions of *bao* are filled with strong emotions. To illustrate, *yi ri wei shi, zhong shen wei fu* ("He who teaches me for one day is my father for life"). In the Chinese culture, the return involves the element of *qing* (human feeling). Third, *bao* is incremental. *Bao* surpasses the concept of "reciprocity." Given the involvement of both care and *qing* in interpersonal exchanges, return should be augmented, as suggested in the expression *ni jing wo yi chi, wo jing ni yi zhang* ("you honor me a foot, and I will in return honor you ten feet"). Fourth, *bao* can be delayed. It does not require an immediate return. Fifth, *bao* is particularistic. That is, any return is measured against the type of relationship. Distinctions are made between insiders and outsiders. Sixth, the nature of giving is emphasized. To illustrate, if someone has saved your life, you need to pay back your gratitude for the rest of your life. Seventh, *bao* is governed by differences in roles. The giver and the receiver view *bao* differently. The majority of givers expect an equivalent return. When the return is not equivalent, both the giver and the receiver consider it unkind. A receiver needs to understand the expectation of returning a favor. When a return is not augmented, it will communicate to the giver the level of gratitude. Eighth and finally, *bao* involves the element of duality. "Exchange and ethics," "exchange and feeling," and "exchange and conformity" define *bao*. Consequently, *bao* goes beyond the notion of exchange and entails rich connotations.

Bao also performs four distinctive functions in Chinese culture (Yang, 1993). First, *bao* is a cultural norm, which enables people to follow the law of causality. It is the social order and an impartial principle. Second, *bao* enables interactions between two people, two families, and two groups to be constantly consolidated and to move in cycles. In the process of such consolidation, firm relationships are established. As a result, the society will become an unbreakable and interconnected whole. Third, *bao* is a way to maintain order in an ethical society. It conveys to people that good will be rewarded with good and evil with evil. It promotes the good and curbs evil. Finally, *bao* cultivates a sense of indebtedness in the Chinese culture. Both the giver and the receiver will always be in an unbalanced relationship. Creditors and debtors define most Chinese relationships.

Yang (1993) argues that research on *bao* still stays at the level of conceptual analysis. He believes that empirical research on *bao* will broaden our understanding of other native Chinese concepts such as *mian zi, ren qing, yuan*, and kinship relations.

Ren Qing

Qu (1993) explains that Chinese interpersonal relationships are expressed in *ren qing, ren lun*, and *ren yuan*. *Ren qing* (human feeling) cannot be equated with the concept of emotion in the Western tradition. The specific focus on ethics in traditional Chinese culture has added two unique dimensions to the feeling/emotion of a person. First, its focus is on interpersonal relationships, not the self. Second, it involves the element of propriety. *Ren qing* thus is a mixture of feelings, relations, and ethics.

Ren lun (human ethics) is very close to the meaning of the present-day term "interpersonal relationships." It involves the observance of proprieties and refers to ordered human relations and their standards (Qu, 1993). Qu indicates that *ren yuan* (human fate) refers to the mandate of heaven, fate, or destiny. It is used to explain interpersonal relationships. To attribute one's situation to *ren yuan* is to seek a satisfactory explanation for oneself and thus to gain balance in life. The explanation of *ren yuan* makes it possible for Chinese to avoid excessive joy or sorrow and to willingly adapt to various interpersonal situations.

Qu (1993) notes that Chinese interpersonal relationships are established on the basis of three deep-rooted foundations: belief in the mandate of heaven, kinship, and Confucian ethics. "Man [woman] proposes, (but) Heaven [God] disposes" (*mou shi zai ren, cheng shi zai tian*) exemplifies the notion of fate in Chinese interpersonal relationships. *Ren qing, ren lun,* and *ren yuan* together form an organic whole. Even though they are mutually inclusive, each performs its unique function. *Ren qing* lies at the core of this system, representing the family-centered orientation of traditional Chinese. *Ren lun* provides rules and regulations for social interactions, and *ren yuan* sets all interpersonal relationships in the framework of accepting them as they are (fate).

Qu (1993) compares how interpersonal relationships operate in Chinese and Western cultures (see Table 2.1 for specific differences). In Western

TABLE 2.1. A Comparison of the Traditional Chinese and Western Interpersonal Relationships

	Traditional Chinese	*Western*
Premise	Linked in hearts	Disconnected in hearts
	Kindred spirits	Different spirits
Method	Experiencing with feelings	Testing with theory
Background	The mandate of heaven	Religion
	Kinship	Individualism
	Hierarchy/order of importance	Justice/equality
Characteristics	Destiny (*yuan*)	God's will (divinity)
	Rules of human feelings (*qing*)	Interpersonal Rules (reason)
	Order of human relationships (*lun*)	Social contract (law)
Manifestations	Blood relationships	Rights and responsibility
	Return greater than give	Equal give and return
	Mutual dependence	Independence
	Other-orientation	Self-orientation
	Submit to the will of heaven and be content with one's life	Strive for progress

culture, interpersonal relationships focus on reason, not feeling, whereas in Chinese culture the emphasis is on feeling, not reason. To Chinese, reason is embedded in feeling. When one is not amenable to feeling, one is not amenable to reason; the former constitutes a more serious offense than the latter. Qu argues that the shift from focusing on self-oriented feelings to relation-oriented feelings and the corresponding rules and regulations in Chinese culture serve to suppress the self-oriented self and give rise to the other-oriented self. In Chinese interpersonal relationships, feeling is more important than reason. The Chinese concept of *ren qing*, however, is not universal. Its meaning and use are influenced by blood relationships. The hierarchical structure on the basis of feelings belonging to blood relationships provokes such bipolarity as insiders versus outsiders, having feelings versus having no feelings, harmony versus conflict, and honesty versus dishonesty. The bipolar tendency helps explain the insider versus outsider and the close versus distant relationship orientation in Chinese culture (Qu, 1993).

PROBLEMS AND CHALLENGES IN CHINESE COMMUNICATION RESEARCH

The study of human communication has made great strides in China in the past two decades. Three major shifts are indicative of such progress, from introduction to application, from acceptance to critical evaluation, and from sporadic research to concerted efforts. Nevertheless, several impediments still exist. First, only a handful of major Chinese universities offer courses in intercultural communication. Lin (1999) attributes the absence of a wide participation to (1) a severe lack of theoretical inquiry that helps establish intercultural communication as a relatively independent area of study, (2) a lack of satisfactory textbooks, and (3) a lack of awareness of the need for intercultural communication as a field of study. Second, researchers do not have a diverse academic background, and most are foreign language instructors (mostly English instructors), Chinese language instructors of non-native speakers, and linguists (Hu, 2000). Consequently, the focus of their research is limited to language and culture, language instruction, translation, and cultural customs. Third, most introduction of and research on intercultural communication has been confined to the field of foreign languages (Lin, 1999). Fourth, the vast majority of the publications in academic journals still focus on critical reviews of research conducted in Western contexts. Finally, there is a tremendous amount of overlap of materials in published articles because university-affiliated academic journals often have a limited circulation.

We think several steps need to be taken to advance intercultural communication research in China. First, more emphasis should be put on testing existing theories and, most important, developing Chinese theories of human communication. Theory development enables a systematic and coordinated analysis of everyday communication behavior. As Lin (1999) concurs, theory building contributes to the vitality of intercultural communication. Second, Chinese scholars must go beyond presenting critical reviews of existing research. They must conduct data-based investigations of communication behaviors in Chinese culture. This proposal is endorsed by Hu (1999), who calls for more data-driven research on a given topic rather than "overview articles" or "articles of a general nature" to further intercultural communication studies. Third, Chinese scholars should apply different methods in their study of Chinese communication. Questionnaires, personal interviews, and texts can be used to explore new topics and to validate existing findings. Last, given the interdisciplinary nature of human communication, collaboration among various disciplines is essential to the study of communication in China, and multidisciplinary teams should join forces in this endeavor.

REFERENCES

Bi, J. W. (1996). *Li mao de wen hua te xing yan jiu* [A study of the cultural characteristics of "politeness"]. *World Chinese Instruction, 1*, 51-59.

Bi, J. W. (1999). Cultural characteristics of indirectness. In W. Z. Hu (Ed.), *Aspects of intercultural communication. Proceedings of China's 2nd conference on intercultural communication* (pp. 335-355). Beijing: Foreign Language Teaching and Research Press.

Brown, P., & Levinson, S. (1987). *Politeness: Some universals in language usage.* Cambridge: Cambridge University Press.

Dodd, C. H. (1995). *Dynamics of intercultural communication* (4th ed.). Madison, W: WCB Brown and Benchmark Publishers.

Du, X. Z. (1999). A tentative comparison of first naming between Chinese and American English. In W. Z. Hu (Ed.), *Aspects of intercultural communication. Proceedings of China's 2nd conference on intercultural communication* (pp. 207-219). Beijing: Foreign Language Teaching and Research Press.

Gao, Y. H. (1998). *Kua wen hua jiao ji neng li de "dao" yu "qi"* [The *"dao"* and *"qi"* of intercultural communication competence]. *Language Instruction and Research, 3*, 39-53.

Grice, H. P. (1975). Logic and conversation. In P. Cole, & J. L. Morgan (Eds.), *Syntax and semantics*, Vol. 3: *Speech Acts* (pp. 41-58). New York: Academic Press.

Gu, Y. G. (1999). Reconstructing humanistic and stylistic traditions in Chinese rhetoric: A contrastive approach. In W. Z. Hu (Ed.), *Aspects of intercultural communication. Proceedings of China's 2nd conference on intercultural communication* (pp. 7-38). Beijing: Foreign Language Teaching and Research Press.

Guan, S. J. (1995). *Kua wen hua jiao liu xue [Intercultural communication studies].* Beijing: Peking University Press.

He, D. K. (1999). A new phase in comparative cultural studies: A review of recently published intercultural communication works. In W. Z. Hu (Ed.), *Aspects of intercultural communication. Proceedings of China's 2nd conference on intercultural communication* (pp. 620-632). Beijing: Foreign Language Teaching and Research Press.

He, Q. Y., & Li, Y. (1998). *Qian tan he zi qi ye de kua wen hua gou tong wen ti* [An introduction to intercultural communication problems in joint venture enterprises]. *Southern Economy, 2,* 57-58.

Hu, W. Z. (1999). Preface. In W. Z. Hu (Ed.), *Aspects of intercultural communication. Proceedings of China's 2nd conference on intercultural communication* (pp. 1-3). Beijing: Foreign Language Teaching and Research Press.

Hu, W. Z. (2000). *Zhong Guo kua wen hua jiao ji yan jiu de hui gu yu zhan wang* [The past and future of research in Chinese intercultural communication]. Plenary address presented at the Deuxieme Seminaire Interculturel Sino-Francais de Canton, Guangzhou, China.

Hu, W. Z., & Gao, Y. H. (1997). *Wai yu jiao xue yu wen hua [Foreign language teaching and culture].* Hunan, China: Hunan Education Press.

Jia, Y. X. (1997). *Kua wen hua jiao ji xue [Intercultural communication studies].* Shanghai: Shanghai Foreign Languages Education Press.

Jia, W. (2000). Chinese communication scholarship as an expansion of the communication and culture paradigm. In D. R. Heisey (Ed.), *Chinese perspectives in rhetoric and communication* (pp. 139-161). Stamford, CT: Ablex Publishing Corporation.

Kim, Y. Y. (1991). Intercultural communication competence. In S. Ting-Toomey & F. Korzenny (Eds.), *Cross-cultural interpersonal communication.* Newbury Park, CA: Sage.

Leech, G. N. (1983). *Principles of pragmatics.* London: Longman.

Lin, D. J. (1996). *Kua wen hua yan jiu [A study of intercultural communication].* Fu Jian, China: People's Press.

Lin, D. J. (1999). *Mei guo kua wen hua jiao ji yan jiu de li shi fa zhan ji qi shi* [The historical development and revelation of intercultural communication in the U.S.]. *Journal of Fu Jian Normal University, 2,* 82-88.

Liu, D. L. (1999). Politeness in correspondence discourse: A contrastive study. In W. Z. Hu (Ed.), *Aspects of intercultural communication. Proceedings of China's 2nd conference on intercultural communication* (pp. 356-369). Beijing: Foreign Language Teaching and Research Press.

Peng, S. Q. (1993). *'Man' yuan yu jie yuan: Zhong guo ren ren ji bu man qing xu biao da fang shi de chu bu tan xi* [Complaints and their resolution: An initial analysis of expressions of Chinese interpersonal discontented sentiment]. In Q. S. Li (Ed.), *A collection of research on Chinese social psychology* (pp. 171-192). Hong Kong: Hong Kong Shi Dai Wen Hua Press.

Qu, X. W. (1993). *Zhong guo ren ji guan xi de te zhi.* [Characteristics of Chinese interpersonal relationships]. In Q. S. Li (Ed.), *A collection of research on Chinese social psychology* (pp. 239-257). Hong Kong: Hong Kong Shi Dai Wen Hua Press.

Wang, H. Y. (1996). *Kua wen hua chuan tong: ru he yu wai guo ren jiao wang [Intercultural communication: How to interact with foreigners].* Beijing: Beijing Languages Institute Press.

Yang, Y. Y. (1993). *Bao: Zhong guo ren de she hui jiao huan guan.* [Bao: A Chinese perspective of social exchange]. In Q. S. Li (Ed.), *A collection of research on Chinese social psychology* (pp. 158-170). Hong Kong: Hong Kong Shi Dai Wen Hua Press.

Yang, Z. H., & Bao, J, Z. (1998). *Lun wen hua jiao liu zhong de fei yu yan xing wei.* [On nonverbal behavior in intercultural communication]. *Journal of Xi'an University of Technology, 14*(4), 439-441.

Zou, M. Q. (1997). *Kua wen hua jiao ji de duo yuan yin su yan jiu.* [On multiple factors of intercultural communication]. *Journal of Yun Nan Nationality Institute* (Philosophy & Social Sciences Edition), 69-75.

Zuo, B. (1993). *Da xue sheng lian mian shi jian ren ding de she hui xin li yan jiou* [A socio-psychological study of the recognition of the concepts of face among college students]. In Q. S. Li (Ed.), *A collection of research on Chinese social psychology* (pp. 122-140). Hong Kong: Hong Kong Shi Dai Wen Hua Press.

3

Chinese Communication Theory and Practice: A Tier-Based Perspective

John H. Powers

Research on the communication practices of Chinese people has been burgeoning in recent years. However, despite the large body of literature, constructing a comprehensive understanding of Chinese communication phenomena is a daunting task, partially because the literature is scattered across many disciplines and partially because no conceptual map exists of how the studies might contribute to a more coherent understanding of Chinese communication. Accordingly, the purpose of this chapter is to begin the process of mapping the conceptual structure of the literature on Chinese communication.

The mapping process is based on an earlier article, which modeled the general intellectual structure of the human communication discipline (Powers, 1995). Based on the idea that the most fundamental concept for defining a "communication" perspective has been the concept of a *message*, the model imagines that communication research may be arranged into four tiers, each with its own primary focus. As illustrated in Figure 3.1, the tiers are arranged hierarchically.

Tier 1 research inquires into the structure and content of the messages that pass between people—investigating the kinds of things people say and do that others consider to be meaningful. Accordingly, tier 1 may be called the *message-centered* tier. Tier 2 research focuses on the communicator of the messages and may, therefore, be called the *communicator-centered* tier. This

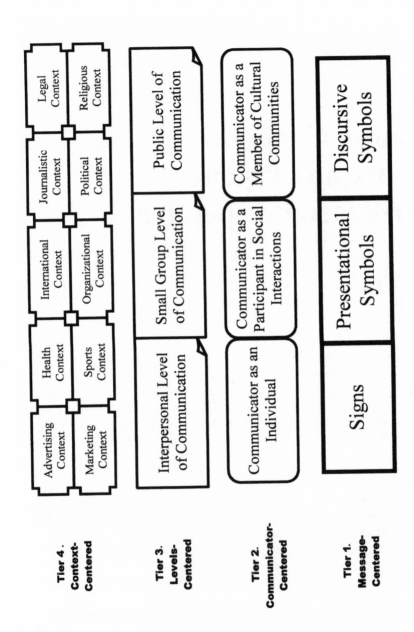

Figure 3-1. The four tiers of human communication theory and research.

tier can be divided into three aspects: the communicator as an individual, as a participant in social interaction, and as a member of a cultural community that is created and changed through communication. Tier 3 research focuses on levels of communication as viewed from some variable criterion, such as the number of people participating in the interaction or the degree of personal information shared among participants. Therefore, tier 3 theory and research may be called the *levels-centered* tier. Traditionally, three levels have been identified: the interpersonal, group, and public. Tier 4 research focuses on the characteristics of various communication contexts and the communication patterns that occur within them. These would include such communication contexts as health, legal, sports, organizational, journalistic, public relations, and advertising. Each such context has its own pattern of expectations for how people will communicate and its own repertoire of communication activities. Thus, tier 4 research may be called the *context-centered* tier. Based on the four tiers of communication research, we can develop a detailed map of the literature on Chinese communication processes, principles and practices.

TIER 1. THE MESSAGE-CENTERED TIER OF CHINESE COMMUNICATION

The message-centered tier of Chinese communication may be divided into two broad categories: sign-based and symbol-based expression. Signs are any expressive phenomena that may be interpreted as indicating the existence of something else—usually some less perceptible portion of an internal or external situation. *Symbols* are interpreted in a radically different way, in that they express the structure and content of someone's ideas. Each of these categories may itself be subdivided into two broad subcategories. Signs may be either actional or artifactual, and symbols may be either discursive or presentational.

Actional signs are those that unfold in time, like a gesture or a smile. *Artifactual* signs, while frequently caused by human actions, are distinctive because their material nature makes them available in a relatively unchanged form over a longer period. *Discursive* symbols include all languages and are characterized by having both a vocabulary and a syntactic system for manipulating the words to express more complex ideas. *Presentational* symbols include all symbolic forms that must "show" the idea that is being expressed. Because presentational symbols have neither a vocabulary nor a formal syntax for manipulating such elements in a standardized way, they must "present" the idea in some physical manner. Chinese communication, of course, uses all of these various forms of expression, as we will now explore.

Research on Chinese Actional and Artifactual Signs

Using the taxonomy just discussed, a variety of Chinese sign behaviors will be surveyed, following the distinction between actional and artifactual signs.

Chinese Actional Sign Systems. Among the studies on Chinese actional signs are Bond's study (1993) on the expression of emotions and Ma's (1999) exploration of Chinese facial expression in relation to ethnic discrimination. While the majority of studies on Chinese actional signs concern the signs spontaneously given off during moment-to-moment interaction, at least some have focused on biologically expressive signs. For example, Chan (1994) investigated the elements of gender display among Hong Kong Chinese.

Chinese Artifactual Sign Systems. An artifactual sign is any material object that can be interpreted as indicating the existence of something else—the communicator's unstated feelings, attitudes, beliefs, social status, and so forth. For example, clothing choices may be taken to signify someone's political beliefs (Kunz, 1996) or the individual's trade, social status, or relationship to the emperor (Szeto & Garrett, 1990).

Research on Chinese Discursive Symbol Systems

Discursive symbolism has at least seven interrelated levels that can have an impact on communicative interaction. These seven levels will be explored in this section.

Oral-Aural/Phonological. Using language in face-to-face interactions is an intrinsically actional phenomenon in which the individual's entire body participates to produce symbolic sounds. While many descriptions of the sounds used in various Chinese dialects have been produced (e.g., Kratochvil, 1998), working out the communicative consequences of the oral features of the Chinese language is equally important for understanding the intricacies of Chinese interaction patterns. The most common approach explores the meanings expressed through intonation patterns and cross-sentence prosody, such as Shen's (1988) work examining the use of prosodic features to identify the topical focus within an utterance and Ho's (1977) exploration of intonation variations used to express interrogative, exclamatory, and declarative meanings. Such studies show how intonation can be used as an interactional resource to accomplish a communicator's goals.

Word Formation/Morphological. Morphology is the study of the forms that words have within a language. As is true with phonological studies, the morphemes of a language can be studied independently of any reference to their communicative consequences. Again, however, Chinese communicators have word formation options available as resources for expressing subtleties of meaning. Accordingly, a number of studies have reported on the interactional meanings of Chinese morphological particles in particular dialect varieties such as Cantonese (Chan, 1998) or in communities such as Singapore (Gupta, 1992).

Lexical/Semantic. Every language provides a repertoire of words that name the categories into which the language's users have divided the world. Because different communities view the world though the lens provided by their unique vocabulary, considerable effort has been expended in exploring the Chinese categorical lexicon. Two reference works are very useful in providing a general orientation: DeMente's (1996) dictionary of China's cultural code words and, more narrowly, Lok's (1995) glossary of PRC political terms, which introduces in historical context many of the words used in Chinese political action, movements, and ideology.

Providing more detail is research explaining how individual words are used. For example, articles have appeared on Chinese *kinship terms* (Huang & Jia, 2000), *personal naming practices* (Blum, 1997), *metaphorical usages* (Ma, 2000), *slang* (Zhou & Wang, 1995), *obscene and profane vocabulary* (Wang, 1994), *Chinese neologisms* (Ching, 1982), *personal address terms* (Cheung, 1990), *abuse terms* (Huang & Warren, 1981), *lexical taboos* (Huang & Tian, 1990), *idioms* (Yee & Smithback, 1991), *personal naming practices* (Lu & Millward, 1989), and philosophical aspects of Chinese naming, especially in its Confucian context (Chang, 1997).

Propositional/Syntactic. Languages also provide a set of syntactic principles for constructing sentences. Although much of the technical syntactic literature has had little impact on understanding the communicative consequences of sentences, a growing literature exists on the communicative use of syntactic resources to develop syntactic genres, especially *question forms* and formulaic sayings such as *proverbs, maxims,* and *slogans* (Gong, 1994). Also relevant to the propositional/syntactical level are studies of Chinese *conditional* sentences (Chierchia, 2000), *counterfactuals* (Eifring, 1988), *presupposition* (Zhang, 1997), and *topic-comment* constructions (Tsao, 1987).

Speech Act/Pragmatic. The relevance of language research to Chinese communication studies is most directly evident at the speech act/pragmatic level of analysis. Pragmatics concerns the linguistic means available for accomplishing a communicator's goals. Among the Chinese speech act/pragmatic phenomena that have been studied are those concerned with *deictic pointing words* (Zhao, 1987), the *assertion of obviousness* (Chappell, 1991), *compliments* (Ye, 1995), *invitations* (Mao, 1992), *greetings and farewells* (Chen, 1991), *politeness* (Gu, 1990), *honorifics* (Hung, 1993), *address forms* (Kroger & Woods, 1992), *opposition markers* in conflict talk (Kuo, 1992), *requests* (L. Huang, 2000), *refusals* (Bresnahan, Cai, & Rivers, 1994), *"rhetorical interrogations"* (Alleton, 1988), and *indirect speech acts* (Biq, 1984).

Macrosemantic/Textual. Languages provide a number of resources for tying two or more utterances together to form larger units of meaning known as macrosemantic texts (Biq, 1988). Such extended texts have been analyzed in a number of ways, including dividing them into distinctive structural types. The most widely studied macrosemantic type is probably the narrative (Hall & Ames, 1995). Williams (1989), for example, investigated the divergent portrayals of the rustication experience in post-Mao narratives, while Lee (1998) has studied the narratives of footbinding. The argument structures used in Chinese texts have also received some scholarly attention in order to discover any relevant differences from Western argument styles and strategies (Zhao, 1999).

Speech Event/Generic. Every community provides a number of recurring speaking occasions that dictate the genre of speaking that is proper for that occasion. For example, Fong's (2000a) analysis of "luck talk" in celebrating the Chinese New Year illustrates a genre of speaking that is responsive to Chinese holiday situations. Similarly, Stuart's (1999) description of Minhe Monguor funeral orations and Lu's (1999) description of *kan dashan* as a genre of party talk both exemplify research on language at the speech event/generic level.

Research on Chinese Presentation Symbol Systems

China has been called "the empire of living symbols" (Lindqvist, 1991), and it is easy to see why. Animal symbolism (Ong, 1993) associated with the Chinese zodiac and the tetragrams of the *I Ching* (Cheng, 1988) are known worldwide. These vast forms of Chinese symbolism are examples of presentational symbolism because they have neither a vocabulary nor a syntax. As mentioned, presentational symbols may be divided into actional and artifactual categories based upon whether they use temporally unfolding behavior or a relatively stable material form.

Presentational Actions

Presentational actions may be divided into three categories: sacred, secular, and the actional fine arts. All three types have been explored by researchers into Chinese expressive behavior.

Sacred Actions. The distinction between the sacred and the secular seems to be universal in communication communities. While usually associated with religious symbolism, the concept of the sacred may be applied more generally to include any action or artifact the community reveres as expressing special meaning. Among the sacred actions reported are Chinese marriage rituals (Lee, 2000) and the ritualized deification of Mao during the Cultural Revolution (Huang, 1997).

Secular Actions. Secular actions may also be used to symbolize a community's ideas. For example, Barme's (1995) provocative title "To screw foreigners is glorious" suggests that cheating non-Chinese people can symbolize patriotic commitment. Work by Saichs (1994) and Lum (1996) examines how activities such as going to discos or performing karaoke can express ideas concerning dictatorship, democracy, and identity. More routinely, research on gift-giving has explored the role that such symbolic actions have in expressing political distance and generational relations (Yan, 1996). Chung (1999) has studied violence as an expressive resource in Taiwan's Congress, while Lik (1976) examined the symbolic meaning of silence in the Chinese philosophical tradition.

The Chinese legal system is in a period of rapid change, and the entire Chinese court system provides a vast actional symbol system (Clarke, 1995). So too are protest movements like the 1989 events in Tiananmen Square (Wasserstrom & Perry, 1992). And recently *qigong* has been treated by the Chinese government as expressing politically subversive ideas (Xu, 1999). Even role models as living examples for action have been self-consciously used by the government to promote social values that their behavior is said to express (Zhang, 1999).

Actional Fine Arts. The role of the actional fine arts was underscored during the Cultural Revolution, both as a source of conflict with the drama *Hai Rui Dismissed from Office* (Wagner, 1993), and as a propaganda tool with the approved Revolutionary Operas (Cheng, 1978). Among the other Chinese actional arts whose expressiveness has been studied are music and song (Jones, 1994), Beijing opera (Lu & Xiao, 2000), live drama (Jerstad, 1967), television drama (Godby, 1999), and feature-length films (Collins & Varas, 1998).

Presentational Artifacts

Parallel to the divisions used in discussing presentational actions, presentational artifacts may be divided into the sacred, the secular, and the artistic.

Sacred Artifacts. For the vast portion of China's history Buddhist and Taoist belief systems, as well as the religions of China's ethnic minorities, have provided a large supply of sacred artifacts for study and interpretation (Cooper, 1977). Moreover, because sacred artifacts need not be religious, public artifacts such as Mao's tomb might be studied to learn how the government and citizens use them for symbolic purposes.

Secular Artifacts. The variety of secular artifacts whose symbolic characteristics have been explored is quite immense. The following is merely a

representative list: big-character posters (Landsberger, 1995), Chinese written characters (Wachtel & Lum, 1991), Chinese food (Chang, 1977), the
goddess of democracy statue (Petress, 1993), museums as symbolic of a
culture's sense of identity (Ho, 1998), snuff bottles (Huntington, 1974),
Chinese silks (Farnworth, 1986), Chinese opera face-painting (Lu & Xiao,
2000), and even Tiananmen Square (Pye, 1990).

Artifactual Fine Arts. Many of China's material fine arts have been studied
for their expressive value. These include comics (Lent, 1995), literary fiction
(Hua, 1999), and painting (Lai, 1992). Galikowski (1998) investigated the
relationship between the artifactual fine arts and politics in modern China.
Moreover, numerous "coffee table" books featuring Chinese fine arts present
excellent photographs of the artifacts as well as providing historical and
interpretive textual notes explicating the meanings expressed.

TIER 2. THE COMMUNICATOR-CENTERED TIER

The tier 1 focus on messages defines the central focus of the communication discipline. Even so, messages are created by people as they go about their
lives in a variety of settings. Accordingly, the second tier of Chinese communication research focuses on the people involved in the communicative interaction. The communicator-centered tier has three major components that
feature the communicator as an individual (tier 2A), as a participant in social
interactions (tier 2B), and as a member of a cultural community (tier 2C).

Tier 2A. The Chinese Communicator as an Individual

Communication research concerning the communicator as an individual
typically emphasizes four themes: (a) the personal characteristics of communicators, (b) the encoding, decoding, and interpretive processes communicators use, (c) the consequences for the communicator receiving the messages,
and (d) the development of the communicator's abilities and repertoire over
the life span.

Communicator Characteristics. There is a common assumption that the
Chinese individual is somehow very different from the Western individual,
even to the point of being "inscrutable" by Westerners (Young, 1982). While
it is doubtful that inscrutability is among the Chinese communicator's personal characteristics, a variety of other characteristics have been explored.
Some studies of the Chinese communicator's characteristics are broadly
conceived and explore the general dimensions of Chinese personality (Bond,
1996), the varieties of Chinese "self" (Wu, 1984), and even personality
development during the Cultural Revolution (Chan, 1985).

In addition to these more general studies of Chinese personality, others report on the relationship between a variety of specific personality character- istics and communication behaviors. Among these communicator character- istics are *assertiveness* (Chan, 1993), *cognitive style* (Chiu, 1972), *communication style* (Farris, 1995), *feelings of estrangement* (Tinberg, 1986), *communicator motives* (Anderson, Martin, & Zhong, 1998), *persuasibility* (Chu, 1967), and *speech apprehension* (Klopf & Cambra, 1980). The goal of such studies is to correlate various personality dimensions with communica- tive strategies in order to explain why communicators make the choices they make. Depending upon the theoretical approach, the communicator's charac- teristics have been described in terms of the communicator's traits, needs, motives, cognitive structures, intentions, goals and plans, attitudes, and so forth.

Encoding, Decoding, and Interpretive Processes. Although scholarship on Chinese encoding processes is fairly scant (see Hayes, 1988, for an example), the decoding and interpretive processes are more widely investigated. For example, Chen (1999) explored how Chinese tones are processed for under- standing speaker meaning. Holbrook and Lu (1969) investigated the intelli- gibility of whispered Chinese, and a number of studies examine the processing of written Chinese (e.g., Jia, 1992; Wong & Chen, 1999), with some making comparisons with how Americans interpret either Chinese characters (Tse & Cavanaugh, 2000) or alphabetic languages. At a higher level of discursive symbolism, Yang, Gordon, Hendrick, and Wu (1999) have explored the language elements that contribute to the comprehension of referring expressions in Chinese.

Consequences and Effects of Communication. Numerous studies have been conducted in the West investigating the effects of message variables on the communicator's subsequent beliefs and behaviors. However, there appears to be little direct influence of this quantitative social scientific tradition in the study of Chinese communication. While many studies investigate the general influence of Chinese culture on various aspects of communication, few examples of traditional Western quantitative social science studies of the type "the influences of X independent variable upon Y dependent variable" seem to exist. Some examples, however, include Bond, Leung, and Wan's (1982) investigation of the social impact of self-effacing attributions, Dong, Tan, and Cao's (1998) study of the socialization effects of American media in China, and Gao's (1998) analysis of the effects of face on Chinese interpersonal communication.

Communicator Development over Time. Communication behaviors are usually acquired over time, develop into mature forms through experience, and perhaps begin to fail as people age. In the Chinese literature, however, this developmental approach seems limited almost exclusively to issues in language acquisition, especially phonological acquisition (Hua & Dodd, 2000), the development of lexical/semantic categories (Jepson, 1989), and second-language acquisition. There are, of course, studies of Chinese child and adolescent development (Lau, 1996) and aging (Kiefer, 1992) that may contribute to understanding issues in Chinese communication development, even if only indirectly. This would seem to be a fertile area for future research in Chinese communication.

Tier 2B. The Chinese Communicator as a Participant in Social Interaction

The second major aspect of tier 2 research focuses on the communicator as a participant in social interaction—with four emphases having emerged in the Chinese communication literature: (a) communicator goals and the strategies available for accomplishing them, (b) the interactive routines communicators typically engage in and the interactional structures that emerge from them, (c) the social relationships created, maintained, and occasionally terminated through communicative interaction, and (d) the mutual and reciprocal effects that communicators spontaneously have on one another.

Communicator Goals and Strategies. Communication scholars generally argue that communication is goal directed. In view of this commitment, a number of studies related to Chinese communicators' goals and strategies have been reported (Chiao, 1989). These include strategies of *refusal* (Bresnahan, Cai, & Rivers, 1994), *assertions of obviousness and disagreement* (Chappell, 1991), and *compliance-gaining strategies* (Chen & Zhong, 2000). Also exploring Chinese communicators' goals and strategies are rapidly growing literatures on *conflict resolution* (Chen & Starosta, 1997) and the use of *code-switching* as a strategic interactional resource in conversational contexts (Millen & Wang, 2000).

Communication Routines and Interactional Structures. Communicative interactions are both spontaneously responsive to moment-to-moment events and yet structured into identifiable types and routines. The literature on Chinese communication contains theoretical contributions in understanding the nature of sequencing routines (Tsui, 1991) in specific situations such as conversational topic and information sequencing (Kirkpatrick, 1993), sequencing related to code-switching patterns (Li & Milroy, 1995), gift offerings and responses (Zhu, Li, & Qian, 2000), and even sequencing in letters of request (Kirkpatrick, 1991).

Social Relationships. Some communication phenomena are intrinsically relational rather than individual. This is generally recognized with a concept such as *credibility*, because credibility exists only where one person attributes it to the other. In the Chinese communication literature, relationships such as *guanxi* have been extensively studied (Kipnis, 1997). So too have *debt-paying* relations (Chang & Holt, 1994), *power and solidarity* relations (Cheung, 1985), *hierarchical* relations (Taylor, 1989), *harmony* relations (Gabrenya & Hwang, 1996), and *face* relations (Chen, 1990; Jia, 1997).

Mutual Effects. A newly emerging literature in general communication theory might be called "mutual effects" rather than simply "effects" research. Mutual effects are those that occur because the communicators are interacting in one another's presence and adjusting their own contributions to whatever the other is doing. Traditional effects research concentrates on *message* effects. Mutual effects, in contrast, are *communicator* effects. In the Chinese communication literature the primary mutual effect that has been studied is *accommodation* (Gong, 2000), which emphasizes the mutual adjustments that communicators make in response to features of the other's communication.

Tier 2C. The Chinese Communicator as a Member of a Cultural Community

The literature on Chinese culture and communication may be divided into three broad themes: (a) the role that communication plays in bringing about cultural patterns, (b) the role that culture plays in bringing about communication patterns, and (c) the nature of specific communication communities within which various communication patterns develop.

Communication as a Cause of Cultural Patterns. Cultures are never static, and part of the reason they change over time is, of course, communication. This is especially true for a rapidly changing culture such as China. Accordingly, a number of works explore from a communication viewpoint the cultural changes that occurred during the Maoist and reform eras (Chu & Ju, 1993) and Tu (1994). A second way of imagining communication as cause of culture is generationally. That is, communication is the process whereby the community brings its culture to each new child. Therefore, studies of Chinese socialization practices are relevant to issues in the communication of culture to the next generation (Wu, 1996).

Communication as a Consequence of Cultural Patterns. Culture is often treated as if it were a relatively stable agent independent of the people who keep it vital through their communicative practices. In this way studies like Hofstede's (1980) *Culture's Consequences* treat culture as an agent capable of causing communication patterns. Research in Chinese communication has explored the role of culture in causing such phenomena as the individualism-collectivism distinction (Lu, 1998a), approaches to human rights (de Bary & Tu, 1998), linguistic determinism (Bloom, 1981), the role of the Chinese writing system in differences between Chinese and American thinking patterns (Guan, 2000), and even the different fates of moveable type in China and the West (Zhou, 1994).

Communication Communities. Communication practices develop in the ways they do partially because there are communities of people who communicate more frequently among themselves than with those outside their community. This principle applies to Chinese communication in two different ways: both internally within various regions of China, to produce different dialects and expressive customs (Qiu, 1992), and externally as Chinese immigration patterns have created communication communities within a variety of countries and international regions (Kluver & Powers, 1999). These immigration patterns have resulted in an extensive body of work on Chinese communities in places such as *America* (Hsu, 1971a), *Australia* (Hornsey & Gallois, 1998), *Britain* (Li & Milroy, 1995), *Canada* (Sachdev, Bourhis, Phang, & D'Eye, 1987), *Hong Kong* (Flowerdew & Scollon, 1997), *Malaysia* (Ward & Hewstone, 1985), *Singapore* (Anderson, 1985; Asuncion-Lande, 1999), and *Taiwan* (Wei & Leung, 1998), as well as more specific communication communities like the Mississippi Chinese in America (Gong, 2000).

TIER 3. THE LEVEL-CENTERED TIER

Communication research is frequently divided into three levels: interpersonal, group, and public. As mentioned earlier, the purpose in identifying levels is to note that communication may vary along a number of dimensions and that as one reaches a critical threshold along these variables, a qualitative change occurs in the nature of the communication observed. Moreover, as communication research reaches the third tier, there is greater interest in how communication interacts with other social and cultural phenomena beyond communication itself.

Tier 3A. The Interpersonal Level of Chinese Communication

The literature on Chinese interpersonal communication reflects the general variety of interpersonal research, but with special attention to the Chinese characteristics of the interactions. Accordingly, some of the research emphasizes how unique Chinese concepts such as *yuan* (Chang & Holt, 1991), *kan dashan* (Lu, 1999), or harmony (Chang, in press) help explain some aspect of Chinese interpersonal communication. Similarly, Yum (1988) has explored how Confucian ideals continue to affect interpersonal relationships and communication patterns throughout the East Asian region.

Other research explores how themes in Western interpersonal literature develop in the Chinese context. Thus, for example, Erwin (2000) investigated the interpersonal communication that occurs on telephone advice hotlines. Chen, Shaffer, and Wu (1997) examined stereotypes of physical attractiveness in Taiwan, while Ma (1996) looked into computer-mediated conversations as a new dimension of intercultural communication. Ma (1990a) has also investigated discontented responses in interpersonal relationships, as well as the role that unofficial intermediaries play in resolving Chinese interpersonal conflicts (Ma, 1992). Because tier 3 research reaches beyond communication itself, there have also been studies of, for example, communication with the elderly (Cai, Giles, & Noels, 1998); and Chen (1995) has compared Chinese self-disclosure patterns with those of Americans. A large amount of interpersonal communication occurs, of course, within the family, and so there is a correspondingly large body of research on family communication (Chen, 1992) or during courtship (Gao, 1991). Such studies provide the basis for exploring issues of relational development in Chinese couples (Chen, 1998) and changes in family value orientations for Chinese residing in the United States (Chen, 1992).

Tier 3B. The Small-Group Level of Chinese Communication

One of the genuine surprises in the literature is the relative absence of studies on Chinese group communication. Surely Chinese group communication should be distinctive, interesting, and worthy of study. However, only three out of 850 items in the database assembled for this chapter can in any way be identified as reflecting current approaches to group communication research. One of these is pedagogical, reporting how metaphors from the *I Ching* may be used to teach small-group discussion (Holt & Chang, 1992); another concerns the role group communication played in creating social pressure in Maoist China (Chu, 1976), and a third concerns small groups and political rituals during the same period (Whyte, 1974). Accordingly, the area of Chinese communication studies that seems most underdeveloped is the field of small-group communication.

Tier 3C. The Public Level of Chinese Communication

Studies of Chinese public communication may be divided into five categories: popular civic discourse, governmental discourse arising from official sources, the rhetoric of Chinese social movements and campaigns, traditional rhetorical criticism, and Chinese rhetorical theory and history.

Popular Civic Discourse. This category of Chinese communication research studies public messages arising from nongovernmental sources as people go about their daily life. Sometimes this discourse arises from interest groups who wish to influence public opinion or government action, and at other times it arises from commercial sources who want to promote their products or services. Among the research on Chinese popular civic discourse have been studies of *letters to the editors* (Chu & Chu, 1981), *religious discourse* (Fulton, 1999), *call-in talk shows* (Chuang & Ma, 1999), *technological discourse* (Cai & Gonzalez, 1997), and *televised soap operas* (Godby, 1999).

Governmental Discourse. Governments frequently communicate with their own citizens and to international audiences. For example, Powers (1999) investigated how China used the Internet to speak to the international community about its human rights record, and Heisey (1999) examined China's public presentations in the United Nations. Communication downward toward the citizens is represented in Cuklanz and Wong's (1999) research on government-produced public service announcements in Hong Kong. In a more historical vein, Hornig (1990) reported on the communication strategies used in the agricultural development efforts during the 1950s.

Movements and Campaigns. An important tradition in public communication research concerns the rise, development, and eventual completion of persuasive campaigns and mass movements. Some examples include Bennett's (1976) study of the Chinese leadership's early mass campaigns, studies of the Cultural Revolution as a mass movement (Huang, 2000), and Han and Hua's (1990) investigation of the messages produced during the 1989 student movement. In addition to government mass-movement rhetoric, there are also studies of smaller campaigns such as China's planned-birth campaign (Cheng, 1991) and the one-child policy campaign (Mosher, 1993). Also in this tradition are studies of how ideological work was used in Chinese communication campaigns (Wang & Wu, 1997), and even how the government used communication to mobilize the nation on behalf of China's bid for the 2000 Olympics (Y. Chen, 1998).

Rhetorical Criticism. There is a sense, of course, in which all study of public communication is rhetorical criticism. However, including this as a separate category focuses attention on the critical analysis of specific rhetorical acts, artifacts, or rhetors. For example, Xiao (1995) has analyzed how the works of Darwin were introduced into China, while Chung (1997) explored the strategies used by Taiwan's KMT party to hold itself together in a time of crisis. Among the specific rhetors whose efforts have been studied are Sun Yat-sen (Xiao, 2000), Mao Zedong (Yan, 2000), and Deng Xiaoping (Qiu, 2000).

Rhetorical Theory and History. Long assumed to be primarily a Western phenomenon, rhetorical theory and history are beginning to find a place in

Chinese scholarship on public communication. Some of the recent work documents rhetoric in various early periods of Chinese history (Lu, 1998b), while others explore how those early traditions influence current Chinese rhetorical practice (Lu, 2000). Contemporary Chinese rhetorical theory has also explored the methods of argument Chinese rhetors use (Kuo, 1994), their applications in particular cases (Zhao, 1999), the cultural influences on Chinese rhetoric such as Confucianism (Gong, 1998) or Taoism (Oliver, 1961), and specific elements of Chinese argumentation such as *pathos* (Garrett, 1993), *ethos* (Gong, 1998), or *topoi* (Xu, 1999).

TIER 4. THE CONTEXT-CENTERED TIER

Communication contexts may be defined as (a) recurring patterns of social circumstances within which communication routinely occurs and (b) to which one's communication practices must adapt if they are to be appropriate. Tier 4 contexts are important because many of the specialties within the communication field differ primarily on the contextual dimension. Specialists in health, organizational, legal, journalism, advertising, and public relations communication are ultimately *contextual* specialists. Because of the sheer quantity of contextually based studies available for every context, only a few representative studies are used to illustrate this section.

Advertising Communication Context. The advertising context focuses on communication related to products and services that the communicators are offering to provide. Advertising communication has explored such issues as advertising for illegal products (Chan, 1995a), the information content of television advertisements (Chan, 1995b), how magazine and television ads reflect Chinese cultural values (Cheng & Schweitzer, 1996), the use of emotion in Chinese advertising (Chan, 1996), presentational design in Chinese patent medicine advertising in Hong Kong newspapers (Wong, 2000), and advertising aimed primarily at Chinese women (Chan, 1997).

Health Communication Context. The health communication context concerns messages related to the profession of medicine, health promotion, and community health. Typical studies have looked at, for example, how the Western medical lexicon can be translated into Chinese (Yallop & Deng, 1993) and how metaphors are used to construct a culturally meaningful concept of illness (Stibbe, 1996). Also investigated was the tier 2B topic of doctor-patient interaction as goal-directed discourse (Gu, 1996) and medical discourse as an example of a more general category of "workplace discourse" (Gu, 1997).

International Communication Context. The international communication context focuses on communication that crosses national boundaries. This would, of course, include studies of intergovernmental communication. But it would also include research investigating the flow of information that passes from one country to another, such as studies of the influence of American television programming on Chinese culture. Several of the studies mentioned in the section on tier 3 public communication are concerned with China's communication practices in the international arena. To these might be added Guan's (1998) exploration of the prospects for cross-cultural communication between China and the West.

Journalism Communication Context. Journalism, especially commercial news, is both one of the mass media and at the same time a contextual specialty within the communication field. As a contextual specialty, journalism participates in all of the lower tiers of communication theory and research, where issues about the nature of journalistic discourse as narrative (Pan, Lee, Chan, & So, 1999), descriptions of news actors (Wu & Hui, 1997), and photographic content of news reports (Kenny, 1993) have all been considered. There have also been studies of such tier 2 topics as the contribution of news reporting to the symbolic construction of the reader's reality (Akhavan-Majid & Ramaprasad, 1998). The journalistic context is so widely studied, in fact, that a separate article using the same structure of categories could profitably be written.

Legal Communication Context. A fertile area for research concerns the communicative aspects of China's legal system (Clarke, 1995), especially as China's legal system feels pressures for transparency and consistency due to China's entrance into the World Trade Organization. MacCormack's (1991) research investigates the tier 2C issue of the role that Chinese values play in traditional Chinese law, while Wu (1995) has investigated the nature of Chinese evidence in situations where English plays a role in Chinese legal systems (as it does, for example, in Hong Kong). This contextual specialty would seem to have considerable potential for future development among Chinese communication scholars interested in the development of China's legal system.

Mass Media Communication Context. Studies of mass-mediated messages can easily be identified at all tiers of the model, depending upon whether they focus on the intrinsic nature of particular tier-1 medium (e.g., radio, television, film), the relation of a particular medium to the individual, interactional, or cultural elements (all tier-2 topics), or the medium's interpersonal, group, or public dynamics (tier 3). That is, when we consider mass media as a *context* of communication, we recognize that, as a large specialty area within communication, it fully participates in all of the lower tiers. In addition to studies of the changing role of mass media in Chinese society (Zhu, 1997), Chinese media research has focused on issues such as television effects (Tsai, 1970), the role of media in political socialization (Wei & Leung, 1998), media history in China (Yu, 1979), crisis communication (Liao, 1980), and the changing functions of the media in the post-Mao era (Robinson, 1981). Although there may be some theoretical controversy over whether the Internet is a *mass* medium, studies of Chinese Internet use (Liu, 1999) should probably also be mentioned here.

Organizational Communication Context. The final context to be mentioned is the organizational context. Communication frequently occurs in large organizations where the communication practices are shaped by the corporate forces at play within the organization. This context is also well represented in the literature, with studies concerned with a broad variety of topics such as Chinese negotiating style (Fang, 1998; Soloman, 1999), the role of face in Chinese organizations (Redding & Ng, 1982), the impact of Confucianism on organizational communication (Chen & Chung, 1994), cultural aspects of organizational conflict resolution (Yu, 1995), the role of cultural values in motivation within the organization, impression management in the workplace (Bilbow, 1997), workplace communication and relationships (Wang & Chang, 1999), and managerial communication (Krone, Chen, Xia, 1997).

CONCLUSION

The purpose of this chapter is to provide a broad map of the literature on Chinese communication practices. In pursuing this goal, a four-tier conceptual structure identifies Chinese sign and symbol behavior as being the most fundamental tier and then proposes that the second tier focuses upon the communicator as an individual, as a participant in social interactions, and as a member of a cultural community that is created, maintained, and changed through communication. The third tier identifies three levels of communication that are distinguishable from one another based on a number of variable criteria that may reach a threshold, whereupon the communication phenomena observed change in identifiable ways. These points of transition are used to distinguish one level from another. The final tier of the model arises because communication phenomena at the three lower tiers are always subject to adaptations in response to the recurring social circumstances that are maintained within a particular communication community. Medical communication differs from legal communication not in some irreconcilable way, but through patterns of communicative co-occurrence and non-occurrence that are distinctive for each context.

Having established the foundations for the tier-based map, the chapter then uses the tier-based structure to illustrate the variety of research conducted concerning Chinese communication practices. However, because the map presented here provides only a preliminary sketch of the various research areas concerned with Chinese communication, only a small selection of the available literature was featured. The next step in developing a greater understanding of Chinese communication would be to develop detailed bibliographic micro-maps of each of the various tier structured areas identified above. In that process, it might be expected that we would be better able to develop comprehensive theories of Chinese communication practices that lead toward more coherent and cohesive explanations of this fascinating area of communication research.

REFERENCES

Akhavan-Majid, R., & Ramaprasad, J. (1998). Framing and ideology: A comparative analysis of U.S. and Chinese newspaper coverage of the Fourth United Nations Conference on Women and the NGO Forum. *Mass Communication and Society, 1*, 131-138.

Alleton, V. (1988). The so-called "rhetorical interrogation" in Mandarin Chinese. *Journal of Chinese Linguistics, 16*, 278-297.

Anderson, C. M., Martin, M. M., & Zhong, M. (1998). Motives for communicating with family and friends: A Chinese study. *Howard Journal of Communications, 9*, 109-123.

Asuncion-Lande, N. C. (1999). Cultural politics of communication policy: A comparative study of Singapore and the Philippines. *Human Communication, 2*(1), 99-122.

Barme, G. (1995). To screw foreigners is patriotic: China's avant-garde nationalists. *The China Journal, 34*, 209-234.

Bennett, G. (1976). *Yungdong: Mass campaigns in Chinese communist leadership.* Berkeley, CA: Center for Chinese Studies.

Bilbow, G. T. (1997). Cross-cultural impression management in the multicultural workplace: The special case of Hong Kong. *Journal of Pragmatics, 28*, 461-487.

Biq, Y.-O. (1984). Indirect speech acts in Chinese polite expressions. *Journal of the Chinese Language Teachers Association, 19*(3), 1-10.

Biq, Y.-O. (1988). From objectivity to subjectivity: The text-building function of *you* in Chinese. *Studies in Language, 12*, 99-122.

Bloom, A. H. (1981). *The linguistic shaping of thought: A study in the impact of language on thinking in China and the West.* Hillsdale, NJ: Erlbaum.

Blum, S. D. (1997). Naming practices and power of words in China. *Language in Society, 26*, 357-379.

Bond, M. H. (1993). Emotions and their expression in Chinese culture. *Journal of Nonverbal Behavior, 17*, 245-262.

Bond, M. H. (Ed.). (1996). *The handbook of Chinese psychology.* Hong Kong: Oxford University Press.

Bond, M. H., Leung, K., & Wan, K. C. (1982). The social impact of self-effacing attributions: The Chinese case. *Journal of Social Psychology. 118*, 157-166.

Bresnahan, M., Cai, D. A., & Rivers, A. (1994). Saying *no* in Chinese and English: Cultural similarities and differences in strategies of refusal. *Asian Journal of Communication, 4*, 52-76.

Cai, D. A., & Gonzalez, A. (1997). The Three Gorges project: Technological discourse and the resolution of competing interests. *Intercultural Communication Studies, 7*, 101-111.

Cai, D. A., Giles, H., & Noels, K. (1998). Elderly perceptions of communication with older and younger adults in China: Implications for mental health. *Journal of Applied Communication Research, 26*, 32-51.

Chan, A. (1985). *Children of Mao: Personality development and political activism in the Red Guard generation.* Seattle: University of Washington Press.

Chan, D. W. (1993). Components of assertiveness: Their relationships with assertive rights and depressed mood among Chinese college students in Hong Kong. *Behavior Research and Therapy, 31*, 529-538.

Chan, G. (1994). Gender display among Hong Kong teenagers. In M. Bucholtz, A. C. Liang, L. A. Sutton, & C. Hines (Eds.), *Cultural performances: Proceedings of the Third Berkeley Women and Language Conference* (pp. 93-101). Berkeley: Berkeley Women and Language Group, University of California Berkeley.

Chan, K.K.W. (1995a). Illegal pharmaceutical advertising in China. *Gazette, 56*, 73-79.

Chan, K.K.W. (1995b). Information content of television advertising in China. *International Journal of Advertising, 14*, 365-373.

Chan, K.K.W. (1996). Chinese viewers' perception of information and emotional advertising. *International Journal of Advertising, 15*, 152-166.

Chan, K. K. W. (1997). Creating advertising that appeals to Chinese women. *Asian Journal of Communication, 7*, 43-57.

Chan, M. K. M. (1998). Sentence particles *je* and *jek* in Cantonese and their distribution across gender and sentence types. In S. Wertheim, A. Bailey, & M. Corston-Oliver (Eds.), *Engendering communication: Proceedings of the Fifth Berkeley Women and Language Conference* (pp. 117-128). Berkeley: Berkeley Women and Language Group.

Chang, H. C. (1997). Language and words: Communication and the *Analects* of Confucius. *Journal of Language and Social Psychology, 16*, 107-131.

Chang, H. C. (In press). Harmony as performance: The turbulence under Chinese interpersonal communication. *Discourse Studies.*

Chang, H. C., & Holt, G. R. (1991). The concept of *yuan* and Chinese interpersonal relationships. In S. Ting-Toomey & F. Korzenny (Eds.), *Cross-cultural interpersonal communication* (pp. 28-57). Newbury Park, CA: Sage.

Chang, H. C., & Holt, G. R. (1994). Debt-repaying mechanism in Chinese relationships: An exploration of the folk concepts of *pao* and human emotional debt. *Research on Language and Social Interaction, 27*, 351-387.

Chang, K.-C. (Ed.). (1977). *Food in Chinese culture: Anthropological and historical perspectives,* New Haven: Yale University Press.

Chappell, H. (1991). Strategies for the assertion of obviousness and disagreement in Mandarin: A semantic study of the modal particles *me. Santa Barbara Papers in Linguistics, 3*, 9-32.

Chen, G. M. (1992). Change of Chinese family value orientations in the United States. *Journal of Overseas Chinese Studies, 2*, 111-121.

Chen, G. M. (1995). Differences in self-disclosure patterns among Americans versus Chinese: A comparative study. *Journal of Cross-Cultural Psychology, 26*, 84-91.

Chen, G. M. (1998). A Chinese model of human relationship development. In B. L. Hofer & J. H. Koo (Eds.), *Cross-cultural communication East and West in the 90s* (pp. 45-53). San Antonio, TX: Institutte for Cross-Cultural Research.

Chen, G. M., & Chung, J. (1994). The impact of Confucianism on organizational communication. *Communication Quarterly, 42*, 93-105.

Chen, G. M., & Starosta, W. J. (1997). Chinese conflict management and resolution: Overview and implications. *Intercultural Communication Studies, 7*, 1-16.

Chen, G. M., & Zhong, M. (2000). Dimensions of Chinese compliance-gaining strategies. *Human Communication, 3*, 97-109.

Chen, J.-Y. (1999). The representation and processing of tone in Mandarin Chinese: Evidence from slips of the tongue. *Applied Sociolinguistics, 20,* 289-301.

Chen, N. Y., Shaffer, D. R., & Wu, C. (1997). On physical attractiveness stereotyping in Taiwan: A revised sociocultural perspective. *Journal of Social Psychology, 137,* 117-124.

Chen, S.-C. (1991). Social distribution and development of greeting expressions in China. *International Journal of the Sociology of Language, 92,* 55-60.

Chen, V. (1990). *Mien tze* at the Chinese dinner table: A study of the interactional accomplishment of face. *Research on Language and Social Interaction, 24,* 109-140.

Chen, Y. (1998). Setting a nation in action: The media and China's bid for year 2000 Olympics. In D. R. Heisey & W. Gong (Eds.), *Communication and culture: China and the world entering the 21st century* (pp. 289-309). Amsterdam: Rodopi.

Cheng, C. Z. (1991). Communication techniques in China's planned birth campaigns. *Gazette, 48,* 31-54.

Cheng, C.-Y. (1988). The *I Ching* as a symbolic system of integrated communication. In W. Dissanayake (Ed.), *Communication theory: The Asian perspective* (pp. 79-104). Singapore: Asian Mass Communication Research and Information Centre.

Cheng, H., & Schweitzer, J. C. (1996). Cultural values reflected in Chinese and U.S. television commercials. *Journal of Advertising Research, 36,* 27-45.

Cheng, P. H. (1978). A comparative value analysis: Traditional versus revolutionary opera. In G. C. Chu (Ed.), *Popular media in China: Shaping new cultural patterns* (pp. 104-124). Honolulu: University of Hawaii Press.

Cheung, S. H.-N. (1990). Terms of address in Cantonese. *Journal of Chinese Linguistics, 18,* 1-42.

Cheung, Y.-S. (1985). Power, solidarity, and luxury in Hong Kong: A sociolinguistic study. *Anthropological Linguistics, 27,* 190-203.

Chiao, C. (1989). Chinese strategic behavior: Some general principles. In R. Bolton (Ed.), *The content of culture: Constants and variants* (pp. 525-537). New Haven, CT: Hraf.

Chierchia, G. (2000). Chinese conditionals and the theory of conditionals. *Journal of East Asian Linguistics, 9,* 1-54.

Ching, E. (1982). From "lover" to "spouse": A glossary of neologisms of the PRC. *Journal of the Chinese Language Teachers Association, 17*(1), 35-65.

Chiu, L. H. (1972). A cross-cultural comparison of cognitive styles in Chinese and American children. *International Journal of Psychology, 7,* 235-242.

Chu, G. C. (1967). Sex differences in persuasibility factors among Chinese. *International Journal of Psychology, 2,* 283-288.

Chu, G. C. (1976). Group communication and development in Mainland China: The functions of social pressure. In W. Schramm & D. Lerner (Eds.), *Communication and change: The last ten years—and the next* (pp. 119-133). Honolulu: University of Hawaii Press.

Chu, G. C., & Chu, L. L. (1981). Parties in conflict: Letters to the editor of the *People's Daily. Journal of Communication, 31,* 74-91.

Chu, G. C., & Ju, Y. (1993). *The Great Wall in ruins: Communication and cultural change in China.* Albany: State University of New York Press.

Chuang, R., & Ma, R. (1999). (Re)locating our voices in the public sphere: Call-in talk shows as a channel for civic discourse in Taiwan. In R. Kluver & J. H. Powers (Eds.), *Civic discourse, civil society, and Chinese communities* (pp. 167-180). Stamford, CT: Ablex.

Chung, J. (1997). Avoiding a "Bull Moose" rebellion: Particularistic ties, seniority, and third-party mediation. In A. Gonzalez & D. V. Tanno (Eds.), *Politics, communication, and culture* (pp. 166-185). Thousand Oaks, CA: Sage.

Chung, J. (1999). Ineffability and violence in Taiwan's congress. In R. Kluver & J. H. Powers (Eds.), *Civic discourse, civil society, and Chinese communities* (pp. 77-91). Stamford, CT: Ablex.

Clarke, D. C. (1995). Justice and the legal system in China. In R. Benewick & P. Wingrove (Eds.), *China in the 1990s* (pp. 83-93). London: Macmillan.

Collins, C., & Varas, P. (1998). Constructing/deconstructing/reconstructing: Chinese film and the (re)presentation of women for the West. In D. R. Heisey & W. Gong (Eds.), *Communication and culture: China and the world entering the 21st century* (pp. 267-288). Amsterdam: Rodopi B. V.

Cooper, J. C. (1977). The symbolism of the Taoist garden. *Studies in Comparative Religion, 11*, 224-234.

Cuklanz, L., & Wong, W. S. (1999). Ideological themes in Hong Kong's public service announcements: Implications for China's future. In R. Kluver & J. H. Powers (Eds.), *Civic discourse, civil society, and Chinese communities* (pp. 93-107). Stamford, CT: Ablex.

de Bary, Wm. T., & Tu, W. M. (Eds.). (1998). *Confucianism and human rights*. New York: Columbia University Press.

DeMente, B. L. (1996). *NTC's dictionary of China's cultural codewords: The complete guide to key words that express how the Chinese think, communicate, and behave.* Lincolnwood, IL: National Textbook Company.

Dong, Q., Tan, A., & Cao, X. (1998). Socialization effects of American television and movies in China. In D. R. Heisey & W. Gong (Eds.), *Communication and culture: China and the world entering the 21st century* (pp. 311-327). Amsterdam: Rodopi.

Eifring, H. (1988). The Chinese counterfactual. *Journal of Chinese Linguistics, 16*, 278-297.

Erwin, K. (2000). Heart-to-heart, phone-to-phone: Family values, sexuality, and the politics of Shanghai's advice hotlines. In D. S. Davis (Ed.), *The consumer revolution in urban China* (pp. 145-170). Berkeley: University of California Press.

Fang, T. (1998). *Chinese business negotiating style*. Thousand Oaks, CA: Sage.

Farnsworth, M. (1986). Symbolism in Chinese silk. *Heritage, 8*, 48-53.

Farris, C. S. (1995). A semeiotic analysis of *sajiao* as a gender marked communication style in Chinese. In M. Johnson & F. Y. L. Chiu (Ed.), *Unbound Taiwan: Closeups from a distance* (pp. 1-29). Chicago: Center for East Asian Studies, University of Chicago.

Fong, M. (2000a). "Luck Talk" in celebrating the Chinese New Year. *Journal of Pragmatics, 32*, 219-237.

Fulton, B. (1999). Freedom of religion in China: The emerging civic discourse. In R. Kluver & J. H. Powers (Eds.), *Civic discourse, civil society, and Chinese communities* (pp. 53-66). Stamford, CT: Ablex.

Gabrenya, W. K., Jr., & Hwang, K. K. (1996). Chinese social interaction: Harmony and hierarchy on the good earth. In M. H. Bond (Ed.), *The handbook of Chinese psychology* (pp. 295-307). Hong Kong: Oxford University Press.

Galikowski, M. (1998). *Art and politics in China, 1949-1984*. Hong Kong: Chinese University Press.

Gao, G. (1991). Stability of romantic relationships in China and the United States. In S. Ting-Toomey & F. Korzenny (Eds.), *Cross-cultural interpersonal communication* (pp. 99-115). Newbury Park, CA: Sage.

Gao, G. (1998). An initial analysis of the effects of face and concern for "other" in Chinese interpersonal communication. *International Journal of Intercultural Relations, 22*, 467-482.

Garrett, M. M. (1993). *Pathos* reconsidered from the perspective of classical Chinese rhetorics. *Quarterly Journal of Speech, 79*, 19-39.

Godby, W. C. (1999). Televisual discourse and the mediation of power: Living room dialogues with modernity in reform-era China. In R. Kluver & J. H. Powers (Eds.), *Civic discourse, civil society, and Chinese communities* (pp. 125-139). Stamford, CT: Ablex.

Gong, D. (1994). *Chinese maxims: Golden sayings of Chinese thinkers over five thousand years*. Beijing: Sinolingua.

Gong, G. (2000). When Mississippi Chinese talk. In A. Gonzalez, M. Houston, & V. Chen (Eds.), *Our voices: Essays in culture, ethnicity, and communication* (pp. 84-91). Los Angeles: Roxbury.

Gong, W. (1998). The role of ethics in persuasive communication: A comparative study of Aristotle's "ethos" and the Confucian "correctness of names." In D. R. Heisey, & W. Gong (Eds.), *Communication and culture: China and the world entering the 21st century* (pp. 3-13). Amsterdam: Rodopi B. V.

Gu, Y. (1990). Politeness phenomena in modern Chinese. *Journal of Pragmatics, 14*, 237-257.

Gu, Y. (1996). Doctor-patient interaction as goal-directed discourse in Chinese socio-cultural context. *Journal of Asian Pacific Communication, 7*, 156-176.

Gu, Y. (1997). Five ways of handling a bedpan: A tripartite approach to workplace discourse. *Text, 17*, 457-475.

Guan, S. (1998). The prospects for cross-cultural communication between China and the West in the 21st century. In D. R. Heisey & W. Gong (Eds.), *Communication and culture: China and the world entering the 21st century* (pp. 15-38). Amsterdam: Rodopi B. V.

Guan, S. (2000). A comparison of Sino-American thinking patterns and the functions of Chinese characters in the difference. D. R. Heisey (Ed.), *Chinese perspectives in rhetoric and communication* (pp. 25-43). Stamford, CT: Ablex.

Gupta, A. F. (1992). The pragmatic particles of Singapore colloquial English. *Journal of Pragmatics, 18*, 31-57.

Hall, D. L., & Ames, R. T. (1995). *Anticipating China: Thinking through the narratives of Chinese and Western culture*. Albany: State University of New York Press.

Han, M., & Hua, S. (1990). *Cries for democracy: Writings and speeches from the 1989 Chinese democracy movement*. Princeton, NJ: Princeton University Press.

Hayes, E. B. (1988). Encoding strategies used by native and non-native readers of Chinese Mandarin. *Modern Language Journal, 72*, 188-195.

Heisey, D. R. (1999). China's rhetoric of socialization in its international civic discourse. In R. Kluver & J. H. Powers (Eds.), *Civic discourse, civil society, and Chinese communities* (pp. 221-236). Stamford, CT: Ablex.

Ho, A. T. (1977). Intonation variations in a Mandarin sentence for three expressions: Interrogative, exclamatory, and declarative. *Phonetica, 34*, 446-456.

Ho, O. (1998). Hong Kong: A curatorial journey for an identity. *Art Journal, 57* (Winter), 39-43.

Hofstede, G. H. (1980). *Culture's consequences: International differences in work-related values*. Beverly Hills: Sage.

Holbrook, A., & Lu, H. T. (1969). A study of intelligibility in whispered Chinese. *Communication Monographs, 36*, 464-466.

Holt, G. R., & Chang, H.-C. (1992). Phases and changes: Using metaphors from *I Ching* to teach small group discussion. *Journal of Creative Behavior, 52*, 95-106.

Hornig, S. (1990). Communication strategies and agricultural development in 1950s China: The early years of the People's Republic of China. *Howard Journal of Communications, 2*, 368-376.

Hornsey, M., & Gallois, C. (1998). The impact of interpersonal and intergroup communication accommodation on perceptions of Chinese students in Australia. *Journal of Language and Social Psychology, 17*, 323-347.

Hsu, F. L. K. (1971). *The challenge of the American dream: The Chinese in the United States*. Belmont, CA: Wadsworth.

Hua, S. (1999). Literature as civic discourse in the reform era: Utopianism and cynicism in Chinese political consciousness. In R. Kluver & J. H. Powers (Eds.), *Civic discourse, civil society, and Chinese communities* (pp. 141-152). Stamford, CT: Ablex.

Hua, Z., & Dodd, B. (2000). The phonological acquisition of Putonghua (Modern Standard Chinese). *Journal of Child Language, 27*, 3-42.

Huang, H., & Tian, G. (1990). A sociolinguistic view of linguistic taboo in Chinese. *International Journal of the Sociology of Language, 81*, 63-85.

Huang, L.-M. (2000). The Chinese way of requesting information in intercultural negotiation. *Intercultural Communication Studies, 9*(2), 107-128.

Huang, S. (1997). Ritual, culture, and communication: Deification of Mao Zedong in China's cultural revolution movement. In A. Gonzalez & D. V. Tanno (Eds.), *Politics, communication, and culture* (pp. 122-140). Thousand Oaks, CA: Sage.

Huang, S. (2000). Power to move the masses in a mass movement: An analysis of Mao's rhetorical strategies during China's cultural revolution movement. In D. R. Heisey (Ed.), *Chinese perspectives in rhetoric and communication* (pp. 207-221). Stamford, CT: Ablex.

Huang, S., & Jia, W. (2000). The cultural connotations and communicative functions of Chinese kinship terms. *American Communication Journal, 3*(3), n.p. [Available: http://www. americancom.org/%7Eaca/acjdata/vol3/Iss3/spec1/huang_jia.html].

Huang, S.-M., & Warren, D. M. (1981). Chinese values as depicted in Mandarin terms of abuse. *Maledicta, 5*(1-2), 105-122.

Huntington, H. E. (1974). Symbolism of Chinese snuff bottles. *Arts of Asia, 4*(2), 42-47.

Jepson, J. (1989). The acquisition of categories in Chinese. *Lingua, 78*(2-3), 193-216.

Jerstad, L. G. (1967). Buddhist proselytization in the Tibetan drama *Drowanzangmu*. *Western Journal of Speech Communication, 31*, 199-210.

Jia, W. (1997-98). Facework as a Chinese conflict-preventative mechanism: A cultural\discourse analysis. *Intercultural Communication Studies, 7*(1), 53-62.

Jia, Y. (1992). Cognitive processes involved in the recognition of Chinese characters. *Diogenes, 157*, 67-87.

Kenny, K. R. (1993). Photographic content in Chinese newspapers. *Gazette, 51*, 149-169.

Kiefer, C. W. (1992). Aging in Eastern cultures: A historical overview. In T. R. Cole, D. D. Van Tassel, & R. Kastenbaum (Eds.), *Handbook of the humanities and aging* (pp. 96-123). New York: Springer.

Kipnis, A. B. (1997). *Producing guanxi: Sentiment, self, and subculture in a North China village*. Durham, NC: Duke University Press.

Kirkpatrick, A. (1991). Information sequencing in Mandarin letters of request. *Anthropological Linguistics, 33*, 183-203.

Kirkpatrick, A. (1993). Information sequencing in modern standard Chinese in a genre of extended spoken discourse. *Text, 13*, 423-453.

Klopf, D., & Cambra, R. (1980). Apprehension about speaking among college students in the People's Republic of China. *Psychological Reports, 46*, 1194.

Kluver, R., & Powers, J. H. (Eds.). (1999). *Civic discourse, civil society, and Chinese communities*, Stamford, CT: Ablex.

Kratochvil, P. (1998). Intonation in Beijing Chinese. In D. Dirst & A. Di Cristo (Eds.), *Intonation systems: A survey of twenty languages* (pp. 417-431). Cambridge: Cambridge University Press.

Kroger, R. O., & Woods, L. A. (1992). Are the rules of address universal? IV: Comparison of Chinese, Korean, Greek, and German usage. *Journal of Cross Cultural Psychology, 23*, 148-162.

Krone, K., Chen, L., & Xia, H. (1997). Approaches to managerial influences in the People's Republic of China. *Journal of Business Communication, 34*, 289-315.

Kunz, J. L. (1996). From Maoism to Elle: The impact of political ideology on fashion trends in China. *International Sociology, 11*, 317-335.

Kuo, S.-H. (1992). Formulaic opposition markers in Chinese conflict talk. *Georgetown University Round Table on Languages and Linguistics, nv*, 388-402.

Kuo, S.-H. (1994). Argumentative strategies in Chinsese political talks. *Proceedings of the National Science Council, ROC. Part C: Humanities and Social Sciences, 4*(1), 88-105.

Lai, T. C. (1992). *Chinese painting: Its mystic essence.* Hong Kong: Oxford University Press.

Landsberger, S. (1995). *Chinese propaganda posters: From revolution to modernization.* Armonk, NY: M. E. Sharpe.

Lau, S. (Ed.). (1996). *Growing up the Chinese way: Chinese child and adolescent development.* Hong Kong: The Chinese University Press.

Lee, C. W. (2000). The rituals of getting married in Singapore. *Human Communication, 3*(1), 41-60.

Lee, W. S. (1998). Patriotic breeders or colonized converts: A postcolonial feminist approach to antifootbinding discourse in China. In D. V. Tanno & A. Gonzalez (Eds.), *Communication and identity across cultures* (pp. 11-33). Thousand Oaks, CA: Sage.

Lent, J. A. (1995). Comics in East Asian countries: A contemporary survey. *Journal of Popular Culture, 29*, 185-198.

Li, W., & Milroy, L. (1995). Conversational code-switching in a Chinese community in Britain: A sequential analysis. *Journal of Pragmatics, 23*, 281-299.

Liao, K.-S. (1980). Mass media and crisis communication in China: Chinese press reactions in the 1962 Sino-Indian border conflict. *Communication Research, 7*, 69-94.

Lindqvist, C. (1991). *China: Empire of living symbols.* Reading, MA: Addison-Wesley.

Liu, D. (1999). The internet as a mode of civic discourse: The Chinese virtual community in North America. In R. Kluver & J. H. Powers (Eds.), *Civic discourse, civil society, and Chinese communities* (pp. 195-206). Stamford, CT: Ablex.

Lok, M. (Trans.). (1995). *A glossary of political terms of the People's Republic of China,* Hong Kong: The Chinese University Press.

Lu, G., & Xiao, X. (2000). Beijing opera during the cultural revolution: The rhetoric of ideological conflicts. In D. R. Heisey (Ed.), *Chinese perspectives in rhetoric and communication* (pp. 223-248). Stamford, CT: Ablex.

Lu, S. (1999). *Kan Dashan* as civic discourse in a Chinese community. In R. Kluver & J. H. Powers (Eds.), *Civic discourse, civil society, and Chinese communities* (pp. 181-194). Stamford, CT: Ablex.

Lu, X. (1998a). An interface between individualistic and collectivistic orientations in Chinese cultural values and social relations. *The Howard Journal of Communications, 9*, 91-107.

Lu, X. (1998b). *Rhetoric in ancient China: Fifth to third century B.C.E.: A comparison with classical Greek rhetoric.* Columbia: University of South Carolina Press.

Lu, X. (2000). The influence of classical Chinese rhetoric on contemporary Chinese political communication and social relations. In D. R. Heisey (Ed.), *Chinese perspectives in rhetoric and communication* (pp. 3-23). Stamford, CT: Ablex.

Lu, Z., & Millward, C. (1989). Chinese given names since the Cultural Revolution. *Names, 37,* 265-280.

Lum, C. M. K. (1996). *In search of a voice: Karaoke and the construction of identity in Chinese America.* Mahwah, NJ: Lawrence Erlbaum.

Ma, R. (1990). An exploratory study of discontented responses in American and Chinese relationships. *Southern Communication Journal, 55,* 305-318.

Ma, R. (1992). The role of unofficial intermediaries in interpersonal conflicts in the Chinese culture. *Communication Quarterly, 40,* 269-278.

Ma, R. (1996). Computer-mediated conversations as a new dimension of intercultural communication between East Asian and North American College Students. In S. C. Herring (Ed.), *Computer-mediated communication: Linguistic, social, and cross-cultural perspectives* (pp. 173-185). Amsterdam: John Benjamins.

Ma, R. (1999). The relationship between intercultural communication and nonverbal communication revisited: From facial expression to discrimination. *New Jersey Journal of Communication, 7,* 180-189.

Ma, R. (2000). Water-related figurative language in the rhetoric of Mencius. In A. Gonzalez & D. V. Tanno (Eds.), *Rhetoric in intercultural contexts* (pp. 119-129). Thousand Oaks, CA: Sage.

MacCormack, G. (1991). Cultural values in traditional Chinese law. *Chinese Culture, 32*(4), 1-11.

Mao, R. L. M. (1992). Invitational discourse and Chinese identity. *Journal of Asian Pacific Communication, 3,* 79-96.

Millen, J. H., & Wang M. (2000). A CMM analysis of Chinese code-switching. *Human Communication, 3*(1), 61-84.

Mosher, S. W. (1993). *A mother's ordeal: One woman's fight against China's one-child policy.* New York: Harcourt Brace.

Oliver, R. T. (1961). The rhetorical implications of Taoism. *Quarterly Journal of Speech, 4,* 27-35.

Ong, H.-T. (1993). *Chinese animal symbolisms.* Petaling Jaya, Malaysia: Pelanduk Publications.

Pan, Z., Lee, C.-C., Chan, J. M., & So, C. Y. K. (1999). One event, three stories: Media narratives of the handover of Hong Kong in cultural China. *Gazette, 61,* 99-112.

Petress, C. K. (1993). The goddess of democracy as icon in the Chinese student revolt. In A. King (Ed.), *Postmodern political communication: The fringe challenges the center* (pp. 99-114). Westport, CT: Praeger.

Powers, J. H. (1995). On the intellectual structure of the human communication discipline. *Communication Education, 44,* 191-222.

Qiu, H. (1992). *Folk customs of China.* Beijing: Foreign Languages Press.

Qiu, J. L. (2000). Interpreting the Dengist rhetoric of building socialism with Chinese characteristics. In D. R. Heisey (Ed.), *Chinese perspectives in rhetoric and communication* (pp. 249-264). Stamford, CT: Ablex.

Redding, S. G., & Ng, M. (1982). The role of "face" in the organizational perceptions of Chinese managers. *Organization Studies, 3,* 201-219.

Robinson, D. C. (1981). Changing functions of mass media in the People's Republic of China. *Journal of Communication, 31* (4), 58-73.

Sachdev, I., Bourhis, R., Phang, S.-W., & D'Eye, J. (1987). Language attitudes and vitality perceptions: Intergenerational effects amongst Chinese Canadian communities. *Journal of Language and Social Psychology, 6*(3-4), 287-307.

Saichs, T. (1994). Discos and dictatorship: Party-state and social relations in the People's Republic of China. In J. N. Wasserstrom & E. J. Perry (Eds.), *Popular protest and political culture in modern China* (pp. 246-267). San Francisco: Westview.

Shen, S. X.-N. (1988). Identifying topic in Chinese through prosodic features. *Journal of the Chinese Language Teachers Association, 23*(2), 33-53.

Soloman, R. H. (1999). *Chinese negotiating behavior: Pursuing interests through "old friends."* Washington, DC: U.S. Institute of Peace Press.

Stibbe, A. (1996). The metaphorical construction of illness in Chinese culture. *Journal of Asian Pacific Communication, 7*, 177-188.

Szeto, M. Y.-Y., & Garrett, V. M. (1990). *Children of the gods: Dress and symbolism in China.* Hong Kong: Urban Council.

Taylor, R. (1989). Chinese hierarchy in comparative perspectives. *Journal of Asian Studies, 48*, 490-511.

Tinberg, H. B. (1986). Language and estrangement: Lessons from the People's Republic of China. *English Journal, 75*(7), 46-50.

Tsai, M. K. (1970). Some effects of American television programs on children in Formosa. *Journal of Broadcasting, 14*, 229-238.

Tsao, F.-F. (1987). A topic-comment approach to the *ba* construction. *Journal of Chinese Linguistics, 15*, 1-54.

Tse, P. U., & Cavanagh, P. (2000). Chinese and Americans see opposite apparent motions in a Chinese character. *Cognition, 74*, B27-B32.

Tsui, A. B. M. (1991). Sequencing rules and coherence in discourse. *Journal of Pragmatics, 15*, 111-129.

Tu, W. M. (Ed.). (1994). *The living tree: The changing meaning of being Chinese today.* Stanford, CA: Stanford University Press.

Wachtel, E., & Lum, C. M. K. (1991). The influence of Chinese script on painting and poetry. *ETC: A Review of General Semantics, 48*, 275-291.

Wagner, R. G. (1993). "In guise of a congratulation": Political symbolism in Zhou Xinfang's play *Hai Rui Submits His Memorial.* In J. Unger (Ed.), *Using the past to serve the present: Historiography and politics in contemporary China* (pp. 46-103). Armonk, NY: M. E. Sharpe.

Wang, J. J. (1994). *Outrageous Chinese: A guide to Chinese street language.* San Francisco: China Books & Periodicals.

Wang, J., & Wu, W. (1997). "Ideological work" as conflict management: A dialectical approach in Chinese communication campaigns. *Intercultural Communication Studies, 7*(1), 83-100.

Wang, S. H.-Y., & Chang, H. C. (1999). Chinese professionals' perceptions of interpersonal communication in corporate America: A multidimensional scaling analysis. *Howard Journal of Communications, 10*, 297-315.

Ward, C., & Hewstone, M. (1985). Ethnicity, language and intergroup relations in Malaysia and Singapore: A social psychological analysis. *Journal of Multilingual and Multicultural Development, 6*, 271-296.

Wasserstrom, J. N., & Perry, E. J. (Eds.). (1992). *Popular protest and political culture in modern China: Learning from 1989.* Boulder, CO: Westview.

Wei, R., & Leung, L. (1998). A cross-societal study on the role of the mass media in political socialization in China and Taiwan. *Gazette, 60*, 377-393.

Whyte, M. K. (1974). *Small groups and political rituals in China.* Berkeley: University of California Press.

Williams, P. F. (1989). Divergent portrayals of the rustication experience in Chinese narrative after Mao. *Contrastes, 18-19*, 89-97.

Wong, K. F. E., & Chen, H.-C. (1999). Orthographic and phonological processing in reading Chinese text: Evidence from eye fixations. *Language and Cognitive Processes, 14,* 461-480.

Wong, W. S. (2000). Establishing the modern advertising languages: Patent medicine newspaper advertisements in Hong Kong, 1945-1969. *Journal of Design History, 13,* 213-226.

Wu, D. Y. H. (1996). Chinese childhood socialization. In M. H. Bond (Ed.), *The handbook of Chinese psychology* (pp. 143-154). Hong Kong: Oxford University Press.

Wu, D., & Hui, H. M. (1997). Personage description in Hong Kong versus mainland Chinese entertainment news discourse. *Text, 17,* 517-542.

Wu, P.-Y. (1984). Varieties of the Chinese self. In V. Kavolis (Ed.), *Designs of selfhood* (pp. 107-131). Cranbury, NJ: Associated University Presses.

Wu, W. (1995). Chinese evidence versus the institutionalized power of English. *Forensic Linguistics: The International Journal of Speech, Language and the Law, 2*(2), 154-167.

Xiao, X. S. (1995). China encounters Darwinism: A case of intercultural rhetoric. *Quarterly Journal of Speech, 81,* 83-99.

Xiao, X. Y. (2000). Sun Yat-Sen's rhetoric of cultural nationalism. In D. R. Heisey (Ed.), *Chinese perspectives in rhetoric and communication* (pp. 165-177). Stamford, CT: Ablex.

Xu, J. (1999). Body, discourse, and the cultural politics of contemporary Chinese Qigong. *The Journal of Asian Studies, 58,* 961-991.

Yallop, C., & Deng, Z. (1993). Medical terminology: A case study of terms in -itis and their equivalents in Chinese and modern Greek. *Linguist, 32*(2), 38-42.

Yan, W. (2000). A critical analysis of three of Mao's early political essays. In D. R. Heisey (Ed.), *Chinese perspectives in rhetoric and communication* (pp. 197-205). Stamford, CT: Ablex.

Yan, Y. (1996). *The flow of gifts: Reciprocity and social networks in a Chinese village.* Stanford, CA: Stanford University Press.

Yang, C. L., Gordon, P. C., Hendrick, R., & Wu, J. T. (1999). Comprehension of referring expressions in Chinese. *Language and Cognitive Processes, 14,* 715-743.

Ye, L. (1995). Complimenting in Mandarin Chinese. In G. Kasper (Ed.), *Pragmatics of Chinese as native and target language* (pp. 207-302). Honolulu: University of Hawaii Press.

Yee, C., & Smithback, J. B. (1991). *Fun with Chinese idioms 1.* Singapore: Federal Publications.

Young, L. W. L. (1982). Inscrutability revisited. In J. Gumperz (Ed.), *Language and social identity* (pp. 72-84). New York: Cambridge University Press.

Yu, F. T. C. (1979). China's mass communication in historical perspective. In G. C. Chu & F. Hsu (Eds.), *Moving a mountain: Cultural change in China.* Honolulu: University of Hawaii Press.

Yu, X. (1995). Conflict in a multicultural organization: An ethnographic attempt to discover work-related cultural assumptions between Chinese and American co-workers. *International Journal of Conflict Management, 6,* 211-232.

Yum, J. O. (1988). The impact of Confucianism on interpersonal relationships and communication patterns in East Asia. *Communication Monographs, 55,* 374-388.

Zhang, M. (1999). From Lei Feng to Zhang Haidi: Changing images of model youth in the post-Mao reform era. In R. Kluver & J. H. Powers (Eds.), *Civic discourse, civil society, and Chinese communities* (pp. 111-123). Stamford, CT: Ablex.

Zhang, Z.-S. (1997). Focus, presupposition and the formation of A-not-A questions in Chinese. *Journal of Chinese Linguistics, 25*, 227-257.

Zhao, H. (1999). Rhetorical adaptability in China's argument for Most Favored Nation status. In R. Kluver & J. H. Powers (Eds.), *Civic discourse, civil society, and Chinese communities* (pp. 251-264). Stamford, CT: Ablex.

Zhao, H. P. (1987). The Chinese pronoun *zan* and its person and social deictic features. *Journal of Chinese Linguistics, 15*, 152-176.

Zhou, H. (1994). Diffusion of movable type in China and Europe: Why were there two fates? *Gazette, 53*, 153-173.

Zhou, Y., & Wang, J. J. (1995). *Mutant Mandarin: A guide to new Chinese slang*. San Francisco: China Books and Periodicals.

Zhu, H., Li, W., & Qian, Y. (1998). Gift offer and acceptance in Chinese: Context and functions. *Journal of Asian Pacific Communication, 8*, 87-101.

Zhu, J.-H. (1997). Political movements, cultural values and mass media in China: Continuity and change. *Journal of Communication, 47*(4), 157-164.

Zhu, Y., & Stuart, K. (1999). "Two Bodhisattvas from the East": Minhe Monguor funeral orations. *Journal of Contemporary China, 8*, 179-188.

II

Metatheoretical Critique

4

A Critical Examination of the Eurocentric Representation of Chinese Communication

Rueyling Chuang and Claudia L. Hale

During the past decade or so, increasing attention has been devoted to understanding both the dynamics of and the problems associated with intercultural encounters and to understanding relational communication from a cross-cultural perspective. There is certainly much that is laudable in these efforts. However, an article published in *Gender in Cross-Cultural Perspective* (see Watson, 1993) serves as a vehicle for highlighting potential problems with respect to research efforts that seek to achieve *verstehen* (situated understanding) concerning the *lifeworld* of non-Euro-American cultures.

In the article just referenced, Watson reported that most Chinese men have many names (e.g., a nickname, a public name, and a pen name), whereas Chinese women do not. Watson further reported that "at marriage the bride loses her *ming* (name) and becomes known by a series of kinship terms such as a *teknomy*—so and so's mother—or when she ages, other people address her simply as 'old woman'" (p. 124). Watson stated that Chinese women do not have names because the selection of "an auspicious, learned name" is difficult and "intellectually challenging" (p. 125).

This conclusion reflects a biased, Euro-American, monologic perspective and perpetuates "orientalism" (Said, 1979). As Jia (2000) noted, the process of applying Western communication theories in an unreflective, uncritical, and uncreative manner to Chinese communication has served to distort Chinese communication and culture to a significant extent. Consequently, such research reproduces "orientalism" in Chinese communication and "fails to re-educate people in the West about exactly how Chinese communicate and why Chinese communicate in given ways" (p. 148).

Watson's study is a clear example of how a scholar (in this particular instance, from the discipline of anthropology) can err by imposing his or her value judgments when interpreting data, thus deriving false conclusions based on outdated information[1] to describe an "exotic" culture. While the naming of Chinese female children did not historically receive as much attention as the naming of Chinese male children, over the past 50 years most Chinese women (at least in China and Taiwan) have not only been given name(s), but they no longer take their husband's family name after marriage. One might argue that this approach is even more "advanced" than American or European traditions, wherein women are expected either to take their husband's family name or to employ a hyphenated combination of their maiden name and their husband's family name.

In point of fact, Chinese names are creatively composed to have a symbolic representation with a specific meaning. This contrasts with the Euro-American practice of taking names from known persons or common sources (e.g., the Bible, historical personalities, etc.). Unlike Euro-Americans, few Chinese have exactly the same first name. Thus, one would not find the Chinese equivalents of popular names, such as Michael or Jennifer, in almost every classroom. Would it be acceptable to claim that the Euro-American practice of using common first names is attributable to lack of "intellectual creativity" and that giving a new name might be too "intellectually challenging" for Euro-Americans?

Our purpose in this chapter is to examine the extent to which cross-cultural/intercultural communication literature perpetuates (false) understandings or (mis)representations of Chinese/Chinese-American communicative behaviors. We argue that the literature concerning Chinese/Chinese-American communication is Eurocentric and does not provide opportunities for the Chinese "voice" to emerge. Our analysis endeavors to reveal how research efforts intended to reveal the Chinese voice have, in fact, muted that voice.

We organize our analysis around four general issues: (1) the role of research in creating/perpetuating stereotypes and ethnicism, (2) the "dualisms" that have dominated cross-cultural/intercultural communication research, (3) explorations of double consciousness and identity and, finally, (4) overlooked areas of concern. Communication theorists Infante, Rancer, and Womack (1990), Kim and Gudykunst (1988), and Asante and Gudykunst (1989) slice the "pie" of cross-cultural/intercultural communication into three or perspectives: covering law/positivistic research; rule-governed/interpretive research, and systems theory. For our analyses, we draw on research conducted within these three approaches as we explore how current research/theory development practices serve either to increase or to hinder our understanding of

Chinese communication. In addition, we argue that, typically, social science research has failed to distinguish between Chinese and Chinese Americans, nor have scholars operating within this perspective offered findings that justify that failure.

CHINESE AS A MUTED GROUP?

Cross-cultural studies like Watson's (1993) are a double-edged sword. On one hand, a study like Watson's can increase our awareness of the inequalities extant in male-female relationships. Watson's study helps us understand how Chinese women's status was historically oppressed in a patriarchal society. Further, Watson's study lends support to Kramarae's (1981) muted group theory by showing how women's voices are silenced in a manmade-language society.

Paradoxically, studies such as that by Watson and muted group theory itself can also be used to support the argument that published cross-cultural research, grounded in a taken-for-granted understanding of Euro-American practices and/or conducted using white middle-class Americans as a comparison group (see, for example, Hall, 1976; Minturn, 1993), is likely to impose white middle-class American standards on other cultures. As Salazar (1991) argued, in "Western intellectual circles" there is a tendency to "romanticize" Third World women's voices and to "conceive of the subjects of the testimonials unproblematically—as always resisting their oppression through various strategies of textual subversion" (p. 93).

The ethnocentric imposition of white middle-class American standards extends even to commentaries concerning language itself. Becker (1991) applied Eurocentric value judgments to Chinese communication in an article in a widely used intercultural communication textbook. Becker claimed that the "ambiguity" of Chinese language (e.g., lack of tenses, lack of plural forms) can be attributed to discoverable "Reasons for the Lack of Argumentation and Debate in the Far East," a phrase that serves both as a title for his article and as a potent description of a particular ideological perspective.

The title of Becker's article and the terminology used to refer to these geographical areas underscore the Eurocentricity of the English language. The very notion of a "Far East" itself implies a Eurocentric standpoint, looking at "oriental" countries through a Western-centered perspective. As Nakayama (1994b) asked, phrases like "Near East," "Middle East," and "Far East" are "near, middle and far from where?" (p. 176).

Within his article, Becker (1991) proclaimed that the Chinese language has no tenses, "unless they are deliberately and awkwardly inserted" (p. 237). One questions the validity of this assertion. Although the Chinese language system does not have verb tenses, most Chinese use adverbial phrases (e.g., yesterday, tomorrow, and now) to indicate specific times. These adverbial phrases come quite naturally in everyday life, and it is not certain that a native speaker of the Chinese language would feel the phrases are "awkwardly inserted" in daily conversation.

Becker cited a literal translation of a typical dialogue from the *Analects* (XVII, 9, in Lau, trans., 1979) of Confucius to support his assertion:

> Confucius: I no desire talk.
> Disciple: If master no talk, what can disciple(s) do?
> Confucius: Does Heaven say anything? (= Heaven rules without language.)

To Becker, such dialogues illustrate that "even the Chinese philosophers were acutely aware of the shortcomings of their own language to reflect anything like the richness of human experience" (p. 237).

Such an analysis might be more worthy of special note if a number of other philosophers did not find their own (Indo-European) languages to be problematic. To begin with, both postmodernism and poststructuralism offer skeptical views of language. Foucault (1977) argued that language (in general) is neither "complete nor fully in control of itself" (p. 19). Foucault's view exemplifies not just postmodern thought, but a Western rhetorical tradition. For example, in *The Sophist* Plato discussed the paradox of language (the notion of "being" and "change is both the same and not the same" [1961, p. 257]). During the Enlightenment, John Locke commented that "the chief end of language in communication [is] to be understood, [and that] words serve not well for that end, neither in civil, nor philosophical discourse" (1975, p. 476). To Locke, words are signs of our ideas. However, due to inherent imperfections and ambiguities, language leads to communication problems. For poststructuralists, language is "an unreliable structure that violates its own rules" (Barney, 1987, p. 179).

Is it fair to point to the "ambiguity" and "shortcomings" of the Chinese language while simultaneously overlooking the assertions of Plato, Locke, Foucault, and others who have argued that Indo-European languages have the same problems? Becker (1991) concluded that, as a result of the "shortcomings" of the Chinese language, many Chinese "medieval philosophers got into arguments which Russell could show to be mere pseudo-problems. . ." (p. 237). Becker seems to imply that the debates engaged in by medieval Chinese philosophers can be explained quite simply through reference to inadequacies within the Chinese language system. We find that problems stemming from language's ambiguity and inadequacy exist in many language systems, not just in Chinese. By neglecting the fact that his criticisms/claims can be applied to many language systems, not just Chinese, Becker's argument contributes to a false understanding of Chinese culture and the complexity of the Chinese language.

Rather than increasing our understanding of Chinese culture, Watson's and Becker's cross-cultural studies perpetuate a variety of (negative) value judgments and "orientalism" that people from a hegemonic culture might have with respect to people from a less dominant culture. The foregoing articles illustrate the practice of employing an unfortunate double standard, that is, placing negative labels on practices within Chinese communication despite their parallels within Euro-American practices.

THE CREATION AND PERPETUATION OF "ETHNICISM"

Van Dijk (1991) argued that elite (mainstream, hegemonic) discourse reproduces ethnicism. Van Dijk defined ethnicism as "a system of ethnic group dominance based on cultural criteria of categorization, differentiation, and exclusion, such as those of language, religion, customs, or world views" (p. 5). Van Dijk further argued that there is a close connection between elite discourse and the perpetuation and reproduction of ethnicism. Power and ideology are embedded in the reproduction of ethnicism. Van Dijk (1993) explained that power can be defined in terms of the type of control elites have over the actions and minds of other people. Although this control might be implicit, "it is usually explicitly implemented by decision making, use of special acts and discourse genres" (p. 66). Van Dijk used, as an example, the study of textbooks as expressions of prevalent stereotypes about immigrant minorities. The works we have examined thus far (Watson, 1993; Becker, 1991) perpetuate selected textbook stereotypes and thus work to distort rather than to help better understand the culture being examined.

Foss and Foss (1994) argue that, for qualitative data to be admissible as evidence for claims about social life, the "researcher should have been deeply involved and closely connected to the scene, activity, or group studied. . . . [Moreover] the researcher should achieve enough distance from the phenomenon to allow for recording of action and interpretations relatively uncolored by what she or he might have at stake" (p. 36). In other words, a delicate combination of intimate knowledge and objective distance is required. The problem appears to be that much of the literature concerning communication practices within the Chinese culture (broadly defined) achieves distance but fails to persuasively exhibit intimate knowledge/understanding.

The ontological proposition of interpretive/qualitative research is that no "pure facts" exist outside of lived experience (Delia & Grossberg, 1977). That position leads to the axiological assumption that a researcher cannot be "purely" objective and free from value judgments. Within this position and the philosophy of interpretive research, no theory can be considered "value-free" (Littlejohn, 1992, p. 33). When the lead author of this chapter, a native Chinese with local knowledge, examines cross-cultural studies like Watson's, she finds that the evidence cited does not withstand informed critical scrutiny.

How can this work speak from the Chinese voice or adequately represent contemporary Chinese experience/ understandings?

As with Van Dijk's argument, Hall (1976) observed that communication research serves to reinforce class divisions while overlooking cultural variations. For example, the concept of a Chinese lack of competence discussed in some communication literature (see, for example, Hammer, 1989) fails to explicate distinctive cultural (and co-cultural) practices. This failure is quite possibly due to the influence of concepts that the dominant (research) culture considers important but that are not endemic to the culture being examined/critiqued. Cooks (1993) has argued that most of the concepts or behaviors of other cultures that deviate from those of the hegemonic culture "are dealt with inadequately (interpreted statistically as cultural variability, e.g., Gudykunst, 1988) in the literature—if at all" (p. 29). Along that same line, Lannamann (1991) suggested that more attention needs to be given to examining the ideological assumptions present in interpersonal constructs and to examining the validity of these constructs within minority groups or across cultures.

THE "DUALISMS" IN INTERCULTURAL STUDIES

The identification of a culture as "high-context" versus "low context" (see, e.g., Hall, 1966, 1976; Gudykunst, 1987, 1988; Gudykunst & Kim, 1984) or as "collectivistic" versus "individualistic" (see, e.g., Hofstede, 1980, 1984; Singelis, 1994; Singelis & Brown, 1995; Triandis, 1986; 1990) has become increasingly popular. These hegemonic, "paradigm-esque" concepts seem to serve as the fundamental starting point for virtually any research based on or exploring issues relevant to culture and communication. This theoretical framework has been popularized in the West and widely used as a "universal mode" of intercultural and international inquiries and often cast in "dichotomized and polarizing terms" (Lu, 1998, p. 91).

The dichotomy of (international) cultural differences can be best exemplified by high/low context cultures and research based on this conceptual framework. Hall's (1966, 1976) ground-breaking conceptualization of culture as high-context (HC) versus low-context (LC) has been cited in numerous studies (e.g., Gudykunst, 1987, 1988; Gudykunst & Kim, 1984; Gudykunst, Yang & Nishida, 1985; Samovar & Porter, 1991). Hall's HC and LC culture schema has proven to be heuristic, as it has served as an organizing construct for studies conducted within a variety of contexts (Gudykunst, Stewart, & Ting-Toomey, 1985; Korzeny, Ting-Toomey & Schiff, 1992; Wiseman & Shuter, 1994).

According to Hall (1976), HC transactions feature preprogrammed information present in the communication "receiver" (that is, "internalized in the person," p. 79) and/or contained in the setting. Only minimal information is present in the transmitted message, that is, in the words. LC transactions are the reverse: Information in the LC culture must be explicitly contained in the transmitted message in order to make up for what is missing in the context or not assumed to be automatically understood by the "receiver." Although Gudykunst and Ting-Toomey (1988) argued that no single culture exists at either extreme of the LC-HC continuum, most intercultural communication researchers have assumed that the American, German, Scandinavian, and Swiss cultures are near the LC end, while most Asian cultures, including China, Taiwan, and Hong Kong, are near the HC end (e.g., Gudykunst, 1983; Sanders, Wiseman & Matz, 1991).

In contrast to the single dualism offered by Hall, Hofstede (1980, 1984) sought to differentiate various cultures based on four dimensions: individualism/collectivism, masculinity/femininity, uncertainty avoidance, and power. Because of its primary impact on efforts to achieve cross-disciplinary understanding of culturally situated communication (see, for example, Hofstede, 1980; Kluckhon & Strodtbeck, 1961; Marsella, DeVos & Hsu, 1985; Triandis, 1986), we will focus on Hofstede's individualism/collectivism duality. Individualism is the extent to which the self is seen as central to activity; this perspective views individuals as primarily responsible for their destinies and as the shapers of their own lives. Conversely, collectivism views individuals as integrally tied to the groups to which they belong; the members of collectivistic cultures have a "we" consciousness. The nature of these differences ought to influence communication and, thus, uncertainty-reduction behaviors.

Gudykunst and Nishida (1989) contended that Hofstede's dimensions of cultural variability are "cross-culturally generalizable" (p. 22). Previous research conducted by scholars who isolated individualism/collectivism as a dimension of cultural variability (e.g., Hsu, 1981; Yang, 1981) seem to confirm Gudykunst and Nishida's assertion. Gudykunst and Nishida (1989) claimed that this work, even though affected by a "Chinese methodological bias" (p. 22), is consistent with Hofstede's individualism-collectivism dichotomy. Gudykunst and Nishida did not explain what they mean by "Chinese methodological bias," leaving us to wonder just what such a bias is.

For the past decade, cross-cultural theorists have endeavored to apply the dualities of LC/HC and individualism/collectivism to explain cross-cultural communication phenomena (see, e.g., Asante & Gudykunst, 1989; Gudykunst & Ting-Toomey, 1988; Samovar & Porter, 1991; Singelis, 1994; Singelis & Brown, 1995; Ting-Toomey & Korzenny, 1991; Triandis, 1986; 1990). While Hall and Hofstede have revolutionized cross-cultural communication studies and have, indeed, provided insightful explanations for the presence of cultural differences, the time has come for us to examine intercultural communication research, as well as the literature of Chinese communication more critically.

The validity of the dominant methods applied in cross-cultural studies, the samples generated, and the conclusions drawn merit attention. The LC/HC and individualism/collectivism dualisms should not be treated as bipolar states, as many cross-cultural/intercultural communication researchers do. Instead, they should be treated as states of flux. Unless the notion of LC/HC and the dichotomy of individualism/collectivism are treated as highly contextual and bounded by the stage or nature of the relationship under investigation, these dualisms will only hinder our understanding of both cross-cultural and intercultural interpersonal relationships.

Research derived from Hall's LC/HC culture schema such as theory of face management (Ting-Toomey, 1988) provides some insightful, fundamental differences between Chinese ("Eastern") and American ("Western") cultures; yet, this research may not account for personal traits and individual differences. It could be problematic to assume that most Chinese tend to be "accommodating" in conflict situations with other Chinese. Further, not all Chinese are inclined to employ an indirect approach. When observing Chinese in their interactions with relatives or acquaintances, one finds that most Chinese are out front and less concerned with tactfulness. For example, some Chinese would find it acceptable to tell a friend—without euphemism—that he/she is too skinny or too fat, while most Americans would say that such directness is "uncalled for" or is "impolite." A Hong Kong or Taiwan pedestrian would be surprised to hear an apology after being bumped by a passerby.

Collier and Thomas (1988) argue that assumptions about culture are based on overgeneralizations, overly simplistic categorizations, or inappropriate assumptions. Hall's categorization and research based on his HC and LC schema are derived from Cartesian linear reasoning, which may not apply to how Chinese position themselves or to Chinese social reality. These examples demonstrate how the "mainstream" or "hegemonic" intercultural communication literature is laden with a worldview taken from a Western tradition.

Skepticism also exists about Hofstede's (1980) research and numerous intercultural communication studies based on his individualism-collectivism dualism. Gudykunst and Ting-Toomey (1988) and their associates, who applied both Hall's and Hofstede's schemas in several of their investigations, offer three cautions regarding Hofstede's studies. First, Hofstede's research sample, constituted by personnel in a multinational organization, might not be representative of other members of the culture. Second, the validity of the items Hofstede used to construct one or two of the indices is questionable, making quantification of attitudes and lived experiences problematic. Third, since Hofstede's theory was developed through an examination of organizational communication, one can not know whether the theory is applicable to communication within non-organizationally based, personal relationships.

In addition to Gudykunst and Ting-Toomey's (1988) arguments against applying organizational communication to an interpersonal context, the Euro-American construct of "relationship" might be very different from the Chinese construct. In Chuang and Krishna's (1994) study of the causes and strategies of relationship termination, most Chinese undergraduate/graduate college student respondents were found to have never terminated a relationship. There are two plausible explanations for this phenomenon. First, unlike American students who start dating at an early age, it is quite conceivable that some Chinese respondents might not have had any romantic involvements prior to the time of the study; consequently, they might not have had an opportunity to engage in the process of romantic relationship termination. Second, Chinese might perceive and define "love" and "relationship termination" differently from Americans. Here again we have a situation in which researchers have sought to explore differences/similarities that are grounded primarily in Eurocentric perceptual biases.

Furthermore, research designs that employ the use of forced-choice questionnaires to investigate Chinese communication are laden with Eurocentric tendencies. Griffin (1994) argued that studies like that of Ting-Toomey, which employ paper-and-pencil Likert scales, attempt to measure types of conflict management styles (e.g., avoiding vs. collaborating) that are fundamentally "Western construct[s]" (p. 425). In a similar vein, Low and Tasker (1991) argued that attitude-rating scales/questionnaires might not be the best way to assess Chinese attitudes since such scales/questionnaires cannot accurately depict the Chinese worldview, which is, in contrast to the Euro-American worldview, non-bipolar in nature.

DOUBLE CONSCIOUSNESS AND IDENTITY

Recently, communication scholars have employed W. E. B. DuBois's "double consciousness" concept to scrutinize ethnic identity via their own bicultural *lebenswelt* (Chen, 2000; Gong, 2000; Ling, 1990; Nakayama, 2000) as well as the discourse produced by Chinese Americans (e.g., Maxine Hong Kingston's "most widely studied work in American literature on college campuses" [Chen, 2000]—*The Woman Warrior*). DuBois (1982) argued that blackness and black consciousness were/are significant components of black reality—they were/are the essence of being black in America. DuBois defined double-consciousness as the myopia of a dual or bipolar consciousness or identity that produces a fundamental alienation in black people; double-consciousness causes black people (and, one could claim, members of any "minority" group) to view themselves both through their own eyes and through the eyes of others. This self-consciousness of alienation is problematic because it embodies both self-disregard and self-liberation. The result is a self in search of its own identity and fulfillment through the presence of the other.

To DuBois, double consciousness not only accounts for the double bind and ethnic identity of African Americans, double consciousness can also be extended to other minority groups (e.g., Chinese immigrants). Ling (1990) wrote that American society maintains its white male hegemony by devaluing those who are "others" (e.g., women, nonwhite ethnic groups, physically challenged people, people with a different sexual orientation). Ling argued that minorities develop a "double consciousness" or positive awareness of themselves and an awareness of the negative perceptions that the hegemonic society has of them.

To Chen (2000), the identity of Chinese Americans is not an "either/or choice, but a both/and transformation; a new kind of integration or sometimes a lack of integration, of two cultural lifeworlds" (pp. 8-9). Chen asserted that, although Chinese Americans might "look like" Chinese, they differ in their thinking. Chen further explained that the conflicts between American-born Chinese and their immigrant parents (conflicts rarely discussed in cross-cultural studies) are "incommensurate"—there is no shared discourse upon which the conflicting ways of life can be adjudicated or even discussed. Ling (1990) cited DuBois's double consciousness as a construct that can be used to gain understanding with respect to multiple cultural insights. That is, the concept of double consciousness can help to construct meanings and increase awareness of the plurality of our cultural interpretations and practices.

DuBois' double consciousness and Chen's explanation of Chinese-Americans' lived experiences illustrate how the dualities of LC/HC and individualism-collectivism fail to contribute to an understanding of people who are "trapped" in two cultures. Cross-cultural theorists (e.g., Hecht, Andersen & Ribeau, 1989; Samovar & Porter, 1991; Ting-Toomey, 1988) assume that the U.S. culture is low-context and individualistic in nature, whereas Chinese culture is at the other end of the spectrum (high-context and collectivistic in nature). It is important to ask: Which ethnic groups in the United States are we talking about? Who are the Chinese? Which Chinese culture? Mainland Chinese? Taiwan Chinese? Hong Kong Chinese? Or Chinese-Americans who grew up in Mississippi and speak with a Southern drawl?

The sense of identity within the Chinese community is another important issue. While Chinese/Chinese-Americans' physical attributes remain similar, they do not share the same lived experiences and identities. One wonders whether a Chinese who immigrated to the United States during the 1950s and lived in downtown Oakland, California, and a capitalist Hong Kong or Taiwan "new" immigrant who bought a $600,000 home in a Los Angeles suburb are able to identify with each other. Moreover, even in Chinese-populated communities—such as Taiwan, Hong Kong, and Mainland China—the political ideology and social structures are drastically different. On American college campuses, one frequently finds that students from various Chinese-populated communities retain social, cultural, and communication practices that create barriers that work against their ability to act together.

The ambiguity of classifying Chinese into HC versus LC and individualistic versus collectivistic cultures does not account for the lived experiences of people who are on the borders of two extremes. To clarify the ambiguities and confusions involved in classifying Asians, Hispanics, and Northern Americans, or Eastern versus Western cultures, provide a critical task for future intercultural communication research.

From this discussion of double consciousness, we turn to Xi's (1994) integration of individualism and collectivism in American and Chinese societies. Xi (1994) cited Carbaugh's (1988) illustration of how Americans try to solve social problems collectively on talk shows (e.g., the Oprah Winfrey Show) through the rhetoric of individualism, and Mechling's (1980) characterization of American boys collectively celebrating their individuality through the metaphor of the Boy Scout campfire. Xi (1994) argued that American individualism and collectivism are interconnected. Xi also used American smoke-free environments to illustrate the collectivistic efforts with respect to personal health and secondhand smoke while, in "collectivistic" Chinese society, this type of public conscious is not prevalent. Thus, Xi contended that both fundamental individualistic and collectivistic elements of culture "are instinctively linked. They cannot be separated from each other in society" (p. 158).

In a similar vein, Lu's (1998) study also challenges the simplification and polarization of the individualism/collectivism construct and the stereotypical categorization of Chinese culture as "collectivistic." Lu brought to light the importance of recognizing sociohistorical contexts and philosophical traditions when studying Chinese communication. Lu modified the individualism and collectivism concept and applied Chinese terms such as *yi* (righteousness, faithfulness) and *li* (utilitarianism and profit) in her study and found that both value systems have influenced Chinese cultural values from the Confucius era to the post-Mao era. Her study indicated that while both traditional Chinese value systems coexist, the value of *yi*, which is associated with other-orientation and collectivism, is declining; while the value of *li*, which is related to personal gain and individualism, has become more pervasive. At the same time, the Chinese value *li* is different from American individualism. Lu noted that even though the value of *li*, which is identified with the schools of Mohism and Legalism in Chinese philosophy, has regained its status in modern China, it is not perceived as a "moral term." Instead, *li* has been associated with negative connections and has a different philosophical basis. Individualism in the United States, on the other hand, is highly celebrated and accepted as a "moral concept" and a "god term" (Lu, 1998, p. 105). She concluded that the individualism/collectivism framework has failed to consider the native point of view and the dynamics of culture change. Her study exemplifies the importance of tracing philosophical and rhetorical traditions and changing social and economic traditions, especially when examining Chinese cultural values and communication.

OVERLOOKED AREAS OF CONCERN

Ellingsworth (1988) argued that, in most intercultural research, the burden of cultural adaptation is placed on the newcomer. Most intercultural communication studies (e.g., Gudykunst & Kim, 1984; Kim, 1991, 1994) emphasize expatriates' or "outgroup" members' "adaptation" and "acculturation" to the (white, mainstream, hegemonic) host culture, while host culture members' adaptation to the increasing presence of expatriates does not receive as much attention.

Moreover, few researchers have discussed adaptation between minority groups. One need only look at the Rodney King riot in Los Angeles or New York's Crown Heights riot to understand that racial tensions merit the attention of cross-cultural/intercultural communication researchers. However, most cross-cultural/intercultural communication studies fail to scrutinize how two "outgroup" members adapt to each other. Studies only discuss how "outgroup" members adapt to the "ingroup" members' culture (see, for example, Gudykunst, 1986; Gudykunst & Kim, 1984).

As Nakayama (1994) argued, discourse is politically inscribed, privileging particular meanings and forms of interacting while undermining others. Nakayama wrote that racialized, gendered, class-based subjects are positioned not in a neutral discourse but in a complex discursive formation that privileges some interests and practices over others. Nakayama re-echoes Cornel West's (1990) belief that cultural practices of domination create "micro-institutional" analyses that "sustain white supremacist discourse in the everyday life of non-Europeans (including the ideological production of the means by which alien normative styles and group perceptions are constituted)" (p. 12). Nakayama (1994) noted that we need an analysis of social difference that includes race, gender, class, or sexual orientation as they express the "forces that sustain relations of domination" (p. 191).

Ellingsworth (1988) concluded that the time dimension is a strong factor in motivating the nature and extent of adaptation. Specifically, the refugee often cannot go home again, and his or her incentive to adjust productively to the new environment is due to a permanent lack of alternatives. Therefore, cultural assimilation and adaptation of refugees should differ from that of international students. International students are often less motivated to adapt to the American host culture, since they have the option to decide to stay in the host culture or to leave. However, intercultural/cross-cultural communication researchers frequently fail to differentiate between these two types of expatriates.

At an even more "micro" level of analysis, intercultural/cross-cultural studies characteristically overlook communication within an ethnic group (e.g., Hellweg, Samovar & Skow, 1991). Lum (2000) determined that regionalism (within the People's Republic of China, Taiwan, Hong Kong, and Southeast Asia) was an important element in facilitating and maintaining diversity in Chinese culture. Lum explained that regionalism among Chinese immigrants is manifested in how they maintain cultural customs or practices and in the dialects or languages they use. Thus, to assume "all Chinese" act in a certain way (as, for example, members of a high-context and collectivistic culture) is problematic. In a similar vein, it would be problematic to lump all Spanish-surnamed ethnic groups (Latinos/Latinas, Chicanos/Chicanas, Mexicans, Cubans, Puerto Ricans, etc.) together and assume that they exemplify a "collectivistic culture" (see, e.g., Hecht, Andersen & Ribeau, 1989; Hofstede, 1984; Gudykunst & Ting-Toomey, 1988).

Nakayama (2000) described the dis/orientation in Asian/Asian American ethnic groups as a dialectical process. He contended that Asian Americans are as diverse as Asians and rejected the notion of "orientals" and how they are often categorized as "other" in U.S. culture (pp. 14-15). Nakayama argued that the lived world of Asian Americans in many regions of the United States is often overlooked. In response to the perception of Asians in America as "perpetual foreigners" (Chan, 1991, p. 187), Nakayama posed the question: What is the Asian American's identity? What does it mean to be a "perpetual foreigner" (due to physical attributes) in one's native country? These compelling questions have not been addressed in most of the "mainstream" and hegemonic intercultural studies of the past decade, whether those studies employed a positivistic/ covering law approach, a humanistic/rule-grounded approach, or systems theory.

We argue that most research based on a social perspective has not clearly distinguished between Chinese and Chinese Americans. Consequently, findings based on the cultural characteristics of Chinese nationals have been employed to offer judgments about Chinese Americans. It is also important to note that current literature produced by Dubios (1982) and Nakayama (1994b, 2000) and other ethnic minority scholars largely deals with United States settings where the European American is the dominant ethnic group and other ethnic groups are marginalized or oppressed. Though their research addresses the power imbalance between different ethnic groups, this work might not apply to Chinese communication. A Chinese-American's (dis)orientation with respect to his/her cultural identity might not relate to a Chinese immigrant's struggle to acculturate to his/her host culture while simultaneously trying to preserve native culture values.

Nor does current research, regardless of methodology, in the dominant communication literature, address a Chinese immigrant's sense of belonging or loss of belonging to his/her motherland. It is only through anecdotal narrative essays, such as Ma (2000), that we see a sojourner's description of his (in this case) intercultural experiences in the United States, Taiwan, and Mainland China as "both-and" and "neither-nor." As he notes, "after spending so many years in North America, I am no longer completely Chinese or Taiwanese, and this change sometimes makes me a stranger in many social situations in Taiwan," a place where Ma was born and raised (p. 102).

CONCLUSION

Our purpose in this chapter has not been to discourage Euro-American scholars who might be interested in conducting cross-cultural/intercultural examinations of communication practices involving Chinese/Chinese-Americans. Rather, we wish to pose a constructive challenge for more fruitful research. We ask that the culture and communicative practices of Chinese/Chinese-Americans be given the same respect that should be accorded to Euro-American culture. There is a need to recognize the complexity of the subject matter being addressed as opposed to adopting "simplifying" processes that seem, unfortunately, typical of the research conducted.

Intercultural communication studies (e.g., Lee & Boster, 1991; Won-Doornink, 1991) have historically examined intercultural interaction not as a life-span process but, rather, as a still-life "snapshot," often with that snapshot taken by having participants fill out a one-time pencil-and-paper questionnaire. In truth, relationships are complex processes and should be approached in a manner that respects that complexity. Duck (1990), for example, described relationships as "unfinished business conducted through resolution of, and dialog about personal, dyadic or relational dilemmas" (p. 9). The appreciation of any relationship as "unfinished business" would seem to require more than a single snapshot. More longitudinal research or critical ethnographic field research needs to be conducted.

A new type of research in intercultural communication would apply an interpretive approach (e.g., hermeneutic phenomenology) and a critical approach (e.g., cultural studies; poststructuralism) to raise the voice of "the other." Lannamann (1991) asserted that an understanding of the role of ideology in interpersonal communication is necessary in order to avoid the perils of reifying cultural practices and legitimizing current social orders through our research findings. Additionally, Bochner (1994) argued that the examination of ideological assumptions helps to protect (intercultural) interpersonal studies from a single, orthodox position that constrains new ideas.

We are certainly not the first nor the only researchers to raise cautions concerning the approach that should be taken when a researcher undertakes the task of engaging in culturally based theorizing (e.g., Tehranian, 1991). Nor are concerns in this area limited to the study of and conclusions drawn about communication within Chinese and/or Chinese-American cultures (e.g., Liberman, 1990). However, through the above critique of the Euro-American literature on Chinese culture and communication, we call all social science researchers to move beyond stereotypes to achieve a more critical and hence better understanding of cross-cultural/intercultural communication processes.

NOTE

1. Some of the documents that Watson relied on for her conclusions were published in the 1920s.

REFERENCES

Asante, M. K., & Gudykunst, W. B. (1989). *Handbook of international and intercultural communication*. Newbury Park, CA: Sage.

Barney, R. (1987). Uncanny criticism in the United States. In J. Natoli (Ed.), *Tracing literary theory* (pp. 177-212). Urbana: University of Illinois.

Becker, C. B. (1991). Reasons for the lack of argumentation and debate in the Far East. In L. A. Samovar & R. E. Porter (Eds.), *Intercultural communication: A reader* (6th ed., pp. 234-243). Belmont, CA: Wadsworth.

Bochner, A. (1984). The functions of human communication in interpersonal bonding. In C. Arnold & J. W. Bowers (Eds.), *The handbook of rhetorical and communication theory* (pp. 544-621). Newton, MA: Allyn & Bacon.

Carbaugh, D. (1988). *Talking American: Cultural discourses on Donahue*. Norwood, NJ: Ablex.

Chan, S. (1991). *Asian Americans: An interpretive history*. Boston: Twayne.

Chen, V. (2000). (De)hyphenated identity: The double voice in *The woman warrior*. In A. Gonzalez, M. Houston, & V. Chen (Eds.). *Our voices: Essays in culture, ethnicity, and communication* (pp. 3-12). Los Angeles: Roxbury Publishing.

Chuang, R., & Krishna, V. (1994, April). *Gender and culture differences in relationship termination: A study of causes and strategies of European American and Asian/Asian American romantic relationship disengagers*. Paper presented at the annual meeting of Central States Communication Association, Oklahoma City.

Collier, M. J., & Thomas, M. (1988). Cultural identity. In Y. Y. Kim & W. B. Gudykunst (Eds.), *Theories in intercultural communication* (pp. 99-122). Newbury Park, CA: Sage.

Confucius (1979). *Analects* (D. C. Lau, Trans.). Harmondsworth, England: Penguin Books.

Cooks, L. (1993, April). *Exploring the opportunities: Where does communication research "fit" in cultural studies?* Paper presented at the Annual Conference of the American Culture Association, New Orleans.

Delia, J., & Grossberg, L. (1977). Interpretation and evidence. *Western Journal of Speech Communication, 41*, 32-42.

DuBois, W. E. B. (1982). *The souls of black folk*. New York: Dodd, Mead.

Duck, S. W. (1990). Relationships as unfinished business: Out of frying pan and into the 1990s. *Journal of Social and Personal Relationships, 7*, 5-28.

Ellingsworth, H. W. (1988). A theory of adaptation in intercultural dyads. In Y. Y. Kim & W. B. Gudykunst (Eds.), *Theories in intercultural communication* (pp. 259-279). Newbury Park, CA: Sage.

Foss, K. A., & Foss, S. K. (1994). Personal experience as evidence in feminist scholarship. *Western Journal of Communication, 58*, 39-43.

Foucault, M. (1977). Preface to progression. *Language-counter memory, practice: Selected essays and interviews*. D. F. Bouchard & S. Simon (Eds.). Ithaca, NY: Cornell University Press.

Gong, G. (2000). When Mississippi Chinese talk. In A. Gonzales, M. Houston, & V. Chen (Eds.), *Our voices: Essays in culture, ethnicity, and communication* (pp. 84-92). Los Angeles: Roxbury.

Griffin, E. (1994). *A first look at communication theory*. (2nd ed.) New York: McGraw-Hill.

Gudykunst, W. B. (1983). *Intercultural communication theory: Current perspectives*. Beverly Hills: Sage

Gudykunst, W. B. (1986). Intraethnic and interethnic uncertainty reduction processes. In Y. Y. Kim (Ed.). *Interethnic communication*. London: Edward Arnold.

Gudykunst, W. B. (1987). Cross-cultural comparisons. In C. Berger & C. Chaffee (Eds.). *Handbook of communication science* (pp. 847-889). Newbury Park, CA: Sage.

Gudykunst, W. B. (1988). Uncertainty and anxiety. In Y. Y. Kim & W. B. Gudykunst (Eds.), *Theories in intercultural communication* (pp. 123-156). Newbury Park, CA: Sage.

Gudykunst, W. B., and Kim, Y. Y. (1984). *Communicating with strangers.* New York: Random House.

Gudykunst, W. B., & Nishida, T. (1989). Theoretical perspectives for studying intercultural communication. In M. K. Asante & W. B. Gudykunst (Eds.), *Handbook of international and intercultural communication* (pp. 17-46). Newbury Park, CA: Sage.

Gudykunst, W. B., Stewart, L. P., & Ting-Toomey, S. (1985). *Communication, culture, and organizational processes.* Beverly Hills: Sage.

Gudykunst, W. B., & Ting-Toomey, S. (1988). *Culture and interpersonal communication.* Newbury Park, CA: Sage.

Gudykunst, W. B., Yang, S. M., & Nishida, T. (1985). A cross-cultural test of uncertainty reduction theory. *Human Communication Research, 11,* 407-454.

Hall, E. T. (1966). *The hidden dimension.* New York: Doubleday.

Hall, E. T. (1976). *Beyond culture.* New York: Doubleday.

Hammer, R. (1989). Intercultural communication competence. In M. K. Asante & W. B. Gudykunst (Eds.), *Handbook of international and intercultural communication* (2nd ed., pp. 247-260). Newbury Park, CA: Sage.

Hecht, M. L., Andersen, P. A., & Ribeau, S. A. (1989). The cultural dimensions of nonverbal communication. In M. K. Asante & W. B. Gudykunst (1989), *Handbook of international and intercultural communication* (pp. 163-185). Newbury Park, CA: Sage.

Hellweg, S., Samovar, L. A., & Skow, L. (1991). Cultural variations in negotiation styles. In S. Samovar & R. Porter (Eds.), *Intercultural communication: A reader* (pp. 185-192). Belmont, CA: Wadsworth.

Hofstede, G. (1980). *Culture's consequences.* Beverly Hills: Sage.

Hofstede, G. (1983). Dimensions of national cultures in fifty countries and three regions. In J. Deregowski, S. Dzuriawiec, & R. Annis (Eds.), *Explications in cross-cultural psychology.* Lisse, The Netherlands: Swets & Zeitlinger.

Hofstede, G. (1984). Hofstede's culture dimensions: An independent validation using Rokeach's value survey. *Journal of Cross-Cultural Psychology, 15,* 417-433.

Hofstede, G. (1991). *Cultures and organizations: Software of the mind.* New York: McGraw-Hill.

Hsu, F. (1981). *Americans and Chinese* (3rd ed.). Honolulu: University of Hawaii Press.

Infante, D. A., Rancer, A. S., & Womack, D. F. (1990). *Building communication theory.* Prospect Heights, IL.: Waveland Press.

Jia, W. S. (2000). Chinese communication scholarship as an expansion of the communication and culture paradigm. In D. R. Heisey (Ed.), *Chinese perspectives in rhetoric and communication* (pp. 139-161). Stamford, CT: Ablex.

Kim, Y. Y. (1991). Communication and cross-cultural adaptation. In L. A. Samovar & R. E. Porter (Eds.), *Intercultural communication: A reader* (6th ed., pp. 383-391). Belmont, CA: Wadsworth.

Kim, Y. Y. (1994). Interethnic communication: The context and the behavior. In S. Deetz (Ed.), *Communication yearbook 17* (pp. 511-538). Thousand Oaks, CA: Sage.

Kim, Y. Y., & Gudykunst, W. B. (1988). *Theories in intercultural communication.* Newbury Park, CA: Sage.

Kluckhohn, F., & Strodtbeck, F. (1961). *Variations in value orientations*. New York: Row, Peterson.

Korzeny, F., Ting-Toomey, S., & Schiff, E. (1992). *Mass media effects across cultures*. Newbury Park: Sage.

Kramarae, C. (1981). *Women and men speaking*. Rowley, MA: Newbury House Publishing.

Lannamann, J. W. (1991). Interpersonal communication research as ideological practice. *Communication Theory, 1*, 179-203.

Lee, H. O., & Boster, F. J. (1991). Social information for uncertainty reduction during initial interactions. In S. Ting-Toomey & F. Korzenny (Eds.), *Cross-cultural interpersonal communication* (pp. 189-212). Newbury Park, CA: Sage.

Liberman, K. (1990). Intercultural communication in central Australia. In D. Carbaugh (Ed.), *Cultural communication and intercultural contact* (pp. 177-183). Hillsdale, NJ: Lawrence Erlbaum & Associates.

Ling, A. (1990). Chinese-American women writers: Four forerunners of Maxine Hong Kingston. In A. M. Jaggar & S. R. Bordon (Eds.), *Gender/body/knowledge* (pp. 309-323). New Brunswick, NJ: Rutgers University Press.

Littlejohn, S. W. (1992). *Theories of human communication* (4th ed.). Belmont, CA: Wadsworth.

Locke, J. (1975). *An essay concerning human understanding*. P. Niddith (Ed.). London: Oxford University.

Low, G., & Tasker, I. (1991). The working of bipolar attitude scales in Chinese. *Educational Research, 33*, 141-151.

Lu, X. (1998). An interface between individualistic and collectivistic orientations in Chinese cultural values and social relations. *Howard Journal of Communications, 9*, 91-107.

Lum, C. M. K. (2000). Regionalism and communication: Exploring Chinese immigrant perspectives. In A. Gonzalez, M. Houston, & V. Chen (Eds.), *Our voices: Essay in culture, ethnicity, and communication* (pp. 235-241). Los Angeles: Roxbury Publishing.

Ma, R. (2000). "Both-and" and "neither-nor": My intercultural experiences. In M. W. Lustig & J. Koester (Eds.), *Among us: Essays on identity, belonging, and intercultural competence* (pp. 100-107). New York: Longman.

Marsella, A. J., DeVos, G., & Hsu, F. L. K. (1985). *Culture and self: Asian and Western perspectives*. London: Tavistock.

Mechling, J. (1988). The magic of the Boy Scout campfire. *Journal of American Folklore, 93*, 35-56.

Minturn, L. (1993). *Sita's daughters: Coming out of purdah*. New York: Oxford University Press.

Nakayama, T. (2000). Dis/orienting identities: Asian American, history, and intercultural communication. In A. Gonzalez, M. Houston, & V. Chen (Eds.), *Our voices: Essay in culture, ethnicity, and communication* (pp. 13-18). Los Angeles: Roxbury Publishing.

Nakayama, T. (1994). Show/down time: "Race," gender, sexuality & popular culture. *Critical Studies in Mass Communication, 11*, 162-179.

Plato (1961). *The Sophist and the statesman* (trans. A. E. Aylor). R. Kolbansky & E. Anscombe (Eds.). New York: T. Nelson.

Said, E. (1979). *Orientalism*. New York: Vintage Books.

Salazar, C. (1991). Third World women's text: Between the politics of criticism and cultural politics. In S. B. Gluck & D. Patai (Eds.), *Women's words: The feminist practice of oral history*. New York: Routledge.

Samovar, L. A., & Porter, R. E. (Eds.). (1991). *Intercultural communication: A reader* (6th ed.). Belmont, CA: Wadsworth.

Sanders, J. A., Wiseman, R. L., & Matz, S. I. (1991). Uncertainty reduction in acquaintance relationships in Ghana and the United States. In S. Ting-Toomey & F. Korzenny (Eds.), *Cross-cultural interpersonal communication* (pp. 79-98). Newbury Park, CA: Sage.

Singelis, T. M. (1994). Bridging the gap between culture and communication. In A-M. Bouvy, F. J. R. van de Vijver, P. Boski, & P. Schmitz (Eds.), *Journeys into cross-cultural psychology* (pp. 278-293). Lisse, The Netherlands: Swets & Zeitlinger.

Singelis, T. M., & Brown, W. J. (1995). Culture, self, and collectivist communication: Linking culture to individual behavior. *Human Communication Research, 21,* 354-389.

Tehranian, M. (1991). Is comparative communication theory possible/desirable? *Communication Theory, 1,* 44-59.

Ting-Toomey, S. (1991). Cross-cultural interpersonal communication: An introduction. In S. Ting-Toomey & F. Korzenny (Eds.), *Cross-cultural interpersonal communication* (pp. 1-8). Newbury Park, CA: Sage.

Ting-Toomey, S. (1988). Intercultural conflict styles: A face-negotiation theory. In Y. Y. Kim & W. B. Gudykunst (Eds.), *Theories in intercultural communication* (pp. 213-235). Newbury Park, CA: Sage.

Ting-Toomey, S., & Korzenny, F. (Eds.) (1991). *Cross-cultural interpersonal communication.* Newbury Park, CA: Sage.

Triandis, H. (1986). Collectivism vs. individualism: A reconceptualization of a basic concept in cross-cultural psychology. In C. Bagley & G. Verma (Eds.), *Personality, cognition, and values: Cross-cultural perspectives of childhood and adolescence.* London: Macmillan.

Triandis, H. (1990). Cross-cultural studies of individualism and collectivism. In J. Berman (Ed.), *Nebraska symposium on motivation 1989* (pp. 41-133). Lincoln: University of Nebraska Press.

Van Dijk, T. A. (1991). *Racism and the press.* London: Routledge.

Van Dijk, T. A. (1993). *Elite discourse and racism.* Newbury Park, CA: Sage.

Watson, R. S. (1993). The named and the nameless: Gender and person in Chinese society. In C. B. Gretteil & C. F. Sargent (Eds.), *Gender in cross-cultural perspective.* Englewood Cliffs, NJ: Prentice Hall.

West, C. (1990). Toward a socialist theory of racism. In C. West, *Socialist perspectives on race.* New York: Democratic Socialists on America.

Wiseman, R. L., & Shuter, R. (1994). *Communication in multinational organizations.* Thousand Oaks, CA: Sage.

Won-Doornink, M. J. (1991). Self-disclosure and reciprocity in South Korean and U.S. male dyads. In S. Ting-Toomey & F. Korzenny (Eds.), *Cross-cultural interpersonal communication* (pp. 116-131). Newbury Park, CA: Sage.

Xi, C. (1994). Individualism and collectivism in American and Chinese societies. In A. G. Gonzalez, M. Houston, & V. Chen (Eds.), *Our voices: Essays in culture, ethnicity, and communication* (pp. 152-158). Los Angeles: Roxbury.

Yang, K. S. (1981). Social orientation and individual modernity among Chinese students in Taiwan. *Journal of Social Psychology, 113,* 159-170.

5

Masculinity Index and Communication Style: An East Asian Perspective

John C. Hwang

Among the different orientations in the study of intercultural and cross-cultural communication, the one that probably receives the most attention is Hofstede's cultural patterns (1984, 1997). Among the four cultural dimensions identified by Hofstede—individualism, uncertainty avoidance, power distance, and masculinity—the first three have been given the most research attention by communication researchers (e.g., Dion & Dion, 1993; Gao, 1991; Gudykunst, 1995; Gudykunst & Kim, 1996; Gudykunst, Yoon & Nishida, 1987; Gudykunst & Nishida, 1994; Matsumoto, 1991; Ting-Toomey, 1994; Triandis, 1995; Yamaguchi, 1994). Although the relationships between masculine cultures and communication styles have received little research attention, many generalizations about their relationships have been asserted and accepted in the field of communication studies. A direct relationship is generally believed to exist between traits of masculine cultures and characteristics of "masculine" communication style (Chen & Starosta, 1998; Dodd, 1998; Jandt, 1998; Lustig and Koester, 1999). The asserted relationship is yet to be closely scrutinized; in fact, published cultural studies seem to suggest a much more complex relationship (see e.g., Gudykunst, Ting-Toomey & Nishida, 1996).

This chapter highlights the main points of Hofstede's masculinity dimension, points out the confusion found in many intercultural communication texts regarding the relationship between Hofstede's masculinity index and "masculine" communication style, and stresses the importance of the emic factor in cross-cultural generalizations. More specifically, this chapter approaches the relationship between Hofstede's masculinity dimension and communication styles from an East Asian perspective—an emic view of how three indigenous philosophies shape the traditional communication style of East Asian cultures.

MASCULINITY AND COMMUNICATION STYLE

Summarizing the results of his classic cross-cultural studies, Hofstede (1984, 1997) asserts that masculine cultures value achievement, materialistic gains, and work performance; have a high degree of differentiation in gender roles; and admire successful achievers. In masculine societies, men are assertive, competitive, and dominant. On the other hand, feminine cultures emphasize nurturing behavior, interdependence, and quality of life; they have fluid gender roles and are sympathetic to the unfortunate. In Hofstede's research, Japan was found to be the most masculine culture, while Scandinavian countries are considered the least masculine.

These attributes of masculinity and femininity suggest an important direct relationship with interpersonal communication. In fact, many communication scholars have extended Hofstede's descriptive labels of dimensions such as "assertiveness" and "dominance" to mean "masculine" communication style and "nurturance" and "people orientation" to mean "feminine" communication style. It is often accepted in the field of intercultural communication that masculine cultures lead to, or at least highly correlate with, "masculine" communication style and that feminine cultures result in "feminine" communication style.

For example, Lustig and Koester (1999) suggest

> Teachers in masculine cultures praise their best students because academic performance is rewarded highly. Similarly, male students in these high-MAS cultures strive to be competitive, visible, successful, and vocationally-oriented. In feminine cultures, teachers rarely praise individual achievements and academic performance because social accommodation is more highly regarded. Male students try to cooperate with one another and develop a sense of solidarity; they try to behave modestly and properly. (pp. 124-125)

Dodd (1998) points out that masculine cultures are more likely to use aggressive styles of communication and that feminine cultures are more capable of reading nonverbal messages and dealing with ambiguity (pp. 93-94). Jandt (1998) suggests that masculine cultures stress assertiveness and competition in communication. Chen and Starosta (1998) draw a similar conclusion: "In masculine cultures, men are expected to be dominant in the society and to show quality of ambition, assertiveness, strength, competitiveness, and material acquisition; thus, the communication styles are more aggressive" (p. 53).

It appears that many authors in intercultural communication equate Hofstede's masculine or feminine labels with corresponding interpersonal communication styles. Intuitively, this line of reasoning makes a lot of sense. After all, as Hofstede's propositions suggest, masculine traits tend to be "dominant" and "assertive," and feminine traits tend to be "nurturing" and "supportive"; thus, their respective communication styles should so reflect.

This line of reasoning leads to several problems: (1) Without a more clear conceptualization of masculine and feminine traits and their corresponding communication styles, our conclusion about their relationships is at best an educated guess. (2) The way we draw conclusions so far risks the danger of shifting level of analysis. (3) Without taking into consideration the unique and mediating influence of emic factors, we may oversimplify the complexity of communication styles in etic generalizations and result in premature closure.

Borden (1991) attempts to clarify the relationship between masculinity and communication style by citing 100 pancultural adjectives associated with male and female gender traits compiled by Williams and Best (1982) and linking these adjectives to a list of masculine or feminine communication characteristics. In essence, Williams and Best (1994) reiterated in their global study of gender roles that men are more likely to be associated with traits such as "aggressive," "initiative," "tough," "bossy," "loud," "rigid," and "show-off" while women, with characteristics such as "submissive," "mild," "modest," "soft-hearted," "shy" "sensitive," and "gentle" (p. 193). Williams and Best's list of gender traits seems to provide more tangible labels than Hofstede's list (1984, 1997) where masculine/feminine communication styles are concerned.

More specifically, Borden (1991) identified the characteristics of "masculine" verbal communication style to include, among others, speaking louder, using more commanding words and expletives language, and being more interruptive, argumentative, and competitive. In contrast, he argues that "feminine" verbal communication traits include providing more self-disclosure, being more supportive, agreeable, and tentative, and doing more listening. The picture painted here is that "masculine" verbal communication style is more active, assertive, dominant, and argumentative while "feminine" style is more passive, receptive, supportive, and tentative. In terms of nonverbal communication, Borden points out that men tend to be more expansive, use more gestures and pointing, and touch more (p. 149). On the other hand, females are more responsive and more facially expressive, more likely to avoid eye contact, smile more, and maintain shorter personal distance in personal interactions.

Citing research conducted primarily in the United States, Wood (1994, 2000) concludes that women's speech displays six identifiable features:

equality, support, focus on feelings and relationship, conversational maintenance, responsiveness, concrete disclosure of personal feelings, and tentative-
ness. Men's verbal communication style, on the other hand, she associates
with efforts to exert control, assert oneself, and enhance power and status.
With regard to nonverbal communication, she asserts that women are more
sensitive to nonverbal communication and display more interest, attention,
and affiliation. Men's nonverbal communication, however, is more likely to
be used for agenda setting, power and status display, commanding territories,
and shrouding emotions from public scrutiny. She argues that these differences are the result of enculturation.

Borden's and Wood's comparisons of communication style between genders show a large degree of agreement. These intergender comparisons certainly are a step in the right direction in helping to delineate the relationship
between gender roles and communication styles; however, the question
whether we can equate "masculine" cultural traits with "masculine" communication style is still unsettled. In fact, the relationship is far more complex
than it appears.

Take Japan, for instance, which ranks number one on Hofstede's masculinity scale. In examining Hofstede's propositions, it is not hard to see why Japan
would rank very high on the masculinity dimension. Even though substantial
social change is taking place in Japan, gender role is still highly differentiated
(Beamer & Varner, 1995). A great majority of Japanese workers regard work
as the center of their lives. A workday can begin or end at anytime beyond
the regular working hours, depending on the amount of work that needs to be
done. After work, another two to three hours of socializing with co-workers
at a social gathering place is not out of the ordinary. As a masculine culture,
Japanese workers see work as the focus of their lives, as Hofstede has
suggested. Using Hofstede's masculine markers and applying them to Japanese culture, it is not difficult to see why Japan would rank extremely high
among masculine cultures.

But the question remains: Can we say that as the most masculine culture,
Japan will show corresponding "masculine" communication traits, that is,
argumentative, direct, aggressive, dominant, vocal, and blunt? Would other
highly masculine cultures such as Austria, Germany, and the Philippines show
similar "masculine" communication traits? The answer to this question is
"yes" and "no."

Most, if not all, communication scholars (Barnlund, 1975, 1989;
Gudykunst & Nishida, 1994; Hall & Hall, 1987; Nishida, 1996; Okabe, 1987;
Tsujimura, 1987) agree that Japanese communication style is indirect, modest, non-argumentative, apologetic, and supportive and shows extreme concern for face saving. Few, if any, would posit that Japanese people manifest
the markers of "masculine" communication style—direct, assertive, blunt,
aggressive, and argumentative. Thus, it is incorrect to classify Japanese verbal
communication style as "masculine."

The Philippines is a highly masculine culture on Hofstede's scale, but Filipino verbal communication style is equally indirect (e. g., *paikot-ikot sa pagsalita* or "beating around the bush"), yielding (e. g., *pakikisama* or "go along with others"), and empathetic (e. g., *makatao* or "concern for the feeling of others") and shows great concern for face saving (*may mukhang ipinakihaharap*) and harmony (*pagkakatugunan*) (Andres, 1994). These are all traits of "feminine" communication style.

In the case of Israel, which is slightly on the feminine side of Hofstede's scale, the *dugri* (straight talk) communication style is highly "masculine"—direct, assertive, and lacking face-concern (Katriel, 1986). In addition, the outspoken verbal rituals of griping (Katriel, 1991), which has become a common practice among the middle-class in Israel, can be considered a "masculine" communication marker as well.

On the other hand, Germany, which is a highly masculine society on Hofstede's scale, manifests traits of "masculine" communication style. German verbal messages are direct, assertive, challenging, and sometimes confrontational, as reflected in *Bresprechung* (discussion) (Friday, 1989).

According to Hofstede's measure, Thailand is a relatively feminine society; its communication style is generally considered "feminine"—indirect, friendly, subdued, supportive, and showing extreme concern for face saving (Fieg, 1989; Knutson, 1994).

We thus find that some countries rated by Hofstede's scale as masculine show "masculine" communication traits, while others actually reveal "feminine" communication markers and vice versa (see Table 5.1).

In Hofstede's research, four other predominantly Confucian societies—South Korea, Hong Kong, Taiwan, and Singapore—rank in the middle of the 50 countries and regions studied. Interestingly, though their masculinity scores differ significantly from that of Japan, they are substantially similar to the Japanese in communication style (see e.g., Chen & Chung, 2000; Kincaid, 1987; Samovar & Porter, 2001).

In sum, equating masculine culture with "masculine" communication style is simplistic and problematic. In addition, within each culture, we should also be cognizant of the potential difference of communication styles between genders—that is, a vast divergence of gender roles is likely to be correlated with a large variance of communication styles between genders.

TABLE 5.1. Masculinity Index and Communication Style

		Masculine Communication Style	
		Hi	Lo
Hofstede's Masculinity Index	Hi	Germany	Japan
	Lo	Israel	Thailand

FEMININITY AND EAST ASIAN COMMUNICATION STYLE

Currently, Western cultures have made significant inroads into East Asian societies. Individualistic traits are becoming more visible in the behavior of younger generations. Nevertheless, the majority of East Asians still share and manifest the traits of a traditional communication style, which have been identified by many communication scholars. For instance, Nishida (1996), summarizing previous studies about Japanese communication style, states that Japanese interpersonal communication tends to be non-argumentative and indirect, emphasizing the use of *sasshi* (empathetic conjecture of the speaker's intention), *ishindenshi* (nonverbal communication of message from heart to heart), and silence. Yum (1987) describes Korean verbal communication as full of implicitness and indirectness and showing a great deal of concern for human relationship. She argues that accommodation and *I-sim jun-sim* (similar to the Japanese concept of *ishindenshin*) are important traits of Korean communication. Among Chinese, similar communication traits are found among members of in-groups (e.g., Bond, 1991; Gao, 1996; Gao, Ting-Toomey, & Gudykunst, 1996; Ma, 1992).

In sum, substantial similarities are found among these three Asian cultures in terms of their traditional communication style: indirectness, non-argumentativeness, face saving, harmony, silence, implicitness, and humbleness. Comparing these characteristics with William and Best's (1994) female gender labels and the feminine communication style outlined by Borden (1991) and Wood (1994), one is likely to characterize Chinese, Japanese, and Korean communication styles as "feminine" rather than "masculine."

EMIC CULTURAL INFLUENCE

The case of Japan presents a particularly interesting question: Why would a highly masculine culture show traits of "feminine" communication style? One important reason appears to be the emic factor—the mediating and overriding effect of a country's unique core culture on its communication style. In fact, a similar "feminine" communication style found among Chinese and Koreans appears to have emanated from shared cultural roots, which render their communication style more "feminine."

Scholars generally attribute the cultural similarities of these countries to three major philosophies: Taoism, Buddhism and Confucianism (Cheng, 1987; Hendry, 1987; Henthorn 1971; Oh, 1958; Tsujimura,1987; Yum, 1987). Interestingly, even though they are different in their emphases, all three philosophies seek to attain harmony—harmony with nature in Taoism, harmony with oneself in Buddhism, and harmony with others in Confucianism. All three philosophies advocate modesty, humbleness, and gentleness, which typify traits of femininity and inevitably shape one's communication behavior. To help provide a better understanding of the kind of communication behavior extolled by these philosophies, and how they mold the communication style of these three cultures, a short summary of their major tenets and their relationships with communication style would be helpful.

Emic Philosophical Influence on Communication Style

Taoism. Among the three common philosophical influences of China, Japan, and Korea, Taoism is probably the most obscure—much less understood by people in the West. But as Professor Lin Yu-tang once said, the most important work of Taoism—*Tao Te Ching*, is probably the one book that should be read above all other Asian literary works, for it has a profound influence on the world view of East Asians (Lin, 1942, p. 579).

In the study of Taoism and its influence on communication style, four points stand out: the awareness of (1) the limit and the relativity (to some extent, the distrust) of verbal language, (2) the importance of the concepts of vacuity, subtlety, tranquility, and silence, (3) the metaphors associated with femininity and softness, and (4) the wisdom of detachment, passivity, and non-action.

The two Taoist classics, *Tao Te Ching* (*Dao De Jing*) and *Chuang Tzu* (*Zhuang Zi*), often allude to two main concepts *yin* and *yang* (the two contrasting cosmic forces). Though bipolar in nature, the two forces are complementary and not necessarily contradictory, because each gives rise to and is contained in the other. *Yang* is generally associated with the masculine qualities of being aggressive, strong, unyielding, firm, forward-pushing, and dominant. *Yin* is associated with being soft, gentle, weak, invisible, flexible, subtle, hidden, tranquil, and receptive and has feminine characteristics (Cheng, 1987). Their interactions result in a continuous, natural creation of all objects and creatures and lead to the unceasing progress of the universe. This process is what I call the three C's of change—contrast, complement, and creation. The working of the three C's, of course, is predicated on the principle of harmony. If we note the global masculine (*yang*) and feminine (*yin*) markers extracted by Williams and Best (1994) and then read the key passages of the two main Taoist classics, we inevitably come away with the impression that Taoism advocates a feminine communication style.

With regard to the Taoist view on communication, let's first focus on the limitation and relativity of language. At the very beginning of the *Tao Te Ching* (translated by Feng, 1972), Lao Tzu (*Lao Zi*) warns against using definitive terms to name an infinite concept, the *Tao*, for no matter how cogent the terms are, no language can describe all the qualities of the *Tao*. In other words, the moment we use language to name and describe it, we set a limit to its boundary and inevitably distort it:

> The Tao that can be told is not the eternal Tao.
> The name that can be named is not the eternal name.
> The nameless is the beginning of heaven and earth.
>   The named is the mother of ten thousand things. (Chapter 1)

This cautious view of language humbles its users. In *Chuang Tzu* (translated by Chan, 1963), the subjective and relative nature of language is even more clearly illuminated:

> There is nothing that is not the "that" and there is nothing that is not the "this."
> Things do not know that they are the "that" of other things; they only know what
> they themselves know. Therefore I say that the "that" is produced by the "this"
> and the "this" is also caused by the "that." This is the theory of mutual
> production. (Chapter 2)

The moral, of course, is that if we must use words to state and describe, we must realize that they are relative and restrictive. Lin (1948) said it well: "Speech by its nature cannot express the absolute" (p. 53). With that in mind, Lao Tzu uses different ways, approaches, and angles to help us understand the *Tao*—for example, subtle suggestions, simple metaphors, and puzzling aphorisms. These aphorisms are generally short, simple, paradoxical, and extremely high-context in nature. Taoist verbal messages thus are inevitably economical and their meanings cryptic. In order words, low-context communication definitely is not a favored communication style of Taoist philosophers.

With regard to verbal communication and argumentation, metaphorically and paradoxically, the *Tao Te Ching* often offers this kind of caution (though it may seem illogical and ludicrous in most of its aphorisms):

> Those who know do not speak.
> Those who talk do not know.
> Keep your mouth closed. Guard your senses.
> Temper your sharpness.
> Simplify your problems.
> Mask your brightness. (Chapter 56)

> Truthful words are not beautiful; beautiful words are not truthful.
> Good men do not argue.
> Those who argue are not good.
> Those who know are not learned.
> The learned do not know. (Chapter 81)

The other Taoist classic, *Chuang Tzu*, is even more explicit and negative about arguments:

Suppose you and I argue. If you beat me instead of my beating you, are you really right and am I really wrong? If I beat you instead of your beating me, am I really right and are you really wrong? Or are we both partly right and partly wrong? Or are we both wholly right and wholly wrong? Since between us neither you nor I know which is right, others are naturally in the dark. (Chapter 2)

From a Western viewpoint, this kind of reasoning may seem odd and absurd. Yet, the Taoist view on silence, language relativity, and argumentation undoubtedly exerts an invisible and immense influence on the communication style of China, Japan, and Korea.

In communication studies, particularly in public relations, being "active" is the sine qua non of our profession. In order to be visible, we should be "active" or, even better, be "pro-active"; the Taoist concept of *wu wei* (non-action) is probably a concept totally alien to most of us in communication studies. After all, action, reaction, and pro-action are all actions. And from the perspective of a "doing" culture, non-action is anathema. Yet from a Taoist point of view, in harmony with nature, nothing (or as little as possible) should be done to interfere with or alter the course of nature (the *Tao*).

The non-action worldview of Taoism can be found in numerous passages in the *Tao Te Ching*, including:

Therefore the sage goes about doing nothing, teaching no-talking.
The ten thousand things rise and fall without cease,
Creating, yet not possessing,
Working, yet not taking credit. (Chapter 2)

Tao abides in non-action.
Yet nothing is left undone. (Chapter 37)

In such a worldview, detachment, simplicity, and non-interference become the norm. With the application of this concept to human relationships, there should be minimal rules and etiquette. Or, to put it in communication terms, Taoism seems to advocate a simple, low-uncertainty-avoidance society.

Probably the most interesting to us is the Taoist emphasis on the qualities of *yin* (frequently found in the metaphors associated with the qualities of softness in women and the purity in infants) and their subsequent manifestations in communication behavior—tranquility, gentleness, yielding, humbleness, lack of visibility, taciturnity, and being non-argumentative, as in the following passages in the *Tao Te Ching*:

The sage is shy and humble—to the world he seems confusing.
Men look to him and listen.
He behaves like a little child. (Chapter 49)

Achieve results,
But never glory in them.
Achieve results,
But never boast.
Achieve results,
But never be proud. (Chapter 30)

Therefore wise men embrace the One [the *Tao*]
And set example to all.
Not putting on a display, they shine forth.
Not justifying themselves, they are distinguished.
Not boasting, they receive recognition.
Not bragging, they never falter.
They do not quarrel, so no one quarrels with them. (Chapter 22)

Great intelligence seems stupid.
Great eloquence seems awkward. (Chapter 45)

The hard and strong will fall.
The soft and weak will overcome. (Chapter 76)

As one of the three most important cultural forces among East Asians, inevitably, the Taoist philosophy on simplicity, taciturnness, humbleness, yielding, and non-argumentativeness leaves a distinct trademark on their communication style.

Buddhism. The second cultural force that helps to shape the communication style of China, Korea, and Japan is Buddhism, particularly Zen Buddhism. Buddhism reached China from India around the first century and became popular after Buddhist scriptures were interpreted with a Taoist twist. Many Taoist terms thus found their way into the teachings of Zen Buddhism, such as vacuity, simplicity, detachment, self-forgetting, and teaching without words. From China, Buddhism was later introduced to Korea and Japan (Chou, 1986; Hendry, 1987; Yum, 1987).

Buddhism posits that life is governed by the Four Noble Truths: Unenlightened life is suffering; suffering is caused by cravings; suffering ceases as craving is extinguished; and selfish craving can be extinguished by following the Eightfold Path.

The Eightfold Path leading to liberation from suffering includes right understanding (accepting the Four Noble Truths), right thought (being free from ill intent, lust, and untruthfulness), right speech (speaking kindly and being free from vain speech, lying, and harsh language), right conduct (being free from killing), right livelihood (not harming others), right effort (promoting good deeds), right awareness (knowing the transitory nature of life and the suffering of an unruly mind), and right meditation (training the mind to rid itself of selfish passions, desires, and sensations) (Burtt, 1982; Kalupah-ana, 1976).

In the Eightfold Path, at least three paths deal directly with intrapersonal or interpersonal communication. Right speech sets the yardstick for proper inter-personal communication; right thought, right awareness, and right meditation deal with the mind's cognitive process or the lack of it to achieve enlightenment.

To catch a glimpse of Buddhist teachings on communication, it is important that we focus on the key passages from the *Dhammapada* (translated by Easwaran, 1985), which is the most important Buddhist scripture for laypeo-ple and thus exerts a much more pervasive influence on the average follower. According to the *Dhammapada* (Path of Truth), right speech is simple and brings peace and harmony to oneself and others:

Better than a speech of a thousand vain
words is one thoughtful word which brings
peace to the mind. Better than a poem of a
thousand vain verses is one thoughtful line
which brings peace to the mind. (8: Thousand)

With regard to the karma of sowing evil seeds of ill thoughts, egotism, and angry words, the Buddha warns that *samskaras* (karmic actions) will bear fruit and be returned in kind:

Hasten to do good; refrain from evil (thoughts). If you
neglect the good, evil can enter your mind. (9: Evil Conduct)

Speak quietly to everyone, and they too will
be gentle in their speech. Harsh words hurt,
and come back to the speaker. If your mind is
still, like a broken gong, you have entered
Nirvana, leaving all quarrels behind you. (10: Punishment)

Conquer anger through gentleness, unkindness
through kindness, greed through generosity,
And falsehood by truth. (17: On Anger)

In terms of right speech, the *Dhammapada* teaches Buddhists to be truthful, humble, harmonious, patient, and gentle:

Him I call a Brahmin [sage] who does not hurt others
with unkind acts, words, or thoughts. (26: The Brahmin)

Neither pleasant words nor a pretty face can
make beautiful a person who is jealous, selfish,
or deceitful. (19: The Person Established in Dharma)

> Best among men are those who have trained their
> mind to endure harsh words patiently. (23: The Elephant)

In terms of the path to enlightenment, the Buddhist emphasis is on self-reliance and inward concentration because enlightenment comes as a result of deep meditation and sudden awakening—not verbal instruction or intellectual arguments. This functions as the basis for *Zen* Buddhism, which, as Thich (1975) states, "teaches a special kind of transmission outside the scripture; it does not depend on words and letters, because understanding Zen is a matter of personal experience, not a matter of book learning" (p. 22). This line of thinking was foreshadowed in the Taoist teaching.

Zen Buddhists insist that Buddhist scriptures (implying the use of verbal communication) are a vehicle of *satori* (enlightenment) and not enlightenment itself. In the practice of Zen, silence (not intellectual debates), meditation, and concentration are paths to enlightenment, because truth is to be found within oneself, not through external instruction. This means that language has limitations and can never convey the whole *dharma* (truth). Scriptures, sermons, and lectures (which consist of words) are but guides that point out the direction of truth and should not be mistaken for truth. Thus, silence or the language of silence becomes the favored way of teaching in Zen Buddhism. As the 27th Patriarch of Buddhism, Bodhidharma, once said (Kalupahana, 1976):

> A special transmission outside the scriptures;
> No dependence upon words and letters;
> Direct pointing at the mind of man;
> Seeing into one's nature and the attainment of Buddhahood. (p. 167)

This becomes the origin of the special kind of nonverbal communication often referred to by East Asians—*I-sim jum-sum* in Korean (Yum, 1987), *ishindensin* (Tsujimura,1987), and *I hsin chuan hsin* in Chinese—all meaning the exchange of meaning without words.

Zen Buddhists by nature are skeptics; they doubt the meaning of words and insist on checking it out themselves through self-discovery and self-enlightenment (Wu, 1979). If they must use words to teach, they use an indirect style—hinting, suggesting, prodding, or even shocking; they use very simple language and leave a lot of room for self-discovery. Their verbal messages, to a person from a low-context culture, sound disjointed, incomplete, and deceptively simple. They may even sound senseless or childish. Buddhists often use *Kung-Ans* or *Koans* (simple and puzzling questions) to break the conventional mind-set and help people "see" the essence of Buddhist nature. For example, to help understand the concept of vacuity, a Zen teacher may ask: "What is the sound of one hand clapping itself?"

In sum, the communication style inculcated by Buddhism is harmonious, gentle, humble, receptive, mild, indirect, taciturn, and simple. These characteristics are quite similar to those of Taoism and closely associated with feminine (*yin*) traits.

Confucianism. Of the three philosophies, Confucianism probably exerts the most direct, explicit influence on the three East Asian cultures. Relatively speaking, it is the most active of the three, advocating the rule of a society by moral codes and rites. These tend to be very specific and well-defined, because Confucius believes in a high-uncertainty-avoidance social structure. In his mind, if human relations are governed by well-defined moral codes founded on the principle of *jen* (benevolence) and harmony, and proper behavior is specified according to *li* (rites), then a society does not need cumbersome laws.

In the *Analects*, one of the most important classics of Confucianism for traditional education and enculturation, we find a plethora of passages defining the parameters of proper communication behavior, for instance (my translation):

The Master said, "A young man should be a filial son at home . . . be careful and trustworthy about his words." (I, 6)

The Master said, "A gentleman seeks no delicious food nor a comfortable home. He acts quickly but is prudent in his speech." (I, 14)

The Master said, "When serving your parents, be patient and gentle in dissuading them from wrongdoings. If they persist, be respectful and avoid the appearance of displeasure. Wait for an opportune time, and try again." (IV, 18)

The Master said, "A gentleman is slow and careful in his speech but quick and diligent in his action." (IV, 24)

The Master said, "Do not look, listen, and speak unless it is consistent with rites." (XII, 2)

The Master said, "A gentleman is ashamed of his words exceeding his deeds." (XIV, 27)

The Master said, "Crafty words ruin one's virtue." (XV, 2)

The Master said, "The Universe proceeds naturally in silence, I am thinking of giving up speech." Tzu Kung [his disciple] said, "If you were to give up speech, where are we going to find truth to follow and pass on?" The Master said, "Heaven never utters a word, yet the four seasons progress unceasingly and the hundred things continue to grow. When has heaven ever said anything?" (XVII, 19)

This last exchange interestingly echoes similar tenets of the Taoist philosophy. Even though Confucius shows no reservation about verbal communication, he advocates proper speech according to rites. He insists that a person's speech should be cautious, proper, trustworthy, and harmonious; his or her words and demeanor should be gentle, mild, and kind, in accordance to the principle of filial piety and benevolence. Further, the centrality of the Confucian philosophy emphasizes *jen*, modesty, and a paucity of desire for material possession and fame. When put to practice, the philosophy is likely to result in a more "feminine" communication style.

In summary, influenced by the three major common cultural forces of Taoism, Buddhism, and Confucianism, the communication style of China, Japan, and Korea tends to be harmonious, non-argumentative, mild, humble, nurturing, and modest; these traits are correlated to what is generally referred to as the "feminine" (*yin*) communication style. These "feminine" communication characteristics are embodied in the following "Personal Motto" written by an ancient Chinese writer and traditionally used to cultivate the moral character of Chinese children. One can readily find the teachings of Confucianism, Taoism, and Buddhism, as well as many "feminine" communication traits, imbedded in the following precepts (my translation):

Personal Precepts
by
Tsue Yuen (77-142 A.D.)

Do not tell on others' weaknesses; do not reveal our own strengths. Do not forget the kindness others rendered us; yet, do not keep scores of what we did for others. Worldly fame need not be sought; kindness and righteousness should be our guide. When actions are taken, only after careful deliberation in the principle of kindness and righteousness, verbal attacks and slander by others will no longer harm us.

Guard against the vanity that surpasses our real ability. To appear as if we were ignorant in spite of our great talent and knowledge is highly regarded by ancient sages. Maintain our purity and integrity in a corrupted environment. Even though our appearance may look dull and unassuming, our heart should always be kind and our mind, open.

Softness and flexibility is the spring of life. Unyielding strength and hardness shorten our life span, as it was cautioned by Lao Tzu. Unyielding strength and power is the goal of an inferior person and ultimately leads to innumerable troubles. Be cautious about our words; be moderate in our diet. Being content is superior to greed. Practice daily self-examination with regularity and we will be as fragrant as a flower.

CONCLUSION

As my analysis shows, using Hofstede's masculinity index as a direct predictor of communication style should be approached with caution. We should not simply use the masculinity score of a country to deduce its communication style without adequately considering emic factors. For instance, three traditional East Asian philosophies—Taoism, Buddhism, and Confucianism—exert a profound influence on the communication style of peoples from China, Korea, and Japan. These philosophies stress harmony, humbleness, gentleness, indirectness, and non-argumentativeness, which are generally considered "feminine" traits. As overwhelming emic cultural forces, these philosophies render their traditional communication styles more "feminine," regardless of their rankings on Hofstede's masculinity scale.

REFERENCES

Andres, T. Q. (1994). *Dictionary of Filipino culture and values.* Santa Monica, CA: Philippine American Library House.

Barnlund, D. C. (1975). *Public and private self in Japan and the United States.* Tokyo: Simul Press.

Barnlund, D. C. (1989). *Communication styles of Japanese and Americans: Images and realities.* Belmont, CA: Wadsworth.

Beamer, I., & Varner, L. (1995). *Intercultural communication in the global workplace.* Chicago, IL: Richard Irwin.

Bond, M. H. (1991). *Beyond the Chinese face.* New York: Oxford University Press.

Borden, G. A. (1991). *Cultural orientation: An approach to understanding intercultural communication.* Englewood Cliffs, NJ: Prentice-Hall.

Burtt, E. A. (Ed.). (1982). *The teachings of the compassionate Buddha.* New York: Mentor.

Chan, W. (1963). *A source book in Chinese philosophy.* Princeton, NJ: Princeton University Press.

Chen, G., & Chung, J. (2000). The "five Asian dragons": Management behaviors and organizational communication. In L. Samovar & R. Porter (Eds.), *Intercultural communication* (pp. 301-311). Belmont, CA: Wadsworth.

Chen, G., & Starosta, W. J. (1998). *Foundations of intercultural communication.* Boston: Allyn & Bacon.

Cheng, C. (1987). Chinese philosophy and contemporary human communication theory. In D. Kincaid (Ed.), *Communication theory: Eastern and Western perspectives* (pp. 23-40). New York: Academic Press.

Chou, H. (1986). *The history of Chinese philosophy.* Taipei: San Ming Publishing Company.

Dion, K. L., & Dion, K. K. (1993). Individualistic and collectivistic perspectives on gender and the cultural context of love and intimacy. *Journal of Social Issues, 49* (3), 53-59.

Dodd, C. H. (1998). *Dynamics of intercultural communication.* New York: McGraw-Hill.

Easwaran, E. (Trans.). (1985). *The Dhammapada.* Tomalis, CA: The Nilgiri Press.

Feng, G. (Trans.). (1972). *Tao Te Ching.* New York: Vintage Books.

Fieg, J. P. (1989). *A common core: Thais and Americans*. Yarmouth, ME: International Press.

Friday, R. A. (1989). Contrasts in discussion behaviors of German and American managers. *International Journal of Intercultural Relations, 13*, 429-445.

Gao, G. (1991). Stability of romantic relationships in China and the Unites States. In S. Ting-Toomey & F. Korzenny (Eds.), *Cross-cultural interpersonal communication* (pp. 99-115). Newbury Park, CA: Sage.

Gao, G. (1996). Self and others: A Chinese perspective on interpersonal relationships. In W. Gudykunst, S. Ting-Toomey, & T. Nishida (Eds.), *Communication in personal relationships across cultures* (pp. 81-101). Thousand Oaks, CA: Sage.

Gao, G., Ting-Toomey, S., & Gudykunst, W. B. (1996). Chinese communication processes. In M. Bond (Ed.), *The handbook of Chinese psychology* (pp. 280-293). New York: Oxford University Press.

Gudykunst, W. B. (1995). Anxiety/uncertainty management (AUM) theory: Current status. In R. Wiseman (Ed.), *Intercultural communication theory* (pp. 255-267). Thousand Oaks, CA: Sage

Gudykunst, W. H., & Kim, Y. Y. (1996). *Communication with strangers: An approach to intercultural communication*. New York: McGraw-Hill.

Gudykunst, W. B., & Nishida, T. (1994). *Bridging Japanese/North American differences*. Thousand Oaks, CA: Sage.

Gudykunst, W. B., Ting-Toomey, S., & Nishida, T. (Eds.). (1996). *Communication in personal relations across cultures*. Thousand Oaks, CA: Sage.

Gudykunst, W., Yoon, Y. C., & Nishida, T. (1987). The influence of individualism-collectivism on perceptions of communication in ingroup and outgroup relationships. *Communication Monographs, 54*, 295-306.

Hall, E., T., & Hall, M. R. (1987). *The hidden differences: Doing business with the Japanese*. Garden City, NY: Doubleday.

Hendry, J. (1987). *Understanding Japanese society*. London: Croom Helm.

Henthorn, W. E. (1971). *A history of Korea*. New York: The Free Press

Hofstede, G. (1984). *Culture's consequences: International differences in work-related values* (abridged edition). Newbury Park, CA: Sage.

Hofstede, G. (1997). *Cultures and organizations: Intercultural cooperation and its importance for survival*. New York: McGraw-Hill.

Jandt, F. E. (1998). *Intercultural communication: An introduction*. Thousand Oaks, CA: Sage Publications.

Kalupahana, D. J. (1976). *Buddhist philosophy: A historical analysis*. Honolulu: The University Press of Hawaii.

Katriel, T. (1986). *Talking straight: "Dugri" speech in Israel Sabra culture*. London: Cambridge University Press.

Katriel, T. (1991). *Communal webs: Communication and culture in contemporary Israel*. Albany: State University of New York Press.

Kincaid, D. (Ed.). (1987). *Communication theory: Eastern and Western perspectives*. New York: Academic Press.

Knutson, T. J. (1994). Comparison of Thai and US American cultural values: *"mai pen rai"* versus "just do it." *ABAC Journal 14* (3), 1-38.

Lin, Y. (1942). *Wisdom of India and China*. New York: Random House.

Lin, Y. (1948). *The Wisdom of Laotse*. New York: The Modern Library.

Lustig, M. W., & Koester, J. (1999). *Intercultural competence: Interpersonal communication across cultures*. New York: Longman.

Ma, R. (1992). The role of unofficial intermediaries in interpersonal conflicts in the Chinese culture. *Communication Quarterly, 40*, 269-278.

Matsumoto, D. (1991). Cultural influences on the facial expression of emotion. *Southern Communication Journal, 56,* 128-137.

Nishida, T. (1996). Communication in personal relationships in Japan. In W. Gudykunst, S. Ting-Toomey, & T. Nishida (Eds.), *Communication in personal relations across cultures* (pp. 102-121). Thousand Oaks, CA: Sage.

Oh, K. (1958). *Handbook of Korea.* New York: Pageant Press.

Okabe, K. (1987). Indirect speech acts of the Japanese. In D. Kincaid (Ed.), *Communication theory: Eastern and Western perspectives* (pp.127-136). New York: Academic Press.

Samovar, L. A., & Porter, R. E. (2001). *Communication between cultures.* Belmont, CA: Wadsworth.

Thich, T. (1975). *Zen philosophy, Zen practice.* Berkeley, CA: Dharma Publishing.

Ting-Toomey, S. (Ed.). (1994). *The challenge of facework.* Albany: State University of New York Press.

Triandis, H. C. (1995). *Individualism and collectivism.* Boulder, CO: Westview.

Tsujimura, A. (1987). Some characteristics of the Japanese way of communication. In D. Kincaid (Ed.), *Communication theory: Eastern and Western perspectives* (pp. 115-125). New York: Academic Press.

Williams, J. E., & Best, D. L. (1982). *Measuring sex stereotypes: A thirty-nation study.* Beverly Hills, CA: Sage.

Williams, J. E., & Best, D. L. (1994). Cross-cultural views of women and men. In W. Lonner & R. Malpass (Eds.), *Psychology and culture* (pp. 191-196). Boston: Allyn & Bacon.

Wood, J. T. (1994). *Gendered lives: Communication, gender and culture.* Belmont, CA: Wadsworth.

Wood, J. T. (2000). Gender, communication and culture. In L. Samvovar & R. Porter (Eds.), *Intercultural communication: A reader* (pp. 170-179). Belmont, CA: Wadsworth.

Wu, J. (1979). *Clarification and enlightenment: Essays in comparative philosophy.* Taichung, Taiwan: Tunghai University Press.

Yamaguchi, S. (1994). Collectivism among the Japanese: A perspective from the self. In U. Kim, H. Triandis, C. Kagitcibasi, S. Choi, & G. Yoon (Eds.), *Individualism and collectivism* (pp. 178-188). Thousand Oaks, CA: Sage.

Yum, J. (1987). Korean philosophy and communication. In D. Kincaid (Ed.), *Communication theory: Eastern and Western perspectives* (pp. 87-98). New York: Academic Press.

Theory and Research in Context

Comparative Studies of Chinese and Western Rhetorics: Reflections and Challenges

Xing Lu

In his book *Comparative Rhetoric: A Historical and Cross-cultural Introduction*, George Kennedy (1998) outlined four objectives in studying comparative rhetoric: (1) to identify similarities and differences of rhetorical traditions, (2) to formulate a general theory of rhetoric applicable to all societies, (3) to develop a terminology of rhetoric that can be used to describe rhetorical practices cross-culturally, and (4) to apply comparative rhetoric to cross-cultural communication.[1] Studies of Chinese rhetoric in the United States in past decades have compared similarities and differences between Chinese and Western rhetorics (Garrett, 1991, 1993a; Hu, 1992; Lu, 1998; Oliver 1971). A set of terminology has been identified from classical Chinese texts and compared with a Western conceptualization of rhetoric and argumentation (Garrett 1993b; Jensen, 1992; Lu & Frank,1993). However, two of Kennedy's objectives still need exploration: Is there a general theory of rhetoric that can be applied to both Chinese and Western rhetorics? What are the implications of comparative rhetoric on intercultural communication between China and the West?

In this chapter, I first review comparative studies of rhetoric by Chinese and American rhetorical scholars. I then identify the areas for further comparative study. Furthermore, I discuss the challenges both Western and Chinese scholars of rhetoric face in engaging studies of comparative rhetoric. Finally, I explore methodological issues in future comparative rhetorical studies and discuss implications of comparative rhetoric for Sino-American communication.

COMPARATIVE STUDIES OF CHINESE AND
WESTERN RHETORICS: A SKETCH

Comparative studies of Chinese and Western rhetorics can illuminate both cultures and enrich the rhetorical repertoire of both peoples. However, the value of comparative rhetoric has been recognized only recently with a series of publications on Chinese rhetoric and attempts to compare Chinese rhetoric with Western rhetoric by Chinese and Western scholars. Actually, for over 2000 years, rhetoric has been considered the property of the West. Prominent rhetorical scholars in the West have claimed that no other cultures have produced a rhetorical system comparable to Western rhetoric (e.g., Murphy, 1983). Robert Oliver's milestone book *Communication and Culture in Ancient India and China* was published in 1971, yet little attention has been paid to studies of Chinese rhetoric, let alone comparative rhetoric, until the 1990s. In this section, I review three stages of comparative studies of Chinese and Western rhetorics in the United States: They are (1) recognition, (2) comparison of differences and similarities, and (3) appreciation and appropriation.

Recognition

Although limited studies of Chinese rhetoric can be found in communication journals of the 1950s (e.g., Crump & Dreher, 1951; Dreher & Crump, 1952), Oliver is the first American scholar to articulate the significance of studying non-Western rhetoric and consistently crusaded and called for the need to study Asian rhetoric. In his article "The varied rhetorics of international relations," published in 1961, Oliver noted that what we know about rhetoric or "new rhetoric" is primarily written by Western men, from Aristotle to Kenneth Burke, which has limited Western scholars in seeing other perspectives and prevented them from conceiving of other systems of values and modes of thinking. He reminded Western scholars that "there is not just one rhetoric—instead, there are many rhetorics. That is to say, there are many different modes of thinking, many different standards of value, many different ways in which influence must be exerted if it is to be effective" (p. 216). In a speech presented at the University of South Dakota, Oliver (1969) lamented that Western arrogance and ignorance of Eastern cultures and rhetoric had not only bred stereotypes and prejudice against Asian people but also made the study of rhetoric and communication incomplete. Oliver reiterated this point throughout seventeen years of correspondence with Vernon Jensen.[2] For example, in the letter he wrote to Jensen on November 9, 1984, Oliver was saddened by the fact that "It has long seemed to me a crying shame, a veritable blot on our profession, that we have equated 'rhetoric' with 'Western rhetoric.' " In another letter, on receiving the news that Jensen's proposal for a seminar on Asian rhetoric was approved by the University of Minnesota,

Oliver commented, "it [the seminar] will make a truly great contribution to Speech education. It has been a sorrow to me that Asian rhetoric has been so wholly neglected. It is heart-warming to know you are plunging into it" (April 4, 1985). Given that the field of rhetoric has been dominated by Eurocentrism for over 2,000 years, Oliver's recognition of Asian rhetoric and call for studies of Asian rhetoric are highly commendable and significant. For Oliver, recognizing Asian rhetoric was necessary to understand and communicate with Asians, to reduce stereotypes and prejudices about Asians, and to enrich Western rhetorical studies.

Comparison of Differences and Similarities

With a pioneering spirit and desire to uncover the implicit meanings of Asian rhetoric, Oliver (1971) introduced classical Chinese rhetoric to his Western audiences with a comparative approach that emphasized differences. For example, Oliver (1971) noted that the West "has been intoxicated with eloquence," while "in sharp and dramatic contrast," the treatises from the East "are virtually bare of tractates on rhetoric" (p. 10). The East, in Oliver's view (1971), "has not been much interested in logic. . . . Clarity of thought itself has been far less favored in traditional literature of India and China than it has been in the West" (p. 10). Furthermore, Oliver contrasts the modes of inquiry of the two cultures, claiming: "Whereas the West has favored analysis and division of subject matter into identifiable and separate entities, the East has believed that to see truth steadily one must see it whole" (1971, p. 10). In essence, Oliver (1971) considered Eastern rhetoric as "peculiarly their own, very different from the tradition that developed in the West" (p. 10).

This emphasis on differences in cultural values and rhetorical practices continued to dominate the subsequent studies of comparative rhetoric. In "Rhetorical emphasis on Taoism," Jensen (1987) identified a few areas of differences in Chinese rhetorical practices, such as deprecation of speech and condemnation of argumentation (a clear contrast to the Western tradition of favoring these two modes of communication). Garrett (1991) extended the comparison of difference, noting that the Chinese place more emphasis on analogical thinking, while the West prefers rational thinking, and that the Chinese audience assumes an active role while the Western focuses on the role of the speaker in a rhetorical situation. Comparing the different conceptualizations of pathos, Garrett (1993a) discovered that the Chinese perceive emotions as an integration of body and mind, considering them normal and natural. The West, by contrast, holds the view that "emotions are constructed as cognitive phenomena" (p. 20); furthermore, emotional appeals are regarded as dangerous and harmful.

The emphasis on differences helped the Western audience make sense of Chinese rhetoric. Studies done by this approach have served to enhance an understanding of Chinese rhetoric in Chinese cultural/social contexts, as well as to offer alternative perspectives on modes of communication and rhetorical strategies. Because rhetoric is culturally based in meanings and practices, recognizing the differences allows us to describe and evaluate a rhetorical system on its own terms and thus reduce the chance of imposing an ethnocentric view of rhetoric onto other cultures. However, this emphasis on differences in the respective rhetorical traditions runs the risk of portraying the Chinese rhetoric as the peculiar Other (Said, 1979; Shome, 1999). Furthermore, such emphasis may have inadvertently reinforced the Orient/Occident distinction and dichotomy, a view long held by Western scholars and early Sinologists (e.g., Forke, 1901/2; Northrop, 1946). As Heping Zhao (1999) states, "Although contrastive rhetoric in its last twenty or so years of endeavor has indeed uncovered certain generalizations that highlight the Otherness of Chinese rhetoric—that may in the end prove to be too limiting to generate much genuine insight." (p. 263).

Studies of comparative rhetoric do not focus only on differences: A few studies also compare the similarities between Chinese and Western rhetoric. For example, Crump (1964) claimed that theories on logic and language proposed by Chinese *Mingjia* (School of Ming) and *Mojia* (School of Neo-Mohism) "resemble so greatly the 'eristic' side of the Greek sophistic [rhetoric]" (p. 99). Dance (1981) discovered that the Chinese Taoist ontology of *yin-yang* echoes Heraclitus's view of change taking place through the interplay of opposites, concluding that "There is an obvious similarity between the Logos of Heraclitus and the Tao of Lao Tzu" (p. 208). After identifying five modes of argument rooted in Asian cultural values,[3] Jensen (1992) concludes that, "the rhetorical differences between East and West are in degree not in kind" (p. 154). Trained in Chinese language and having the competency to read classical Chinese, Garrett (1993b) identifies rhetorical terms such as *"bian"* (argumentation, disputation) and *"shui"* (persuasion) embedded in the Chinese Mohist text and compares similar and different meanings of rhetoric and argumentation with those in Western texts. A more extensive discussion of the similarities between Chinese and Greek rhetoric is offered in Xing Lu's 1998's award-winning book, *Rhetoric in Ancient China, Fifth to Third Century B.C.E.: A Comparison with Classical Greek Rhetoric*. While acknowledging certain areas of differences, Lu (1998) discovered, through a careful examination of cultural contexts and philosophical/literary texts produced before 200 B.C.E. that both Chinese and Greek thinkers considered rhetoric as the art of persuasion with a strong emphasis on ethos, both used rhetoric to engage deductive and inductive reasoning, and both rhetorical systems addressed various psychological appeals. This comparison of both similarities and differences allows room to develop a universal sense of rhetoric and recognizes culturally specific meanings of rhetoric. It aims to discover the common ground, rather than promote polarization between China and the West.

Appreciation and Appropriation

Leading American rhetorical scholars on Asian rhetoric are keenly aware of the significance of studying Chinese rhetoric to benefit Western rhetoric. For Oliver (1971), studying Asian rhetoric offers "invitations to inquiry" and "new modes or channels of investigation" (p. 6). Jensen (1992) echoes Oliver, reiterating that Asian rhetoric would "broaden and deepen our insights into the study of argumentation" (p. 153). Garrett (1991) concurs that by recovering Asian rhetorical tradition, "the Western tradition can be re-examined, refined, and enriched" (p. 304). In the introduction to his recently edited book *Chinese Perspectives in Rhetoric and Communication,* D. Ray Heisey (2000) states that his motive for compiling a volume of Eastern perspectives on communication is "to advance our own Western thinking" and "for the benefit of all of us" (p. xix).

For these reasons, attempts have been made to incorporate and integrate Chinese and Western rhetorics to shed light on each other. In his article "The Tao of Speech," Dance (1981) provides a great example of such integration by combining the Chinese notion of Tao and the Greek notion of Logos. He argues that the functions of speech (Logos) offers the source of human mind and spirit from birth to death and "serves as a 'path,' as a 'tao,' to our becoming ever more human and increasingly humane" (p. 211). After examining the conceptualization of pathos as explicated in classical Chinese texts and various Chinese persuasive contexts, Garrett (1993a) suggests that the West could learn from the Chinese by developing a more integrated and holistic approach to emotional education through the creation of a cultural environment and comprehensive self-cultivation. In another study, Garrett (1993c) introduced the ancient Chinese practice of "pure talk" (a type of witty conversation of the cultural aristocracy from 200 to 600 C.E.). The use of wit by "pure talkers" and the functions of witty conversations, according to Garrett, parallel "the game of wit practiced in the African-American community and the exploitation of wit among gay men known as 'camp'"[4] (p. 312). In both cases, Garrett (1993c) observes that wit is not used just for pleasure, but functions "to construct a community, to create an alternative source of ego-reinforcement, and to sharpen a weapon to be wielded against the outside world [the dominant group]" (p. 312). Garrett's work not only informs the Western readers of the Chinese rhetorical tradition of "pure talk" but also demonstrates the cross-cultural functions of this rhetorical form.

A more recent study on Chinese rhetoric by Steven Combs (2000) is another example of appreciation and appropriation in comparative rhetoric. From his analysis of Sun Zi's *The Art of War,* a classical Chinese text on warfare, Combs discovered that the principle of parsimony (extreme economy in the expenditure of resources) employed as war strategies can be applied to persuasive communication in the areas of conflict management, strategic positioning of the speaker and audience, and holistic assessment of a rhetorical situation. Combs' work is significant not only because it helps the Western audience appreciate Chinese rhetorical texts and recognize their benefits to Western rhetoric but also because it exemplifies a universal appropriation of cross-cultural texts. As Combs (2000) keenly concludes, "Although *The Art of War* illustrates the culturally based nature of rhetorical theory, this analysis demonstrates that many cultural differences in Chinese communication practices are intelligible to Westerners. The text cannot be homogenized or fully subsumed within the Western rhetorical tradition, but it can help bridge understandings of East/West rhetorical theories and practices" (p. 292-293). In the same article, Combs makes several additional cross-cultural connections from *The Art of War* to Aristotle's concept of ethos, Perelman and Olbrechts-Tyteca's notion of preassumptions, and Kenneth Burke's theories of identification. This trend of cultural adaptation and appropriation of Chinese rhetoric has served as a link between rhetoric and intercultural communication studies.

In sum, studies of comparative rhetoric have moved from focusing on differences to examining both similarities and differences. The mode of inquiry has advanced from a dichotomized approach to an integrated perspective. The task of comparative rhetoric has broadened to include discovering both the culturally specific meanings and the universal applications of cross-cultural rhetoric. The value of these comparisons lies not only in the illumination of respective rhetorical traditions but also in the appropriation of the foreign rhetorical tradition to explain and address contemporary communication phenomena in each culture.

AREAS AND CHALLENGES IN COMPARATIVE STUDIES BETWEEN CHINESE AND WESTERN RHETORICS

Even though strides have been made in the study of Chinese rhetoric and its comparison to Western rhetoric, many areas still deserve further attention. I will first identify these areas of comparative study and then I will delineate the challenges Chinese and Western rhetorical scholars face in doing comparative studies.

Areas of Comparison

There are many areas of comparison between Chinese and Western rhetorics. However, given what has been done, the next two major areas of comparison that need exploring are (1) parallels of major historical periods when philosophical and religious shifts took place and (2) major rhetorical texts produced in each culture.

The research done so far primarily focuses on the time period of the fifth to third centuries B.C.E. Needless to say, this is the richest period of thought and rhetorical practice, when prominent philosophers and rhetoricians emerged in both ancient China and ancient Greece. However, it is important to examine how the rhetorical canons or concepts formulated in this time period developed in subsequent years and how the development is influenced by social/political contexts in each culture. For example, in the Judeo-Christian time period in the West, diversity of thought gave way to the dominance of Christianity. A rich body of rhetorical theories was reduced to stylistic devices (decorum, tropes, and figures). Rhetoric was no longer used as a tool to discover truth and new knowledge, but to defend Christianity and to persuade people to believe in God. Around the second century A.D., Chinese emperor Han Wu Di adopted Dong Zhongshu's (179-104 A.D.) advocacy of abandoning all other schools of thought and privileging Confucianism as the dominant political philosophy for China. After this, diversity of thought was suppressed and different philosophical views were condemned. As a result, rhetoric, which played multiple roles and flourished in the Pre-Qin period (221 B.C.E.), was narrowed down to embellishment of words and linguistic styles.

While church fathers led by St. Augustine successfully Christianized rhetoric in the medieval period in the West, Buddhism was adopted and appropriated in China and integrated with Taoism and Confucianism, thus becoming the dominant religion for Chinese people. A comparison and contrast of religious transitions in both cultures and the role rhetoric played in facilitating and appropriating the transitions deserve scholars' attention. Adding to the list of comparative rhetoric is the area of disputation among thinkers within each tradition. Humanists and scholastics were divided during the medieval period, and conflicts occurred among church fathers on the conceptualization of truth and use of rhetoric; similarly, debates between Han Yu (768-824) and Liu Zhongyuan (773-819) were argued for and against the adoption of Buddhism during the Tang Dynasty (618-907).[5] Another internal conflict was that between Zhu Xi (1130-1200) and Cheng Liang (1143-1194) on whether China should adopt an idealistic or a realistic orientation as its political philosophy during the Song Dynasty (960-1279).[6] Contrast can also be made between the flourishing of rhetoric during the Renaissance period in the West and the impact of *Wenzi Yu* (Suppression of Rhetoric) during the Ming Dynasty (1381-1621) and the Qing Dynasty (1662-1911) in China. These comparisons enable us to search for a theory of universal rhetoric that addresses similar rhetorical exigencies in parallel periods of human history. They also prompt us to examine how indigenous cultural forces influence the perception and practice of rhetoric.

In addition, rhetorical texts of two cultures provide rich data for comparison. A number of rhetorical texts from the pre-Qin time period have been examined in the current scholarship on Chinese rhetoric (e.g.,

Combs, 2000; Garrett, 1983; Kirkwood, 1992; LaFargue, 1994; Raphals, 1992; Richards, 1991; Rieman, 1980; Zhao, 1994). However, hardly any studies have been done on the comparison of these texts with Western texts. For example, comparisons can be made between Confucius's *Lun yu* (*The Analects*) with Plato's *Phaedrus* regarding the moral characteristics of speakers, between Aristotle's *Rhetoric* and *Mojin* (the Mohist Canon) by Late Mohists on the similarities and differences of the two logical systems, between Aristotle's *Rhetoric* with *Xunzi* concerning ethos and the rational approach of rhetoric and with *Han Feizi* on various psychological appeals, and between Western rhetorical texts featuring technical and strategic elements with Chinese texts of similar focus such as *Strategies of Gui Guzi* and *The Art of War*. These comparisons will illuminate the diverse modes of persuasion and rhetorical practices in both cultures and inform us on how rhetoric was conceptualized in each culture in response to its own political and social contexts.

Moreover, a number of other influential Chinese rhetorical texts produced in subsequent years have not been well explored rhetorically. These are *Lun heng* (Discussion of balance), *Shishou xinyu* (New accounts of tales in the new world), *Liu zhu tan jin* (Buddhist sutra), *Wenxing diaolong* (Cultivating the mind and carving the dragon), *Huai Nanzi* (Explanation of Huai Nanzi), *Cai gen tan* (Vegetable roots of Tan), *Yan tie lun* (Disputes over salt and iron), and *Shou yuan* (The garden of talks). These texts, produced in different time periods in Chinese history, used various rhetorical styles and persuasive strategies to record and respond to the social/political situation at each particular time. Studies of these texts from a rhetorical perspective will provide new topic areas for further comparisons in rhetorical expressions and the employment of rhetorical techniques in cross-cultural situations.

Challenges

Rhetorical scholars face at least four challenges in engaging a comparative study of Chinese and Western rhetorics. First and foremost is the lack of agreement on terminology and concepts. Lu (1998) identified seven terms (*bian, shou, shui, yan, ci, jian, and ming*) that all share some similarities with the Greek sense of rhetoric but find no direct equivalent in the Greek conceptualization of rhetoric. Rhetorical scholars should continue to search for similar or different meanings for terms in the respective rhetorical texts. At the same time, scholars may have to settle for the notion that rhetorical terms and concepts can also be culturally specific and derived from their own linguistic, social, and philosophical contexts. In fact, there is not even consensus or agreement among the Chinese academic community on the meaning of these terms. For example, Lu linked the word "rhetoric" with several similar meanings in Chinese texts and contexts, while scholars in Mainland

China still perceive "rhetoric" as limited to a single idea of modification of terms and stylistic devices *(xiu ci)*.

The second challenge rhetorical scholars face is the different approaches in the study of rhetoric. In the United States, works on Western rhetorical traditions trace the evolution of the discipline to its social, political, and religious contexts. Rhetoric is associated with the discovery of truth, perceived as a fundamental value of a democratic society, and focused on the impact messages and images have on attitude and action. By contrast, in the list of books published since the 1930s in China on *xiu ci* (modification of names), emphasis has been mostly placed on stylistic devices, modes of speech, and features of language. Even Chen Wangdao's (1932) landmark book *Xiouci xue fafan* (Introduction of rhetoric) concentrates largely on the features of Chinese language itself, its types and practical usage. As observed by Hu Shuzhong (1992), Chinese rhetorical scholars examine rhetorical features from a microperspective, while Western scholars approach the study from a macroperspective that links rhetoric with ethics, politics, and epistemology. It seems that contemporary Chinese studies on rhetoric are limited by the term "*xiu ci.*" To broaden the understanding of rhetoric, Chinese scholars must search for other terms that embrace more complex meanings and diverse practices of rhetoric.

While American scholars have demonstrated appreciation for Chinese rhetoric and attempted to appropriate Chinese rhetoric in the interpretation and understanding of Western rhetoric, the same efforts have not been made by Chinese scholars residing in China. Because studies of rhetoric are limited to *xiu ci* only, few Mainland Chinese scholars are familiar with Western theories and practices of rhetoric. The popular Chinese journal *Speech and Eloquence* is devoted primarily to speech practices rather than theoretical and historical comparisons. Hu Shuzhong's 1993 publication of *Comparative Studies in English and Chinese Rhetoric* introduced Western rhetorical tradition in only general terms and placed heavy emphasis on the comparison of tropes and figures of speeches. Rhetoric as a mode of criticism in the analysis of discourse and images in political and social contexts is hardly known to the Mainland Chinese. Only in recent years have Changfu Chang and others (1998a, 1998b) begun a collective effort to translate into Chinese a set of articles on rhetorical criticism by American scholars. These translations will help broaden the Chinese perspective of rhetoric and enhance the understanding and application of rhetorical modes of criticism. Furthermore, Chinese scholars need to develop their own modes of rhetorical criticism that are suited to the Chinese contexts and rooted in Chinese rhetorical tradition.

As shown in Lu's book (1998), the Chinese term "*bian*" has been conceptualized by classical Chinese thinkers with diverse meanings that resemble closely the term "rhetoric" as conceived by ancient Greeks. Like Greek rhetoric, *bian* was closely associated with ethics, politics, emotions, and epistemology when the political environment was relatively free and relaxed.

However, when political control was tight and dissidents were persecuted, *bian* was diminished to stylistic devices and modes of speech, similar to those during the period of the Roman Empire and Christian domination in the West.

The third challenge rhetorical scholars face is the translation of rhetorical texts. Chinese scholars face the challenge of understanding English texts as well as the original Greek and Latin rhetorical texts from the West. Western scholars face the challenge of understanding the Chinese language, especially the classical Chinese language. Few translated texts dealing with rhetorical theories and practices are available in both cultures, even though efforts have been made by Western scholars to translate Chinese texts. However, one has to be cautious when using the translations for the interpretation of rhetorical meanings. For example, as Garrett (1999) sharply pointed out, "Stephen Mitchell's recent translation of *The Way and the Power [Daode jing]* may leave something to be desired for some scholars." However, the disappointing fact is "he 'translated' this text without knowing any Classical Chinese, and arrived at his English-language version by dint of relying on other translations" (p. 62). For those scholars not equipped with two languages, expert opinions should be consulted to avoid pitfalls.

This leads to the last challenge rhetorical scholars face in studying comparative rhetoric between China and the West: the lack of exchange and collaboration between Chinese and Western scholars. In the past, pioneering scholars such as Oliver and Jensen singlehandedly conducted and wrote up the research themselves. Writings on rhetoric by Chinese scholars were also largely by single authors. To this day, there is hardly any scholarly collaboration between Chinese and Western scholars on this topic. As a result, both sides remain unaware of their counterparts' publications and studies, let alone exchange ideas and research findings. This situation was discussed by David Frank (2000) as he observed that many scholars work in isolation. He urges rhetorical scholars to seek broader collaborations in developing their research programs. Such a collaboration, according to Frank, "can play an important role in helping other scholars, students, and generally educated public better understand the nuances of Chinese rhetorical practices" (p. 3). I would add that it will also help scholars in China understand the roles, functions, and scopes of Western rhetoric. The collaborative research between Lu and Frank (1993) is such an example. Clearly, comparative rhetoric will be more meaningful and beneficial if such a collaboration is established and continued.

FUTURE PROSPECTS AND IMPLICATION ON CROSS-CULTURAL COMMUNICATION

In the past, the study of rhetoric was dominated by a Eurocentric orientation. However, in the twentieth century, the emergence of studies in Chinese rhetoric began to challenge the Eurocentric view. Now in the twenty-first century, in a global world where people from different cultures contact each other on a daily basis, comparative studies of rhetoric and communication become increasingly significant in providing information and facilitating meaningful interaction between diverse cultures. In this section, I discuss two issues: (1) methodology in the study of cross-cultural rhetoric and (2) comparative rhetoric and Sino-American communication.

Methodology in the Study of Cross-Cultural Rhetoric

Lu (1998) notes, "The challenge that rhetorical scholars will face in the twenty-first century is not simply to dismantle the notion that only Greek rhetoric legitimately belongs within the rhetorical canon, but, more importantly, to produce unpolarized, subtly nuanced, postethnocentric intellectual discourse and multicultural modes of rhetorical inquiry" (p. 308). To this end, rhetorical scholars have been exploring approaches that make the study of cross-cultural rhetoric intelligible and useful to people of both cultures.

Shuter (1999) proposed what he termed "a ground approach" in the study of rhetoric of other cultures. Such an approach, according Shuter, "allows the discourse to reveal itself to the critic, rather than having the critic 'squeeze' rhetoric into the predetermined categories and schemes" (p. 16). This approach questions the ethnocentric assumptions of scholarship on comparative rhetoric, relies primarily on original cultural texts, and considers the impact of social/political contexts for the meanings of Chinese rhetoric and its comparison with Greek rhetoric. Such an approach also helps Western audiences unpack some stereotypes about Chinese culture and reach a better understanding of contemporary Chinese communication behavior. Garrett (2000), on the other hand, calls for an openness to foreign concepts as they "may allow the researcher to notice aspects of a phenomenon that she would not see otherwise" (p. 54). In fact, Garrett believes that "the foreign term or category is more illuminating than misleading" (p. 54).

However, Garrett cautions the researcher that "usefulness, appropriateness, and fit of terms should always be in question and should never be assumed, and that their application must always bear a burden of proof when applied outside their original cultural context" (p. 54). Such rhetorical appropriation is exemplified in Xiaosui Xiao's 1995 study of Yan Fu's appropriation of Western concepts and adaptation to the Chinese audience through his translation of Thomas Huxley's *Evolution and Ethics*. Intercultural communication takes place when foreign ideas are rhetorically adapted and modified by the native interpreter to his or her fellow citizens. Xiao concludes that this is a process of "rhetorical translation, a process which is guided by sensitivity to a particular historical situation and to a given cultural tradition" (p. 95). Yan Fu's successful rhetorical appropriation suggests, according to Xiao (1995), that intercultural rhetorical studies may be "initiated by the 'taker' or 'host culture' rather than by the 'giver' or 'quest culture.'" Xiao further explains, "this means that in this kind of intercultural communication the native interpreter, not the original author, is the real speaker to the native audience, though he or she may think of himself or herself as merely speaking for a foreign school of thought" (p. 94). It is Yan Fu's rhetorical translation, not Huxley's original works, that makes Huxley's thinking appealing to the Chinese audience in an intelligible, sensible, and meaningful way.

In offering suggestions on the domains of comparison, Garrett (2000) points out the problem of using limited views of the Western definition of rhetoric as the framework to search for conceptualized Chinese rhetoric. Instead, researchers should define rhetoric broadly to include discursive and symbolic practices that are rooted in Chinese texts and cultural contexts. This approach opens more avenues for more specific comparisons of rhetorical practices, rhetorical concepts, and modes and settings of persuasion.

In sum, by employing the proposed methods, we can identify additional areas of similarities and differences between cultural values and rhetorical practices, and we can enrich our understanding of rhetoric as a symbolic human activity that has universal appeal as well as distinct cultural characteristics. Given the increased contacts and communication between nations and cultures, a general theory of rhetoric such as that envisioned by George Kennedy will emerge, and its application/implication to cross-cultural communication will be immense.

Comparative Rhetoric and Sino-American Communication

I agree with George Kennedy that comparative rhetoric must help illuminate the process and achieve goals of intercultural communication. Through comparative rhetoric we come to understand the areas of rhetorical practices or modes of persuasion that are rooted in specific cultural values and that are likely to cause stereotypes and misunderstandings in intercultural contexts. For example, after the collision between a U.S. spy plane and a Chinese fighter jet on April 1, 2001, the Chinese government demanded an apology, while the United States only offered "regrets." Conflict between the two countries intensified as both sides failed to understand the function of apologetic rhetoric rooted in each culture. For the Chinese, apologies are used to ease tension, save face, and reach a peaceful resolution. For Americans, apologies mean culpability, which involves litigation and liability. For example, in American car insurance policies, the holder is advised not to apologize when involved in an accident.

China and the Chinese people have been portrayed in negative and undesirable terms in Western discourse and are the subject of Orientalism. Chinese people are considered peculiar (Takaki, 1989); Chinese language is regarded as linguistically inferior and not suited for civilization (Becker,

1986), and Chinese thinking is believed to be unsystematic and disorderly (Northrop, 1946). China is portrayed as "evil, a menace, not following the international rules" (Song et al., 1996, p. 82). The "China Threat" theory still very much informs and influences U.S. foreign policy toward China (Krauthammer, 1995). On the other hand, Chinese also stereotype and demonize Americans, calling them "foreign devils" and "ghosts of hegemony" and accusing them of "having an ulterior motive of blocking China from advancing to a better life" (Song et al., 1996). Anti-American sentiments escalated with the U.S. bombing of the Chinese embassy in Yugoslavia and the U.S. spy plane's clash with a Chinese jet that caused the loss of the Chinese pilot. Sino-American relations have been shadowed by mistrust, accusations, and defensiveness over issues such as intellectual property, human rights, and trade policies.

Many factors contribute to the causes of these stereotypes and prejudice. One factor certainly is the lack of understanding, tolerance, and appreciation of each other's rhetorical traditions and communication styles. Comparative studies between Chinese and Western rhetoric can help dispel or reduce these stereotypes. For example, Shijie Guan's (2000) comparative study of the differences between Chinese and American thought patterns and relationships with their respective languages sheds light on Sino-American cultural differences. Moreover, Heping Zhao's study (1999) exemplified both the Chinese flexible rhetorical strategies in gaining "most favored nation" status and their shared rhetorical characteristics with the West. More comparative studies of this nature are needed to enhance the understanding and appreciation of each other's rhetorical practices.

Through comparative studies of Chinese and Western rhetoric, both Chinese and Western scholars can learn from each other's rhetorical perspectives as well as contribute to new rhetorical theories. Further, comparative rhetoric does not just help with understanding other cultures' values and rhetorical strategies; more important, it enriches and illuminates one's own cultural and rhetorical practices. For instance, researchers can use a rhetorical theory or framework from a foreign culture to analyze and critique the rhetorical practices of their own culture. Garrett (1993b, 1993c) and Combs (2000) have employed Chinese rhetoric to render a better understanding of Western rhetoric. Numerous studies by overseas Chinese scholars have used a Western rhetorical framework to analyze Chinese rhetorical practices. For example, in her 1998's study, Lu applied Kenneth Burke's dramatism to analyze the rhetoric of anti-American sentiments in the Chinese bestseller *China Can Say No*. She also used a cultural/ideological mode of criticism developed by American scholars in the analysis of communist propaganda for the purpose of political and ideological control (Lu, 1999). This mutual appreciation and appropriation of each culture's rhetoric makes Kennedy's vision of a general theory of rhetoric applicable to all societies.

CONCLUSION

In this chapter, I review and address the four objectives proposed by Kennedy (1998) in studying comparative rhetoric in the case of comparative studies between Chinese and Western rhetorics. I also discuss the method-ological issues in comparative rhetoric that Kennedy did not include in his comparative rhetoric framework. Rhetorical scholars currently face new challenges in adopting the methodology of uncovering native perspectives as well as appropriating foreign rhetorical concepts for the purpose of informing and illuminating rhetorical traditions of Western and non-Western cultures. However, it is worth the effort if we try to advance our knowledge of communication and to maintain world peace. In conclusion, I would like to pay tribute to Oliver, who initiated the studies of non-Western rhetoric and paved the way for comparative rhetoric and intercultural communication through his pioneering works. Oliver should be pleased to know that the torch he ignited has been carried on. I hope that more comparative studies of rhetoric will emerge to enhance and enrich our understanding of human communication.

NOTES

1. While the book offers a general introduction to the rhetoric of some cultures (Australian aborigines, American Indians, Ancient Near East, China, and India), it sheds little light on methodological issues, as it does not really engage in comparative studies of the rhetorical traditions of these cultures.

2. Vernon Jensen kindly forwarded to me all the letters he and Robert Oliver wrote to each other between 1983 and 2000 before Oliver passed away. In these letters, they discuss many issues ranging from Asian rhetoric to American politics, from intellectual exchange to personal growth, from academic works to family updates.

3. There are five modes of argumentation: (1) argument from the authority, (2) argument by analogy, (3) argument by examples, (4) less reliance on deductive reasoning, and (5) adaptation to audience. Garrett's 1983 study identified four primary modes of Chinese argumentation: (1) argument by authority; (2) argument by a deductive chain, (3) argument from consequences; and (4) argument by comparison.

4. According to Garrett (1993c), "camp" is a conversational art in which the talker is aware of the rule of playing and behaving. The playful nature of camp is characterized by competition, exaggeration, and aggression (p. 312).

5. Both Han and Liu were literary elites and imperial officials in the Tang Dynasty. Han held conservative views of Confucianism and opposed the adoption of Buddhism in China. Liu, on the other hand, advocated the integration of Confucianism, Taoism, and Buddhism.

6. Zhu and Cheng were well-known imperial scholars for their time. Chu advocated building an orderly society through Mandate of Heaven and conformation to ideal social norms and moralistic principles (tian li). Cheng emphasized pragmatism and criticized Chu's theory as unrealistic and empty rhetoric. All these thinkers were intellectual elites as well as well-known rhetoricians. They made proposals to the emperor on how to rule China and what kind of political philosophy and religion he should adopt.

REFERENCES

Becker, C, (1986). Reasons for the lack of argumentation and debate in the Far East. *International Journal of Intercultural Relations 10*, 75-92.

Chang, C.F., et al. (1998a). Trans. *Dangdai xifang xiuci xue: Piping meshi yu fang fa [Contemporary Western rhetoric: Critical paradigms and methods]*. Beijing: China Academy of Social Science Publishing House.

Chang, C. F., et al. (1998a). Trans. *Dangdai xifang xuici xue: Yanjiang yu huayu piping [Contemporary Western rhetoric: Speech and discourse criticism]*. Beijing: China Academy of Social Science Publishing House.

Chen, W. D. (1932). *Xiuci xiu fafan [Introduction of rhetoric]*. Shanghai, China: Big River Books.

Combs, S. (2000). Sun-zi and *The art of war:* The rhetoric of parsimony. *Quarterly Journal of Speech, 86*, 276-294.

Crump, J. I., & Dreher, J. (1951). Peripatetic rhetoric of the Warring Kingdoms. *Central States Speech Journal, 2*, 15-17.

Crump, J. I. (1964). *Intrigues: Studies of Chan-kuo ts'e*. Ann Arbor: University of Michigan Press.

Dance, F. E. (1981). The Tao of speech. *Central States Speech Journal, 32*, 207-211.

Dreher, J., & Crump, J. I. (1952). Pre-Han persuasion: The Legalist School. *The Central States Speech Journal, 3*, 10-14.

Forke, A. (1901-2). The Chinese sophists. *Journal of the North China Branch of the Royal Asiatic Society, 34*, 1-100.

Frank, D. (2000). Research on Chinese rhetoric and communication.*Newsletter of the Association for Chinese Communication Studies*, Spring Issue.

Garrett, M. (1983). *The 'Mo-Tzu' and the 'Lu-Shih Ch'un-ch'iu': A case study of classical Chinese theory and practice of argument*. Ph.D. Dissertation, University of California, Berkeley.

Garrett, M. (1991). Asian challenge. In S. Foss, K. Foss, & R.Trapp (Eds.), *Contemporary perspectives on rhetoric* (pp. 295-306). Prospect Heights, IL: Waveland.

Garrett, M. (1993a). Pathos reconsidered from the perspective of classical Chinese rhetorical theories. *Quarterly Journal of Speech, 19*, 19-39.

Garrett, M. (1993b). Classical Chinese conceptions of argumentation and persuasion. *Argumentation and Advocacy, 29*, 105-115.

Garrett, M. (1993c). Wit, power, and oppositional groups: A case study of "pure talk." *Quarterly Journal of Speech, 79*, 303-318.

Garrett, M. (1999). Some elementary methodological reflections on the study of the Chinese rhetorical tradition. In A. Gonzalez and D. V. Tanno (Eds.), *Rhetoric in intercultural contexts* (pp. 11-17). Thousand Oaks, CA: Sage Publications.

Guan, S. (2000). A Comparison of Sino-American thinking patterns and the function of Chinese characters in the difference. In D. R. Heisey (Ed.), *Chinese perspectives in rhetoric and communication* (pp. 25-43). Stamford, CT: Ablex.

Heisey, D. R. (2000). Introduction: Chinese perspectives coming of age in the West and serving as a balance in theory and practice. In D. R. Heisey (Ed.), *Chinese perspectives in rhetoric and communication* (pp. xi-xx). Stamford, CT: Ablex.

Hu, S. Z. (1992). *Yinghan xiuci bijiao yanjiu [Comparative studies in English and Chinese rhetoric]*. Shanghai, China: Foreign Language Education Press.

Jensen, V. (1987). Rhetorical emphasis of Taoism. *Rhetorica, 5*, 219-232.

Jensen, V. (1992). Values and practices in Asian argumentation. *Argumentation and Advocacy, 28*, 155-166.

Kennedy, G. (1998). *Comparative rhetoric: A historical and cross-cultural introduction.* New York: Oxford University Press.

Kirkwood, W. G. (1992). Revealing the mind of the sage: The narrative rhetoric of Chuang Tzu. *Rhetoric Society Quarterly, 22,* 6-19.

Krauthammer, C. (1995). Why we must contain China. *Time,* July 31, p. 72.

LaFargue, M. (1994). *Tao and method: A reasoned approach to the Tao Te Ching.* Albany: State University of New York Press.

Lu, X. (1998). *Rhetoric in Ancient China, fifth to third century B.C.E.: A comparison with Classical Greek rhetoric.* Columbia: University of South Carolina Press.

Lu, X. (1998-1999). Rhetoric of nationalism and anti-Americanism: A Burkean analysis of *China can say no. Intercultural Communication Studies 8(2),* 163-176.

Lu, X. (1999). An ideological/cultural analysis of political slogans in Communist China. *Discourse & Society, 10,* 487-508.

Lu, X., & Frank, D. (1993). On the study of Ancient Chinese rhetoric/*bian. Western Journal of Communication, 57,* 445-463.

Murphy, J. (1983). *A synoptic history of classical rhetoric.* Davis, CA: Hermograras Press.

Northrop, F. S. C. (1946). *The Meeting of East and West.* New York: Macmillan Company.

Oliver, R. (1961). The varied rhetorics of international relations. *Western Speech, 25,* Fall, 213-221.

Oliver, R. (1969). Sacred cows, Asian and American. *Vital Speeches of the Day,* August 15, 668-672.

Oliver, R. (1971). *Communication and culture in ancient India and China.* New York: Syracuse University Press.

Oliver, R. (1984). *Letter to Vernon Jensen,* November 9th.

Oliver, R. (1985). *Letter to Vernon Jensen,* April 4th.

Raphals, L. (1992). *Knowing words: Wisdom and cunning in classical traditions of China and Greece.* Ithaca, NY: Cornell University Press.

Richards, I. A. (1991). Mencius through the looking glass. In A. Bertthoff (Ed.), *Richards on rhetoric: I.A. Richards' selected essays 1929-1974.* New York: Oxford University Press.

Rieman, F. (1980). Kung-sun Lung, designated things and logic. *Philosophy East and West, 30,* 305-319.

Said, E. (1979). *Orientalism.* New York: Vintage Books.

Shome, R. (1999). Postcolonial interventions in the rhetorical canon: An 'Other' view. In J. Lucaites, C. M. Candit, & S. Candall (Eds.), *Contemporary rhetorical theory: A reader* (pp. 591-608). New York: The Guilford Press.

Shuter, R. (1999). The cultures of rhetoric. In A. Gonzalez & D. V. Tanno (Eds.), *Rhetoric in intercultural contexts* (pp. 11-17). Thousand Oaks, CA: Sage Publications.

Song, Q., Zhang, Z. Z., Qiao, B., Zheng, Y., & Gu, Q. S. (1996*). Zhongguo ke yi shuo bu [China can say no].* Beijing: Chinese Cultural Federation Press.

Takaki, R. (1989). *Strangers from a different shore: A history of Asian Americans.* New York: Penguin Books.

Xiao, X. (1995). China encounters Darwinism: A case of intercultural rhetoric. *Quarterly Journal of Speech 81,* 83-99.

Zhao, H. (1994). Rhetorical invention in *Wen xin diao long. Rhetoric Society Quarterly, 24,* 1-15.

Zhao, H. (1999). Rhetorical adaptability in China's argument for "Most Favored Nation Status." In R. Kluver & J. H. Powers (Eds.), *Civic discourse, civil society and Chinese communities* (pp. 251-263). Stamford, CT: Ablex.

7

"The Assimilation of Western Learning": An Overlooked Area of Intercultural Communication

Xiaosui Xiao

"Western learning" was the phrase that set afire the hearts of many ardent Chinese and sent their thoughts into flight a century ago. But ten years ago, when I started to explore how modern Western ideas were assimilated in China, the "assimilation of Western learning" had not become a subject of study for either Chinese or Western communication scholars. What particularly compelled me to mine this forgotten land were the rhetorical questions: How did this assimilation occur? How did fundamental concepts in the West such as "struggle," "equality," and "science" cross international and linguistic boundaries and make their way into Chinese discourse? What role did Chinese rhetorical tradition play in this process? To answer these questions I have conducted a series of rhetorical analyses during the past decade. The purpose of this chapter is to review a selected group of these studies. This review, I believe, can help draw more scholars and students of Chinese communication to this fertile area, which has yet to be fully exploited.

The "assimilation of Western learning" here refers specifically to the introduction and popularization of modern Western ideas in China after the Opium Wars (1839-1861). This cross-cultural process reached its heights during the Reform Movement (1890s) and the May Fourth New Cultural Movement (1915-1925). It had an enormous impact on the course of modernization in China. The process of assimilating Western ideas virtually consists of an unbroken chain of rhetorical events. Among them, four stand out as the most important landmarks in the process. The first is the debate in the Imperial Court over the nature of the Opium Wars, in which the reform-minded literati-officials finally persuaded the throne to adopt an open policy toward the technological aspect of Western learning. The second is Yan Fu's "translation" of Thomas Huxley's *Evolution and Ethics* in the Reform Movement. The third is Tan Sitong's writing of the first Chinese "manifesto of egalitarianism," *A Study of Humanity* (1899-1901). The last is the May Fourth radicals' defense of an omnipotent concept of science in the 1923 nationwide debate between science and metaphysics. The four events play an extremely significant role in the development of the intellectual interaction between China and the West. They have successfully introduced and popularized in China a wide range of Western terms and concepts, including "machine," "technology," "industry," "struggle," "evolution," "progress," "equality," "democracy," "science," "law," "essence," "matter," and the like. Moreover, as this chapter will reveal, the strategies used by the Chinese introducers to signify and legitimize these foreign terms and concepts had a profound impact on the way in which China has responded to Western challenges.

The four works to be reviewed in this chapter, entitled respectively "Rhetorical Situation Revisited" (Garrett & Xiao, 1994), "China Encounters Darwinism: A Case of Intercultural Rhetoric" (Xiao, 1995), "The Hierarchical *Ren* and Egalitarianism: A Case of Cross-Cultural Rhetorical Mediation" (Xiao, 1996), and "Tao-Preaching and the 1923 Scientistic Campaign" (Xiao, 1998), are studies of these four rhetorical events.[1]

A UNIQUE APPROACH

Historians in the English-speaking world have provided comprehensive studies of these events and have produced influential works such as Ssu-yu Teng and Reischauer Fairbank's *China's Response to the West: A Documentary Survey, 1839-1923* (1954), Mary C. Wright's *The Last Stand of Chinese Conservatism: The Tung-chih Restoration* (1957), Benjamin Schwartz's *In Search of Wealth and Power: Yen [Yan] Fu and the West* (1964), James R. Pusey's *China and Charles Darwin* (1983), and Hao Chang's *Chinese Intellectuals in Crisis: Search for Order and Meaning (1890-1911)* (1987). These works have been extremely useful reference guides for me. Their analyses of the historical situations in which the reform-minded literati-officials, the first Chinese Darwinist Yan Fu, and other spokespersons of Western learning found themselves help one to understand the radical change of their thoughts. What is more significant is that these studies, with the exception of a very early one by Teng and Fairbank, have tried to go beyond the simple "Western impact versus Chinese response" model that dominated the early Western study of modern Chinese history in the 1950s and 1960s. Schwartz was not the only one to discover that "[t]he 'response to the West' was itself carried

on within the setting of the intellectual currents of the Chinese world"
(Schwartz, 1964, p. 6).

However, historians have examined these events of intellectual encounter
between China and the West within their disciplinary context, often from the
perspective of the history of ideas. They have been concerned with the
interaction between two cultural systems of thought rather than with the
interaction between the speaker and the audience. For them, the most important question about the encounter is what particular tendencies of the Chinese
intellectual tradition preoccupied the Chinese spokespersons of Western
learning, who were then responding to certain definite strands within the
complex of eighteenth- and nineteenth-century European thought. For me, the
perspective of the history of ideas cannot explain how the assimilation of
Western learning, which is essentially a communication and rhetorical event,
occurred in China at the time. The cases considered in my study are intricate
processes of cross-cultural communication taking place in a given cultural
and discursive environment. They involved a tense dialogue between two
cultural forms of discourse and demanded the participation of a large Chinese
audience. The cases thus need to be reexamined from a communication and
rhetorical perspective. Such a perspective requires special focus on the
conditions that made possible meaningful transaction and communication
between the persuader and the audience. The rhetorical critic is concerned
with how the audience is guided to understand and accept the persuader's
ideas and how the persuader adapts consciously to the audience's worldview.

The four rhetorical studies to be reviewed here illustrate a unique approach
not only to the studies of these four significant events but also to cross-cultural communication study in general. Current intercultural communication
studies tend to focus on only two lines of research. One examines the
interpersonal dimensions of communication to discover how people from
different cultures interact face-to-face. The other line of research on cross-
cultural communication takes a mass-media standpoint, emphasizing on issues such as the effects of Western international broadcasting, the new world
information order, the use of new technologies for the instantaneous worldwide transmission of information, the international telecommunications marketplace, and so forth. The four rhetorical studies, however, focus on the
intellectual dimension of intercultural transaction. The cross-cultural exchange of ideas is an important form of intercultural communication. Here,
foreign ideas and thoughts usually take the form of written texts. Not only do
native interpreters often have to play a crucial role in the reading of these
foreign ideas and thoughts, but various historical, social, and rhetorical
factors also affect the process of interpretation. The interaction between the
foreign ideas and the reading public of the local culture thus constitutes one
of the most profound chapters in intercultural communication. The modern
history of East-West communication has shown that the furthest-reaching
influence from the West did not come from its technology or its goods, but

from its thought. Regrettably, this form of communication has been over-looked by mainstream intercultural communication scholars.

THEORETICAL FRAMEWORK

The four rhetorical studies differ from each other in their focus of study. "China Encounters Darwinism" concentrates on the rhetor's translating skills, while "The Hierarchical *Ren* and Egalitarianism" examines the rhetor's use of metaphor. "Rhetorical Situation Revisited" is concerned with the rhetor's interaction with his or her discursive tradition, whereas "Tao-preaching and the 1923 Scientist Campaign" is more interested in the discursive game the rhetor plays in his or her argument.

Despite this difference in focus, they are all products of operations within the same general theoretical framework, which I call the framework of "the rhetoric of signification." This framework draws on some of the critical theories of cultural studies. It has four basic assumptions.

Assumption One. The assimilation of Western learning is a process of signification or a process of meaning-building. The introduction of Western learning takes place in either of two situations: the introducers use old symbols or old vocabularies and build a new meaning on top of them, or they introduce new symbols from the West. Even in the second situation, the foreign symbols would signify nothing to the native audience unless they were given a meaning.

Assumption Two. Signification is a site of social struggle. According to Stuart Hall (1982), every social group or social class has its own ideological standpoint when it participates in signifying practice—it signifies events in a particular way. Thus, signification is by no means a peaceful process. As a result of the struggle over meaning, one social group or social class (usually the one that has power) comes to claim the power to signify. With this power it legitimizes and institutionalizes its preferred way of signification, making it the dominant discourse. But this power to signify always faces challenges from non-dominant discourses.

Assumption Three. From the perspective of struggle over meaning, signifi-cation inevitably involves the critical role of rhetoric. Whether a dominant discourse can claim itself as the only correct account or whether a non-dom-inant discourse can break the monopoly of meaning held by the dominant discourse depends largely on the use of signifying strategies. A dominant discourse has to rely upon metaphor, metonymy, and other rhetorical mecha-nisms to "imprison" the existing vocabularies within a mainstream meaning system. A non-dominant discourse also has to use these mechanisms to liberate or, in Hall's term, "dis-articulate" these vocabularies from their places within an established meaning system and re-associate them with a different meaning system (1982, p. 78). Furthermore, in order for a strategic and reasonable struggle to gain the power to signify, a non-dominant discourse has to maintain a kind of ambiguous relationship with a dominant discourse. For example, it may need to use the popular topics and vocabularies of a dominant discourse to gain entrance to the world of public discourse.

Assumption Four: The native interpreter and advocate of a foreign practice of signification, often representing the force of reform in his or her society, plays a crucial part in a cross-cultural process of signification. This is because a cross-cultural process of signification, like the assimilation of Western learning in China, is usually initiated by the host culture, not by the guest culture. In this process the native interpreter and advocate of a foreign practice of signification often acts as an active player rather than a passive receiver. Thus, if an introduced foreign practice of signification is made to appear meaningful in a cultural context, it is not necessarily due to the rhetoric of the original speaker but to the rhetoric of the native interpreter and advocate of this foreign practice.

Viewed from this standpoint, the four selected cases are all cases of struggle for signification. In these cases, the Chinese propagators of Western ideas attempted to establish new meaning systems by introducing Western learning as a new practice of signification.

CASE STUDIES

"Rhetorical Situation Revisited"—An Analysis of the Opium-Wars Discourse

This series of research started with a study on "the Opium-Wars discourse." After the tragic defeats in the Opium Wars had greatly embarrassed China, the ominous but unavoidable term "the Opium War" began to be heard in the Imperial Court debates. Its meaning became the point at issue. The Court was subsequently divided into different camps depending on how they defined it.

Our study found that almost 20 years after the First Opium War (1839-1842), the court's discussions on the "War" were still very much in line with the dominant Confucian discourse. It was generally agreed that the "War" should be defined as an intrusion from greedy and vicious "barbarians." It was based on this definition that the court decided to show infinitely royal graciousness to these "uncivilized barbarians." Thus the cession of Hong Kong, as well as other concessions, was not a dishonor for China at all, but a magnanimous favor given to the barbarians.

This account gave way to a different one following the Second Opium War (1857-1860), when the leaders of the Foreign-Affair Movement (*Yangwu*

Yundong, 1865-1890) like Prince Gong, Zeng Guofan, and Li Hongzhang—the first generation of modern Chinese propagators of Western learning—strove to advocate reform. These men replaced the term "barbarian" (*yi*) with "overseas" (*yang*), suggesting that the West was another world of civilization. They also admitted that the "War" marked a "shameful, tragic loss" for Imperial China. They then redefined China's circumstance after the Wars as "a truly unprecedented situation in the past several thousand years." Meanwhile, however, these reformers' explanation of the situation did not suggest a radical departure from the Chinese political discourse tradition. They, instead, looked backward to the statecraft tradition and spoke in the highest terms of some seventeenth-century scholars who stressed "knowledge for practical purposes" (e.g., Gu Yanwu). The new explanation not only provoked a sustained feeling of urgency among the Chinese literati-officials but also created a sense of crisis in meaning, for the dominant Confucian discourse was no longer assumed to be the only correct and legitimate account.

This explanation of China's critical situation had a far-reaching impact. It created a breakthrough and opened up the prospect of a new practice of signification. It thus created favorable conditions for a later flux of new discourses in China.

"China Encounters Darwinism"—An Analysis of an Early Chinese Evolutionist Discourse

In the 1890s, the rising Western-minded intellectuals—leaders and activists of the ensuing Reform Movement—began to challenge both the cosmic and the ethical bases of the established Confucian meaning system. Yan Fu's *Heavenly Evolution* (1898) and Tan Sitong's *A Study of Humanity* (1899-1901) represented these two tendencies. These two influential works are thus the second and third cases in this series of studies.

Heavenly Evolution, a "translation" of the British Darwinist Thomas Huxley's lecture *Evolution and Ethics* (1894), is the first Chinese version of a Darwinian work. My close examination of the two texts shows that the Chinese version is a re-creation rather than a translation in many aspects. The translator claimed that he only paraphrased the original. But he in fact added a great many of his own opinions. Nonetheless, there is no doubt that he introduced a key Darwinian idea: Living species evolve because of their struggle for existence.

Apparently, Yan was trying to go against the mainstream Confucian explanation of evolution, which considered harmony to be the key to the evolutionary process of life, rather than the so-called struggle for existence. But surprisingly, Yan's "translation" achieved great success at the time. After the publication of *Heavenly Evolution*, as the *People's Journal* reported in 1905, "the ideas of things' struggle and heaven's selection have struck root in men's hearts. The people's spirits have taken on an altogether new aspect"(cited in

Fang, 1981, p. 103). How could Yan possibly justify and popularize such an iconoclastic explanation? This was the central question of my analysis.

I found that Yan chose to interpret (signify) the Darwinian term "struggle" in a way that the mainstream Confucian meaning system could not possibly reject. He first defined "struggle" in the sense of a collective fight for the survival of a whole nation. He then placed this notion of struggle between two processes that the Chinese had generally perceived as inevitable and holy. One was the cosmic process of generation and regeneration; the other was the ethical process that led to the heavenly selection of virtue and the elimination of vice. Yan reminded his countrymen of the missing link between these two sacred processes, namely, the struggle for existence. The heavenly process of generation and regeneration forced all races to compete for existence. The result of this competition was the survival of the ethically best. Through this connection, "struggle" had a divine meaning—it was not only natural, but also just.

"The Hierarchical *Ren* and Egalitarianism"—An Analysis of an Early Chinese Egalitarian Discourse

Tan Sitong's *A Study of Humanity* (1899-1901) is, like Yan's *Heavenly Evolution*, a great intellectual achievement of the Reform Movement. For me, the treatise provides another good example of how a radical but skillful explanation could at once damage and protect a dominant meaning system. In this treatise, Tan picked "humanity" (*ren*), a god-term in Confucian ethics, as his target. He tried to associate it with the idea of equality, thus putting himself in direct confrontation with the dominant explanation and the mainstream meaning system of tradition. The Confucian tradition had long assumed that a perfect world of humanity had to be maintained by a system of hierarchical relations. What Tan tried to abandon was not just a traditional explanation, but also the core of Confucian ethical codes—the doctrine of the Three Bonds (between ruler and subject, father and son, and husband and wife).

My study reveals that, to make his non-traditional egalitarian interpretation of humanity acceptable, Tan used a signifying strategy that was very different from Yan's. He tried to develop a new space within this term's established range of meanings. For the Neo-Confucianists after the eleventh century, in addition to its classical meanings of benevolence and love, "humanity" also signified a cosmic state of interconnectedness. It is from this new meaning that the Neo-Confucianist came to suggest that the world of humanity was a great organic unified whole. The Neo-Confucian sense of interconnection became the breakthrough point for Tan. In *A Study of Humanity*, Tan stretched the notion of interconnection to such an extent that it introduced a whole new view of the world. From this worldview, all things in the world were so organically and holistically interconnected that they were, in essence, equally important to the whole that they belonged to. Here was the idea of equality.

Tan did not have to appeal to Western sages, as Yan had, to propagate the egalitarian gospel. He discovered equality in one of the most common and most important concepts in Chinese culture.

"Tao-Preaching and the 1923 Scientistic Campaign"—An Analysis of an Early Chinese Scientistic Discourse

By the time of the May Fourth era (1915-1925), advocates of the radical New Cultural Movement were no longer satisfied with the Reform leaders' reinterpretation of the time-honored terms of Chinese culture. Instead, they tried to replace the old terms with new terms and to introduce the non-traditional concepts of science and democracy as the foundations of a new symbolic world. Thus occurred the 1923 nationwide debate over whether science was adequate for dealing with the fundamental questions of human life. The defenders of science in the debate promoted quite an effective campaign for an omnipotent notion of science and thus ended up creating a new icon for worship by the young, open-minded Chinese of the time.

The scientific campaign, the fourth and the last case marks a more radical stage in the struggle for signification. In this stage, the defenders of science did not want to attach the concept of science to any of the key terms of Chinese culture. For them, none of the traditional systems of learning could be called a "science." "Science," a resounding name for a modern system of knowledge, had to make a clean break with all that had conventionally signified traditional learning. For this reason, traditional learning as a whole had to have a name that contrasted with "science." Thus, it came to be called "metaphysics" (*xuanxue*).

My study shows that in order to justify the use of "science" in the sense of a legitimate system of knowledge the defenders of science still relied to a certain extent on the established meaning system of their tradition, although they tried to turn away from the core of its symbolic system. According to this meaning system, a system of learning found its fundamental meaning and value in explaining the *dao* of Heaven and the *dao* of men. The defenders of science adapted to this recognized hierarchy of meaning by speaking of science as essentially a system of knowledge about the *dao* (the Way) of the cosmos and the *dao* (the Way) of human life. For them, science exceeded all traditional systems of learning merely because it was the only reliable account of *dao*. It can be said that the defenders of science made a strategic concession to the established meaning system, in exchange for its recognition of the cultural legitimacy of the "scientific god."

A FERTILE FIELD

The foregoing review demonstrates that a cross-cultural transaction of ideas, like the assimilation of Western learning in China or in other non-Western societies, is primarily a process of intercultural communication that has to be studied from a communication and rhetorical standpoint. Further, this cross-cultural process can be understood in the light of the rhetoric of signification. Viewed from the perspective of such a rhetoric, Western learning is a new cultural practice of signification. The introduction of any given aspect of Western learning will unavoidably change the existing Chinese meaning system as a whole and thus will meet resistance from the established system. The introducer, then, will have to fight and communicate strategically and skillfully in order to make the introduced signifying practice acceptable to a dominant Chinese discourse.

The intellectual encounter between the East and the West provides a new and rich continent for intercultural communication scholars. Here, they can explore how Western ideas have been introduced to China, Africa, the Middle East, South-East Asia, Latin America, and other non-Western societies, especially over the past two or three hundred years, during which time this introduction became an enduring fashion for the people there. The question of how Eastern ideas have been introduced to the West is, of course, equally worthy of study. For an intercultural communication scholar, it is particularly important to know whether there are general rules determining the process of the East-West exchange of ideas.

The four case studies reflect only my preliminary attempts to pursue the ignored rhetorical question concerning how modern Western ideas came to be popularly accepted in China. The assimilation of Western learning in China as a promising sub-area of study is only beginning to be explored. This chapter proposes a theoretical framework for examining this rhetorical process. It does not mean, however, that a rhetorical study of the "struggle for signification" is the only feasible approach to this particular process of cross-cultural communication. The process can certainly be looked at from other communication and rhetorical perspectives.

The scope of my study is, of course, limited. Due to limits of time and knowledge, I can select only a few cases for study. Many other important cases have regrettably been left out of the list of my previous study. For instance, some Western theories of anarchism were popular for a while during the May Fourth New Cultural Movement. Marxism came to dominate Chinese thought throughout most of the twentieth century after this movement. During the past twenty years China has been introducing theories of the market economy from the capitalist West. I have not seen any communication and rhetorical study exploring such rich topics as anarchism, Marxism, and capitalism in China, although they have been intriguing areas of study to historians, sociologists, and political scientists.

"The assimilation of Western ideas" can be seen as a "heteromorphic phenomenon" in intercultural communication. It raises questions that usually do not exist in a "normal" process of cross-cultural communication. For instance, in the case of the assimilation of Darwinism in China, who is the real speaker, Huxley or his Chinese spokesman Yan Fu? If the native Yan is the real speaker, can he be counted as an intercultural communicator? Can scholars of intercultural communication afford to ignore him? It may also be necessary to ask a hypothetical question: What could Huxley learn from Yan's success, supposing the former wanted to deliver a speech on evolution to a Chinese audience in a meaningful and effective way?

NOTE

1. The first work originated as a paper I presented at the 1992 annual convention of the American Society of Rhetoric. Professor Mary Garrett and I revised it into a journal article published later in the *Rhetoric Society Quarterly*, vol. 24, pp. 30–40. (1994).

REFERENCES

Chang, H. (1987). *Chinese intellectuals in crisis: Search for order and meaning (1890-1911)*. Berkeley: University of California Press.

Fang, H. (1981). *Zhongguo jindai baokan shi [The modern history of Chinese periodicals]* (Vol. 1). Taiyuan: Renmin.

Garrett, M., & Xiao, X. (1994). The rhetorical situation revisited. *Rhetoric Society Quarterly, 24,* 30-40.

Hall, S. (1982). The rediscovery of "ideology": Return of the repressed in media studies. In M. Gurevitch, T. Bennett, J. Curran, and J. Woollacott (Eds.), *Culture, society and the media* (pp. 56-90). London: Routledge.

Pusey, J. R. (1983). *China and Charles Darwin*. Cambridge, MA: Council on East Asian Studies, Harvard University.

Schwartz, B. (1964). *In search of wealth and power: Yen Fu and the West.* Cambridge, MA: The Belknap Press of Harvard University.

Teng, S., & Fairbank, R. (1954). *China's response to the West: A documentary survey, 1839-1923.* Cambridge, MA: Harvard University Press.

Wright, M. C. (1957). *The last stand of Chinese conservatism: The Tung-chih restoration.* Stanford: Stanford University Press.

Xiao, X. (1995). China encounters Darwinism: A case of intercultural rhetoric. *Quarterly Journal of Speech, 81,* 83-99.

Xiao, X. (1996). The hierarchical *ren* and egalitarianism: A case of cross-cultural rhetorical mediation. *Quarterly Journal of Speech, 82,* 38-54.

Xiao, X. (1998). The 1923 scientific campaign and tao-preaching. Paper presented at the 1998 annual convention of the International Communication Association.

8

Research on Chinese Communication Campaigns: A Historical Review

Jianglong Wang

One can not fully understand the Chinese and Chinese communication in the People's Republic of China (PRC) without understanding the mechanism of Chinese communication campaigns. For the PRC Chinese, participating in communication campaigns (*yun dong*, the Chinese term for campaigns) had, in fact, been a way of life in the latter half of the twentieth century, since the founding of the PRC in 1949. The importance of understanding communication campaigns in the PRC has been pointed out by many (e.g., Townsend, 1967; Bennett, 1976; Cell, 1977; Liu, 1981; Wang & Wu, 1997-98). Cell (1977), for example, succinctly captured the significance and value of understanding Chinese campaigns when he stated: "To comprehend how China changed, how it has accomplished so much in so short a time, there is no single institution more important to understand than the campaign (p. 1)."

Primarily for purposes of understanding PRC Chinese, a considerable amount of research has been conducted by scholars from different disciplines to study Chinese communication campaigns in various historical periods (Yu, 1964, 1967; Cell, 1977; Chen, 1979; Liu, 1981; Bishop, 1989; Wang, 1994; Huang, 1996; Wang & Wu, 1997-98). Given this large body of research, the immediate concern of this chapter is to provide a general overview of the most influential research on Chinese communication campaigns from a historical perspective. Significant studies on Chinese communication campaigns are gathered and reviewed. Foci of this historical review are thus placed on the strength, limitations, significant issues, and future directions of Chinese communication campaign research. In the remainder of this chapter, I first define the concept of Chinese communication campaign and delineate the types of Chinese campaigns. I then continue to examine specific Chinese campaign research with emphases placed on analyzing and understanding research findings and implications. Further, I specify the challenges facing future Chinese campaign research, and, finally, I conclude this chapter with a general evaluation on research conducted in this area.

CHINESE COMMUNICATION CAMPAIGNS

Although scholars in the West have made an effort to distinguish "campaigns" from "movements" (Paisley, 1981; Salmon, 1989), to the Chinese, however, the term *yun dong* is an inclusive phrase, denoting both purposefully organized campaigns and spontaneously spread social movements. For instance, while the government-sponsored "Great Leap Forward" campaign of 1958 is called by the Chinese "*da yiao jin yun dong* (the Great Leap Forward)," the spontaneously spread national movement to mourn over the death of their beloved leaders in 1989 is named "*qun zhong ai dao yun dong* (The Mass Mourning Movement)."

Defining Chinese Communication Campaigns

In the West, the term "communication campaign" has also been interchangeably used with other similar concepts like "information campaign," "media campaign," and "public campaign," to mention just a few. However, all campaigns are typically considered as having a set of purposive activities organized by one sponsoring party to solicit desired attitudinal and/or behavioral changes in another party within a certain period of time (Rogers, 1973; Rice & Paisley, 1981; Rogers & Storey, 1987; Rice & Atkin, 1989; Backer, Rogers, & Sopory, 1990). Cell (1977), while studying mass campaigns in the PRC, offered the following definition for mass mobilization campaigns in the PRC: "Formally defined, the mass mobilization campaign in China is an organized mobilization of collective action aimed at transforming thought patterns, class/power relationships and/or economic institutions and productivity."(p. 7).

The mass mobilization campaigns Cell referred to include all major campaigns organized and implemented in the PRC since its founding (1949) to 1975, a span of time covering more than a quarter of the twentieth century (see Cell, 1977, pp. 187-191, for a list of the specific campaigns included in his study).

In China, given the governing system of one ruling party, almost all campaigns sponsored by the Chinese government and its ruling party carried with them a political undertone and, as such, they usually required deep involvement and wide participation from its people. To a large extent, this definition of mass campaign in the PRC is fairly representative, for it has included the most salient characteristics of Chinese communication campaigns. The purpose of using the term "mass mobilization campaign," as pointed out by Cell (1977), is to "emphasize the dual components of organization and mass participation" in Chinese communication campaigns.

Types of Communication Campaigns in China

With the general understanding of Chinese communication campaigns as a set of organized activities usually sponsored by the government and often having political implications, researchers attempted to divide Chinese communication campaigns further into categories. Yu (1967) was one of the earliest researchers who categorized Chinese campaigns into three groups: economic, ideological, and struggle campaigns. While acknowledging the difficulty he encountered in separating Chinese campaigns into distinctive categories, Yu (1967) believed that economic campaigns in the PRC most often had as their purpose economic reform, while ideological campaigns were aimed at "remolding the thoughts" of the PRC people. Struggle campaigns such as the "suppression of counterrevolutionaries" campaign (zhen fan yun dong) targeted at "resolving antagonistic contradictions."[1]

Another way of categorizing the Chinese communication campaigns was proposed later by Liu (1981), who suggested that campaigns in the PRC be divided into two major types with seven subcategories. Taking them as a whole, Liu (1981) considered Chinese campaigns as either "political-ideological" or "developmental-informational" in nature. Considering their objectives, Liu (1981) further divided Chinese campaigns into seven kinds, including campaigns for (1) class struggle, (2) denunciation of purged political figures, (3) studying political ideology, (4) emulating model workers, (5) promoting policies, (6) correcting harmful public opinions, and (7) distributing public information.

Although presentation of categories of communication campaigns often entails the risk of oversimplifying the complexity and interrelatedness of Chinese communication campaigns, categorization does provide those interested in Chinese campaign studies with a roadmap showing distinguishable characteristics of various communication campaigns in the PRC.

RESEARCH IN CHINESE COMMUNICATION CAMPAIGNS

In the beginning, interest in studying Chinese campaigns started with the founding of the PRC in 1949. The primary motivation then was to understand the power and mechanism with which the Chinese Communist Party and its government successfully organized its people in the course of their revolution (Yu, 1967; Lewis, 1968; Schurmann, 1968). As China's revolution progressed, the Chinese and Chinese society seemed to have changed a great deal within a short period of time after the party's founding. Interest in researching Chinese communication campaigns became stronger, and the primary concern was the reasons for the success of these communication campaigns. Many believed these campaigns were fundamentally responsible for the political, social, and economic achievements made in the PRC. Research on Chinese communication campaigns has therefore focused on (1) the theoretical and ideological foundations, (2) the campaign pragmatics, and (3) the utility of Chinese communication campaigns.

Theoretical and Ideological Foundations

Chinese communication campaign researchers began their journey by probing into the foundations upon which the Chinese communists were able to win their revolution in a seemingly quite impossible situation. They initiated research by tracing the theoretical foundations with which the Chinese communication campaigns operated. Under the influence of focusing on political aspects of the country (which was typical of social science research in Chinese issues at the time), researchers on Chinese communication campaigns also considered the Chinese case to be a political one (Starr, 1973). They started tracing the origin of Chinese communication campaigns to the Yenan Period, in which one of the most famous first campaigns, *"zhen feng yun dong,"* was operated under the leadership of Chairman Mao Zedong, then the chairman of the Chinese Communist Party (CCP) (Cell, 1977). By carefully examining this famous campaign, researchers found that the communist ideology, "Mao Zedong thought," to be specific, was the main cornerstone for all Chinese communication campaigns. Under the ideological guidance of Mao Zedong, China was to be known to the world for its communication campaigns, because immediately after the *"zhen feng yun dong"* in Yenan, Mao (1967) declared in 1943:

> From now on, such campaigns should be launched everywhere in the first month of every lunar year, and in the course of them the pledges to "support the government and cherish the people" and "support the army and give preferential treatment to the families of the soldiers who are fighting the Japanese" should be read out time and time again. (Volume III, p. 134)

To many Chinese, Mao Zedong thought and Chinese revolution are inseparable; without the guidance of Mao Zedong thought, China could not have won its revolution and the PRC would not have been founded (Starr, 1973).

As an integral part of China's revolution, the operation of communication campaigns was, indeed, "revolution at work,"[2] which should be rightly placed under the leadership of Chairman Mao and his CCP. Chinese communication campaign researchers found that central to Mao's ideology on Chinese campaigns is what Liu (1981) termed "his two-step-flow theory of leadership." In other words, consistent with his view on the universality of contradictions and his view on correctly resolving both antagonistic and non-antagonistic conflicts in the Chinese society (Wang & Wu, 1997-98), Mao believed that campaigns were the best vehicle to transform policies formed at the top into actions of the masses at the grassroots level.

Mao (1968) himself considered this process of transforming Party policies into the action of the masses as a dialectical process between the leaders and the led. That is, Party leaders go to the masses, listen to their interests and concerns, and then form relevant policies aimed at representing the masses' interests and taking care of their problems. Mao later further developed this method for his CCP's political communication with the Chinese people, which became known as the "mass line." Lewis (1963) believed that Mao was the first Chinese leader to utilize this strategy (i.e., the strategy of mass line) to establish a reciprocal and organized relationship between political leaders and the masses in China.

Specifically, Lewis (1963) found that the implementation of Mao's "mass line" was a process consisting of four interrelated steps of (1) perception, (2) summarization, (3) authorization, and (4) verification. While perception refers to a stage at which political leaders perceive the "objective social conditions" of their communities, summarization is for leaders at lower levels to report their firsthand observations to leaders at higher levels. When local leader's "objective reports" are brought to the attention of leaders at higher levels, it is up to them to form policies as well as programs aimed at solving the problems or resolving the conflicts. This is the third step of authorization. Then, when formed policies and/or programs are carried out (usually through the channels of communication campaigns), the final stage of verification occurs, at which effects of policy and/or program implementations are verified. Of particular interest to campaign researchers, though, is not the functions of "mass line" in the CCP and its government's political work, but how "mass line" has been applied to the operation of communication campaigns in the PRC.

Campaign Practices

In addition to mapping out the theoretical and ideological foundations of Chinese communication campaigns, researchers have also paid attention to the pragmatics of running Chinese communication campaigns. Their foci were primarily on organization, processes, strategies, and effects of Chinese communication campaigns.

Organization of the Chinese campaigns. In his study on the operation of the family-planning campaign in the city of Shanghai, China, Wang (1989) discussed in detail how the Chinese family-planning campaign (a major off-and-on national campaign in the PRC) was organized. Wang (1989) noted that sitting on top of the campaign organizational chart was the State Family Planning Commission (SFPC), which was in charge of all the affairs of the campaign in the nation. Wang (1989) continued to describe the levels of organizations in the campaign:

> Under the SFPC are the Family Planning Commissions (FPC) at the provincial level, and beneath these are the Family Planning Committees for cities and regions. At the bottom of this *campaign organizational chart* [italics added by the author] are the Family Planning Groups for factories, schools, neighborhoods, etc., which are considered "the basic units" by the Chinese (pp. 8-9).

Members of the Family Planning Groups, according to Wang (1994), were the campaign agents who work face-to-face on the targets of the campaign— individual couples of childbearing age. Obviously, through this tightly-knit organizational scheme, campaign targets and campaign runners (top leaders at the SFPC that form the policies and programs for the campaign) are directly connected with each other. Although there may be variations of campaign organizations as scopes of campaigns vary, this vertical organizational scheme, from the top of the Chinese political structure down to the local political leaders at the grassroots level, is quite common and representative of all Chinese communication campaigns.

Campaign processes. Liu (1981) believed that the running of Chinese communication campaigns was comparable to that of the presidential election campaigns held in the United States. "On the whole, a typical Chinese campaign is, structurally speaking, not too different from the presidential election campaigns . . . . in the United States" (p. 202). Specifically, Liu (1981) described four sequential steps employed by the Chinese in operating their communication campaigns. The first of these four steps is the creation of an ad hoc organization solely devoted to affairs of the campaign, like the SFPC mentioned by Wang (1989) in the family planning campaign. The second campaign step is the training of activists, people who are enthusiastic about the campaign, like volunteers in U.S. presidential election campaigns. The difference, however, lies in the selection of campaign activists/volunteers. In China, campaign activists are selected by two criteria, that is, the person must have both knowledge of the campaign and political reliability.[3] Having been selected, they are then trained to be the agents of the campaign, who should be thoroughly familiar with the policies and programs of the campaign and be willing to work with campaign targets face-to-face. With the ad hoc campaign organization in place and campaign agents trained, the

Chinese are ready to move into the third step of a campaign, which is to choose a community to test-run the program. Liu (1981) compared this step to the practice of "canvassing" in U.S. presidential election campaigns. Important lessons, if any, learned from the "test-run" of the campaign are then applied to the revision and redesign of the campaign before "positive experiences of the campaign" are spread onto the nation in full speed. Finally, comes the conclusive step of the campaign, when policies and programs are carried out in the campaign and expected effects are believed to have been achieved.

Campaign strategies. In recent history, though a variety of communication strategies were employed in Chinese communication campaigns, researchers found that persuasion, coercion, personal influence, compliance-gaining, group pressure, and ideological work (Townsend, 1967; Teiwes, 1971; Chen, 1979; Bennett, 1976; Cell, 1977; Taplin, 1981; Rice & Atkin, 1989; Wang, 1989, 1994; Wang & Wu, 1997-98) are the principal strategies utilized by the Chinese. Coercion as a campaign strategy was primarily used in struggle campaigns to resolve antagonistic contradiction found in the Chinese society (Teiwes, 1971), for Mao (1967) advocated:

> As for members of the reactionary classes and individual reactionaries, so long as they do not rebel, sabotage or create trouble after their political power has been overthrown, land and work will be given to them as well in order to allow them to live and remold themselves through labor into new people. If they are not willing to work the people's state will *compel* them to work [italics added by the author]. (Volume IV, p. 419)

Also, Teiwes (1971) tried to distinguish the Chinese practice of coercion and persuasion by comparing the practices in two communist countries at the time—the Soviet Union and the PRC. While coercion was more generously applied in Russia, China was "more subtle in combining the two methods" of coercion and persuasion and demonstrated "much greater willingness to rely on persuasive techniques" (Teiwes, 1971, p. 16).

In addition, Teiwes (1971) and Wang (1989) believed that the Chinese applied group pressure most often in their campaigns. In most cases, group pressure was brought to bear through social and relational networks surrounding campaign targets, such as familial and workplace social and relational networks of the targets. While Chinese strategic use of group pressure in communicative activities has long been noticed by researchers (e.g., Whyte, 1974; Rice & Atkin, 1989). Rice and Atkin (1989), for instance, believed that the Chinese might have been the heaviest users of group pressure in communication campaigns. Others in the field (Huang, 1967; Liu, 1981; Howkins, 1982; Wang, 1989; Bishop, 1989; Wang & Wu, 1997-98) seem to concur with the functions of groups in Chinese communication campaigns for "small groups have been so 'routinized' in Chinese political life that most Chinese have learned to adapt to this ritual" (Liu, 1981, p. 213).

Coupled with group pressure, another often-employed strategy in Chinese communication campaigns is personal influence. Typically, in the running of their communication campaigns, the Chinese make full use of real people to influence the attitudes and/or behaviors of their campaign targets. These real people are often ones who have personal appeals to campaign targets or whose past life experiences are ones to which the targets can easily relate. Their personal influence is brought to bear to influence campaign targets' attitudes and/or behaviors in line with those advocated by the campaign in question. Numerous cases of using personal influence in Chinese campaigns were found (e.g., Liu, 1971; Wang, 1994). For instance, in the national campaign of socialist education from 1963 to 1964, "*she hui zu yi jiao yu yun dong*," many converted targets of the campaign, who had suffered from their past ignorance of the principles of socialist practice, for purposes of exercising their personal influence, came to tell their own stories to those not yet changed in the campaign (Yu, 1967). Liu (1981) also described a vivid case of personal influence in China's birth control campaign, in which women who suffered from having large families with many children were brought to tell their "bitterness" to couples who were still thinking of having more kids.

A further salient strategy employed in Chinese communication campaigns is persuasive compliance gaining. Wang (1994), in his case study on the family planning campaign in Shanghai, for instance, has outlined the specific compliance-gaining strategies utilized by the family-planning campaign agents in the neighborhoods, factories, and universities of the city. Taken as a whole, Wang (1994) discovered the compliance-gaining strategies employed by various agents in the campaign included (1) social and monetary rewards as well as sanctions, (2) campaign agents' political and personal appeals, (3) campaign agents' special knowledge (such as being a gynecologist) of family planning, (4) campaign agents' legitimate appeals (like those coming from authoritative campaign agents), and (5) appeals from influential significant others (such as influences from parents who support the policy of the campaign) of the campaign targets.

In addition to coercion, group pressure, personal influence, and compliance-gaining strategies, Chinese communication campaign researchers also found out that ideological work (*si xiang gong zuo*) is a unique Chinese political strategy commonly applied in the operation of their communication campaigns (Wang, 1989, 1994; Wang & Wu, 1997-98). For example, Wang and Wu (1997-98) found that "ideological work" was a dialectical conflict management strategy applied in Chinese communication campaigns for purposes of resolving non-antagonistic contradictions. "Ideological work" conducted in communication campaigns, according to Wang & Wu (1997-98), is a process in which persuasive work such as "heart-to-heart talks" with campaign targets are performed. Specifically, the process of conducting "ideological work" included five sequential steps outlined as "(1) understanding influential factors, (2) analyzing processual levels of the work, (3) mastering feelings, reasons, and exemplary behaviors, (4) employing knowledge or expertise, and (5) changing social norms for the group" (Wang & Wu, 1997-98, p. 89).

Although identification and categorization of Chinese campaign strategies is a worthwhile endeavor, one must understand these strategies are deliberately and arbitrarily categorized by campaign researchers for different reasons and purposes. As such, overlapping of strategy divisions appears to be inevitable in certain cases.

Effects of campaigns in the PRC. In the literature of Chinese communication campaign research, systematic evaluations with reliable and valid measurements are seriously lacking. Researchers in the past depended on mostly anecdotal reports, official Chinese government publications, and other less-reliable sources to gauge the effectiveness of communication campaigns in the PRC. One study claims that most of the Chinese campaigns aimed at changing targets' attitudes have achieved minimum or superficial effects, while most campaigns targeting behavioral changes have accomplished campaign objectives temporarily (Bishop, 1989), primarily because of campaign targets' reluctance to reveal their true feelings.

> But in case Chinese propagandists do want to test the effectiveness of their persuasion, they have to face the fact that as a rule people in totalitarian nations do not reveal their true feelings in the open. Most go along or adapt to the system out of necessity. That is why, in special occasions like the "Hundred Flowers Blooming" campaign in 1957 or the Cultural Revolution of 1967-68, one witnesses hitherto unseen conduct and opinion that the authorities suppressed earlier coming back in force. What proves to be a real cost to the whole nation is that the public's "seeming compliance" is not limited to "political" or ideological matters but applies also to campaigns designed for genuine public good. (Liu, 1981, pp. 217-218)

Elsewhere, however, Liu (1971) believed that the Chinese had achieved overall success in their earlier campaigns because of people's enthusiasm in the rule of the CCP and the new people's government. As people's enthusiasm waned with the communist system, the effectiveness of the Chinese communication campaigns was gradually reduced. In Liu's words:

> Popular enthusiasm for the Communist regime, meanwhile, inevitably waned. Consequently, the mass campaigns gradually lost their effectiveness. Though the campaigns still were useful for linking the media with face-to-face communication, they became too intrusive to be received by the people favorably. They have created a constant sense of anxiety among cadres and general resentment among

the public. The Party had overplayed the campaigns, and that reduced their effectiveness. (Liu, 1971, pp. 111-112)

Not surprisingly, this resentment from the Chinese masses toward large-scale national campaigns, particularly for those political struggle campaigns, eventually made the CCP led by Deng Xiaoping[4] seek a drastic reduction of campaigns, especially those struggle campaigns used for fractional partisan politics.

The Utility of Chinese Communication Campaigns

In addition to gaining knowledge of the Chinese and the way in which Chinese politicians communicate with their people, campaign researchers have on their agenda also the purpose of discovering what Chinese communication campaign experiences may mean to others in the world. Cell (1977), for instance, believed that the Chinese communication campaign experiences could be summarized as having "five points." He considered that (1) the Chinese campaign system as a whole is a "utilitarian method for China's goal of socialist transformation; (2) campaigns in the PRC can be divided into different types with "economic, struggle, and ideological" ones as the most apparent; (3) while struggle campaigns in China were most effective in dealing with antagonistic contradictions in the Chinese society, other types of campaigns seemed to be effective in handling non-antagonistic contradictions amongst the Chinese; (4) economic campaigns "show greater levels of achievements and lower levels of shortcomings compared with other types of campaigns" in China; and (5) ideological campaigns, given their unrealistic objectives in most cases, "produce the lowest level of achievements" (Cell, 1977, p. 172).

Further, while pointing out that China could not "provide the blueprint for action for other societies," Cell (1977) held the view that "the success of the Chinese" in running their communication campaigns had positive utility for many others in developing countries.

> The Chinese have brought forcefully and dramatically to the world's attention a vibrant, dynamic, alternative strategy for economic, political, and social change. The social scientists wishing to lay claim to the universality of development theory can no longer ignore the Chinese example. They must reckon directly with this very different strategy and the implications it poses for other strategies of social, political, and economic change. (p. 175)

Liu (1981), however, advocated that the most important negative lessons from the Chinese campaign experiences were that, first, China's communication campaigns had "excessively emphasized 'collective' benefits at the expense of 'individual' benefits," which may not be applicable or even productive for campaigns in countries like the United States. Second, some Chinese campaigns suffered from "lack of credibility," which often misled campaign participants. In other words, campaign participants were negatively influenced by the exaggerated effectiveness of campaign results. Lastly, the overuse of "small groups" (group pressure) in Chinese communication campaigns has greatly reduced their impact. On the other hand, Liu (1981) felt that positive lessons from the Chinese campaigns included "the emphasis on personal participation in persuasion campaigns." That is, the way Chinese turned persuaded campaign targets into persuaders who would influence campaign targets to change has utility for campaign designers elsewhere in the world. Another positive lesson was the Chinese campaigns' "flexibility in operation," which refers to Chinese campaign organizers' ability to quickly mobilize "a large number of activists" and turn them into campaign agents who could then be dispatched to "every corner of a locality to disseminate the message" (Liu, 1981, p. 223) of the campaigns.

CHALLENGES FACING FUTURE CHINESE COMMUNICATION CAMPAIGN RESEARCH

Research on Chinese communication campaigns has been fruitful in achieving its objective of gaining understanding of the Chinese people and the way in which China's ruling party, the CCP, communicates with the Chinese masses via its special method of running communication campaigns based on Chinese political "mass line." Findings of Chinese communication research not only have informed us of the theoretical and ideological foundations of Chinese campaigns but also have revealed the specific strategies with which the Chinese have effectively operated their campaigns. Campaign researchers appear to be in consensus that the Chinese communication campaigns as a whole have been constructive and successful in respect to their contribution to China's political/ideological, economic, and social development, although there are some negative lessons from the Chinese communication campaign experiences. Research findings further demonstrated the usefulness, benefits, and implications of China's positive and negative campaign experiences to the social and economic development of other countries in the world, particularly developing countries in the Third World.

As revealed by this review, one major challenge facing Chinese communication campaign research appears to be the practice of separating the running of communication campaigns from its cultural contexts. Most research on Chinese campaigns, it seems safe to postulate, was conducted under the assumption that Chinese communication campaigns can be understood without comprehending any elements of Chinese culture. Although some attention has been paid to the impact of China's political and economic systems on the operation of Chinese campaigns, little has been done to examine social and, more important, cultural influences upon ideology and practice of running Chinese communication campaigns. From a social and cultural perspective, for instance, how could the theoretical and ideological foundations of Chinese communication campaigns possibly be connected with the traditions of Chinese society and Chinese culture?

Another significant challenge facing Chinese campaign research is the lack of a longitudinal method of assessing the effectiveness of Chinese communication campaigns. Most evaluative campaign studies, for instance, were done as a snapshot of a particular campaign at a given time, based either on eyewitnesses' descriptions of the campaigns or on official reports published by the CCP or the Chinese government. Consequently, the reliability and validity of these assessments are jeopardized.

Further challenges for Chinese campaign researchers include the search for indigenous campaign concepts such as "mass line" (*qun dong lu xian*), "ideological work" (*si xiang gong zou*), "heart-to-heart talk" (*tan xin*), and so on. Searching for the meanings and applications of such native conceptualizations of Chinese communication campaigns and campaign operation will help to reveal meaningfully the mechanism of Chinese communication campaigns, on the one hand, and significantly deepen our knowledge of the Chinese campaigns, on the other. Also, although researchers (e.g., Wang, 1997) have started comparing the running of Chinese campaigns with the operation of campaigns in the United States, more comparative studies of Chinese campaigns should be done with those run in other countries of the world, particularly with those run by developing countries. Such comparative campaign studies will not only help demonstrate similarities and/or differences of campaigns in different countries but, more important, also contribute to our understanding of the functions of cultures in operating communication campaigns by making culture a salient factor.

Also revealed by this review is the dearth of researchers' efforts in generating theories of Chinese communication campaigns, although there was apparent interest in Chinese campaign ideologies and theoretical foundations. This shortage of Chinese campaign theories, however, may be attributable to (1) campaign researchers' pragmatic orientation toward problem solving and campaign strategy focus and (2) their foci on communist political ideologies, principles, and/or guidelines reflected in such orthodox thinking as Mao Zedong thought.

For purposes of advancing our knowledge of Chinese communication campaigns, future research on Chinese campaigns would benefit from focusing on the roles played by Chinese culture in the operations of Chinese communication campaigns. It would be important and worthwhile for researchers to develop longitudinal studies on Chinese campaigns in order to assess both the long- and the short-term effects of campaigns in the PRC. Moreover, of particular value to the advancement of Chinese campaign studies are the search for an indigenous conceptualization of campaigns and of the running of campaigns in China.

CONCLUSION

This review, from a historical perspective, provides a general overview of studies on Chinese communication campaigns. Various dimensions and different aspects of important research on campaigns in the PRC are carefully examined. Emphases have been placed on evaluating research findings as well as on understanding their implications for the benefit of advancing research on Chinese communication campaigns.

During the latter half of the twentieth century, particularly since the founding of the PRC, the Mainland Chinese were utilizing communication campaigns as the most effective vehicle for achieving their goals in socialist revolution and construction. Campaigning has subsequently become such an established institution in the PRC that an adequate understanding of the Chinese cannot possibly be reached without first acquiring the knowledge on how the Chinese run their communication campaigns. Research on Chinese communication campaigns started with a pragmatic orientation to better understand the Chinese and their government in the PRC. Foci of campaign researchers have thus been placed on (1) the theoretical and ideological foundations of Chinese communication campaigns; (2) campaign organization, processes, strategies, and campaign effects; and (3) the utility of Chinese communication campaigns worldwide.

Although past research on Chinese communication campaigns has been insightful and informative in aiding the world to gain a better understanding of the theoretical foundations and the practical functions of campaigns run in the PRC, Chinese communication campaign research is faced with significant challenges before knowledge in this area can advance further. Major challenges include but are by no means limited to (1) examining the impacts and influences of Chinese culture on the operation of Chinese campaigns, (2) investigating and discovering indigenous Chinese campaign concepts, (3) measuring campaign effects in the PRC more accurately with internal and external validity, (4) conducting comparative campaign studies grounded in indigenous cultures and traditions, and (5) generating theories for Chinese communication campaigns. Successfully facing these challenges in Chinese campaign research remains as part of a significant research agenda for students and scholars of Chinese communication campaigns.

NOTES

1. The late chairman of the Chinese Communist Party, Mao Zedong, believed that there are basically two types of contradictions in the PRC: those among its people and those among

the Chinese people and their enemies (c.f. Wang & Wu, 1997-98). While contradictions among the Chinese people are grouped as non-antagonistic, those between the people and their enemies are defined as antagonistic contradictions.

2. To magnify the importance of Chinese communication campaigns in the course of the Chinese revolution, Charles P. Cell named his book on Chinese campaigns *Revolution at Work: Mobilization Campaigns in China.*

3. The official phrase for the two criteria is "being both red and knowledgeable." Being red means the person must be politically reliable. For instance, he or she must be a member of the CCP and/or an enthusiast of the campaign who supports the policies and/or programs being implemented by the campaign (see Liu, 1981; and Wang, 1989, for more details on the selection of campaign activists/agents).

4. After the death of Mao Zedong in 1976, when Deng Xiaoping finally smashed the "Gang of Four" and reassumed his leadership of the CCP, he called on the CCP to cease launching large-scale national campaigns and for the nation to concentrate its efforts on realization of "four modernizations" of the country. Quite paradoxically though, Deng was later accredited as the general architect of the "four modernizations" program (Lu, 1999). To many, this "four modernizaitons program" is in essence an economic construction campaign modeled similarly to those run in the Mao era.

REFERENCES

Backer, T., Rogers, E., & Sopory, P. (1990). *Impact of organizations on mass media health behavior campaigns* (final report). Los Angeles: Human Interaction Research Institute.

Bennett, G. (1976). *Yundong: Mass campaigns in Chinese communist leadership.* Berkeley, CA: Center for Chinese Studies.

Bishop, R. (1989). *Qi Lai! Mobilizing one billion Chinese: The Chinese communication system.* Ames: Iowa State University Press.

Cell, C. (1977). *Revolution at work: Mobilization campaigns in China.* New York: Academic Press.

Chen, P. (1979). China's birth control action programme, 1956-1964. *Population Studies, 14,* 141-158.

Howkins, J. (1982). *Mass communication in China.* New York and London: Longman.

Huang, S. (1996). *To rebel is justified: A rhetorical study of China's cultural revolution movement 1966-1969.* Lanham, MD: University Press of America.

Huang, Y. (1967). *Birth control in communist China.* Kowloon, Hong Kong: Union Research Institute.

Lewis, J. (1963). *Leadership in communist China.* Ithaca, NY: Cornell University Press.

Lewis, J. (1968). Leader, commissar and bureaucrat: The Chinese political system in the last days of the revolution. In P. Ho & T. Tang (Eds.), *China in crisis* (pp. 449-481). Chicago: University of Chicago Press.

Liu, A. (1971). *Communications and national integration in communist China.* Berkeley: University of California Press.

Liu, A. (1981). Mass campaigns in the People's Republic of China. In R. Rice & W. Paisley (Eds.), *Public communication campaigns* (pp. 199-223). Beverly Hills, CA: Sage.

Lu, X. (1999). An ideological/cultural analysis of political slogans in communist China. *Discourse & Society, 10* (4 October), 487-508.

Maitland, C. (1998). Global diffusion of interactive networks: The impact of culture. *The Electronic Journal of Communication, 8* (3 & 4). (File: Maitland V8N 398).

Mao, T. (1967). *Selected works of Mao Tse-Tung* (vols. I-IV). Peking: Foreign Languages Press.

Mao, T. (1968). *Quotations from Chairman Mao Tse-tung.* Peking: Foreign Languages Press.

Paisley, W. (1981). Public communication campaigns: The American experience. In R. Rice & W. Paisley (Eds.), *Public communication campaigns* (pp. 15-40). Beverly Hills, CA: Sage.

Rice, R., & Paisley, W. (1981). (Eds.). *Public communication campaigns.* Beverly Hills, CA: Sage.

Rice, R., & Atkin, C. (1989). (Eds.). *Public communication campaigns* (2nd ed.). Newbury Park, CA: Sage.

Rogers, E. (1973). *Communication strategies for family planning.* New York: Free Press.

Rogers, E., & Storey, D. (1987). Communication campaigns. In C. Berger & S. Chaffee (Eds.), *Handbook of communication science* (pp. 817-846). Newbury Park, CA: Sage.

Salmon, C. (1989). *Information campaigns: Balancing social values and social change.* Newbury Park, CA: Sage.

Schurmann, F. (1968). *Ideology and organization in communist China.* Berkeley: University of California Press.

Starr, J. (1973). *Ideology and culture: An introduction to the dialectic of contemporary Chinese politics.* New York: Harper & Row Publishers.

Taplin, S. (1981). Family planning communication campaigns. In R. Rice & W. Paisley (Eds.), *Public communication campaigns* (pp. 127-142). Beverly Hills, CA: Sage.

Teiwes, F. (1971). *Rectification campaigns and purges in communist China.* Unpublished doctoral dissertation, Columbia University, New York.

Townsend, J. (1967). *Political participation in Communist China.* Berkeley: University of California Press.

Wang, J. (1989). *Communicating the policy of "one child per family" in Shanghai: An analysis of the family planning groups' communication strategies* Unpublished doctoral dissertation. Northwestern University, Evanston, IL.

Wang, J. (1994). Campaign agents' communication competence and the success of a family planning campaign: A case study. *World Communication, 23(2),* 68-76.

Wang, J. (1997, Nov.). *The impact of culture upon communication campaigns: A comparative study of American and Chinese communication campaigns.* Paper presented at the International Conference of East-West Communication, Hong Kong, the PRC.

Wang, J., & Wu, W. (1997-98). "Ideological work" as conflict management: A dialectical approach in Chinese communication campaign. *Intercultural Communication Studies, 7*(1), 83-100.

Whyte, M. (1974). *Small groups and political rituals in China.* Berkeley: University of California Press.

Yin, J. (1998). Selling to the middle kingdom: Culture is the key. *Asian Journal of Communication, 8* (2), 41-69.

Yu, F. (1964). *Mass persuasion in communist China.* New York: Praeger.

Yu, F. (1967). Campaigns, communication and development in communist China. In D. Lerner & W. Schramm (Eds.), *Communication and change in developing countries* (pp. 195-215). Honolulu: East-West Center.

9

Balancing Ideals and Interests: Toward a Chinese Perspective of Development Communication

Yanru Chen

PRELUDE: OLD CONCEPTS TAKE ON NEW MEANING IN CHINA

It has been nearly four decades since American historian Daniel Boorstin (1961) set forth his famous dichotomy of "ideal versus image," that is, that the Graphic Revolution brought about by television had led Americans gradually to think in terms of images rather than ideals. It then followed that the once-glorious "American dream" had become an "American illusion." Yet today's mass communication industry in China has precisely just entered the era of "images" and "interests" (referring to both audience tastes and media financial profits), in contrast to "ideals" such as socialism, collectivism, patriotism, and heroism consistently and persistently promoted by the state government. In fact, whether or not the mass media in China, the main producer of culture, should be regarded as an industry or should be "industrialized" has been an issue much debated among academic experts, government officials, and media practitioners since 1999 (*Chinese Cultural Press*, November 11, 1999). The best solution suggested was for the media content to satisfy both "customers (audiences) and cadres (government officials)." Chang and Chen (1999) go a step further to conceptualize the Chinese media as being in a position "between the market and the state." Here we see that Western and Chinese views of current Chinese mass communication converge at one point—in striving to balance between "ideals" and "interests." This is an apparent gap in the existing research in both development communication and Chinese communication.

DEVELOPMENT COMMUNICATION: WHY THE CHINESE GAP?

In the half century or so of scholarship in development communication, a branch of communication studies that has grown since the end of World War II, China has somehow eluded the focused attention of Western scholars. Western scholars have by and large not examined the interplay between communication and development in China in the same way that they studied it in other developing countries (the classic example being Schramm, 1964). Of many possible reasons, two seem to stand out. During the decades when development communication witnessed swift development in both scholarship and practice, China was closed against most of the developed world and labeled itself one of the leading nations of the Socialist Bloc. Scholars studying China at the time treated it as a Communist country such as the former Soviet Union and East European countries, not as a developing country by Western definitions. The second reason is that although in the recent years of economic reform China began to identify itself as the largest developing nation in the world, most experts with Western training who specialize in China still examine mass communication phenomena in this country within the traditional Western propaganda model. Conspicuously missing from the scholarship in development communication is a model truly based on current China that is open to modification as development unfolds in China. The result of efforts to build such a model will not only be meaningful to Chinese communication research but also contribute to the larger field of development communication.

This chapter draws upon Western and Chinese concepts of development and development communication, research findings in Chinese communication, and recent empirical cases in China's market economy era to shed light on the new perspective that reflects on the area of "culture, development, and communication in China." A chief argument underpinning this chapter is that China fits only into the unique model of socioeconomic development "with Chinese characteristics" as proposed by the late paramount leader Deng Xiaoping and upheld by the current party and state leaders. The newest challenge to China as well as to development communication is the task of reconciling, if possible, the two seemingly opposing ends embodied in the oxymoron of a "socialist market economy." A market economy drives individuals and institutions, including the mass media, toward personal (or institutional) and short-term pursuits of *interests* that often oppose the greater *ideals* of national development and social equality. In the presence of such strong forces that seem to run against the principles of socialism, the Chinese government must continue to uphold the socialist ideology that is the basis of its legitimacy.

Indeed, China is undertaking an unprecedented transition in its economic structure from a Stalinist, planned model to a socialist market economy model. This means that Chinese society is undergoing an unprecedented transformation. According to a synthesis of development theories, economic growth and development ought to be accompanied by corresponding structural changes. To ensure optimal development, the two types of changes must be compatible. From the modernization model that prevailed in the 1950s and 1960s to the ensuing dependency model to the world-system model (Mowlana, 1990), theories of development have come a long way. However, no matter how swiftly such theories may evolve, they are still outpaced by China's startling changes in the last two decades. Recently, a Chinese scholar (Chen, 1999) reviewed the various models of modernization (a concept not to be equated with development) and observed that there are four modernization models.

The first model is the North-American–European model, exemplified in the cases of the United States and Western Europe, including the British Commonwealth, a model characterized by laissez-faire economic policy. The second is the Germany-Japan-South Korea model, which emphasizes government intervention in basically privatized economies; its exemplary countries have experienced a relatively shorter period of the "modernization birth pain." The third is the Stalinist model adopted by the former Soviet Union and its followers in the socialist bloc during the decades preceding the 1990s. Its rigidity in planning and inflexibility in structure have proved to be major hindrances to bona fide modernization. The fourth is usually called the "mixed model," mostly followed by the Latin American countries until the recent past, which was marked by a high economic growth rate coupled with great disparity between the rich and the poor, the urban centers and the rural areas. On the whole, the third and fourth models are gradually phasing out from the world scene.

It may not be fruitful to debate what model could fit China—China's development provides a model in its own right, which, combined with communication, is the central concern of this chapter. But it is worth mentioning that for the first three decades following the founding of the People's Republic in 1949, China attempted to follow the Soviet model of development. But the process was disrupted by the Cultural Revolution (1966-1976), a clash between ideal and reality, an overzealous ideal having pushed reality too fast, and hence reality shifted further and further away from the ideal until the two became irreconcilable.

Before moving on to the topic of development communication, it is necessary to clarify a few concepts. First of all, economic growth does not necessarily mean economic development, the latter encompassing structural changes. Second, economic development does not necessarily mean social development, let alone social progress. In other words, growth is not equated with development and development with, progress. It is the greatest temptation for those studying one or another aspect of development or development communication to confuse these concepts. Third, development is not equated with modernization, the latter often being mistaken for Westernization—modernization seen from a Western perspective.

How do we define development, then? Taking an eclectic approach and synthesizing across a wide range of definitions (e.g., summaries in Goulet, 1971; Mowlana, 1990; Schramm, 1964), the author of this chapter attempts to put forth the following definition:

Development is the process through which a nation's human resources are optimally mobilized to maximize constructive use of material resources and symbolic resources, leading to a state of individual and collective material and spiritual being that affords optimal opportunity for the fulfillment of personal potential and personality.

Then what is development communication? It becomes clear and easy if we define it in terms of its main task: *Development communication is the process of mobilizing a nation's symbolic resources and human resources to attain to the ideal of development.* To experts, it may be evident that this definition is an effort to transcend and depoliticize the "socioeconomic-political" type of boundaries within which preceding scholars used to operate when dealing with the thorny concepts of development and development communication. Also, the currently proposed definitions show that development and development communication are closely intertwined, serving each other.

It is time to return to the questions and challenges that gave rise to this chapter. How does development communication play its role in current China in the face of challenges from the conflict between China's professed *ideal* of development, that is, shared prosperity, and the conflicting *interests* of different participants in developments, between whom there is a widening gap between poverty and prosperity? This is a question confronting not only communication scholars and the Chinese propaganda apparatus but also the Chinese government. Hence it is justified to say that this study is both empirically and theoretically grounded.

Classic studies include research on the role of communication in China's radical social change between 1949 and 1976 (Chu, 1977), propaganda campaigns during the same period (Cell, 1977), mass mobilization such as the propagation of the family planning policy (Bishop, 1989), the history of China's media (Chang, 1989), and the interplay between communications and national integration in China between 1949 and 1970 (Liu, 1971). It should be noted that culture as a factor is to an increasing extent figuring into the interwoven processes of communication and development and will be duly touched upon in this chapter. The cultural factor is significant in Chinese development and communication because the Chinese cultural and philosophical tradition has always emphasized the potential conflict and possible reconciliation between *yi* (righteousness and justice) and *li* (interests). This pair of concepts can be translated into the tension between "ideals" and "interests" in contemporary China.

The 1990s witnessed drastic changes in China's social structure, including the communication apparatus, affording the maturing overseas community of Chinese communication researchers greater opportunity for substantive research. The chunk of literature on Chinese communication produced in the 1990s focuses on a number of areas pertinent to the problems and issues that have arisen during China's modernization drive. Chan (1993, 1994, 1995) explores the tension between government control of the media through the implementation of party ideology and the increasing media independence that accompanies commercialization of the Chinese media industry. This is an inevitable issue that emerges from a burgeoning market economic system. Writings on the role of communication in China's development process are really scanty, mainly including the works of Chen (1991a, 1991b) and Shi and Zhang (1991), which are mostly reviews rather than in-depth empirical analyses.

With the development of satellite TV and the Internet, some researchers focus on one or another aspect of the issue of regulating China's expanding new media technology (e.g., Hao, 2000; Hong, 1998; Lee, 1998; Tan, 1998; Ure, 1998). Advertising and consumerism, by-products of a market economy, have also attracted some scholars' attention (Wang, 1996, 1997a, 1997b, 2000; Wei & Pan, 1999).

Relatively scanty is research in several topic areas. The first, "thought work," which is part of propaganda work targeted at transforming the norms and values of the masses so that they will comply to the demands of the national development plan, has only recently been touched upon (Lynch, 1999). Ng (1998, 1998/1999) elaborates on the influence of traditional Chinese cultural values on current patterns of persuasion. Another noteworthy area that has not received sufficient attention is the role of the mass media in communication campaigns such as the bid for year 2000 Olympics (Chen, 1998b). Speaking of campaigns, an almost forgotten practice in communication campaigns in China is the making of national role models (moral exemplars), who are exalted through the media for the masses to emulate. Chen (1999b) provides an interesting look into the process of making three national role models through the media during the market economy era. She observes that the media now played a greater role in the making of models, while in the pre-reform era who should become a role model depended more on the state leaders' will.

A look at the existing research reveals that the studies are more or less done at a *micro* level of analysis, dealing more with specific problems, tensions, and challenges than the efforts made by the Chinese government, the media, and the public in combating these issues. In addition, the explanations offered by both Western scholars and overseas Chinese scholars for the communications phenomenon in current China are not Chinese but rather Western.

This summary brings the discussion back to where it started: Is there any possibility and plausibility for building a Chinese perspective of communication that might have greater power in explaining the continuous changes in China?

As was said earlier, China is in every way a developing country, and the Chinese government consistently and persistently professes and practices the belief that communication must serve national development (Jiang, 2000). Therefore, it is imperative to take a quick glance at some major issues in Chinese development communication that might serve as building blocks for our new perspective.

CHINESE DEVELOPMENT COMMUNICATION: CHALLENGES AND RESEARCH AGENDA

There is a lack of theoretically informed and empirically grounded research on the relationship between communication and national development in current China. The year 1992 is usually considered the watershed year marking the official sanction of accelerated expansion of the market economy nationwide, following the promulgation of "socialism with Chinese characteristics" as the party's guiding ideology. It seems that most scholars have neglected a vitally important fact: The Chinese media are by and large in the grip of the party and the state, and hence it is both relevant and imperative to examine the *guided functions* of mass communication in the process of national development. The results of such research may well provide useful lessons for other developing nations.

The author ventures to further clarify the definition of development communication suggested in earlier sections of the chapter. It can be conceptualized as a process of activating a nation's *symbolic resources* through the media and other communication channels to mobilize the nation's *human resources* in order to maximize the constructive use of *material resources* and in turn to achieve the ultimate goal of development—the emancipation and fulfillment of each individual human being and the preservation and strengthening of the whole nation. Here questions may be directed to the definition of symbolic resources. Broadly speaking, symbolic resources are mainly products of two types of interactions—interaction between human beings and their material environment and interaction between human beings. Cultural anthropologists may twist the wording and offer the alternative term "culture."

Learning from the late Wilbur Schramm's simplistic style of reasoning on media effects, we may try to give a simpler example here to illustrate the point. Mount Everest is the highest mountain peak in the world, located in the China-Nepal borderlands. When it stands there all by itself, it is not part of China's symbolic resources. But after Chinese athletes have ascended to the peak, their action of conquest becomes part of the nation's symbolic resources, signifying national strength and pride. Every nation possesses such or other symbolic resources. But does every nation realize its potential power to mobilize the masses? The answer may require a global study. However, we can say with assurance about the Chinese case that the Chinese government, media, and educators have become increasingly aware of the power of symbolic resources. Chen (1998b; 1999a) documents such evidence in her studies of communication campaigns in China such as Beijing's bid for the year 2000 Olympics, which invoked much of China's symbolic resources to create a most presentable image of the nation and arouse a sense of national pride among the population.

Since the early 1990s, China has been confronted with the failures and problems in many other socialist countries, and the Chinese government has been calling upon the propaganda apparatus, especially the media, to invoke the nation's historical and cultural heritage to cultivate among the masses a spirit of patriotism, collectivism, and socialism (Chen, 1999a; 1999b). How might this be done most effectively? This is a pressing question to be addressed by concerned scholars.

The preceding are some issues in current Chinese communication identified by other scholars. Combining these issues with China's current reality of interplay between communication, development, and culture, this chapter attempts to abstract from them several "larger" dichotomies that might serve as main references for researching Chinese communication in the Reform Era. As the author understands it from China's empirical cases of development communication, such dichotomies require a balance on the part of development communication planners and the media to balance between each pair of factors.

The first balance required is that between *preserving cultural tradition* and *promoting economic modernization*. The conflict between these two parallel processes manifests itself through the media. The Chinese government explicitly expects the media to help with both tasks, which seem compelling in the most recently proposed and planned "development of the Chinese west." The Chinese Midwest, which has been charted by the Central Government to include ten provinces and one city directly under the Central Government, has bounteous cultural heritage (potential symbolic resources) combined with a relatively underdeveloped economy. There is a great gap between living conditions in the populous coastal provinces in eastern China and those in the western inland provinces. The media have been reporting that the norms and values of the population in the Chinese west are yet to be changed to facilitate economic change.

A dilemma confronts the media: If they magnify the rich traditions of folk cultures in the western provinces, which inevitably embody certain important values guiding lifestyles and thought patterns, such messages may unwittingly sanction the cultural status quo in this economically backward region and hinder change. If the media emphasize the necessity for all-round changes from values to lifestyles to economic structure, the distinct and unique characteristics of the western cultural tradition are likely to be submerged in the current of change and may no longer be powerful symbolic resources to distinguish this region's identity.

Perhaps one solution is to replay the age-old trick of tapping the western cultural tradition as symbolic resources and simply attempt to utilize these very resources to mobilize change. However, that attempt may be utopian, because experience in other developing countries has indicated that unless there is an overall change in the entire cultural milieu, the spiritual universe in which a people live, economic growth, though possible, may not bring about a balanced social development (Zhang, 1992). The classic issue of tradition versus modernization is presenting itself to the Chinese media today as it did to many other developing nations. Maybe future research in Chinese communication should look into the successes and failures in other countries in this regard so that China might learn from their cases.

The second requirement for balance is that between *promoting the socialist ideal* and *facilitating the implementation of a market economy policy*. As this chapter makes clear from the beginning, Marxist-Leninist-Mao (Zedong)-Deng (Xiaoping) ideals for socialism are the basis of the Chinese government's legitimacy; that is, as long as the Chinese Communist Party (CCP) is governing China, its guiding ideology has to be socialism. Yet precisely in order to rescue the socialism that had reached the brink of collapse shortly before the Reform Era began in 1978, the market economy has to be the dominant policy governing the national life—not only economic life, but also cultural production and consumption. This implies the infiltration of capitalist culture imported mainly through the media from the Western developed nations. With the rapid growth and expansion of the Internet, a larger segment of the urban youth population will before long be further exposed to Western ideologies that may seem more conveniently compatible with the intensive competition in a market economy.

The prospect that China may soon join the World Trade Organization (WTO) will only compound the situation. There is limited room for optimism in this sphere, for the media are facing the mammoth task of reconciling the cognitively dissonant ideal and policy. However, the current picture is not all that gloomy. The anti-corruption campaign spearheaded by the media and formally launched by the party in the last two or three years is an effort at reducing the spiritual detriment of the loopholes in an immature market economy. Undoubtedly, in the foreseeable future China will gradually perfect its legal system as well as its organizational channels of regulation and social control. Until then, the media, such as China Central Television (CCTV), which is best known for its main program "Topic in Focus," will continue to wield great power as a Chinese-style watchdog of the government. The General Bureau of Radio, TV, and Film under the State Council has persisted in exercising control over the overall planning of TV drama production and important news programs. At least the prime time slots in CCTV's Channel One are always filled with news and entertainment programs that magnify the "keynote" of promoting "socialist spiritual civilization," including government-endorsed mainstream values and behaviors that are theoretically compatible with the socialist ideal. Interestingly, though, some programs in between straight news and entertainment, such as TV dramas, while promoting the endorsed values, always set their story plots against the backdrop of the whirlwind of change in social life under the market economy policy (Chen, 1998; Chen & Hao, 1997). Can we call such juxtaposition a "balance"?

The third requirement for balance is that between *protecting China's national cultural identity* and *promoting adaptation to the globalization of the economy*. Admit it or not, China is currently a socialist *country* in a capitalist international *market*. Like it or not, globalization is not only penetrating the economic sphere but also threatening the cultural boundaries of many nations, especially the developing nations, which have more to lose than to gain from globalization. The expansion of the Internet and its pervasiveness in the urban centers of developing countries have been duly observed by concerned scholars. But more in-depth studies with breadth are also needed to forecast the greater influence of Western cultural values on the people of developing countries through the Internet. Some optimists have labeled the Internet "the place where the globe meets." But reversing the lyrics of a favorite childhood song, the author of this chapter would counter that it is simply not true that "the more we get together, the happier we will be."

What about intercultural conflicts rooted in cultural differences? China experts in this area of research may start paying more attention to problems of intercultural communication on the Internet. However, one trend is certain and pervasive enough to alarm us: There is an imbalance between Americans' knowledge of China and the Chinese knowledge of America. There are numerous McDonalds and KFCs in China, together with American movies and TV programs and stories of American sports stars. The language barrier in Internet communication and the predominant use of English only aggravate the situation. The knowledge about American culture that an average Chinese youth acquires may not necessarily condition his or her heart/mind positively and may well erode the Chinese cultural values that the government, the school, the media, and the family strive to inculcate in him or her.

But to shift our angle of thinking: Should China stop or prevent the expansion of the Internet and other media connections with the outside world on the grounds that they may carry and convey negative influences? The answer is apparently no. In order to survive in a global market still dominated by developed capitalist countries, China simply has to continue promoting the policy of "opening up" the country to the outside world, mainly through the media and interpersonal exchanges. The young generation of Chinese will grow up in the age of the Internet, and they may get to know Michael Jordan and become his admirers before they learn to admire China's own national heroes. This reality may well prove the greatest challenge to the Chinese media as well as educators. The national news and entertainment media, which jointly launched a Patriotic Education Campaign in the early 1990s to remind the Chinese youth "we are Chinese," will surely have a role to play in combating negative cultural influences through the Internet and other mass media. But meanwhile the media have to continue to gear up the Chinese population to be "global-minded."

A most recent example of China's success in the twenty-seventh Olympic Games in Sydney, Australia, illustrates such a mixture of assertion of national identity with a sense of being a member of the international community. The Chinese media gave saturation coverage to the processes of contest, conquest, and coronation of the Chinese athletes, with lengthy commentaries on the significance of their accomplishments to China's national pride and nation building. This may be seen as a feasible way of balancing between cultivating the sense of "being Chinese" and promoting participation in international competition—so that China can assert itself as a strong nation among the world of nations.

The fourth requirement for balance is that between *projecting a positive, encouraging image of the society/population, promoting a shared ideal*, and *maintaining objective representation of China's social reality*. The ideal of reform is better social equality on the basis of shared prosperity. Yet the gap between the rich and the poor is ever widening as economic reform deepens. It is a well-known fact that in the year 1999 alone more than 12 million workers were laid off by their large or medium-size state-owned enterprises, which are going through the throes of structural reform and market adaptation. Strategically, it was simply a must to render so many once-dedicated workers jobless. How should the media handle this delicate issue of unemployment, which is a reality, and yet seems to run against the long-term ideal of socialism, that is, shared prosperity and equal opportunity for personal fulfillment for everyone? The image of the "unemployed worker" in CCTV's 1999 Chinese New Year's Eve show was a highly positive and optimistic one, full of understanding and willingness to identify with the state's greater ideal at the cost of individual interests (Dai, 1999).

In fact, to the observant eye, the national media contents are replete with similar images. This is only one example. In February-March 2000, CCTV Channel One gave its prime time slot to a TV drama serial, "The Making of a Hero," adapted from a classic novel by an author of the former Soviet Union and featuring the themes of heroism, collectivism, patriotism, and socialism. Immediately, the national media released report upon report on how enthusiastically different generations of the Chinese population welcomed this program, and many audience members were shown expressing their appreciation of and identification with the emotional image and spiritual world of the hero. Underlying the promotion was a latent message. No matter what harsh reality we face and no matter how many setbacks we encounter in our socialist reform and reconstruction, we ought to be determined in our faith in the socialist ideal and persist in performing our duties as an act of loyalty to our nation. If this was what the audience "read" out of the TV drama, its heroic image had fulfilled the function of conveying an ideal as a possible weapon with which to combat the harsh reality facing many Chinese people today.

Here we might say with caution that perhaps Daniel Boorstin's (1961) dichotomy of ideal versus image was a bit too extreme, for, after all, the modern media are powerful and handy enough to be employed to transmit ideals through images. Of course, the issue is whether the audience consumes the image alone or with the ideal.

Idealism is a necessity, if not a last resort, in the presence of highly unsatisfactory realities. A society going through economic reform and cultural change cannot be too satisfying to many of its members, and under such circumstances a unifying ideal is a good aid in mobilizing the people to work for a common goal, which certainly includes their own interests in the long run. Here is where the media have a major role to play in what can be called "development communication." The importance of fostering a strong sense of a shared ideal among the people has been repeatedly emphasized by state leaders, academic experts/theoreticians, and the media (see *Guangming Daily* Tuesday editions for the year 2000). The ideal cannot be created out of nothing. It has to be based on China's symbolic resources and has to be a "realistic ideal." Such an ideal can render the reporting of "reality" somewhat "idealistic." That is the delicate art of striking a balance between media-made image, government-endorsed ideal, and social reality.

Having thus disposed of the major dilemmas challenging the media in Chinese development communication today, we are still not fully assured that such balancing acrobatics will succeed. However, the specified areas of interest can become major areas of research for scholars in Chinese communication. Systematic content analyses that reflect upon the relationship between the media and social change may shed light on one or all of these areas. Longitudinal or cross-sequential surveys of the correlation between people's values and media content can further clarify our confusion as to what impact the mass media can have on the Chinese audience today. Whether or not the impact of Western cultural values spread through the media is offsetting the positive values promoted by the Chinese state is another problem area that calls for empirical research. A looking-glass should also be inserted into the newsroom of the Chinese media and the TV program production studio to unveil what structure lies behind the image-making and ideal-manufacturing business. In succinct words, "macro" and "in-depth" studies should be the order of the day. To achieve these ends in Chinese communication research, some initial theorization may be necessary.

TOWARD A CHINESE PERSPECTIVE OF DEVELOPMENT COMMUNICATION

If we still follow the tradition of mainstream literature on development communication, the role and function of the media should be our primary concern with Chinese development communication today. However, the social and cultural milieu in which the Chinese media function has drastically changed. We have to accept the fact that cultural *pluralism* is becoming a new reality paralleling China's economic development. As a social trend as well as a social ideal, pluralism has been advocated in some Western countries at one time or another. Yet a larger segment of the Chinese population had been previously conditioned to accepting "one view and one voice"—the view and voice of the central authority. Chinese people have to understand that it only befits human nature to pursue pluralism, apart from political or ideological considerations.

One thing is certain: The Chinese media are no longer *mere* propaganda machines or robots. Although the media are still under the leadership of the CCP and owned by the government, the latter no longer imposes ideologies upon the population through the media. Rather, the media strive to balance between the market and the state, the market being the media's main source of financial support. There are cases of exception, of course. The propaganda campaign against the Falungong Movement was launched in July 1999 and has been carried on right into the twenty-first century. Practically all the news media around the country are running reports and comments that are in tune with the party's definition of the case and its development.

The *guidance function* of the media might constitute part of Chinese development communication theory. The function refers to creating a general atmosphere for public opinion to be relatively freely aired, within certain bounds that are not as strict as that in the past.

This function of the media is coupled with two other complementary lines of communication that promise to endure for a long time in the course of development: "thought work" done mainly through organizational channels and the anti-corruption campaign. "Thought work" is an old CCP tradition of seeking to transform or reform people's thinking and in turn to change their behaviors in order to be in line with the ideal and goal of national development. Since early 2000, the state and party leaders have repeatedly emphasized its importance and the need to adapt the work style to meet the demands of people's psychological needs in a changeable and impetuous market economy. Therefore, the national media have identified many examples that illustrate what is successful thought work. It is no longer ideological bombardment, but consists of sincere efforts by thought workers to help the target mass members solve their problems, for example, to help unemployed workers find new jobs and adjust to them (CCTV serial news reports since July 2000 on "Enhance Thought Work"). In other words, thought work, which used to emphasize the indoctrination of *ideals*, is now focusing on awakening the people's sense of interests and the desire to strive for such personal *interests*. Perhaps this is an old principle of communication manifesting itself in China's new situation.

As for the anti-corruption campaign, the media often play the role of watchdogs spearheading public opinion, unearthing cases of corruption and bringing them to the attention of central-government leaders. Several such cases of corruption by high-level cadres have been exposed since the beginning of 2000. President Jiang Zemin has probably realized the gravity of the threat of corruption to the legitimacy of the CCP. He has recently set forth his "three representations theory." He maintains that the CCP should always represent the direction in which advanced production forces work; the CCP should always represent the direction of advanced cultures; the CCP should always represent the interests of the greatest number of the people. These three dimensions coincide with the trichotomy of "material resources, human resources, and symbolic resources" set forth in this chapter and in the author's earlier work (Chen, 1999a). Ever since Jiang presented his "new" perspective on the role of the CCP, the anti-corruption campaign has been intensified, at least in the manner of communication. The media have to face mass discontent with the malfunction of the bureaucracy and yet the reporting focuses on the positive side: how many corrupt officials have received just punishment by the law, and the like (see reports at the cctv.com.cn website). The entertainment media programs featuring anti-corruption events always end with the punishment of the corrupt officials. For example, according to CCTV reports, the film and TV drama "Choice between Life and Death" aired in September 2000 has fanned much public discussion and hope for success in the campaign. In other words, the media, while airing public sentiment against corruption, nonetheless provide and create a *leading opinion* that guides public opinions.

If we accept the fact that the *guidance function* is fulfilled mainly by the news media, the entertainment media (or the entertaining dimension of each medium) are partially responsible for the *cultural diversity* in China today. Under the general guided direction, there is unprecedented freedom of speech by Chinese standards, evidenced by the increase in the number of popular publications of all kinds and the mushrooming of TV variety shows that feature themes undreamed of before by the Chinese audience, such as sexuality and extramarital love. As a result, a great variety of interests are fulfilled.

The preceding is merely the first step toward a Chinese perspective of development communication that does justice to current China. This chapter proposes from the beginning that a new model of Chinese communication be built and offers a few building blocks. The essence of the Chinese media's function is to balance between ideals and interests in a fast-developing economy and fast-changing society where ideals are constantly clashing with interests and where different interests are often clashing with each other under the pretext of advocating different ideals. The catchword for the interplay between Chinese media, culture, and development is "development-guided pluralism in communication." More research to explore and elucidate on this fascinating research program is much anticipated.

REFERENCES

Bishop, R. L. (1989). *Qi Lai: Mobilizing one billion Chinese—The Chinese communication system*. Ames: Iowa State University Press.

Boorstin, D. J. (1961). *The image: A guide to pseudo-events in America*. New York: Vintage Books.

Cell, C. (1977). *Revolution at work: Mobilization campaigns in China*. New York: Academic Press.

Chan, J. M. (1993). Commercialization without independence: Trends and tensions of media development in China. In J. Y. Cheng & M. Brosseau (Eds.), *China Review, 1993* (pp. 25.1-25.21). Hong Kong: The Chinese University Press of Hong Kong.

Chan, J. M. (1994). Media internationalization in China: Processes and tensions. *Journal of Communication, 44*, 70-88.

Chan, J. M. (1995). Calling the tune without paying the piper: The reassertion of media control in China. In C. K. Lo & M. Brosseau (Eds.), *China Review 1995* (pp. 5.1-5.6). Hong Kong: The Chinese University Press of Hong Kong.

Chang, T. K., & Chen, Y. (1999). Between the state and the market: Regulating TV in China. Unpublished paper, a revised version of which was presented to the AEJMC annual convention.

Chang, W. H. (1989). *Mass media in China: The history and the future*. Ames: Iowa State University Press.

Chen, L. (1991a). The door opens to a thousand blossoms: A preliminary study of communication and rural development in China (1979-1988). *Asian Journal of Communication, 1*, 103-121.

Chen, L. (1991b). Culture, politics, communication and development: A tentative study on the case of China. *Gazette, 48*, 1-16.

Chen, T. (1999). *Shehui fazhan lilun moshi yanjiu (Theoretical models of social development)*. Xiamen, China: Xiamen University Press.

Chen, Y. R., & Hao, X. (1997). Conflict resolution in love triangles: Perspectives offered by Chinese TV dramas. *Intercultural Communication Studies, 7*(1),133-148.

Chen, Y. R. (1998a). In search of the essential woman in national development: China's first TV drama series on women, by women, for women. *Journal of Development Communication, 9*(2), 1-17.

Chen, Y. R. (1998b). Setting a nation in action: The media and China's bid for year 2000 Olympics. In D. R. Heisey & W. Gong (Eds.), *Communication and culture: China and the world entering the 21st century* (pp. 289-310). Amsterdam: Editions Rodopi B. V.

Chen, Y. R. (1999a). Reviving the national soul: Communications and national integration in China's market economy era. Doctoral dissertation, Nanyang Technological University, Singapore.

Chen, Y. R. (1999b). Creating a new model, creating a new nation: The media and the making of role models in China's market economy era. *Journal of International Communication, 6* (2), 90-105.

Chu, G. C. (1977). *Radical change through communication in Mao's China.* Honolulu: University of Hawaii Press.

Dai, J. H. (1999). *Yinxing shuxie: Jiushi niandai zhongguo wenhua yanjiu [Invisible scripts: Research in the Chinese culture of the 1990s].* Nanjing: Jiangsu People's Publishing House.

Goulet, D. (1971). *The cruel choice: A new concept in the theory of development.* New York: Atheneum.

Hao, X. (2000). Party dominance vs. cultural imperialism: China's strategies to regulate satellite broadcasting. *Communication Law and Policy, 5,* 155-182.

Hong, J. (1998). China's satellite technology: Developments, policies, and applications. In P. S. N. Lee (Ed.), *Telecommunications and development in China* (pp. 171-199). Cresskill, NJ: Hampton Press, Inc.

Hong, J. (1998). *The internationalization of television in China: The evolution of ideology, society, and media since the reform.* Westport, CT: Praeger.

Jiang, Z. M. (2000). *Speech at the national conference on thought and political work.* Beijing: People's Publishing House.

Lee, P. S. N. (Ed.). (1998). *Telecommunications and development in China.* Cresskill, NJ: Hampton Press.

Liu, A. P. L. (1971). *Communications and national integration in Communist China.* Berkeley: University of California Press.

Lynch, D. C. (1999). Dilemmas of "thought work" in fin-de-siecle China. *China Quarterly,* no. 157, 173-201.

Mowlana, H. (1990). *The passing of modernity: Communication and the transformation of society.* White Plains, New York: Longman.

Ng, R. M. C. (1998). The influence of collectivism-individualism on persuasion in Chinese and American cultures. In D. R. Heisey and W. Gong (Eds.), *Communication and culture: China and the world entering the 21st century* (pp. 71-82). Amsterdam: Editions Rodopi B.V.

Ng, R. M. C. (1998/1999). The influence of Confucianism on Chinese persuasion: The past, the present, and the future. *Human Communication, 2,* 75-86.

Schramm, W. (1964). *Mass media and national development: The role of information in the developing countries.* Stanford, CA: Stanford University Press.

Shi, H., & Zhang, Y. (1991). Communication and development in China. In F. L. Casmir (Ed.), *Communication in development* (pp. 177-197). Norwood, NJ: Ablex.

Tan, Z. (1998). The impact of foreign linkages on telecommunications and development in China. In P. S. N. Lee (Ed.), *Telecommunications and development in China* (pp. 263-280). Cresskill, NJ: Hampton Press, Inc.

Ure, J. (1998). China's telecommunications: Options and opportunities. In P. S. N. Lee (Ed.), *Telecommunications and development in China* (pp. 245-262). Cresskill, NJ: Hampton Press, Inc.

Wang, J. (1996). The siren songs of consumption: An analysis of foreign advertisements in two mainland Chinese newspapers, 1985-1993. *Gazette, 56,* 201- 219.

Wang, J. (1997a). From four hundred million to more than one billion consumers: A brief history of the foreign advertising industry in China. *International Journal of Advertising, 16,* 241-260.

Wang, J. (1997b). Through the looking-glass of foreign ads in China. *Asian Journal of Communication, 17,* 19-42.

Wang, J. (2000). *Foreign advertising in China: Becoming global, becoming local.* Ames: Iowa State University Press.

Wei, R. & Pan, Z. (1999). Mass media and consumerist values in the People's Republic of China. *International Journal of Public Opinion Research, 11*, 75-96.

Yu, F. T. C. (1963). *Mass persuasion in Communist China*. London & Dunmow: Pall Mall Press.

10

Chinese Health Communication in the Old and New Millennia

Mei-ling Wang

At the close of the last millennium, the Western medical community began to take an interest in the Chinese ethnomedical system. *The Journal of the American Medical Association* published a special issue in 1997 that offered empirical confirmation of the effectiveness of some Chinese medical treatments. In November 1997, the National Institutes of Health formally recommended acupuncture for treating various health problems such as headaches, pain, and post-chemotherapy complications. Despite the proven effectiveness of some Chinese ethnomedical methods in the treatment of some chronic illnesses, the philosophy behind these methods can be esoteric to foreigners (Morse, 1978).

In fact, the Chinese ethnomedical system has a long history of application. The Chinese ethnomedical system evolved in the course of four thousand years of Chinese history and was based on clinical observations of major illnesses and diseases. The system subscribes to a set of assumptions that emphasize the concept of "holistic well-being," in humans' interaction with the natural, spiritual, and social worlds. Overall, the Chinese ethnomedical system is grounded in the philosophy that one's well-being is intricately linked to one's communication behavior at intrapersonal, interpersonal, and social levels. Therefore, the Chinese ethnomedical system was not just an archaic set of beliefs suitable only for anthropological studies but a complex health system that has been closely related to Chinese social communication behavior for more than four millennia.

The purpose of this chapter is, first, to provide a detailed account of earlier Chinese health communication research by surveying the major assumptions and theories underlying the Chinese ethnomedical system and, second, to articulate the impact that this research tradition is likely to exert on health communication research in the West. In the end, this chapter attempts to illustrate the idea that how individuals interpret their health status and the course of treatment they pursue reveals important information about human communication behavior in their social life. When the intercultural dynamics between the Occident and Orient increase in the medical field because of the common desire to improve human health, research on Chinese health communication is likely to offer some solutions to this intercultural challenge of healing.

CHINESE ETHNOMEDICAL SYSTEM: A SYNOPSIS

While the Western medical system sees the immediate causes as the origins of disease/illness, the Chinese medical system looks for underlying and ultimate causes as the major explanations for sickness (Ho & Lisowski, 1997; Bowers & Purcell, 1974; Hugard & Wong, 1968; Kaptchuk, 1983). In Chinese ethnomedical theory, illness is explained in concepts similar to those in Western humoral pathology, which was developed into an elaborate medical theory under Hippocrates. According to humoral pathology, the body has four liquids–humors: blood, phlegm, yellow bile, and black bile—and good health results from the balance of humors in the body (Foster & Anderson, 1978). Yet, the Chinese concept of balance of humors is very different from the Western idea of chemical or biochemical balance. In the Chinese view, the concept of balance seeks the balance between coldness and hotness and between moistness and dryness, and balance is also about neutralizing the toxic levels of various foods and balancing all emotional experiences. That is why Chinese medicine practitioners place an emphasis on the flow of qi (the energy flow in the body) (Maduro, 1983; Mitchell, 1983; Muecke, 1983). Physical discomfort is believed to be caused by an imbalance of qi, which can be cured by such corrective measures as acupuncture or coining. When it comes to remedies, the Western system resorts mostly to synthetic chemicals as medicine, but the Chinese approach tends to rely on herbs as measures releasing tensions in the body and the work of the mind (Maduro, 1983; Mitchell, 1983; Muecke, 1983).

HISTORY OF CHINESE ETHNOMEDICAL SYSTEM

The history of Chinese ethnomedical system is a history of discovery of the workings of nature in relation to the metaphysical and physical aspects of human existence (Bowers & Purcell, 1974; Ho & Lisowski, 1997; Hugard

& Wong, 1968; Kaptchuk, 1983; Lampton, 1974; Liu, 1988; Lu, 1991; Maciocia, 1994; McNamara, 1996; Meng & Zhou, 1999; Morse, 1978; Said, 1981; Wong & Wu, 1936; Yang & Li, 1993). Archaeological evidence shows that the Chinese appeared in the northern part of China nearly a million years ago. Deriving from their empirical observation, the Chinese came up with a set of rules and beliefs regulating diet and social relations, which became the philosophical underpinnings of the Chinese ethnomedical system. Chinese written language came into existence sometime between the twenty-first century B.C. and 476 B.C., which facilitated in no small way the documentation of their healing experience. Sporadic documentation of Chinese medical knowledge was discovered from writings on turtle shells (Meng & Zhou, 1998). For example, *The Classic of Mountain and Sea* recorded methods of health promotion and illness prevention. *The Book of Rites* published in the Zhou Dynasty (1122-255 B.C.) included more listings of medicinal plants in its medical repertoire. Herbs were formally classified into grass, trees, worms, stone, and cereals. With the publication of *Nei jing* (Yellow Emperor's classics of internal medicine), written by a group of physicians during the Feudal Period (618 B.C. to 476 B.C.), the Chinese healing methods began to be integrated into a more organized system of knowledge (Wong & Wu, 1936). It includes 162 chapters of discussions of anatomy, physiology, pathology, diagnostics, therapeutics, and health prevention. The many clinical observations and proposed solutions in *Nei jing* became the major guiding principles for the Chinese therapeutic system. For example, the hot-cold theory in explaining the etiology of diseases was first mentioned in *Nei jing.*

After *Nei jing, The San Han Lun* (Essay on typhoid) by Zhong-jing Zhang (150-219 A.D.), published during the Three Kingdoms Era, integrated discussions of Chinese ethnomedical theories from ancient practitioners, treatment procedures, prescriptions, and specific medical property of herbs into a more comprehensive system of therapeutics in clinical settings. The other important book on herbs was the *Classic of the Agriculture Emperor's Materia Medica* (or the *herbal*), published in the East Han Dynasty (25-220 A.D.), which lists 365 herbs, including 252 plants, 67 uses of animal parts, and 46 minerals, for 170 diseases.

From the Tang Dynasty (618-907), medical research received increasing attention from the royal court. In the Tang Dynasty, the Royal Medical Institute categorized therapeutics into internal medicine, pediatrics, external medicine, dentistry, ear problems, and oral hygiene. Research based on clinical observations and empirical experiences resulted in advancement in therapeutics in specialty treatment. For example, Zou Hou Fang provided detailed discussions of such infectious diseases as measles and rabies. The *Etiology of All Diseases,* written in 610 A.D., was the first book devoted to detailed discussion of symptoms and diagnosis of 1,700 diseases. *The qien qin yao fang* (One thousand ounces of gold classic), written by Sun Shu Mao in 652 A.D., was one of the largest encyclopedias on Chinese ethnomedical system. Li's *Ben Cao Gang Mu* (Classification of herbs and plants), which lists a total of 1,892 herbs and 1,110 pictures of the herbs, offers in-depth discussion of the diagnostics and treatment of all different diseases. The most important contribution of the book was the invention of a classification scheme for diagnosing diseases in internal organs as well as offering discussions of medical ethics, therapeutic effects of food, pediatrics, and obstetrics and gynecology. Chinese knowledge of pharmaceutics was much advanced by this book.

After the Tang Dynasty (618-907), intense interest in specialty treatment was reflected in the medical practice and research in the beginning of the Song Dynasty (960-1127). Etiology of diseases and illnesses received a more refined classification. The first monograph on obstetrics and gynecology was written by Kao Yin in *Quian pao* (Essence of gynecology), but the most comprehensive discussion on gynecology was written by Tzu-ming Chen in the 24-volume *Fu Jen Liang Fang* (Prescriptions for women). The earliest discussion on pediatrics appeared in *Lu Sin Jing* (Fontanel). These discussions provided a deeper understanding of specialty treatment in the Chinese ethnomedical system.

Pharmaceutics made the greatest stride during the Yuan Dynasty (1279-1368), when various writings on the toxicology and therapeutic effects of food and medicine were published, including the *Historical Collection of Herbal Prescriptions* by Shen Wei Tang. In the mid-sixteenth century A.D., vaccine was used to prevent infectious diseases. But one of the most important contributions to the Chinese herbal repertoire was made by Shi-Zen Li's *An Outline of Materia Medica* in 1578 A.D., a most comprehensive guide to Chinese herbal medicine. This voluminous collection, which took more than thirty years to complete, totaled more than 1.9 million words in 52 volumes. A total of 1,892 herbs were classified into 16 categories, which were further divided into a total of 62 subcategories. In addition, a list of 8,160 prescriptions was included for different diseases. Li's works crystallized the most useful medical knowledge that the Chinese had learned from Mother Nature.

PHILOSOPHICAL, CULTURAL, AND COMMUNICATIVE SOURCES

Discussion of the Chinese ethnomedical system cannot be separated from the cultural and philosophical framework in which the Chinese medicine is embodied. Among all cultural beliefs Taoist philosophy, Confucianism, and Buddhism have the most influence on the system (Fu, 1994; Lin, 1993; Meng & Zhou, 1999). Taoism espouses the idea of not violating the law of nature in living one's life (Fu; 1994; Lai, no date; 1994; Sivin, 1995; Wong & Wu,

1936; Yang & Li, 1993). Confucianism emphasizes the importance of moderation, balance, and harmony in social life (Lin, 1993). Buddhism, introduced to China about 67 A.D., brought Chinese attention to the mind-body connection in relation to health (Wong & Wu, 1936). Under the teachings of Buddhism, the importance of mental health in relation to physical well-being received increasing attention from medical practitioners.

Because of the influence of these philosophical beliefs, the Chinese ethnomedical system theorizes that the forces of nature have specific effects on humans. These ideas are reflected in health-maintenance behavior. These include, first, the concept of flow of qi (the energy flow in the body). The Chinese believe that a flow of energy, qi, exists in the body and is the driving force of life. Qi influences all human activities, such as circulation, metabolism, and immunity. The blocking of this energy can lead to health problems. Second is the concept of balance. The idea of balance in its most inclusive sense is central to human health. Balance is discussed in terms of equilibrium among all atmospheric elements, emotions, intake of foods, and mind-and-body balance. Third is the concept of heat, which is unique in Chinese medicine because the level of heat in one's body is considered to be central to one's health. Acute diseases, such as inflammatory and infectious diseases, are related to the level of heat in one's body. Lack of or excessive heat invites health problems. Fourth is the dialectic relationship between mind and body. In the Chinese system, mind and body have a reciprocal dynamic to keep the human health in equilibrium. The mind plays a strong role in regulating human health, but a weakened body can speed up the deterioration of the mind. It is believed that there is a direct link in the relationship among mind, stress, and health. In this system, stress is considered to be the worst enemy to human health because it can throw off homeostasis. Fifth is the emphasis on tracing the cause of diseases/illnesses. It is believed that the biggest taboo in dealing with disease/illness is treating the symptoms, instead of the root, of the problems. The saying "treat the head when head aches and treat the foot when the foot aches" can cause long-term negative effects on health. As a result, preventive care is important because, if not cured, a small irritation can develop into a major health threat. According to this view, one does not lead a rugged lifestyle and expect medicine to provide a quick fix of the problem.

Chinese ethnomedical practices are related to some assumptions behind Chinese social and cultural behavior. First, the idea of taking the middle of the road, or "*zhong yong*," is one of the most important philosophical principles underlying Chinese discussions of what constitutes a fine, moral person and what constitutes appropriate social behavior. For example, a well-rounded person is someone who is expected to know his or her center and conducts his or her behavior in such a way that shows balance in every aspect of life. Accordingly, the most ideal state of life is one in which the individual masters the art of *zhong* (the middle). There are two concepts operating here:

one is *the center*; the other is *balance in the middle*. For example, one is expected to act "right in the middle of every rule" (*zhong gui zhong ju*) and to walk "without haste or retard" (*bu ji bu xu*). One is supposed to "have an appropriate amount of eating and drinking" (*yin shi shi zhong*). One's appearance is a reflection of the thoughts "in the center of one's mind" (*cheng yu zhong, xing yu wai*). Illness is likely to result if one loses the balance of "body and mind" (*shen xin shi tiao*). Emotional instability or lacking balance in "mind and spirit" spells trouble ahead.

Second, a related concept to the idea of *zhong* is the emphasis on restraint or modesty, that is, a dislike of extremes, in everyday behavior. Chinese medical practitioners tend to emphasize the importance of restraint, "not too much or too little of anything," in keeping one's health. The concept of restraint permeates every aspect of the Chinese way of life. For example, the Chinese believe that one should be cautious in every utterance, treating it as gold to be lost in careless chats with people, "*jin yan shen xing.*" Ill consequences are likely to occur as a result of excess of words, "*yan duo bi shi.*" Excessive desires, "*zong yu,*" such as eating or drinking with abandon, hurt one's flow of energy and one's concentration. Restraint should also be exercised in one's emotional expressions: excessive anger "arouses the burning fire attacking the heart" (*nu huo gong xin*); extreme joy leads to unexpected sadness, "*le ji shen bei*"; and excessive worries invite illness, "*ji yu cheng ji.*" Emotion-wise, a fine person is one who displays no excessive suspicion or worry (*bu yi bu ju*).

Third, the Chinese ethnomedical system is modeled after the course of Nature and therefore reverence for Nature or the natural course of life is deemed essential to guide one's physical existence. In practice, this means that one should not temper one's health with unnatural ways of life or means of treatment. The philosophical underpinnings of the ethnomedical concept of "revering Nature" can be found in common beliefs about what constitutes an ideal mode of social existence in everyday life. On a more abstract level, reverence for natural law is then translated into an attitude of "following the flow of life," or "*shun qi zi ran,*" a tendency to adjust oneself to the events of life instead of trying to change the course of life by drastic means.

Fourth, the ethnomedical belief that one's energy flow, heat level, or mind-body equilibrium is likely to be disrupted by events of conflict or emotional distress reflects the importance of "harmony" in one's social life to maintain one's mental and physical sanity. Harmony (*he*) comes hand in hand with peace (*ping*). An ideal state of existence and social relationship is manifested in physical or metaphysical harmony, so-called "peace under heaven" (*tian xia tai ping*), which results from balance, restraint, and following natural law. Harmony is manifested in one's talking in appropriate volume, soft and agreeable pitch, and pleasant facial expressions (*he yan yue se*). Harmony is also reflected in the way individuals treat each other, which ideally is underscored by respect and good and natural manners, *ping shi zi ran.* During one's interaction with others, one is supposed to demonstrate "a serene mind with a harmonious flow of energy" (*xin ping qi he*). Beyond interpersonal communication, harmony is a major concern in all aspects of social life. For example, a well-situated residence is one that has "the harmony of wind and water" (*feng shui tiao he*). A happy family is one characterized by members who get along with one another harmoniously, "*jia he wan shi xing.*" The development of a nation should be guided by peace and stability as a whole.

Fifth, as discussions about Chinese ethnomedical beliefs have revealed in the previous section, treatment of diseases/illnesses and pregnancy-related issues emphasized tracing the cause of health-related problems, "*gen ben.*" Scrutinizing the "origin" or the "core" (*gen*) of a disease/illness or curing the cause of a disease, "*zhi ben,*" is the most important principle in Chinese therapeutics.

This idea of tracing the true cause of illnesses/diseases is closely linked to Chinese philosophical beliefs about what constitutes a being and what is expected of a moral being. For example, the Chinese believe that an individual's social behavior has to be derived from a moral core ("*dao de zhi gen ben*"). The way truth is pursued or a problem is researched is analogous to "the tracing of the roots of a tree" (*zhu gen jiu yuan*). The emphasis on the cause and origin of all physical phenomena has to do with the belief in "the cycle of cause and effect" in personal conduct and social relationships. It is widely believed that everything one does or says inevitably breeds some consequences in one's life, the phenomenon of "reaping melons when the seeds of the melons have been sowed, reaping beans when the seeds of beans have been sowed," namely, "*zhong gua de gua, zhong dou de dou.*"

CROSS-CULTURAL DIALOGUE IN HEALTH COMMUNICATION

The growing interest in Chinese ethnomedical beliefs provides fertile ground for communication research. To begin with, the health communication research as currently defined in the West is a relatively new discipline. The *Journal of Health Communication* did not exist until the beginning of 1990s. The study of health communication tends to be designated in the "applied communication" corner because of the supposedly utilitarian nature of the discipline. The significance of the discipline is even less appreciated in public health or medicine because communication, even in its broadest sense, is deemed to have little relevance to health problems. The knowledge of health communication, like web-page design or carpentry, is used as a practical tool at its best that helps facilitate the day-to-day clinical operations of health professionals, especially the physicians, the top of the medical echelon of command. In this context, health communication is considered one small area of applied communication that is limited to the discussion of such localized concerns as "compliance and persuasion," "empathetic expression," or "patient assertivenss" skills. Of course, one cannot deny that in mass communication and public relations, more ambitious attempts have been made to apply health communication concepts to health promotion campaigns through the use of mass media in reducing health risks and promoting health maintenance practices. Some, in attempting to increase the intellectual depth of the discipline, even delve into the critical inquiry of the power relationships between the medical institutions and the health care seekers, but this epistemological territory has already been claimed by medical sociologists. The way human health is conceptualized in the existing biomedical model makes little room for health communication to claim higher legitimacy in health sciences. In the traditional biomedical model, health problems center around the discussions of immediate causes of problems, such as germs and viruses. Day-to-day social communication problems do not enter into the picture of diagnostics.

However, under the Chinese ethnomedical system, health communication would be based on a very different conceptual system because communication itself is deemed to have clinical relevance. This view is very different from the basic assumption of biomedicine, which sees microorganisms as the major pathological agents. The concerns for tracing the cause of the problem, balance and harmony, and mind-and-body connection portends research built on entirely different philosophical bases without having to create another intellectual hegemony or perpetuate another kind of paradigmatic thought. So how would the study of health communication be approached differently in this framework?

First, in this framework, health communication is much broader in scope and more profound in depth. It is not limited to the study of isolated variables, such as compliance-gaining in face-to-face encounters or a one-way, magic-bullet model of persuasive effects, although they can be integrated into the Chinese system. It is not just about searching for antecedent conditions to fulfill some positivist predictions of some simple causal models. Prevailing theories of health communication have been deeply influenced by the positivist traditions in the United States. We cannot deny that this research has produced some significant results in illuminating the interrelationships of some psychological constructs and has generated some functional utility in the field. For example, research on compliance gaining has helped health professionals become more effective in persuading their patients to follow a certain treatment regimen. Yet, as the health care system in the United States is going through a major overhaul, the conventional model of health communication needs rethinking, especially in the relationship between health care clients and providers. The current health care paradigm is under severe criticism, even by health professionals themselves. McCord (1986) noted that the term "compliance" may soon become obsolete due to the negative and authoritarian connotations. The old model envisions health care seekers as empty vessels who give control over their health to the experts, who then decide all life-and-death matters with absolute authority. Beyond the philosophical pitfalls, the model lacks intellectual originality and authenticity. To be more exact, it is an intellectual copycat from other disciplines.

The Chinese ethnomedical system suggests that health communication is a more encompassing area of study than this paradigm. In a nutshell, human health is affected by communication behavior, and communication behavior reveals important information of human health. The interrelationship between the two concepts is much more dynamic than as they are currently defined, and the possibilities for research are abundant and unlimited. This new model concerns philosophical discourse about interpersonal relations, social relations, and the metaphysical worlds, especially the role of spirituality in health maintenance. Health communication is the site at which humans articulate their empirical knowledge, their culture-conditioned behavior, and their understanding of their psychological and spiritual well-being. Health communication is about cross-cultural encounters, how differences in belief and value systems are translated into differences in health-seeking behavior. For example, the way that health problems are talked about in the West reveals a culture steeped in technology and mechanical innovations. In contrast, the way health maintenance is articulated in Eastern cultures reveals a reverence for the natural course of things. More important, how these differences are expressed reveal important clues for individuals' vulnerabilities for certain illnesses and related diagnostics. Clinically relevant information can be obtained from one's communication of diet and health complaints, which might lead to a discovery of culturally relevant solutions. The Chinese ethnomedical system suggests that health communication can be studied at the macro level as well as the micro level.

Second, as the Chinese ethnomedical system has suggested, communication has its health consequences. As mentioned earlier, in the Chinese ethnomedical system, extreme emotions cause possible damage to one's immunity. This truth has been verified by modern medical research in that the immune system is compromised when one has high stress levels. What and how one communicates are closely related to one's mental or physical state of well-being. Finding out one's behavioral antecedents helps clinical diagnosis. In this model, health communication is placed at the center of any given clinical encounter. Knowledge of communication is more than a convenient tool, like a surgical knife, that induces patients' compliance to health professionals' orders. The content of communication itself is the center of clinical interviews.

Third, health communication is a transactional model. It is not a one-direction, compliance-gaining model designed only to allow the expression of the voice of one party in the interactions, as the traditional paradigm asserts. The traditional health communication model sees clinical encounters as a one-way communication process, in which the medical authority provides diagnosis, treatment method, or verdict on the fate of the patients. The expert knowledge or order is a monopoly that is not to be challenged. In that model, health communication is to facilitate the establishment and consolidation of this authority by inducing absolute compliance from health care seekers. In its extreme, coercion is even used to induce compliance. The Chinese ethnomedical model suggests that the patient should be placed at the center of this communication encounter because all the physical evidence revealed from the patient, be it the nonverbals, the colors of the complexion, energy levels, posture, paralinguistics, or verbals are the foci of clinical interest. Chinese medicine practitioners have long been instructed to revere their patients because it was the clinical evidence from these patients that provided the best learning opportunities for health professionals (Meng & Zhou, 1999).

Fourth, related to the previous point is the idea that health communication is a model of cooperation, not a model of conflict. It is *not an impersonal model*, but an *interpersonal model* of communication. In this model, health care seekers and health providers work together to solve a health problem. recent health care reform in the West has pitted patients against health professionals. Both parties have been trying to delineate in unambiguous terms the responsibilities and rights of both sides. When treatment results are not satisfactory or when trust is breached, they resort to legal suits to resolve the medical problem. The talk of empowerment of patients or enhancing the patients' rights that emerged relatively recently in the United States to challenge medical institutions or health insurance enterprises is a welcome move to reverse the power imbalance in the health care setting. However, the Chinese ethnomedical system sees health-related knowledge manifested in humans' day-to-day living experience. The knowledge itself is nothing esoteric or mysterious. Of course, that is not to say that everyone can be good in treating all health problems.

The Chinese equivalent of the word "physician" (*dai fu*) connotes the most brilliant and most altruistic of all individuals and is a profession suitable only for those most committed to the well-being of the ill. Yet, this system sees all individuals equally capable of engaging in health prevention or maintenance behavior. It presumes that except inherited problems, when one engages in the "right" preventive behavior, it is very unlikely that one would be subject to a state of illness or disease. In this model, the patients themselves, who have intimate knowledge of their health status, are fully engaged with health professionals when it comes to the treatment of health problems. Patients become the most astute observers of their own health and are encouraged to participate in the diagnostic process. The health professionals offer their opinions and prescriptions, but during the process, the patients are encouraged to understand their own conditions. Coercion is not necessary because if the patients have the most intimate knowledge of their health status, they are regarded as equally responsible for any health decision made in the clinical setting. What the physicians do is to help them understand the medical conclusion and related treatment provided by the physicians.

Fifth, health communication is about communication ethics. Influenced by the ethnical requirement of high moral responsibility and virtue for those who serve the public, the Chinese ethnomedical system demands the highest moral standard from health professionals. This system is not only about curing diseases, it is also a framework of how individuals should be treated when they are ill. The major principles of interpersonal relations are moral dignity and respect, which transcend all distinctions and associations. Several assumptions underlie these two ideas (Meng & Zhou, 1999). Most important, the physicians are held to the highest moral standards in their interactions with patients. Above all, physicians should respect every living human life, or in the words of Sun Shi Mao, the esteemed physician of the Tang Dynasty, life should be valued as more important than a thousand pieces of gold. This respect is demonstrated through the acts of *"ren,"* treating all lives as one's own, and *"ce yin,"* or commiseration, seeing others' suffering as one's own, in the physicians' interactions with the patients. Also, the physicians are expected to act without selfish intentions. The physicians should act and communicate with the uttermost humility and caution.

Moreover, the physicians should keep all patients' medical records in strict confidence. These ideas should not be too alien to modern health professionals. They actually have their modern counterpart in the West, such as in the Hyppocratic oath, that the physicians should act according to the following principles: beneficence, the principle that health professionals should do whatever that is in the best interest of the patient, respect, honesty, informed consent, confidentiality, and fidelity (Tindall, Beardsley & Kimberlin, 1994). What the Chinese ethnomedical system suggests is that the principles underlying the art of curing and healing are not too different from those that correct the ills of human communication. The study of health communication is not about how manipulation of certain words or psychological triggers facilitate one party's goal in a communication dyad. It is about assuming responsibility and acting in ways that contribute to equilibrium in a communication situation. Communication in this model is egalitarian and reciprocal and as a result, it is less likely to lead to conflict or misunderstanding.

CONCLUSION

The renewed interest in the Chinese ethnomedical system in the West not only sheds light on new possibilities of treating intractable, chronic health problems, but it also opens up new possibilities and new directions to re-evaluate the health communication discipline as currently defined in the West. This discussion was designed to provide "une ebauche" of the history, philosophical grounding, and implications for future research in health communication. Yet, this discussion was by no means intended to diminish the value of existing health communication research, because doing so would not befit the spirit of the Chinese ethnomedical system. Instead, it was meant to offer a new way of examining social experiences, seeing things in ways that broaden the intellectual horizon of the health communication discipline, seeing things in ways that might provide solutions to the problems in the real world. In the spirit of the new millennium, when humans aspire for new intellectual height and crave for ingenuity in improving the health of our fellow homo sapiens, rethinking the existing health communication paradigm offers exactly such an opportunity.

REFERENCES

Benedict, R. (1959). *Patterns of culture*. NewYork: Longman.
Bowers, J. Z., & Purcell, E. F. (1974). *Medicine and society in China*. New York: Josiah Macy Jr. Foundation.
Clark, M. (1983). Cultural context of medical practice. *The Westem Journal of Medicine, 139* (6), 806-810.
Eisenberg, D. (1995). *Encounters with qi: Exploring Chinese medicine*. New York: Norton.
Eisenberg, L., & Kleinman, A. (Eds.). *Relevance of social science for medicine*. Dordrecht: Reidel.
Farquhar, J. (1994). *Knowing practice: The clinical encounter of Chinese medicine*. Boulder, CO: Westview.
Foster, G. M., & Anderson, B. G. (1978). *Medical anthropology*. New York: Wiley.
Friedman, H. S., & DiMatteo, M. R. (1979). Health care as interpersonal process. *Journal of Social Issues, 35* (1), 1-11.
Fu, W. K. (1994). *Zhong guo yi xue shi (The medical history of China)*. Taipei: Ji Ying.
Geertz, C. (1973). *The interpretation of cultures*. New York: Basic Books.
Griswold, W. (1994). *Cultures and societies in a changing world*. Thousand Oaks, CA: Pine Forge Press.
Harre, R. (1979). *Social being: A theory for social psychology*. Oxford: Basil Blackwell.
Harre, R., & Secord, P. F. (1973). *The explanation of social behavior*. Oxford: Basil Blackwell.
Helman, C. G. (1984). *Culture, health, and illness*. Bristol, England: John Wright & Sons, Ltd.
Ho, P., & Lisowski, F. P. (1997). *A brief history of Chinese medicine*. Singapore: World Scientific.
Hugard, P., & Wong, M. (1968). *Chinese medicine*. (Trans. from French by B. Fielding). New York: McGraw-Hill Book Company.
Jelliffe, D. B. (1967). Parallel food classifications in developing and industrialized countries. *The American Journal of Clinical Nutrition, 20*, 279-281.
Kaptchuk, T. J. (1983). *The web that has no weaver: Understanding Chinese medicine*. New York: Congdon & Weed.
Keesing, R. M. (1981). *Cultural anthropology: A contemporary perspective*. New York: Holt, Rinehart & Winston.

Kleinman, A. (1980). *Patients and healers in the context of culture.* Berkeley: University of California Press.

Lai, Z. H. (no publication date). *Lao Zhuang zhe xue yen jiou (The study of Lao zi and Zhuang zi).* Tainan, Taiwan: Dzong Heh Publisher.

Lampton, D. M. (1974). *Health, conflict and the Chinese political system.* Ann Arbor, MI: Center for Chinese Studies.

Landy, D. (1977). *Culture, disease, and healing: Studies in medical anthropology.* New York: Macmillan.

Lin, Y. (1993). *Zhong Guo wen hua yu zhong yi xue (Chinese culture and Chinese medicine).* Fujien, China: Fujien Science Publisher.

Lipson, J. G., & Melies, A. I. (1983). Issues in health care of Middle Eastern patients. *The Western Journal of Medicine, 139* (6), 854-861.

Liu, Y. (1988). *The essential book of traditional Chinese medicine. Volume I: Theory.* (Trans. by T. Y. Fang and L. Chen). New York: Columbia University Press.

Lu, H. (1994). *Chinese herbal cultures.* New York: Sterling Publishing Co.

Maciocia, G. (1989). The practice of Chinese medicine: The treatment of diseases with acupuncture and Chinese herbs. New York: Churchill Livingstone.

Maduro, R. (1983). Curanderismo and Latino views of disease and curing. *The Western Journal of Medicine, 139* (6), 868-874.

Matsumoto, K. (1983). *Five elements and ten stems.* Higganum, CT: Paradigm.

McCord, M. A. (1986). Compliance: Self-care or compromise?. *Topics in Clinical Nursing: Patient compliance and outcomes, 7* (4),1-8.

McNamara, S. (1996). *Traditional Chinese medicine.* New York: Basic Books.

Meng, J. C., & Zhou, J. Y. (1999). *Zhong yi xue gai lun (An overview of Chinese medical science).* Taipei, Taiwan: Ji Ying.

Mitchell, M. F. (1983). Popular medical concepts in Jamaica and their impact on drug use. *The Western Journal of Medicine, 139* (6), 841-847.

Morse, W. R. (1978). *Chinese medicine.* Reprinted from 1938 edition. New York: AMS Press.

Muecke, M. A. (1983). In search of healers—Southeast Asian refugees in the American health care system. *The Western Journal of Medicine, 139* (6), 835-840.

Pellegrino, E. D. (1963). Medicine, history, and the idea of man. In J. A. Clausen and R. Straus (Eds.), *Medicine and society: The annals of the American Academy of Political and Social Science 346,* 9-20. New York: Basic Books.

Porkert, M. (1974). *The theoretical foundations of Chinese medicine: Systems of correspondence.* Cambridge, MA: MIT Press.

Said, H. M. (1981). *Medicine in China.* Karachi, Pakistan: Hamdard Academy.

Shen, T. Y. (1994). *The basis of traditional Chinese medicine.* Hong Kong: Commercial Press.

Sivin, N. (1995). *Medicine, philosophy and religion in ancient China.* Hampshire, England: Variorum.

Snow, L. F. (1983). Traditional beliefs and practices among lower class black Americans. *The Western Journal of Medicine, 139* (6), 820-827.

Tindall, W. N., Beardsley, R. S., & Kimberlin, C. L. (1994). *Communication skills in pharmacy practice.* Philadelphia: Lea & Febiger.

Witte, K. (1991). The role of culture in health and disease. In L. A. Samovar and R. E. Porter (Eds.), *Intercultural communication: A reader* (6th ed., pp. 199-207). Belmont, CA: Wadsworth.

Wong, K. C., & Wu, L.-T. (1936). *History of Chinese medicine.* Shanghai, China: National Quarantine Service.

Yang, S. S., & Li, J. J. (1993). *Li Dong-yuan's treatise on the spleen and stomach.* Boulder, CO: Blue Poppy Press.

Yum, J. O. (1991). The impact of Confucianism on interpersonal relationships and communication patterns in East Asia. In L. A. Samovar and R. E. Porter (Eds.), *Intercultural communication: A reader* (6th ed., pp. 66-77). Belmont, CA: Wadsworth.

11

What We Still Need to Know about Chinese Negotiation

Deborah A. Cai and Leah Waks

The opening of China to the world, both politically and economically, has led to an increase in research attempting to explain how Chinese negotiate. Currently, there are nearly one hundred books and articles specifically related to Chinese communication at the negotiation table. Two-thirds of the literature is prescriptive (Cai & Drake, 1998), providing advice based on experience of practitioners who have negotiated with Chinese or are Chinese (Blackman, 1997; Chan, 1998; Chang, 1991; Davidson 1987; Davies & Clarke, 1994; de Keijzer, 1992; Eiteman, 1990; Fang, 1999; Huang, 1990; Lavin, 1994; Liu, 1995; Melvin, 1995; Nair & Stafford, 1998; Pye, 1982, 1986, 1992; Solomon, 1985). On one hand, the literature is highly repetitive; on the other, there is little empirical research on negotiation processes used by the Chinese (Adler, Brahm, & Graham, 1992; Swierczek, 1990). Of the empirical studies available, most compare American and Chinese negotiators in the context of individualistic and collectivistic cultures (Adler et al., 1992; Graham, Kim, Lin, & Robinson, 1988; Lee, 2000; Lee & Lo, 1998; Leung, 1987).

In this chapter we provide six research questions (RQs) as a plan for research on Chinese negotiation in the twenty-first century: RQ1: What does negotiation mean to the Chinese? RQ2: How does the Chinese view of time affect negotiation? RQ3: What reasoning processes are used to prepare and process arguments? RQ4: How do Chinese negotiators think about decisions? RQ5: How do Chinese negotiators view the relationship with foreign negotiators? RQ6: Are the findings generalizeable? Before addressing each research question, we present a summary of approaches to studying Chinese negotiation.

OVERVIEW

General interest in the study of Chinese negotiation began in the 1960s (Lall, 1968; Solomon, 1985; Young, 1968) and increased dramatically in the 1980s (Frankenstein, 1986; Graham, 1985, 1986; Knutsson, 1986; Pye, 1982; Shenkar & Ronen, 1987; Tung, 1982a, 1982b). Research presents two major explanations for Chinese negotiation (Blackman, 1997; Fang, 1999; Pye, 1982, 1992). One view is that Chinese negotiation is influenced predominantly by the Chinese hierarchy and bureaucracy (Blackman, 1997; Faure, 1999; Pye, 1982). The other view is that Chinese negotiation is influenced predominantly by Confucianism (Shenkar & Ronen, 1987; Seligman, 1990; Yum, 1988). Both the bureaucratic-hierarchical approach (Blackman, 1997; Faure, 1999; Pye, 1982) and the Confucian approach (Chen, 1993; Seligman, 1990; Shenkar & Ronen, 1987) point to culture as the primary shaper of structure, process, strategies, and outcomes of negotiation between the Chinese and their foreign partners.

Pye (1982) argues that Chinese negotiation is anchored in both Confucianism and a communist-socialist system that is bureaucratic and hierarchical, which explains the "hypercautious attitudes and endless suspicions of Chinese" (p. 17). He maintains that with the liberalization of China these cultural characteristics are more pronounced and have a greater impact on the success or failure of negotiation (1992).

Although communism has certainly affected the culture of modern China, Chinese culture is anchored in several traditions in addition to Confucianism, such as Taoism, Legalism, Mohism, and Buddhism, which have seemingly opposing philosophies (Lu, 1998). Confucianism has been identified with the value of *yi* (benevolence, faithfulness, and empathy). Guided by this value, Chinese are expected to take responsibility for their family and group members and conform to social norms (Lu, 1998). Taoism and Legalism have been identified with the value of *li* (profit and utilitarianism), where self-interest and material gain serve as primary goals and motivation. In practice, this value can be traced to ancient persuasive practices aimed at promoting self-interest and personal gain, though these practices may take a very subtle form. The notions of *yi* and *li* can be viewed as opposing thinking patterns that lead to seemingly contradictory behaviors (Chu, 1991). They may also be interpreted as dialectically connected, accommodating one another to achieve both individual and group goals.

This dialectic of influences (Janosik, 1987) results in apparent contradictions. Some writers portray Chinese negotiations as a time of relationship building (Shenkar & Ronen, 1987) or cooperative endeavors aimed at maximizing benefits for all parties (Adler et al., 1992), while others present them as competitive and confrontational (Blackman, 1997; Faure, 1999; Pye, 1982). Faure (1998) argues that Chinese negotiation is more a confrontation than a peaceful discussion, in which Chinese bring to the negotiation national culture (Pye, 1982), organizational culture (Hofstede, 1980), and professional and local culture (Graham, 1996).

In brief, dialectical cultural constraints have shaped the slow pace, procedures, changing tactics, and prolonged decision-making process of Chinese negotiations (Blackman, 1997; Faure, 1999; Pye, 1982, 1992). Chinese negotiation also is influenced by Confucian philosophy on the nature of relationship, the collective commitment to work together in harmony, and emotional restraint (Chen, 1993; Deverge, 1986; Seligman, 1990; Shenkar & Ronen, 1987; Yum, 1988). The Confucian approach interprets Chinese negotiation behavior as stemming from issues of "face," relationship, and the quest for mutual benefits (Brunner & Wang, 1988).

Little empirical research has been conducted to understand the specific relationship between the process of negotiation and the strategies employed that affect the structure, process, and outcome in Chinese negotiation. The following research questions provide a guide for further research on the influence of Chinese culture on negotiation.

RESEARCH QUESTIONS

RQ1: What Does Negotiation Mean to the Chinese?

A basic question receiving surprisingly little attention in existing literature is whether the Chinese and their foreign counterparts conceptualize negotiation similarly (see Faure, 1998, for a notable exception). Western literature on negotiation makes a distinction between integrative (win-win) and distributive (win-lose) negotiation, promoting the benefits of a "problem-solving" approach. The potential for a win-win solution, however, may be a Western mindset. Several authors note that Chinese perceive trade negotiations with the West primarily as a zero-sum situation of extreme competitiveness (Chang, 1991; Lavin, 1994; Lee, 2000; Shenkar & Ronen, 1987). Chan (1998) notes that the "long prevailing zero-sum thinking is so deeply rooted in the Chinese hierarchy that MNCs [multinational corporations] have to work harder during negotiations" (p. 74). The Chinese bargaining style is said to be one of aggressive haggling (Lee, 2000).

One way to answer this research question is to compare negotiation metaphors used by Chinese and American negotiators. Lakoff and Johnson (1980) contend that metaphors are a basic tool used to conceptualize our experiences. Gelfand and McCusker (in press) argue for comparing cultural metaphors of negotiation because metaphors provide a conceptual scheme that defines the context of negotiating. In the West, some metaphors for negotiation include game, chess match, and dance (Lakoff & Johnson, 1980). Each metaphor provides a coherent cognitive frame and implies related behaviors for negotiating.

Based on interviews with Chinese negotiators, Faure (1998) suggests two predominant metaphors for Chinese negotiation. The first, "mobile warfare," focuses on confrontation and conflict, action and outcome. The second, "joint quest," suggests that negotiation is a shared exploration into unknown territory. The nature of this joint quest will depend on whether the foreigner is a "barbarian" or is "civilized," which is defined by the foreigner's knowledge and understanding of the Chinese culture.

Faure (1998) provides several Chinese metaphors that describe the choice of strategies by Chinese negotiators. "Luring the tiger down from the mountain" emphasizes the need to combat and weaken the opponent. "Killing the chicken to warn the monkey" is a coercive act designed to frighten the opponent. "To take the firewood under the cauldron" refers to the need to eliminate the opponent's source of energy. "Taking advantage of a fire to commit a robbery" relates to the strategy of sowing dissension by speaking to different negotiators separately. And "borrowing a corpse for the return of the soul" alludes to the Chinese assumption that foreign negotiators are indebted to the Chinese on account of the past. These metaphors emphasize tactics including "harassment, destabilization, exhaustion, and squashing" (Faure, 1999, p. 201). The value of and emphasis on strategic thinking is deeply rooted in Chinese culture, with origins in both Taoism and Confucianism. Taoist thought, which encourages the conquering of an enemy without battle, pervades the influential writings of Sun Tzu in *The Art of War*, written over 2,000 years ago (Fang, 1999).

The implications of this research question are far reaching. Answers to questions about who is sent to negotiate, what authority a negotiator has at the negotiation table, and especially the process of negotiating are all influenced by how we understand the concept of negotiation itself. Although rhetorical roots for answering these questions can be found in Confucian teaching, as many researchers on Chinese culture suggest, the cultural foundations are also found in the writings of ancient philosophers such as Lao Zi, Sun Zi, and Mo Zi. The dialectic of strategy and relationship must be understood in its holistic nature, where strategy and relationship are integrally related. Future research should examine how strategy and relationship interact with each other in a variety of relational contexts and situations.

Is negotiation a zero-sum game for the Chinese? Highlighted in the quoted metaphors is the Chinese framing of negotiation as a zero-sum competition rather than a give-and-take exercise (Chan, 1998; Faure, 1998, 1999; Pye, 1982). Use of stalling tactics and delays, lack of concession making, and making extreme demands are cited as difficulties in negotiating with the

Chinese and are perceived by Western negotiators as competitive tactics (Chang, 1991; Lavin, 1994; Lee, 2000; Pye, 1982; Shenkar & Ronen, 1987). But whether these tactics are indeed competitive or only perceived as competitive by Western negotiators are two separate issues.

Attribution theory predicts that we assign cause to behavior, which in turn determines our own emotions and behaviors (Kelley, 1972). Cultural assessments are at risk of attribution biases (Morris & Peng, 1994); North Americans may make dispositional attributions of Chinese actions (i.e., Chinese are competitive) but justify their own actions as situational (i.e., this is our cultural way of doing things). Faure (1999) cites several Chinese behaviors that may be perceived as competitive in U.S. culture that would not be perceived as such in Chinese culture: little eye contact, lack of a private place to discuss business, making extreme demands, and issuing "take it or leave it" positions. Chan (1998) adds to this list the leaking of information to play companies off each other and the lack of disclosing information. Faure further points out that American behaviors such as emotional outbursts and direct threats, among others, may be perceived as equally competitive and unacceptable to the Chinese.

Future research should address the conditions under which negotiation is perceived as a zero-sum game by the Chinese; whether this perception can be altered to be a cooperative, variable-sum game; what tactics are perceived as competitive both by Chinese negotiators and their foreign counterparts; and the attributions made by both Chinese and foreign negotiators about specific communication tactics and strategies.

RQ2: How Does the Chinese View of Time Affect Negotiation?

"The Chinese have a longer range view of things and are in less of a hurry. They have a different definition of timeliness and insist that 'investment' in a relationship cannot be hurried" (Chan, 1998, p. 88). Although this view is echoed by other writers (Chang, 1991; Faure, 1999; Shenkar & Ronen, 1987), it raises at least three questions: (a) Do Chinese have a long-range view of negotiation? (b) what is their perspective on timeliness? and (c) what goes into building an enduring relationship? The last question will be addressed later in the chapter.

What is the Chinese view of timeliness? The Western view of time is said to be monochronic, or linear, with dates and scheduling taking high priority, whereas the Chinese view of time is polychronic, with emphasis on relationship and end-results (Hall, 1976; Warrington & McCall, 1983). Macleod (1988) compares the two perspectives: "Apparently, Chinese see life as a flowing stream and we (Americans) see it as a string of incidents, much like a string of beads. We finger one, finish with it, and want to have it tidily counted off so we can go on to the next; they see every incident . . . as simultaneously blending into each other before and after, and so nothing ever ends" (p. 73).

A recurring charge to Western negotiators doing business in China is to expect the process will take time (Davies & Clarke, 1994; Warrington & McCall, 1983). Western negotiators report frustration, however, with the length of the decision-making process (Lindsay & Dempsey, 1983; Swierczek, 1990). Lengthy negotiations can seem to go nowhere for long periods of time but then result in agreements at the last moment before the Western negotiator returns home (Chang, 1991; Hendryx, 1986). Attempts to explain the Chinese sense of timing include the following: inexperience of the negotiators (Pye, 1982), risk aversion (Chan, 1998; Leung & Leung, 2000), need to firmly establish a relationship (Lee & Lo, 1998), and the scholarly way of taking time to think (Davies & Clarke, 1994). Chinese negotiators may also be aware of the foreign propensity to be impatient and thus use the Chinese pace as a tactic (Lavin, 1994; Nair & Stafford, 1998; Pye, 1982; Stewart & Keown, 1989). Davies and Clarke (1994) suggest that "taking the time to conduct business at the 'Chinese pace' may be the single most important thing for Westerners to learn" (p. 38).

Research has yet to examine causal explanations related to the "Chinese pace." Interpreting the use of time as a stalling tactic at times may be a misperception based on Western expectations. Theoretical implications for the "Chinese pace" also need to be explored, ranging from the appropriate use of silence and pauses (Adler et al., 1992; McLaughlin, 1984) to the length of negotiation phases (Holmes, 1992; Leung & Leung, 2000).

What is the Chinese view of the concept of time? The second question gets at the broader conceptual view of time suggested by Kluckhohn and Strodtbeck's (1961) value orientations regarding the place of humans in history and the future. On July 1, 1996, Hong Kong returned to China. Accounts of the event in the United States, however, generally failed to grasp how important the reclaiming of Hong Kong was to the Chinese people. Although the United States focused on the economic value of regaining Hong Kong, there was little attention paid to the emotional and patriotic value of the event. This difference in perspectives is due to the relative value that 150 years has in the course of history for Americans and Chinese.

The Western perspective views time as short or long along a linear contin-uum. From this perspective, U.S. negotiators focus on separate issues and short-term goals (Kirkbride & Tang, 1990). In contrast, Chinese take a long-term perspective, looking far into the future and past. In a comparison of planning processes between U.S. and Taiwanese negotiators, Cai (1998) finds that participants from the United States gave greater consideration to short-term goals than to mid-range or long-term goals. But participants from Taiwan gave significantly more attention to long-term goals than did the U.S. participants. Graham and Herberger (1983) note that Americans often manage negotiations sequentially, separating issues and dealing with them one at a time. In contrast, East Asian negotiators take a more holistic approach, with no settlements reached on specific issues until the end of the negotiation. Conceptually, these are two different ways of thinking, not only about time but also about how to reason about the world as a whole. Future theorizing should explore the implications of taking a "long-term perspective" toward negotiating, and research can examine the effectiveness of holistic versus specific arguments in Chinese negotiation.

RQ3: What Reasoning Processes Are Used to Prepare and Process Arguments?

We first draw attention to the problem of understanding cognitive processes from a cross-cultural perspective. Based on their research, Pan, Kim, and Vanhonacker (1995) conclude that American executives have a higher need for cognition than Chinese executives. These researchers propose that "low need for cognition cultures" are more likely to accept the effectiveness of a top-down approach to decision making. In other words, this research implies that high power distance (Hofstede, 1980) and the Chinese emphasis on hierarchy result in a low need for cognition among Chinese.

But is it the case that Chinese have a lower need for cognition than Americans, or is the measure of "need for cognition" (see Epstein, 1990, and Cacioppo & Petty, 1982) biased toward Western reasoning processes? Redding (1980) contrasts the richness of Chinese cognitive processes with Western thought, arguing that "it is necessary to counteract the tendency for Westerners to look down upon the 'non-scientific' approach as primitive" (p. 132). Instead, research should determine how to conceptualize "need for cognition" from a Chinese perspective and develop cross-culturally appropriate measures for this concept.

Differences in U.S. and Chinese reasoning processes are often addressed in the Chinese negotiation literature, but without research to support the differences or their implications for negotiating (Nadler, Nadler, & Broome, 1985). Walker (1990), for example, demonstrates that reasoning by Americans stresses detail and proof, tends to be more legalistic, and is more likely to be focused on pragmatic and practical issues. In contrast, reasoning by Chinese is more likely to use emotion and imagery and tends to be more ambiguous. Further, Chinese purportedly emphasize principles over details and universals over specifics without separating specifics from the whole or dealing with issues in isolation (Graham & Herberger, 1983; Kirkbride & Tang, 1990; Kirkbride, Tang, & Westwood, 1991; Solomon, 1987; Ting-Toomey, 1988). Whereas Western thinking emphasizes inductive logic and an emphasis on causality, Chinese thinking emphasizes deductive logic, context, and even intuition (Redding, 1980).

In a series of studies comparing how Euro-Americans and Chinese reason about persuasive arguments, Peng and Nisbett (1999) demonstrate that Western rational thought is quite different from Chinese dialectical thought. In other words, when presented with arguments that seemed contradictory, the Chinese resolved these contradictions by retaining elements from both sides and thus choosing a middle perspective. Euro-Americans resolved the contradictions by polarizing the arguments and determining a "correct" position. Peng and Nisbett further demonstrate that Chinese prefer dialectical, or contradictory, arguments to Western logical arguments.

With argumentation as a central feature of negotiating, it is not surprising then that Lavin (1994) observed in a particular negotiation that

> none of the U.S. arguments ever "worked." The Chinese never conceded one point in the debate. No U.S. statistic, no citation of international law, no familiarity with international trade or commercial practice mattered in the end. Knowledge was not power. Even if U.S. arguments worked as exercises of logic, they could not work as exercises of negotiation. (p. 19)

Future research can examine how Chinese perceive the effectiveness of inductive versus deductive arguments, how Chinese process strong and weak arguments, and what type of data is most often used and what type is perceived to be the most influential in negotiation.

RQ4: How Do Chinese Negotiators Think About Decisions?

Pye gives us the following description of Chinese decisions:

> In contrast to American practices, the Chinese do not treat the signing of a contract as signaling a completed agreement; rather, they conceive of the relationship in longer and more continuous terms and they will not hesitate to suggest modifications immediately on the heels of an agreement. Their expectation is that agreements will set the stage for a growing relationship in which it will be proper for China to make increasing demands on the other party. (Pye, 1982, pp. xi-xii)

The point versus process theories of decision making highlight two different cultural perspectives (Cai & Adrian, 1999; Hesselgrave, 1978). *Decision-point* is the view that reaching a specific agreement is the essential goal of decision making; once an agreement is reached, it remains a stable act on which the rest of the business relationship is built. From this perspective, the *point* of decision is the primary focus and once achieved, it is considered a violation to overturn the decision or back out of the agreement. In contrast, *decision-process* is the view that decision making is a process that occurs in stages. Deliberation occurs prior to determining the agreement, but even once an agreement has been reached, dissonance may result in returning to deliberate once again. From this perspective, the decision itself is not of primary importance; instead, the process of deciding and redeciding is of greater value. Whereas Americans focus on the point of agreement when the contract is signed and "real business" can begin, Chinese focus on the process of negotiating a business relationship, in which reaching an agreement and signing a contract is only one part.

Lavin (1994) argues that "the real negotiations with China often begin once the agreement is signed" (p. 21). Chen (1993) further points out that "for the Chinese, contracts are expected to change and promises may be broken; only a strong personal relationship is more reliable and often indispensable for the implementation of a contract" (p. 148). Chinese negotiators are often viewed negatively for requesting last-minute changes in an agreement. Such negative evaluations miss the possibility of a cultural explanation that merits attention. Future research can test how Chinese view last-minute changes in agreements, how the relationship is affected when changes are made after a decision has been reached, and whether Chinese perceive last-minute changes in a contract as a strategy.

RQ5: How Do Chinese Negotiators View the Relationship with Foreign Negotiators?

The importance of relationship, negotiator status, "face," and *guanxi* (the value of relationships as a social resource) are cited as necessary concepts to understand when negotiating with the Chinese (Chang & Holt, 1991; Chen, 1993; Gannon & Associates, 1994; Gilsdorf, 1997; Hu & Grove, 1991; Pye, 1992; Ralston, Holt, Terpstra, & Yu, 1997; Shenkar & Ronen, 1987; Solomon, 1987; Tse, Francis, & Walls, 1994). Chan (1998) notes the distrust Chinese have for strangers, suggesting that "earning the term 'old friends' should be a trader's goal in the negotiation exercise" (p. 84). But what it means to be "friends" or to establish a long-term relationship needs to be understood beyond Western interpersonal expectations.

Almost any discussion of Chinese communication highlights the value of collectivism (i.e., the importance of group over individual goals and needs) and its manifestation in *guanxi* (Ford, LaTour, Vitell, & French, 1997; Shenkar & Ronen, 1987). But these concepts often are described without appreciation for cultural nuances. *Guanxi* is generally explained in terms of moral affiliation, family-type obligations, bonds of friendship, harmony in relationships, relationship over contract, and embedded social networks (Chan, Ko, & Yu, 2000; Downing, 1992; Lee & Lo, 1998; Warrington & McCall, 1983). One author provides the following explanation of the concept:

> These *guanxi* have significantly greater impact on business than comparable "old boys networks" do in the United States, and the Chinese are far more overt about

it. As one article comments, it is sometimes hard to know who really has the authority to make a negotiated commitment stick, but a quick solution is to cozy up to someone important on the local scene. (Li, 1996, pp. 1060-1061)

We draw attention here to three aspects of relationship that merit further attention in negotiation research: *guanxi*, in-group membership, and collectivism.

What is guanxi? The comparison of guanxi to Western social networks or familial ties misses the strength of the extended ties inherent in this concept. Further, it is an oversimplification to compare *guanxi* to collectivist concern. A more accurate picture of *guanxi* may be drawn from Massett's (1999) cross-cultural research on the transitivity rule in social networks. In any culture, individuals have links to other individuals within their social network, who in turn have links to their own network of relationships. Consider the example that Person A is linked to Person B and Person B is linked to Person C. Within individualist cultures, Person A has no obligations to Person C nor personal rights to request assistance from Person C. Although Person B may introduce Persons A and C, their rights and obligations to each other would result only from these two individuals choosing to establish a direct relationship. In contrast, within collectivistic cultures, the rule of transitivity applies: If A equals B and B equals C, then A equals C. In other words, because Person B is linked to both Person A and Person C, Persons A and C share the same rights and obligations that Person B has in both relationships.

Massett (1999) found support for the transitivity rule in social networks in Mexico and for non-transitive networks in the United States. Future research examining the transitive nature of *guanxi* relationships also should investigate the expectations of rights and obligations related to such relationships. Chan (1998) provides for the likelihood of transitivity in *guanxi* relationships, noting that strangers met through relatives, good friends, or colleagues may be more accepted among Chinese because of *guanxi*. Chan also notes that being a friend brings both privilege and responsibilities; the negative side is that the Chinese may make seemingly unreasonable demands on friends. Research should explore whether foreign negotiators and business partners are held to these same relational expectations. In other words, can foreign negotiators reach the status of in-group or do they retain the status of foreigner despite apparent relational bonds?

Can foreigners be in-group members? The Western view of the negotiation relationship is generally based on egalitarian expectations of collaborating between parties who view each other as relatively equal. Western companies may believe they have a slightly superior role because they feel they are providing much needed capital and technology to the Chinese.

But from a Western perspective, as long as both sides continue to benefit, the relationship should proceed (Cai & Adrian, 1999). Yet, the commitment to interpersonal relationships within Chinese culture may not translate to relationships across national boundaries. On one hand, Chinese negotiators may actually trust their foreign counterparts more than people from their own country, because of a reverence for foreigners and foreign products. But on the other hand, the benefits and commitments to in-group relationships may not apply to international partners. Although discussions of Chinese values emphasize harmony in relationships, *guanxi*, and long-term commitment to established relationships, it is possible that, despite good working relationships and apparent friendships, international negotiators may remain, at least to a certain degree, members of the out-group. Given their long history and societal development, the Chinese cultural view of China as *zhong guo* (Middle Kingdom) and the rest of the world as *wei guo* (star nations) may be stronger than is generally recognized by foreign negotiators.

Second, although the reasons for establishing international relationships may vary, the long-range goals may be more specific, such as acquiring technology and capital to become self-sufficient. The risk of introducing technology into developing nations only to be cut off from the partnership is not new to Western companies seeking international joint ventures (Bleeke & Ernst, 1993). The seemingly premature dissolution of an apparently "successful" relationship can leave Western negotiators distrusting the pursuit of future partnerships. But from the Chinese perspective, once primary goals are met, dissolution of the partnership may be viewed as a natural progression of the relationship. Differing goals and notions about relationships may be misleading to both parties (Cai, in press). Future research should move beyond current assumptions about in group and out group to examine how relationships are established, how trust is built and maintained, expectations related to psychological and physical needs within established relationships, and Chinese perspectives on long-term relationships in foreign alliances.

How do culture and context interact? The Western overemphasis on collectivism and relational harmony in the Chinese negotiation literature may be misleading Western negotiators who forget that negotiation is a context that is inherently competitive as both sides strive to achieve their own goals. Further, although relational goals in negotiation should not be ignored, the primary focus of negotiation is on instrumental, or measurable, rather than relational goals (Wilson & Putnam, 1990). In Cai's (1998) study, pre-negotiation plans were coded for three types of goals: instrumental, relational, and identity. Results showed plans by both U.S. and Taiwanese participants focused primarily on instrumental goals, with no significant differences between the two groups on relational or identity goals. Future research can examine how Chinese balance instrumental, relational, and identity goals in different conflict and bargaining contexts.

Any generalizations about Chinese culture should be understood within the context of negotiation (Janosik, 1987), examining how culture interacts with the structural features of negotiation (Faure, 1999). Negotiator role is one such structural feature shown to override the effects of culture (Cai, Wilson, & Drake, 2000; Graham, Mintu, & Rodgers, 1994; Lee, 2000). Cai and Donohue (1997) demonstrate that facework is determined less by culture than by negotiator role. In traditional Confucian hierarchical culture, the buyer should achieve better outcomes than the seller, yet market conditions of contemporary China give rise to a "seller's market" so that sellers may outperform buyers (Adler et al., 1992). Contextual features such as role, time limits, number of issues and how they are linked, and the cultural composition of the bargaining dyad, whether intra- or intercultural, should be studied for interactions with Chinese culture (Cai et al., 2000).

RQ6: Are the Findings Generalizeable?

Finally, researchers need to begin clarifying the distinctions of being "Chinese." Cai and Fink (2000) found Asian women to be significantly more individualistic than Asian men. Faure (1999) and Graham (1996) note differences between people from northern and southern China, describing northern Chinese as more cooperative and equity oriented, and southern Chinese as more competitive, not minding unbalanced outcomes as long as they are beneficial. Vast differences exist between northern and southern China, from structures of lineage relationships to business practices. Shenkar and Ronen (1987) offer a warning about overgeneralizing between the Chinese countries/communities of Hong Kong, Taiwan, Singapore, and China because of variations in geography, language, and religion and their level of industrial development. We need to move beyond the generalizations found in the existing literature on Chinese negotiation to a discussion of specific Chinese cultural groups spread across countries and regions. There is much work to be done to begin distinguishing communication and negotiating behavior across different populations of Chinese people. Future studies should compare people from the wide variety of Chinese communities worldwide with the goal of understanding how "Chinese culture" has been adapted globally and what aspects of Chinese culture are pervasive.

Existing literature on Chinese negotiation is repetitive: "Nearly all studies indicate that foreign negotiators should try to understand the Chinese culture and to develop interaction, *guanxi,* and long-term relationships with the Chinese" (Chan, 1998, p. 93). Even so, there is still much that we do not know about Chinese negotiation. The questions provided in this chapter highlight several major areas for future research on Chinese negotiation. There are many questions still to be addressed and many more questions to be answered.

REFERENCES

Adler, N. J., Brahm, R., & Graham, J. L. (1992). Strategy implementation: A comparison of face-to-face negotiations in the People's Republic of China and the United States. *Strategic Management Journal, 13*, 449-466.

Blackman, C. (1997). *Negotiating China: Case studies and strategies*. St. Leonards, Australia: Allen & Unwin.

Bleeke, J., & Ernst, D. (1993). The way to win in cross-border alliances. In J. Bleeke & D. Ernst (Eds.), *Collaborating to compete: Using strategic alliances and acquisitions in the global marketplace*. New York: John Wiley & Sons.

Brunner, J. A., & Wang, Y. (1988). Chinese negotiating and the concept of face. *Journal of International Consumer Marketing, 1*, 27-43.

Cacioppo, J. T., & Petty, R. E. (1982). The need for cognition. *Journal of Personality and Social Psychology, 42*, 116-131.

Cai, D. A. (1998). Culture, plans, and the pursuit of negotiation goals. *Journal of Asian Pacific Communication, 8*, 103-123.

Cai, D. A. (in press). Looking below the surface: Comparing subtleties of U.S. and Chinese cultures in negotiation. J. Weiss (Ed.), *Tigers roar: East Asia's recovery and its impact*. Armonk, NY: M. E. Sharpe.

Cai, D. A., & Adrian, A. (1999, May). Culture and decision making in international alliances: U.S. and China. Paper presented at the annual conference of the International Communication Association, San Francisco.

Cai, D. A., & Donohue, W. A. (1997). Determinants of facework in intercultural negotiation. *Asian Journal of Communication, 7*, 85-110.

Cai, D. A., & Drake, L. (1998). The business of business negotiation: An intercultural perspective. *Communication Yearbook, 21*, 153-190.

Cai, D. A., & Fink, E. L. (2000, June). Conflict styles and culture: A reconsideration of avoidance in the dual concern model. Paper presented at the annual conference of the International Association of Conflict Management, St. Louis.

Cai, D. A., Wilson, S. R., & Drake, L. (2000). Culture in context: Individualism/collectivism, negotiator role, framing, and paths to integrative agreements. *Human Communication Research, 26*, 591-617.

Chan, A. C. F. (1998). Business negotiation with the Chinese: Evidences from China, Taiwan, and Hong Kong. In K. Leung & D. Tjosvold (Eds.), *Conflict management in the Asia Pacific: Assumptions and approaches in diverse cultures* (pp. 73-121). New York: John Wiley & Sons.

Chan, H. L., Ko, A., & Yu, E. (2000). Confucianism and management. In O. H. M. Yau & H. C. Steele (Eds.), *China business: Challenges in the 21st century* (pp. 179-192). Hong Kong: Chinese University Press.

Chang, J. L. J. (1991). Negotiation of the 17 August 1982 U.S.-PRC arms communiqué: Beijing's negotiating tactics. *The China Quarterly, 125*, 33-54.

Chang, H. C., & Holt, G. R. (1991). More than relationship: Chinese interaction and the principle of *kuan-hsi*. *Communication Quarterly, 39*, 251-271.

Chen, M. (1993). Understanding Chinese and Japanese negotiating styles. *The International Executive, 35*, 147-159.

Chu, C. N. (1991). *The Asian mind game*. New York: Rawson Associates.

Davidson, W. H. (1987). Creating and managing joint ventures in China. *California Management Review, 29*, 77-94.

Davies, I., & Clarke, G. (1994, March). The art of war between friends: Successfully negotiating with the Chinese. *Law Society Journal*, 38-42.

de Keijzer, A. J. (1992). *China: Business strategies for the '90s*. Berkeley, CA: Pacific View Press.

Deverge, M. (1986). Negotiation with the Chinese. *Euro-Asia Business Review, 5,* 34-36.

Downing, R. (1992). The continuing power of cultural tradition and socialist ideology: Cross-cultural negotiations involving Chinese, Korean, and American negotiators. *Journal of Dispute Resolution* (1), 105-132.

Eiteman, D. K. (1990). American executives' perceptions of negotiating joint ventures with the People's Republic of China: Lessons learned. *Columbia Journal of World Business, 29,* 59-67.

Epstein, S. (1990). Cognitive-experiential self-theory. In L. Pervin (Ed.), *Handbook of personality theory and research* (pp. 165-192). New York: Guilford Press.

Fang, T. (1999). *Chinese business negotiating style.* Thousand Oaks, CA: Sage.

Faure, G. O. (1999). The cultural dimension of negotiation: The Chinese case. *Group Decision and Negotiation, 8,* 187-215.

Faure, G. O. (1998). Negotiation: The Chinese concept. *Negotiation Journal, 14,* 137-148.

Ford, J. B., LaTour, M. S., Vitell, S. J., & French, W. A. (1997). Moral judgment and market negotiations: A comparison of Chinese and American managers. *Journal of International Marketing, 5*(2), 57-76.

Frankenstein, J. (1986). Trend in Chinese business practice: Change in the Beijing wind. *California Management Review, 29,* 148-160.

Gannon, M. J., & Associates. (1994). *Understanding global cultures: Metaphorical journeys through 17 countries.* Thousand Oaks, CA: Sage.

Gelfand, M. J., & McCusker, C. (in press). Culture, metaphor, and negotiation. In M. Gannon & K. L. Newman (Eds.), *Handbook of cross-cultural management.* New York: Blackwell Publishers.

Gilsdorf, J. W. (1997). Metacommunication effects on international business negotiating in China. *Business Communication Quarterly, 6,* 20-37.

Graham, J. L. (1996). Vis-à-vis: International business negotiation. In J. L. Usunier & P. N. Ghauri (Eds.), *International business negotiations* (pp. 69-90). Oxford: Pergamon.

Graham, J. L. (1986). The problem solving approach to negotiations in industrial marketing. *Journal of Business Research, 14,* 549-566.

Graham, J. L. (1985). Cross-cultural marketing negotiations: A laboratory experiment. *Marketing Science, 4,* 130-146.

Graham, J. L., & Herberger, R. A. (1983, July/August). Negotiators abroad: Don't shoot from the hip. *Harvard Business Review,* 160-168.

Graham, J. L., Kim, D. K., Lin, C. Y., & Robinson, M. (1988). Buyer-seller negotiations around the Pacific Rim: Differences in fundamental exchange processes. *Journal of Consumer Research, 15,* 48-54.

Graham, J. L., Mintu, A. T., & Rodgers, W. (1994). Explorations of negotiation behaviors in ten foreign cultures using a model developed in the United States. *Management Science, 40,* 72-95.

Hall, E. T. (1976). *Beyond culture.* New York: Doubleday.

Hendryx, S. R. (1986, July-August). The China trade: Making the deal. *Harvard Business Review,* 75-84.

Hesselgrave, D. (1978). *Communicating Christ cross-culturally.* Grand Rapids, MI: Academie.

Hofstede, G. (1980). *Cultures consequences: International differences in work related values.* Beverly Hills, CA: Sage.

Holmes, M. E. (1992). Phase structures in negotiation. In L. L. Putnam & M. E. Roloff (Eds.), *Communication and negotiation* (pp. 83-105). Newbury Park, CA: Sage.

Hu, W. Z., & Grove, C. L. (1991). *Encountering the Chinese: A guide for Americans.* Yarmouth, ME: Intercultural Press.

Huang, Z. D. (1990). Negotiation in China: Cultural and practical characteristics. *China Law Reporter, 6,* 139-145.

Janosik, R. J. (1987). Rethinking the culture-negotiation link. *Negotiation Journal, 3,* 385-395.

Kelley, H. H. (1972). *Attribution in social interaction.* Morristown, NJ: General Learning Press.

Kirkbride, P. S., & Tang, S. F. Y. (1990). Negotiation: Lessons from behind the bamboo curtain. *Journal of General Management, 16,* 1-13.

Kirkbride, P. S., Tang, S. F. Y., & Westwood, R. I. (1991). Chinese conflict preferences and negotiating behaviour: Cultural and psychological influences. *Organization Studies, 12,* 365-386.

Knutsson, J. (1986). Chinese commercial negotiating behaviour and its institutional and cultural determinants: A summary. In *Chinese culture and management* (pp. 18-31). Brussels: Euro-China Association for Management Development.

Kluckhohn, E. R., & Strodtbeck, E. L. (1961). *Variations in value orientations.* Evanston, IL: Row, Peterson.

Lakoff, G., & Johnson, M. (1980). *Metaphors we live by.* Chicago: University of Chicago Press.

Lall, A. (1968). *How communist China negotiates.* New York: Columbia University Press.

Lavin, F. L. (1994). Negotiating with the Chinese: Or how not to kowtow. *Foreign Affairs, 73,* 16-22.

Lee, D. Y. (2000). Retail bargaining behaviour of American and Chinese customers. *European Journal of Marketing, 34,* 190-206.

Lee, K. H., & Lo, T. W. C. (1998, Summer). American businesspeople's perceptions of marketing and negotiating in the People's Republic of China. *International Marketing Review,* 41-51.

Leung, K. (1987). Some determinants of reactions to procedural models for conflict resolution: A cross-national study. *Journal of Personality and Social Psychology, 53,* 898-908.

Leung, T. K. P., & Leung, S. M. (2000). Negotiating joint ventures in China: The relationship between bureaucracy and strategy. *Asia Business Law Review, 27,* 20-29.

Li, J. C. Y. (1996). Strategic negotiation in the greater Chinese economic area: A new American perspective. *Albany Law Review, 59,* 1035-1080.

Lindsay, C. P., & Dempsey, B. L. (1983). Ten painfully learned lessons about working in China: The insights of two American behavioral scientists. *Journal of Applied Behavioral Science, 19,* 265-276.

Liu, S. S. (1995). A comparison of pharmaceutical promotional tactics between Hong Kong and China. *Journal of Business & Industrial Marketing, 10,* 34-43.

Lu, X. (1998). An interface between individualistic and collectivistic orientations in Chinese cultural values and social relations. *The Howard Journal of Communications, 9,* 91-107.

Macleod, R. K. (1988). *China, Inc.: How to do business with the Chinese.* New York: Bantam.

Massett, H. A. (1999). *The effects of culture and other-orientation on personal communication networks and behavioral intentions: A comparison between the United States and Mexico.* Unpublished doctoral dissertation, University of Maryland, College Park. (Dissertation Abstracts 9957185).

McLaughlin, M.L. (1984). *Conversation: How talk is organized.* Beverly Hills, CA: Sage.

Melvin, S. (1995). Getting started. *The China Business Review, 22*(3), 21-24.

Morris, M. W., & Peng, K. P. (1994). Culture and cause: American and Chinese attributions for social and physical events. *Journal of Personality and Social Psychology, 67,* 949-971.

Nadler, L. B., Nadler, M. K., & Broome, B. (1985). Culture and the management of conflict situations. In W. Gudykunst, L. Stewart, & S. Ting-Toomey (Eds.), *Communication, culture, and organizational processes.* Newbury Park, CA: Sage.

Nair, A. S., & Stafford, E. R. (1998). Strategic alliances in China: Negotiating the barriers. *Long Range Planning, 31,* 139-146.

Pan, Y. G., Kim, D. H., & Vanhonacker, W. R. (1995). The need for cognition: A comparative study of American and Chinese business executives. *Journal of International Consumer Marketing, 7*(3), 95-106.

Peng, K. P., & Nisbett, R. E. (1999). Culture, dialectics, and reasoning about contradiction. *American Psychologist, 54,* 741-754.

Pye, L. W. (1992). The Chinese approach to negotiating. *The International Executive, 34,* 463-468.

Pye, L. W. (1986, July/August). The China trade: Making the deal. *Harvard Business Review,* 74-80.

Pye, L. W. (1982). *Chinese commercial negotiating style.* Santa Monica, CA: Rand Corporation.

Ralston, D. A., Holt, D. H., Terpstra, R. H., & Yu, K. C. (1997). The impact of national culture and economic ideology on managerial work values: A study of the United States, Russia, Japan, and China. *Journal of International Business Studies, 28,* 177-207.

Redding, S. G. (1980, May). Cognition as an aspect of culture and its relation to management processes: An exploratory view of the Chinese case. *Journal of Management Studies,* 127-148.

Seligman, S. D. (1990). *Dealing with the Chinese: A practical guide to business etiquette.* London: Mercury.

Shenkar, O., & Ronen, S. (1987). The cultural context of negotiations: The implications of Chinese interpersonal norms. *The Journal of Applied Behavioral Science, 23,* 263-275.

Solomon, R. H. (1985). *Chinese political negotiating behavior: A briefing analysis.* Santa Monica, CA: Rand Corporation.

Solomon, R. H. (1987). Friendship and obligation in Chinese negotiating style. In H. Binnendijk (Ed.), *National negotiating styles.* Washington: Department of State.

Stewart, S., & Keown, C. F. (1989). Talking with the dragon: Negotiating in the People's Republic of China. *Columbia Journal of World Business, 28,* 68-72.

Swierczek, F. W. (1990). Culture and negotiation in the Asian context: Key issues in the marketing of technology. *Journal of Managerial Psychology, 5,* 21-28.

Ting-Toomey, S. (1988). Intercultural conflict styles: A face-negotiation theory. In Y. Y. Kim & W. Gudykunst (Eds.), *Theories of intercultural communication* (pp. 213-235). Newbury Park, CA: Sage.

Tse, D. K., Francis, J., & Walls, J. (1994). Cultural differences in conducting intra- and inter-cultural negotiations: A Sino-Canadian comparison. *Journal of International Business Studies, 25,* 537-555.

Tung, R. L. (1982a). *U.S.-China negotiations.* New York: Pergamon.

Tung, R. L. (1982b). U.S.-China negotiations: Practices, procedures and outcomes. *Journal of International Business Studies, 13*(2), 25-37.

Walker, G. B. (1990). Cross-cultural argument in international negotiation: Values and reasoning at the Law of the Sea conference. In F. H. Van Eemeren, R. Grootendorst, J. A. Blair, & C. A. Willard, (Eds.), *Proceedings of the Second International Conference on Argumentation.* Amsterdam: SICSAT.

Warrington, M. B., & McCall, J. B. (1983). Negotiating a foot into the Chinese door. *Management Development, 21*(2), 3-13.

Wilson, S. R., & Putnam, L. L. (1990). Interaction goals in negotiation. In J. A. Anderson (Ed.). *Communication yearbook 13* (pp. 374-406). Newbury Park, CA: Sage.

Young, K. T. (1968). *Negotiating with the Chinese Communists: The United States experience, 1953-1967.* New York: McGraw-Hill.

Yum, J. O. (1988). The impact of Confucianism on interpersonal relationships and communication patterns in East Asia. *Communication Monographs, 55*, 374-388.

12

Advertising with Chinese Characteristics: The Development of Advertising in China, 1979–1999

Zhihong Gao

Ever since 1979, when China embarked on a voyage of economic reforms, the Chinese economy has been developing at a fantastic speed. According to China State Statistics Bureau ("China sees," 1998), the nation's gross domestic product has grown at an annual rate of 9.8 percent for the last 20 years. Growing together with the economy is the purchasing power of the Chinese people and the huge potential of the Chinese consumer market. Advertising, an integral part of China's economic reform package, has also undergone rapid development over the years.

The development of Chinese advertising is often quoted by the proud Chinese as an index of their economic achievements and praised by Western scholars and politicians as a flagship of how far China has voyaged on a road to capitalism. Yet, the advertising environment in China is often characterized by foreigners as "difficult and perplexing" (Donath, 1980), "fraught with problems" (Boudot, 1988), and full of "pitfalls" ("Hard sell," 1994); consequently, international businesses that want to enter the market are advised to lower their expectations and remain patient. Facing such a contradiction, one has to wonder about the true picture of Chinese advertising.

The purpose of this chapter is to adopt an institutional approach to Chinese advertising and analyze its development in the larger social-economic context. It is my argument that the social foundation that has provided the fertile soil for modern advertising in capitalist society is missing in China and that, conditioned by its own historical-social context, Chinese advertising has developed characteristics of its own. The chapter will consist of three parts: (1) the social foundation of Chinese advertising, (2) the general development of Chinese advertising, and (3) an industry of Chinese characteristics.

THE SOCIAL FOUNDATION OF CHINESE ADVERTISING

In the West, modern advertising emerged at the end of the nineteenth century as a result of industrialization and urbanization on a massive scale (Pope, 1983; Schudson, 1984). After more than a century's development, advertising has established itself as a major social institution and plays an important role in Western society. Economically, advertising provides information in respect to products and services to facilitate the efficient functioning of the market and informed consumer judgment. In addition, advertising has also penetrated into various social sectors and, through advertising dollars and sponsorships, finances a whole range of social institutions.

It is safe to say that advertising is a product of capitalism, and its philosophical roots can be found in the idea system of classical liberalism and its major economic institution, the market system (Rotzoll & Haefner, 1996, p. 30). According to classical liberalism, human beings are rational and self-interested; as individuals they participate in the market and take care of their own interest by serving others well. In a free-market economy with perfect competition, the invisible hand of the market will order things accordingly, and the government should interfere as little as possible.

Yet, as my analysis will demonstrate, the ideology of classical liberalism is generally missing in Chinese society, and the development of Chinese advertising has been based upon a dramatically different social foundation.

From 1949, when the People's Republic of China was founded, until 1977, the Chinese economy was tilted toward heavy and military industries, and consumer goods production was largely ignored. Meanwhile, ideology played a prominent role in Chinese politics, and Chinese society was extremely politicized. In order to reinforce its communist worldview, the Chinese Communist Party (CCP) systematically destroyed traditional belief systems such as Confucianism, Buddhism, and Taoism and replaced them with new traditions and a new historical memory codified in communist ideological categories and language (Schurmann, 1968; Solomon, 1972).

The success of Chinese communist propaganda was largely attributed to the development of a closed communication system in the country. All the media in the country were directly financed and controlled by the CCP and its affiliated organizations. The general headquarters of the Chinese communication network was the Propaganda Department of the Central Committee. Because "the propaganda program was an integral part of the

Party's policy, a decision on economics or other areas of development also prescribed a coordinated propaganda strategy" (Liu, 1971, p. 41). In such a case, it is not surprising that the Propaganda Department administered a wide range of issues, from science to education, from mass media to literature and art, and from public health to sports. Actually, no aspect of life in Communist China had an independent existence, as all were subjected to strong central control.

In 1978, when a new government headed by Deng Xiaoping came into power, the country began to reorient its development and thus embark on a road of economic reform and rapid growth. Meanwhile, attracted by its cheap labor and huge market potentials, many transnational corporations set up operations in the country, bringing with them Western technologies and thoughts. Consequently, the Chinese people are enjoying increasing access to the outside world in terms of both commodities and information. Yet, confronted with the various challenges for democracy, the regime still upholds its socialist ideology and redefines its economic system as a "socialist market economy with Chinese characteristics." Similarly, the Chinese media, though having gained some autonomy in management, are still firmly controlled by the party.

We can see that China represents a dramatically different case from developed Western countries. Before 1979, China was economically underdeveloped and suffered from serious material insufficiency; in such a context, plain living was strongly advocated by the party and widely accepted by the people as a traditional virtue. Meanwhile, the CCP exercised totalitarian control over various social sectors, including the economy, the media, and the arts, and the capitalist West with its bourgeois thoughts and lifestyles was condemned without reserve. It is important to understand that it was against such a bleak and gray background that commercial advertising was reintroduced into the country in 1979.

Even today, despite its rapid industrial development, China is still primarily agricultural, and there is no significant affluence or industrial overproduction. Central planning has been the dominant feature of the economy for decades, and a market economy is merely a new experiment recently implemented by the government. Ideologically, the government still upholds socialism and advocates the development of public goods, and the friendly probusiness atmosphere of classical liberalism is generally missing in the society. Culturally speaking, China is still collectivistic in orientation, where group interest commands a higher priority than individual interest and traditional values such as conformity and harmony are still widely celebrated. So, it is safe to say that the economic, social, and ideological foundations, which have provided the fertile soil for the growth of advertising in capitalist society, do not consistently prevail in China. Yet, since its reintroduction in 1979, advertising has been developing rapidly in the country.

THE GENERAL DEVELOPMENT OF CHINESE ADVERTISING

Modern advertising in China dates back to the early part of the twentieth century, and the 1930s is said to be the "old golden time" of Chinese advertising (Xu, 1989). Introduced by foreigners, advertising at that time primarily served foreign businesses to promote Western products in China (Wang, 1997).

From the establishment of the People's Republic in 1949 up to the advent of the Cultural Revolution, the communist state tolerated the existence of advertising in the country out of pragmatic considerations (Bishop, 1989; Chu, 1982). Between 1966 and 1978, advertising completely disappeared from the Chinese media as a result of the Cultural Revolution. According to the socialist orthodoxy, "advertising is a necessary evil for the capitalist countries caused by over-production and under-consumption"(Chu, 1982, p. 40); the goal of socialism is to get rid of such a capitalist evil.

After ten years' absence, advertising returned to China in 1979 as part of the state's efforts to develop its economy. Commercials were first broadcast on Shanghai Radio in January 1979; at the same time, magazine, newspaper, and movie advertisements reappeared, and billboards and shop-window displays were restored (Bishop, 1989, p. 141). Most important of all, Chinese television also began to air commercials and accept international advertising. In December 1979, *The People's Daily* announced that it would accept advertisements of foreign concerns (Chu, 1982). Consequently, the images of foreign commodities, such as Coca-Cola, Swiss watches, and Japanese airlines, began to penetrate Chinese daily life.

Though the advertising industry in China had a late start, it has been developing at a strikingly high speed (Cheng, 1996; Song & Wong, 1998). Since the 1980s, advertising has become one of the fastest-growing industries, with an overall 30-40 percent annual growth. Its total turnover had reached 150 million Chinese *yuan*[1] in 1982, 845 million in 1986, 6,780 million in 1992, and 53,783 million in 1998 (Anonymous, 2000). In terms of total advertising spending, China ranked 36th in 1990 in the world and jumped to ninth in 1997, with ad spending of $5.6 billion (Song & Wong, 1998).

The growth of advertising agencies in China is also astonishing. In 1979, there were only a dozen advertising agencies, most of which, such as Beijing Advertising Co. and Shanghai Advertising & Decorating Co., were established by the government as official bodies to handle export advertising. The number of agencies has grown significantly over the years: by 1992 there were about 16,683 agencies; in the late 1990s, there were more than 60,000 agencies employing more than 587,000 people (Anonymous, 2000).

Chinese television advertising has experienced the most rapid development and has become the most popular advertising medium. Before 1979, Chinese television had never carried advertisements, and its funding was provided entirely by the state. Now a large proportion of television programming finance comes from advertising revenue. For instance, in 1992, China Central Television (CCTV) gathered almost 500 million *yuan* from advertising revenue, and in 1999 the figure reached 4,714 million. Other media such as radio and newspapers, though not as rich as television, also harvest good revenue from advertising. The People's Radio of Qingdao, a coastal city of about 1 million urban residents, collected 29 million *yuan* in advertising revenue in 1999 (Anonymous, 2000).

Facing the rapid growth of the advertising market and the various new problems, the Chinese government has also been making vigorous efforts to regulate the industry. In 1982, it issued "Provisional Regulation for Advertising Management," which was replaced in 1987 by "Regulation for Advertising Management." In 1994, China issued its "Advertising Law." Besides the basic advertising law, the administrative body of Chinese advertising, the State Administration for Industry and Commerce (SAIC), also issued numerous orders over the years to regulate the advertising market.

Despite its rapid growth, Chinese advertising still contains a lot of problems and contradictions, and it would be naive and over-optimistic to celebrate its fast growth as an emblem of victorious capitalism in China. In many ways, the development of advertising in China has been closely tied to and reflected the legacy of Chinese socialist economy and politics and thus taken on some unique characteristics.

AN INDUSTRY OF CHINESE CHARACTERISTICS

Chinese advertising shares many similarities with its Western counterparts. However, since its reintroduction into the country in 1979, Chinese advertising has also developed some unique characteristics.

An Institution Born out of Macroeconomic Imbalance

Advertising in a capitalist society is seen as the institution of affluence because it provides a primary solution to the problem of overproduction through promotion of consumption. However, in China the reintroduction of advertising was not preceded by material abundance. On the contrary, in the late 1970s China ranked among the poorest Third World countries. Primarily a socialist command economy, the country had witnessed a strong centralized monopoly over commerce, serious macroeconomic imbalance, extremely severe material shortage, and slow growth of living standards. Rationing of daily commodities was a prevalent practice. For instance, in 1976 rationed retail commodities reached 77 items (Solinger, 1984). It is in such a historical context that advertising was reintroduced into the country in 1979.

The essential goal of China's economic reforms is to promote economic growth and increase the living standard of the people. However, in the process of reform and reorientation, the country has repeatedly witnessed macroeconomic imbalance between demand and supply. For example, during the initial stage of the reform, namely from 1979 to 1983, the rapid increase in household income led to dramatically increased demand for consumer goods and consequently a high inflation rate. To readdress the problem, the government, on one hand, increased its imports of agricultural and manufactured consumer goods to meet the increased demand; on the other hand, it adopted an austerity wage policy to restrict the growing demand. As a result of these measures, China experienced substantial trade deficits and the living standard of the people lagged behind. The scenario repeated itself in the late 1980s and the first half of the 1990s (Naughton, 1995).

Given the fact that China was repeatedly confronted with imbalance between growing demand and insufficient supply, the role advertising plays in the country becomes extremely dubious. As there was no free market with abundant commodities to begin with, advertising only helped worsen the imbalance between demand and supply. In such a light, the reintroduction of advertising in 1979 can be seen as premature. Even in the 1980s, as the government still practiced a dual-track pricing system[2] and tried to reduce the pressure of increased demand, advertising counteracted the objectives of the government policies by promoting consumption and affecting demand.

Similarly, advertising plays a rather paradoxical role in promoting domestic industries. Compared to gigantic transnational corporations, Chinese domestic enterprises are small in scale and weak in finance, and rising advertising expenses have become a barrier to entering competition with international companies on the same level. The local businesses do not seem to have many choices: They either channel all their finance disproportionately to advertising in a desperate effort, while ignoring research and product development, or watch their market share grabbed away by international competitors through well-financed advertising campaigns. Even though the government has adopted some policies to protect domestic enterprises from international competition, such policies are limited in effect as well as under constant attack from foreign business interests.

The Socialist Role of Advertising in China

Given the macroeconomic imbalance and the dubious role advertising plays in the economy, one has to wonder why the government reintroduced advertising into the country in the first place. The answer is, Chinese advertising at its initial stage assumed a very different role from that of its Western counterpart. More specifically, advertising functioned as an essential ideological tool to facilitate the country's policy reorientation.

In its ideological reorientation, the communist state first managed to give advertising a legitimate status and elevate it from being an evil of capitalism to an aesthetic art of socialism. A quotation from a Shanghai newspaper provides an adequate illustration of this new dimension of advertising in socialist China:

> We should use advertising as a means to educate and assist people and to promote understanding and cement ties between the masses and production and sales departments. Advertising is an art involving a wide selection of the people. Good advertising can make our cities beautiful, lift our spirits and make us feel proud of a thriving socialist economy or culture in a cheerful artistic atmosphere. (Quoted in Anderson, 1981, p. 12)

From this quotation we can see that, besides its economic function, advertising in China also serves an educational and propaganda purpose. Advertisements about various consumer products help break the linkage between socialism and austerity and cast the country in the glamourous light of material prosperity. In such a light, the contrast between China and Western developed countries gradually diminishes in terms of consumer goods: Most luxury commodities have found their way to China and are loudly advertising their availability through various means.

The propaganda function of advertising in China often puzzles and even irritates Westerners. In fact, Chinese advertising has been designated by the government as an important tool to build a "socialist spiritual civilization"; as a result, regulations require that companies either produce advertisements for or donate space to Communist Party propaganda (Forney, 1997). Thus, it is not uncommon to see some public-interest advertisements standing out among product advertisements in the media. The content of these ads may range from environmental protection to family planning and from social morality to nationalistic sentiments.

If advertising in capitalist society fulfills the ideological function of capitalist realism (Schudson, 1984), advertising in socialist China can similarly be seen as part of socialist-realism rhetoric, which beautifies as well as says "I love you" to the socialist regime. However, a contradiction emerged as many early advertisements in China promoted Western luxury products, which were either unavailable in the market or too expensive for the Chinese. One has to expect that the advertising of Western products extolled capitalism to the Chinese and consequently undermined the legitimacy of socialism in the country.

As Chinese advertising has developed, especially as an increasing amount of international advertising has appeared on the horizon, the contradictions involving advertising's economic role and its ideological baggage have intensified. In order to hurdle the negative impact of advertising and uphold the socialist ideal, China has issued rigorous ethical standards in its advertising law and subjected advertisements to censorship (Cheng, 1996; Peerenboom, 1995). Meanwhile, the regime keeps emphasizing the positive role of advertising in constructing both socialist material and spiritual civilizations. Given the rapid development of Chinese consumer goods industries, more and more domestic firms begin to advertise their products on various media. In such a context, it is possible for the advertising of domestic brands to boost the national pride of the Chinese and to consequently implicate itself in the regime's rhetoric of "socialist market economy with Chinese characteristics."

The Media Are in Control

There is a dialectic relationship between advertising and the media in China in that the development of advertising, to a large extent, is conditioned by the mass media system of the country, and advertising in its turn also promotes the development of the media.

Whereas in the West the media are usually privately owned and operate for profit, in China the media used to be exclusively owned and financed by the state and function primarily as the propaganda apparatus of the CCP. The Chinese media system is made up of four levels: On the top there are the party's central media organs, such as China Central Television, China People's Radio, and *The People's Daily*; these media tend to have large audiences and enjoy national monopolies; each ministry also has its own organ or trade publications. The other three levels are regions (31 provinces), local cities (450), and counties (approximately 1,900) (Huang, 1994). On the whole, the Chinese media are closely affiliated with the Chinese administration system and enjoy limited autonomy.

In the era of economic reforms, the Chinese media have acquired some new dimensions. While serving the country's drive toward market development, they are also undergoing a rapid process of commercialization; and as the state has decreased its subsidy to the media, advertising has become their primary source of revenue (Zhao, 1998). For example, in 1993 *Wen Hui Daily*, a prestigious newspaper in Shanghai, gathered 85 percent of its $7 million revenue from advertising; *The People's Daily*, though still formally controlled by the party, has become financially independent (Lazarick, 1994). There is also increasing competition between the national, provincial, and local media. A direct result of media commercialization is the erosion of the socialist ideology and the increasing pluralization of media content (Fang, 1998; Zhao, 1998). However, the state ownership of the media still remains unchallenged.

Unlike the situation in the West, where advertisers hold strong leverage over the commercial media, in China, thanks to government monopoly, it is the media's market (Geddes, 1993). As a result, it was quite legitimate for the media to adopt a three-tier rate system and charge domestic companies, joint ventures, and foreign companies totally different rates; the media could have their own in-house ad agencies and enjoy monopoly profit (Song & Wong, 1998). Though these practices have gradually faded out, it is still quite common for advertisers to deal with the media directly in terms of media buying, and agencies have a much diminished role in the market. Meanwhile, because there are limited media outlets and consequently limited advertising space, advertisers have to wait two to three months to get into the media (Song & Wong, 1998; Yatsko, 1997). The Chinese media people are quite happy that "advertisers have to wait in line" (Lazarick, 1994), but to ad agencies, the media have become the biggest hurdle for the further development of Chinese advertising.

It is true that, backed up by big ad money, the Chinese media have become financially independent of the state and have as a result gained more autonomy, but it is still too early to celebrate this as progressive. In fact, the limited autonomy gained from the state is often compromised by pressures from commercial interests; money instead of politics is increasingly reshaping the Chinese media according to the model of Western commercial media. Many Western scholars have pointed out the inadequacy of commercial media in the Western countries (Herman & McChesney, 1997; McChesney, 1999). After in-depth analyses of the Chinese media, Zhao (1998) warns the media reformers "not to equate reform with commercialization or reduced reform to commercialization" (p. 182); rather, China needs to explore other alternative forms of media that will promote true democracy in the country.

Complex Administration System of Advertising

Bureaucracy has been a marked characteristic of the Chinese government ever since ancient times. The communist system has not only failed to eradicate bureaucracy in its practice, but also has, to some extent, generated its own more complicated bureaucratic administration system. Advertising, though reborn in the late 1970s, has become a victim of Chinese bureaucracy.

Ad agencies in China fall into two categories: those that handle domestic advertising and are affiliated with the ministries of culture or light industry and those that are affiliated with the Ministry of Foreign Trade and Economic Cooperation (MOFTEC).[3] Meanwhile, it is up to the State Administration for Industry and Commerce (SAIC) to supervise and regulate advertising practice. In order to do business in China, ad agencies must apply to the SAIC for licenses; if approved, they need to register with the Regional Administration for Industry and Commerce (RAIC) where they will locate. In other words, to set up operations in China at a national level, an ad agency needs to apply to MOFTEC and then apply for a license with the SAIC; if an agency wants to set up regional offices, it has to apply to the regional department of MOFTEC, then register with the SAIC through the RAIC, and finally obtain a license from the RAIC (Swanson, 1997). Because advertising is a lucrative and fast-growing business sector, government ministries and bureaus are fighting for its control ("Media circus," 1998). Such bureaucratic competition will only make the scenario of Chinese advertising even more complex.

When it comes to advertising censorship, the same problems occur. Though China has issued its advertising law, it is the regional administrations' responsibility to enforce the law. So, in order to air an ad in different provinces, an ad agency has to send the ad to each provincial committee for advertising regulations for content review. Outdoor advertising is even more complicated; for example, in Beijing, each district has its own vetting committee (Forney, 1997). Censorship is often sporadic. The fact that an ad has been approved in one province does not guarantee its approval in others. In such a climate, it is quite difficult as well as frustrating to carry out national campaigns.

The advertising administration bodies also tend to set up their own in-house ad agencies, and such practices often put outside agencies at a disadvantage. For instance, Chaoyang District in Beijing has joined the outdoor advertising business: They first pitched propaganda but then shifted to paid advertising, and ads run on light boxes (a special advertising medium usually lit at night in the public squares) have a higher chance of being approved (Forney, 1997).

Though advertising is administered by a complex bureaucratic system, advertising regulations in the country tend to be vague and problematic. When the state government has no clear policies on a certain issue, the provincial governments often set up their own rules and regulations. For instance, the state does not have relevant policies concerning internet advertising, and many provinces have issued licenses to companies involving in the business. Recently, the central government decided to put web advertising on hold and ordered those provinces to cancel their licenses ("China puts web ads on hold," 1999).

In recent years, the government has gradually centralized the administration and supervision of advertising. For instance, China Advertising Association (CAA), which is affiliated with SAIC, has been recognized as the only national advertising trade association in the country; China Advertising Association of Foreign Trade and Economic Cooperation, which is affiliated with MOFTEC, joins CAA as a member.

CONCLUSION

Since 1979, China has come a long way in institutionalizing advertising as mass communication, and the development of Chinese advertising is impressive in many ways. However, despite all the astonishing figures and numbers, there are contradictions inherent in Chinese advertising, which, though a transplant from capitalist society, has been conditioned by the social-economic conditions of the country and thus developed its own characteristics.

In some aspects, Chinese advertising has served as a democratizing force and contributed to the general economic and social development in the country. However, it is necessary to notice that advertising alone cannot undertake the task of transferring China into a civil society, for two basic reasons. First, advertising is a product of capitalism and inherits the pro-business bias of the system. The solution provided by advertising is limited to consumption and preconditioned on access to financial power. Second, advertising, as a social institution, is conditioned by its social-political environment. This is especially true in China. Though economic reforms in the country have made remarkable progress, the government has been reluctant to implement fundamental political reforms. In such a context, media reforms are far from thorough and revolutionary. Rather, the government still maintains its monopoly over media, and private or foreign ownership of media is generally prohibited. Without the complete autonomy of the media and without guarantee of freedom of speech, advertising is still confined to the business sector, and advocacy of unorthodox ideas through advertising on the media is still impossible.

For future research, it will be productive to investigate how scholars in China reflect the development of Chinese advertising in the past two decades. More specifically, what kind of discourse have they borrowed from the West to analyze Chinese advertising? What kind of discourse have they developed from socialist theories to accommodate Chinese politics? What are their conclusions, and how do they define the future development of Chinese advertising? By focusing on the debate on advertising in China, we can obtain valuable insights into the evolution of Chinese advertising as well as Chinese society as a whole.

NOTES

1. One hundred U.S. dollars equaled RMB189.26 yuan in 1982, 345.28 yuan in 1986, 551.49 yuan in 1992, and 828.98 yuan in 1997 (China Statistics Bureau, 1998).

2. Under the dual-track system, a single commodity has both a (typically low) state-set planned price and a (typically higher) market price (Naughton, 1995, p. 8).

3. Foreign agencies are affiliated with MOFTEC.

REFERENCES

Anderson, M. H. (1981). China's "great leap" toward Madison Avenue. *Journal of Communication, 31*, 10-22.

Anonymous, (2000). *Twenty years of Chinese advertising* (2000). Beijing: China Statistics Press.

Bishop, R. L. (1989). *Qi lai! Mobilizing one billion Chinese.* Ames: Iowa State University Press.

Boudot, E. (1988). Chinese puzzles for foreign advertisers. *Asian Business, 24*, 82-85.

Cheng, H. (1996). Advertising in China: A socialist experiment. In K. T. Frith (Ed.), *Advertising in Asia.* Ames: Iowa State University Press, 73-102.

China puts web ads on hold. (1999, March 4). *Ad Age International Online,* http://www.adage.com/international/daily/index.html

China sees rapid economic development over past 20 years. (1998, September 22). http://www.chia-embassy.org/Cgi-Bin/Press.pl?rapiddev

Chu, J. (1982). Advertising in China: Its policy, practice and evolution. *Journalism Quarterly, 59*, 40-45+.

Donath, B. (1980). Peddling to the PRC. *Industrial Marketing, 65*, 74-77.

Fang, B. (1998, May 7). Colourful crusaders. *Far Eastern Economic Review*, 13.

Forney, M. (1997, July 10). One sign, two systems. *Far Eastern Economic Review*, 72-73.

Geddes, A. (1993, January 18). China TV ad rates soar, though still a bargain. *Advertising Age*, I-3, I-30.

Hard sell. (1994, October 31). *Business China, 20*, 4-5.

Herman, E. S., & McChesney, R. W. (1997). *The global media*. London: Cassell.

Huang, Y. (1994). Peaceful evolution: The case of television reform in post-Mao China. *Media, Culture and Society, 16*, 217-241.

Lazarick, L. (1994). Boom times for a sort of controlled Chinese press. *Editor & Publisher, 127*, 70 +.

Liu, A. P. (1971). *Communications and national integration in Communist China*. Berkeley: University of California Press.

McChesney, R. W. (1999). *Rich media, poor democracy, communication politics in dubious times*. Urbana: University of Illinois Press.

Media circus. (1998, January 19). *Business China, 24*, 5-7.

Naughton, B. (1995). *Growing out of the plan: Chinese economic reform, 1978-1993*. Cambridge, U.K.: Cambridge University Press.

Peerenboom, R. (1995). Truthful touting. *China Business Review, 22*, 26-27.

Pope, D. (1983). *The making of modern advertising*. New York: Basic Books, Inc.

Rotzoll, K. B., & Haefner, J. E. (1996). Advertising in contemporary society: Perspectives toward understanding. Urbana: University of Illinois Press.

Schudson, M. (1984). *Advertising, the uneasy persuasion*. New York: Basic Books.

Schurmann, F. (1968). *Ideology and organization in Communist China*. Los Angeles: University of California Press.

Solinger, D. J. (1984). Chinese business under socialism. Berkeley: University of California Press.

Solomon, R. H. (1972). Communication patterns and the Chinese revolution. In Y. Wei (Ed.), *Communist China* (pp. 283-293). Columbus, OH: Charles E. Merrill.

Song, T. B., & Wong, L. (1998). Getting the word out. *China Business Review, 25*, 22-25.

Swanson, L. A. (1997). China myths and advertising agencies. *International Journal of Advertising, 16*, 276-283.

Wang, J. (1997). From four hundred million to more than one billion consumers: A brief history of the foreign advertising industry in China. *International Journal of Advertising, 16*, 241-260.

Xu, B. Y. (1989). The role of advertising in China. Working paper. Urbana: Department of Advertising, University of Illinois.

Yatsko, P. (1997, January 23). Not the people's daily. *Far Eastern Economic Review*, 52.

Zhao, Y. (1998). *Media, market, and democracy in China*. Urbana: University of Illinois Press.

IV

Challenges of Glocalization

13

The Interface Between Culture and Technology in Chinese Communication

Ringo Ma

The International Institute for Management Development (IMD) in Lausanne, Switzerland, ranks "all key players in the world economy" in terms of their "competitiveness" and publishes the rankings in the *World Competitiveness Yearbook* annually (International Institute for Management Development, 2000). Among the 47 nations or regions being ranked in 1999, at least six are heavily influenced by Confucianism. The six nations or regions and their ranks are Singapore (2), Hong Kong (7), Japan (16), Taiwan (18), The People's Republic of China (29), and South Korea (38). The recognition of their economic success can be traced back to the 1980s when Hong Kong, Singapore, South Korea, and Taiwan came to be known as "Asia's Four Little Dragons," whereas Japan had been called the "Big Dragon of Asia" for many decades (Reed, 1986). Since then scholars have tried to answer whether there is a link between their economic success and Confucianism as their common cultural heritage. The following agreement was reached among the participants in the Workshop on Confucian Humanism hosted by the East-West Center in Honolulu, Hawaii:

> There was some agreement that the Confucian tradition itself was not primarily oriented toward the development of wealth and power but may have offered a setting conducive to the nurturing of such ambitions. For example, Confucian institutions appear to have fostered social and political attitudes that encouraged

rapid economic development once the seeds of free enterprise were planted by some other means. (Tu, Hejtmanek & Wachman, 1992, p. 2)

The explanation is at odds with some commonly accepted theories. Barry, Child, and Bacon (1959), for example, argue that in "Appollonian" (pastoral and agricultural) societies, as opposed to "Dionysian" (hunting and fishing) ones, conformity and obedience are emphasized in child training and there is a fear of innovation. In their notion of value orientations, Kluckhohn and Strodtbeck (1960) have proposed that change is valued in "future-oriented" but not in "past-oriented" cultures. Because Confucian societies lean more toward "Appollonianism" and "past orientation" in many respects, they were expected to be slow in the adoption of technology. In reality, however, they have proven to be more "advanced" than many other nations in this regard. In fact, both "infrastructure" (including "basic infrastructure" and "techno-logical infrastructure") and "science and technology" are ranked in the top "Competitive" list among the eight "Competitive Input Factors" used by the IMD (International Institute for Management Development, 2000). Inclusion in the top "competitiveness" list indicates high scores on the two factors.

This chapter aims to explore how traditional values and modern technology are interfaced in communication among Chinese people. Chinese culture is represented by all the Confucian nations or regions included in the IMD rankings except Japan and South Korea. Previous research suggests some major differences in communication between East Asians in Confucian soci-eties and North Americans (e.g., Ting-Toomey, 1985, 1988; Yum, 1988). While the creation and management of technology concern only a small portion of the population in any society, most people cannot avoid adopting technology in their communication with others. I will argue in this chapter that the pervasive adoption of new technology in communication by Chinese people all over the world can be viewed from the following three perspectives: use of technology as cultural practice, use of technology as cultural change, and use of technology as cultural adaptation. Communication technology has the potential to both reinforce and alter their traditional values. It may also be used to make smoother their adaptation to a new environment.

THE RELATIONSHIP BETWEEN CULTURE AND TECHNOLOGY

The relationship between culture and technology has been addressed from various perspectives. Check (1996) contends that information technology can encourage families to stay home to telecommute, run a family business, or home school their children and thus strengthen the traditional family. Ma (2000) notes that intercultural communication via the Internet is able to demystify some cultural differences exaggerated through state-sanctioned media programs and to empower the underrepresented in human society. Therefore, the global society is moving toward a state with more "local diversity within international homogenization" (p. 99).

The negative impact of technology on culture is a major theme of numerous publications. Umble (1992) reported the refusal of Amish people to have telephones in their individual households because gossip as a necessary consequence of telephone conversation would make social harmony difficult to maintain. Demac and Sung (1995) pointed out the "high social costs associated with the world of advanced communication technology" (p. 291):

> In general, there is a growing gap between the potential of technology to give people better control over their lives and the drive by others to use it for profit and centralizing control. This gap makes it all the most difficult to know if the introduction of new technology equals progress. (p. 291)

They offered an example of such centralizing control at workplace: "Secretaries now work on machines that monitor when they begin work, when they take breaks, how many keystrokes they type, and if they meet their quotas" (p. 282).

One of the most famous scholars on the pessimistic view of technological determinism is Neil Postman (e.g., 1985, 1992), who (1992) created the term "Technopoly" (a word capitalized throughout his book) to refer to a society in which the primary goal is efficiency and technical calculation is regarded as superior to human judgment. He used the term to describe how our culture is dominated by technology:

> Technopoly is a state of culture. It is also a state of mind. It contains in the deification, which means that the culture seeks its authorization in technology, finds its satisfactions in technology, and takes its orders from technology. This requires the development of a new kind of social order, and of necessity leads to the rapid dissolution of much that is associated with traditional beliefs. (p. 71)

While Postman (1992) maintains that culture is subservient to and controlled by both invisible (I.Q. scores, statistics, polling, etc.) and visible (television, computers, etc.) technologies, Winston (1995) notes that the effects of technology are the result of how they are used, and how they are used depends on the social conditions in which they are created or introduced. Compared with the "technological determinist," view which stresses "the role of media technology in governing the content of communication," "cultural determinist accounts tend to deny technology this determining role" (p. 56). Winston argues that "social and economic factors are the dominant factors in supporting or blocking the utilization of technology, and making human action the prime mover of change" (p. 55).

Schwartz and Ewald (1968) write that "however slow the change that takes place, nothing in culture is permanent" and "given sufficient time, many small changes may add up to major shifts in cultural systems" (p. 433). They describe how the adoption of a new object can lead to a major change for human society:

> When culture changes, it is real action that changes. Thus, when a Latin American peasant woman abandons her primitive grindstone in favor of a commercially operated power grinder, it is her behavior as an occupant of the status of wife or housekeeper that changes. Because of this change in real action, in time the norms for that structural position may also change. Insofar as this change may alter the relationship between husband and wife, the change in real action also modifies the real structure of that society. (p. 453)

They conceptualize "sociocultural changes as an adaptive process" (p. 452) and assert that "change is a never ending process of readjustment and readaptation, as man [sic] responds behaviorally to ever changing circumstances" (p. 454). O'Connor and Downing (1995) also note that "culture is simultaneously an ongoing progress and an active process of communication and understanding" (p. 10).

After reviewing some popular and academic discourse, McOmber (1999) identified the following three definitions of technology: "technology as instrumentality," "technology as industrialization," and "technology as novelty" (pp. 140-145). While "technology-as-industrialization represents the most typical understanding of technology in academic debates over the role of technology in society," in popular discourse, however, "technology often has little to do with 'the technological society' in the sense of the culture that arose alongside industrial production" (p. 149). "An intermingling of the other two definitions" is sometimes found in popular discourse (p. 149). At the end of his essay, a definition of "technology-as-cultural practice" is proposed to bridge the gap: "From such a perspective, every dimension of the Internet, from its very existence to its overall purposes as an entertainment or educational medium to the contents of specific Web pages, is an outcome of human choices, regardless of whether choices are intentionally made" (p. 150).

Boczkowski's (1999) study of the Argentine Mailing List, "a national virtual community composed mostly of Argentine people living abroad" (p. 87), disclosed a mutual shaping of users and technologies. The mutual shaping that took place on the list included hardware capabilities, national identities, processes of collective remembering, software configurations, and coordination practices. The "mutual shaping" theme is compatible with many definitions of "culture." According to Geertz (1973), "man [sic] is an animal suspended in webs of significance he himself has spun" and culture refers to those webs (p. 5). Therefore, he continues, "the analysis of it to be . . . not an experimental science in search of law but an interpretive one in search of meaning" (p. 5). The statement was made to justify the interpretive approach to studying culture, but it also reminds us that meanings are socially constructed in a given culture. When the interface between culture and technology is viewed from this perspective, members of a culture are adapted to an increasingly technology-oriented environment as a result of newly constructed meaning for technology. A recent example is presented in McMillan and Hyde's (2000) case study in the formation of organizational conscience through communication when technological innovation and changes were evaluated and adopted at Wake Forest University. At the moment, though "many millions of dollars are being spent to keep [their] students on the cutting edge of the computer revolution," they are "fearful of what may be happening to an ancient art whose moral function entails helping people to 'know together' (*conscientia*) what ought to be" (p. 42). In other words, technology is what members of a culture interpret it to be. The resolved meaning of technology can vary with time and place.

The review of current literature reveals a multidimensional relationship between culture and technology. Any single perspective is unable to completely map out the interface between the two. A "mutual shaping" and "ever-changing" view seems to provide a realistic approach to the study of the relationship between the two. In the next section of this chapter, three perspectives will be proposed to address this interface in Chinese communication.

USE OF TECHNOLOGY AS CULTURAL PRACTICE IN CHINESE COMMUNICATION

Although most devices of technology were not created in Chinese society, the way they are used by Chinese people can nevertheless be very "Chinese." Under many circumstances the traditional values of Chinese people are reinforced with these devices. The following are some easily identified situations in which technology has become cultural practice:

In order to maintain interpersonal harmony and face, Chinese tend to communicate in a more indirect manner than North Americans (Ting-Toomey, 1985, 1988; Yum, 1988). Their use of intermediaries to resolve conflicts was found pervasive (Ma, 1992). Furthermore, they have been cautioned against excessive use of verbal messages for more than two thousand years through Confucian and Taoist teachings (Becker, 1986). With the assistance of technology, direct confrontation can be easily avoided in many ways. Negative responses in business negotiation, for example, can be sent via facsimile transmission, while positive ones are notified through phone calls.

The high demand for karaoke in Chinese society is more or less associated with some communication patterns in the Chinese culture, such as the empha-

sis on *guanxi*.[1] While establishing *guanxi*[2] remains important in modern
Chinese society, it is done more and more frequently in a technologically
enhanced environment—a karaoke box. Ma and Chuang (in press) note the
following:

> Business people from other parts of the world are perhaps familiar with the
> technology used in karaoke and knowledgeable about the emphasis of *guanxi* in
> the Chinese culture, but they may be surprised at seeing the joint product of
> modern technology and traditional values in a small karaoke box.

In other words, the device of technology actually enables Chinese to fulfill
their communication goals in a more traditional fashion. This is probably why
karaoke has become so popular in Chinese communities all over the world.

Bond and Hwang (1986) identified six categories of face-enhancing and
face-saving behavior in Chinese society. Among the six is "enhancing other's
face":

> In addition to enhancing his or her own power image, an individual may adopt
> some tactics of ingratiation to enhance the resource allocator's face so that the
> latter might reciprocate by allotting resources in a way to benefit the ingratiator.
> The tactics include presenting compliments of sufficient credibility and sponta-
> neity. (p. 246)

On the computer-mediated chat list, one noticeable difference has been
found between Americans and Chinese with regard to compliments: Americans tend to compliment other members through sending a personal message
while Chinese usually make a public announcement. Complimenting another
person in the public sphere is an example of enhancing another's face.
However, with the power of the Internet, the compliments can reach even
more people. The effect of "face-enhancing" thus multiplies.

The family has always been basic and important to Chinese. Nevertheless,
the Confucian doctrine of filial piety may have been replaced by the over-
protection of children by parents today. It is especially important for parents
to locate their teenage children after school. The best solution is to give the
child a cellular phone; thus the parent-child relationship remains very close
even when the child is socializing with peers.

USE OF TECHNOLOGY AS CULTURAL CHANGE IN CHINESE COMMUNICATION

As previously discussed, Chinese people may use technology to preserve
some traditional values. However, their culture can, as a result of technology
adoption, be steered in a new direction as well. Although the cultural change
as reflected in Chinese thinking and behavior can be attributed to many

political, social, and economic factors the adoption of new technology is usually a major facilitator. As Lum (2000) notes in his introduction to media ecology, "change in the dominant form of communication media in society may facilitate large-scale cultural changes" (p. 3).

The practice of expressing oneself more strongly on computer networks than one would in face-to-face communication, commonly known as "flaming," has been reported in previous studies (e.g., Kiesler, Siegel, & McGuire, 1984; Kim & Raja, 1991). The Internet has also altered the behavior of Chinese people in similar fashion. Disrespect and directness on call-in talk shows and bulletin board systems (BBS) replaced politeness and implicitness as observed in traditional face-to-face interactions. For example, several cases have been reported in Taiwan in which a university teacher or administrator decided to bring an action of libel against some students for the message they posted on campus BBS. Any major election in Taiwan generates numerous messages of personal attack in explicit forms on the Internet or talk shows. Recently, a male student in Chengdu (a major city in Central China) announced his need for a "one-night stand" sex partner on the Internet. Furthermore, sex-related topics and self-disclosure have become common among users of the Internet. However, sex was a taboo subject in Mao's era. College students in Mainland China were not even allowed to date before the 1980s.

As the hierarchical nature of communication is diluted, the faultless image of national leaders can no longer be maintained through state-controlled mass media. President Lee Teng-hui of Taiwan was cursed daily on the Internet before he stepped down on May 20, 2000. In September 1999, after a major earthquake in Central Taiwan, the landing of the helicopter Lee took for a trip to the devastated area caused the blowing away of some tents used by earthquake victims. One victim approached him and complained about the collapse of her tent. Lee was unpleasant in response to her complaint. After the film clip of Lee's set-to with the woman was aired for the first time on Formosa TV, Lee's image protectors tried to stop the showing on the island. However, a digitized video clip of the scene was immediately circulated on the Internet. In other words, the more Lee's image was protected, the more frequently the video clip was watched, and the more he became negatively perceived. In contrast, emperors of China were never seen in person by ordinary people. Mao's eight-time public appearances and meetings with the Red Guards during the Cultural Revolution were unprecedented, thus treated like a religious homage.

USE OF TECHNOLOGY AS CULTURAL ADAPTATION IN CHINESE COMMUNICATION

Kim (1988) notes that "international migration represents a situation in which the newly arrived individuals are required to cope with substantial cultural change" (p. 8). The term "cross-cultural adaptation" refers to "the complex process through which an individual acquires an increasing level of 'fitness' or 'compatibility' in the new cultural environment" (p. 9). While many factors are considered in Kim's (e.g., 1995, 1996) model of cross-cultural adaptation, it is perceived to be simplistic from the critical perspective. As Hegde (1998) notes, Kim's research assumes that "the individual is responsible for his or her participation in the new society" (p. 35): "Kim's view, that people can embrace an intercultural identity development if they are open-minded and resilient enough to endure stress, seems too optimistic in a world in which hegemonic structures systematically marginalize certain types of difference" (p. 36).

When describing postcolonialism, During (1995) also notes that "postcolonialism is regarded as the need, in nations or groups which have been victims of imperialism, to achieve an identity uncontaminated by universalist or Eurocentric concepts and images" (p. 125). The perspective suggests that members of minority groups need to negotiate their cultural identity through communication, instead of developing a new identity through assimilation as implied in Kim's theory. Cultural adaptation is thus different from cultural practice or cultural change. In cultural practice an existing culture faces no threat to its survival from other cultures. Technology simply enhances the practice of the culture. In cultural change, the change in a current culture is the direct consequence of technology adoption. It is a "natural change" that takes place in a unique social and historic context. Cultural adaptation, however, refers to a situation in which a culture has to negotiate with other cultures for survival. Any resultant change in cultural adaptation is thus not self-initiated.

For many Chinese who live in a non-Chinese society, technology can help them find how to adapt to the new culture and how to negotiate their cultural identity. Their access to the Internet not only keeps them updated about their home country but also provides them with useful information for survival as well as emotional and moral support from one another. Liu's (1999) study of the Chinese virtual community in North America found the following:

> [Chinese Ethnic Internet] was used as a mode of civic discourse for Chinese-related issues in their host countries. It united Chinese immigrants all over North America to speak out for justice and protect the Chinese culture. The actions taken in the CBS incident [a program suggesting that the Chinese community was full of potential spies for the "mainland Chinese government"] and the Vancouver Sun incident [a distorted report on a Chinese figure skater] are just examples of things that happened in the past and set examples for similar things that will happen in the future. (p. 205)

Liu's content analysis of the Id-line list, a virtual community consisting of communication scholars in the Association for Chinese Communication Studies, yielded seven categories of topics: "community-building," "humor," "professional issues," "cultural topics," "community protection," "personal subjects," and "China-related politics" (p. 201). The seven categories reflect the issues of both cross-cultural adaptation and cultural identity. Liu also emphasizes the social functions that computer-mediated communication performs among Chinese communication scholars in North America: "Indeed, jokes, humorous stories, witty remarks, and poems are well appreciated on Id-line. They make people laugh, help them ease their cross-cultural stress, release their academic pressure, and pique their interest into active participation" (pp. 202-203).

In other words, Chinese people can empower themselves in many ways in a non-Chinese society through the use of technology. Whether their culture will be preserved or altered in the future may not be their primary concern. However, they do need to find out how to survive in an environment in which their voices tend to be muted.

MOVING TOWARD AN ECLECTIC VIEW OF CULTURE AND TECHNOLOGY

In Chinese communication, a multifaceted relationship between culture and technology is implied in the three perspectives proposed in this chapter: use of technology as cultural practice, use of technology as cultural change, and use of technology as cultural adaptation. While culture is viewed as a driving force behind the adoption of technology in the first perspective, cultural change becomes the consequence of technology in the second. From the third perspective, cultural values are sustained and cultural identities are negotiated through the utilization of technology. In other words, both "technological determinist" and "cultural determinist" views are taken into account under certain circumstances. The "readjustment or readaptation" theory is also valid when survival in a new or changing environment becomes an issue to members of Chinese culture.

Economic and political factors must be considered in each of the three perspectives to provide a more complete picture of the relationship between culture and technology. The fast adoption of communication technology is largely facilitated by the fast economic development in Chinese societies. The rapid economic boom has created a strong demand for entertainment as well as information, and thus a rampant need to consume modern technology in everyday life. That is why Internet service providers, karaoke boxes, and cellular phones have been mushrooming in all Chinese societies. People in Taiwan are much more critical toward their national leaders now than they were years ago largely because they live in a free and democratic society. They are not afraid of saying anything to their national leaders. The various forums on the Internet make it easier for them to practice freedom of speech.

As a consequence of the convenience provided by the Internet, on which face-to-face confrontation can be avoided, they have gradually shifted away from their traditional pattern of indirect communication. Sometimes they even go to the other extreme—arguing ad hominem through crude language.

One definition of technology assumed in popular and academic literature, according to McOmber (1999), is "techonology as industrialization." From this perspective, "technology is as much an event as a set of practices or objects" (p. 143). He states that one often finds this definition at work "among those who speak on behalf of global development or modernization" (p. 143). It suggests that "the process of industrialization always passed through the same stages in all cultures, with democracy as the inevitable outcome of increased urbanization, literacy, and media exposure" (p. 143). While the concept that "technology is an event" can apply to the situation in which Chinese use technology for cultural adaptation, their goal is not limited to "global development or modernization." In addition to becoming more globalized, they can re-gain their cultural identity and find tips for survival in a non-Chinese society from their fellow Chinese. In other words, technological advancement does not necessarily cause the fading away of non-European or non-United States cultures.

CONCLUDING REMARKS

Although previous studies of culture and technology tend to be biased toward either optimistic enrichment or pessimistic determinism theory, the cases presented in this study suggest that the interface between culture and technology cannot be resolved in a unidimensional theoretical framework. The research evidence presented in this chapter has illustrated a close relationship between culture and technology in Chinese communication in three aspects: (1) technology has been used to preserve traditional Chinese culture, (2) technology has facilitated culture change in Chinese societies, and (3) technology has enabled an expansion of discursive space in which overseas Chinese can adapt to a new cultural environment and empower themselves.

Culture is communication. Whether technology is a welcome addition or intrusive monster to an existing society has to be resolved in a common-sensing process. A piece of technology that is applauded in one culture may become a symbol of evil in another. Within the same society, a symbol of evil may be transformed into a sign of blessing at a later time. As emphasized in the article entitled "Keeping Technology in Perspective," included in the American Federation of Teachers' *AFT On Campus*: "what faculty see as a tool for enhancing learning, administrators may see as a tool for cutting costs and capitalists may eye as a tool for making money" ("Keeping Technology in Perspective," 2000, p. 21). That suggests that the meaning of technology should evolve through continued negotiation in the academic world. By the same token, the status of a particular piece of technology in a given culture is also determined by the members of the culture through communication. How culture and technology are interfaced in Chinese communication, therefore, is contingent upon the meaning assigned to technology by Chinese people in a given social and historical context. A new technology can start with being intrusive and non-traditional and end up enhancing cultural values. It can be used for an adaptive purpose at the beginning but becomes integrated in the culture later. One who takes an extreme position is unlikely to obtain a full picture of this complex relationship. Only through multiple perspectives can their interface be meaningfully conceptualized.

NOTES

1. The *pinyin* system of romanization is used to transliterate Chinese names and special Chinese terms in this chapter.

2. *Guanxi* transliterated under the *pinyin* system is equivalent to *kuan-hsi* under the Wade-Giles system. The Chinese term *guanxi* has a range of meaning, including "relationship," "relation," and "connection."

REFERENCES

Becker, C. B. (1986). Reasons for the lack of argumentation and debate in the Far East. *International Journal of Intercultural Relations, 10,* 75-92.

Barry, H., III, Child, I. L., & Bacon, M. K. (1959). Relation of child training to subsistence economy. *American Anthropologist, 61,* 51-63.

Boczkowski, P. J. (1999). Mutual shaping of users and technologies in a national virtual community. *Journal of Communication, 49*(2), 86-108.

Bond, M. H., & Hwang, K. K. (1986). The social psychology of Chinese people. In M. H. Bond (Ed.), *The psychology of the Chinese people* (pp. 213-266). Hong Kong: Oxford University Press.

Check, C. J. (1996). Technology will strengthen the traditional family. In O. W. Markley & W. R. McCuan (Eds.), *America beyond 2001: Opposing viewpoints*. San Diego: Greenhaven Press.

Demac, D. A., & Sung, L. (1995). New communication technologies and deregulation. In J. Downing, A. Mohammadi, & A. Sreberny-Mohammadi (Eds.), *Questioning the media: A critical introduction* (2nd ed., pp. 277-292). Thousand Oaks, CA: Sage.

During, S. (1995). Postmodernism or postcolonialism. In B. Ashcroft, G. Griffiths, & H. Tiffin (Eds.), *The postcolonial studies reader* (pp. 125-129). New York: Routledge.

Geertz, C. (1973). *The interpretation of cultures*. New York: Basic Books.

Hegde, R. S. (1998). Swing the trapeze: The negotiation of identity among Asian Indian immigrant women in the United States. In D. V. Tanno & A. González (Eds.), *Communication and identity across cultures* (pp. 34-55). Thousand Oaks, CA: Sage.

International Institute for Management Development. (2000). World competitiveness yearbook. Retrieved April 17, 2000, from the World Wide Web, at https://www.imd.ch/wcy/wcy1999.cfm?section=wcy&select=wcy&CFID=6250 &CFTOKEN=26532347

Keeping technology in perspective. (2000, May/June). *AFT on Campus, 19*(8), 21.

Kiesler, S., Siegel, J., & McGuire, T. W. (1984). Social psychological aspects of computer-mediated communication. *American Psychologist, 39*, 1123-1134.

Kim, M. S., & Raja, N. S. (1991). *Verbal aggression and self-disclosure on computer bulletin boards.* Paper presented at the annual meeting of the International Communication Association, Chicago.

Kim, Y. Y. (1988). Preface. In Y. Y. Kim & W. B. Gudykunst (Eds.), *Cross-cultural adaptation: Current approaches* (pp. 7-17). Newbury Park, CA: Sage.

Kim, Y. Y. (1995). Cross-cultural adaptation: An integrative theory. In R. L. Wiseman (Ed.), *Intercultural communication theory* (pp. 170-193). Thousand Oaks, CA: Sage.

Kim, Y. Y. (1996). Identity development: From culture to intercultural. In H. B. Mokros (Ed.), *Interaction and identity* (pp. 347-369). New Brunswick, NJ: Transaction Books.

Kluckhohn, F., & F. Strodtbeck (1960). *Variations in value orientations.* New York: Row, Peterson.

Liu, D. (1999). The Internet as a mode of civic discourse: The Chinese virtual community in North America. In R. Kluver & J. H. Powers (Eds.), *Civic discourse, civil society, and Chinese communities* (pp. 195-206). Stamford, CT: Ablex.

Lum, C. M. K. (2000). Introduction: The intellectual roots of media ecology. *New Jersey Journal of Communication, 8*, 1-7.

Ma, R. (1992). The role of unofficial intermediaries in interpersonal conflicts in the Chinese culture. *Communication Quarterly, 40*, 269-278.

Ma, R. (2000). Internet as a town square in global society. In G. M. Chen & W. J. Starosta (Eds.), *Communication and global society* (pp. 93-106). Boston: Peter Lang.

Ma, R., & Chuang, R. (in press). Karaoke as a form of communication in the political and interpersonal contexts of Taiwan. In L. Lu, W. Jia, & D. R. Heisey (Eds.), *Chinese communication studies: Contexts and comparisons.* Westport, CT: Greenwood.

McMillan, J. J., & Hyde, M. J. (2000). Technological innovation and change: A case study in the formation of organizational conscience. *Quarterly Journal of Speech, 86*, 19-47.

McOmber, J. B. (1999). Technological autonomy and three definitions of technology. *Journal of Communication, 49*(3), 137-153.

O'Connor, A., & Downing, J. (1995). Culture and communication. In J. Downing, A. Mohammadi, & A. Sreberny-Mohammadi (Eds.), *Questioning the media: A critical introduction* (2nd ed., pp. 3-22). Thousand Oaks, CA: Sage.

Postman, N. (1985). *Amusing ourselves to death: Public discourse in the age of show business.* New York: Elisabeth Sifton Books/Viking.

Postman, N. (1992). *Technopoly: The surrender of culture to technology.* New York: Afred A. Knopf.

Reed, D. (1986, September). Asia's four Little Dragons. *Reader's Digest*, 131-135.

Schwartz, B. M., & Ewald, R. H. (1968). *Culture and society: An introduction to cultural anthropology.* New York: Ronald Press.

Ting-Toomey, S. (1985). Toward a theory of conflict and culture. In W. B. Gudykunst, L. P. Stewart, & S. Ting-Toomey (Eds.), *Communication, culture, and organizational processes* (pp. 71-86). Beverly Hills, CA: Sage.

Ting-Toomey, S. (1988). Intercultural conflict style: A face-negotiation theory. In Y. Y. Kim & W. B. Gudykunst (Eds.), *Theories in intercultural communication* (pp. 213-235). Newbury Park, CA: Sage.

Tu, W., Hejtmanek, M., & Wachman, A. (Ed.). (1992). *The Confucian world observed: A contemporary discussion of Confucian humanism in East Asia.* Honolulu, HI: The East-West Center.

Umble, D. Z. (1992). The Amish and the telephone: Resistance and reproduction. In R. Silverstone & E. Hirsch (Eds.), *Consuming technologies* (pp. 183-194). London: Routledge.

Winston, B. (1995). How are media born and developed? In J. Downing, A. Mohammadi, & A. Sreberny-Mohammadi (Eds.), *Questioning the media: A critical introduction* (2nd ed., pp. 54-74). Thousand Oaks, CA: Sage.

Yum, J. O. (1988). The impact of Confucianism on interpersonal relationships and communication patterns in East Asia. *Communication Monographs, 55,* 374-388.

14

Computer-Mediated Communication: Internet Development and New Challenges in China

James Jinguo Shen

One cannot hope for positive repercussions from new technologies except on the condition that they will be taken up in the creative practices of individuals and collectives.

Felix Guattari, 1992, 2

As China continues its modernization drive into the twenty-first century, computer-mediated communication (CMC) has become one of the most significant fields in Chinese communication. While economic reform has prompted repeated calls for the transformation of the political system in the last two decades, online communication has already provided a new arena for Chinese people to improve their info-practice (communication practice via information technology) in the shifting context.

This chapter examines Chinese Internet development and its impact on the Chinese communication system. It explores how the Chinese online communication creates an alternative mass medium and polysemic sociocultural meanings, and how cyberpractice brings the challenges and opportunities to the Chinese media reform. To a certain extent, the study also addresses the academic concerns about how people come to practice and understand new technology and how the technology is practiced across cultures (Lewis, 1999, p. 2).

"Computer mediation" in this chapter refers to the mass communication mediated via state-owned or privately owned computer networks that link

Chinese universities, urban areas, and the rest of the world. It implies a special communication relationship via the technology for "a much larger share of communication and thus of our contact with others and our environmental reality" (McQuail, 2000, pp. 64-65).

INTERNET DEVELOPMENT

As globalization promotes informatization (social movement for rapid information diffusion) via the ever-expanding computer networks, the Chinese online population has experienced exponential growth since 1998. Although the central government was often caught in the dilemma between telematic (computer-related information network) improvement and information control, the national modernization agenda prioritized the advancement of the telecommunications infrastructure (Hao, Zhang, & Huang, 1996; Li, 1996; Lu, 1997; He, 1998; McIntyre, 1998; Mueller, 1997; Zhao, 2000). In this technophile milieu, e-mail messaging and other online services led to the rise of the early netizens in most metropolitan areas, who in turn increased the rapid diffusion of Internet communication among millions of computer newbies.

It should be noted that the number of Chinese Internet users has sky-rocketed since 1998 (see Table 14.1). Considering that people in China often share Internet accounts, the actual number of cyber practitioners may be more than the estimate. If China keeps up the momentum of Internet development, its Internet population will become the second largest or, probably, the largest in the world by 2005 (CND, 2000; Anonymous, 2000).

Netizen Demographics

In June 1998, 60 Gallup investigators conducted an independent survey in both major urban and rural areas of China on the new consumption styles of

TABLE 14.1. Rapid Growth of Chinese Online Population

Time	Chinese Internet Users
July 1998	1.175 million
End of 1998	2.1 million
July 1999	4 million
End of 1999	8.9 million
July 2000	16.9 million
End of 2000	22.5 million
2003	33 million

Sources: China Internet Network Information Center, Hong Kong–based Big Brains, IDC, and Washington-based Strategy Group.

the Chinese people. They discovered that in Beijing, the capital city of China, one-third of the people inthe age group 18-29 had online experience, and this ratio was four times greater than for the age group 40 and above.[1] According to the survey by the China Internet Network Information Center in January 2001, 70 percent of Chinese Internet users were aged between 18 and 30, and nearly 70 percent of the users have two-year or four-year college degrees or master's degrees; 63 percent of them were single and earned between 500 and 2,000 Chinese yuan (US$61-241) per month. Noticeably, the female users increased from 7 percent in 1999 to 30.4 percent at the end of 2000 (CNNIC, 2001).

Other media research indicated that with the booming Chinese market for e-business in the late 1990s, a greater number of younger, less educated people were also enticed to join the online communication, which was once an exclusive communication field for the educated class. That change confirms the fact that recent online practitioners are an increasingly young segment of the entire Chinese population (Greenberg, 2000, p. 1).

Noticeably, Chinese Internet users largely concentrate in big cities and provinces such as Beijing, Shanghai, and Guangdong. In contrast, netizens in most remote areas totaled less than 1 percent. By 1998, only 1.7 percent of the residents in major cities had had access to information via the Internet, and only 20 percent of the netizens spent more than ten hours a week on the Internet (CND, 1999). In 2000, however, online access became more available to urban dwellers, and an average user spent 13.7 hours online each week (CNNIC, 2001).

To a large extent, the increase of online communication in the urban areas is attributable to a series of reductions of Internet dial-up access fees, which before 1999 equaled 35 percent of salary for an average user in Beijing (CND, 1999). In December 2000, ISP competition in China brought the access fees down to only one Chinese *yuan* (US$ 0.12) per hour, which is merely 25 percent of the charge a year earlier (Anonymous).

Internetwork

In July 1999, 1.46 million computers in China were connected to the Internet. One year later the total of computer hosts reached 6.5 million, and the number jumped to 8.92 million at the end of 2000 (CNNIC, 2000, 2001). In the last ten years China has established four major authorized networks: China Education and Research Network (CERNET), ChinaNet (CHINANET), China Academy of Sciences Network (CSTNET), and China Golden Bridge Net (CHINAGBN). In December 2000, China was connected with the rest of the world via six major networks: CSTNET, CHINANET, CERNET, CHINAGBN, UNINET, and CNCNET (CNNIC, 2001).

CERNET is the first nationwide education and research network in the country; it is also China's first nationwide Internet backbone. Funded by the government and managed by China's State Education Commission, it was designed to connect all of the 1,075 colleges and universities as well as some primary and high schools in the country. It is now linked to many external networks, such as the HARNET in Hong Kong, DFN in Germany, and the Internet in the United States (via Sprintlink) (Li, 1996; Xu et al., 1997; CNNIC, 2000). In March 1999, China's largest commercial ISP, CHINANET, was connected to other Asian countries by AIH's Pan-Asian Backbone via a 2 Mbps fiber-optic line (CND, 1999).

Chinese academic institutions play a leading role in the development and deployment of Internet communication network. Beijing-based Tsinghua (Qinghua) University, which is known as China's MIT, hosts CERNET. Tsinghua updated its computer network after three years' investment of 43 million Chinese yuan (US$5.2 million). In early 1999 it connected 7,500 computers and 2,500 e-mail subscribers (CND, 1999).

Embrace of Informatics

In China's new wave of the government reform in 1999, the Internet was used to connect 60 percent of local government departments, which controlled 80 percent of public information sources or over 3,000 databases (*Xinhua,* 1999).

The public net surfing fervor led to the establishment of various online magazines and newspapers as well as Chinese online bookstore www. bookbuilding.com.cn. New online services and activities include personal financing, voice mail, voice-over-IP, flight inquiries, taxi service, global news, the latest movies, weather forecasts, world time and hotel and dinner reservations, international marriage service, semen website, net pageant, and net survival open competition (Anonymous, 2000). Even online lottery kiosks became available in Guangzhou in 1999 (CND, 1999). In order to streamline with the global Internet, some Chinese websites, such as www.readworld.com and www.muzi.net, provide the free service of English-to-Chinese translation for Chinese people to enjoy the global Internet culture.

As a conspicuous urban phenomenon in the age of information explosion, thousands of Internet cafés opened in Chinese cities. Currently, Shanghai alone has more than 2,000 Internet cafés, the first of which was opened in May 1996. When those Internet cafés became the third major online access location after residential homes and offices, they were extremely popular among college students, local residents, and international visitors. When the former American president Bill Clinton went to Shanghai in July 1998, he visited one of the Internet cafés and surfed the net for news reports about his Chinese visit (*Xinhua,* 1999).

In spite of the early development of Chinese Internet communication, the Chinese online access rate is still much lower than that in the developed nations, where ubiquitous Internet access is available to almost all. Computer-mediated communication in China remains an intellectual power practice because access is largely available to the educated elite in big universities and urban areas. In that sense, college students are a leading age group in promoting Chinese online communication.

TSINGHUA UNIVERSITY CASE

In order to explore concrete Internet practices in China, the author conducted a survey among graduate students of Tsinghua University in the late spring of 1999. The fifteen questions covered many research issues, such as the demographic features of the student group and their routine online practices and main purposes for Internet use. Questions were raised to investigate when and where they first used the Internet, how they rated Internet content, what languages they used for Internet communication, how they communicated via the Internet with people in other countries, and what they thought of online information control (censorship), cybersex, hate speech, and the major impact of the Internet on their personal communication and life. Thanks to the assistance of Dr. Yagang Fan, a professor from Tsinghua University and visiting scholar at Harvard University, the English questionnaire was distributed among 100 graduate and doctoral students in both art and science departments. With the collection of 57 questionnaires from science departments and another 30 from the English department, the 87 percent return rate enhanced the data validity for the research analysis.

The graduate students of Tsinghua University are comprised of top students from various prestigious Chinese universities and colleges. Upon their graduation, their leadership role in the IT revolution and media reform will be manifested in many fields across the country. It is not coincidental that many of the current reform leaders in the Chinese government are Tsinghua alumni. To this date, Premier Zhu Rong-ji still assumes the role of the honorary dean of the Business Administration College of Tsinghua.

The graduate students under investigation were mostly aged 21 to 25, and the diffusion of computer-mediated communication among them had already reached what Rogers called "a critical mass" (Rogers, 1983). Although their Internet practices may differ from the rest of the Chinese online population because of their elite status and easy online access, their Internet experiences constitute representative anecdotes of online communication among Chinese people.

Cyber Practicality

The research discovered that most of the Chinese students heard of the Internet between 1993 and 1995 and began to use it two or three years later. The university was the predominant locale for their initial experimental practices. To this date, it is still their primary work field for online communication. As the campus network was expanded and updated, they used the Internet one to three times a week in early 1999.

For most Chinese students, the main purpose of Internet use was for studies and talking with friends. With e-commerce clicking into cyberspace, online shopping was no longer a new concept to them in name, but still a new cyberpractice in deed.

Among those industrious college students, news and new technology were the most popular categories for Internet visits. Given the nature of the transborder medium, which more easily circumvents official censorship, the news on the Internet not only covers more of the popular subjects on the global and the local but also embodies a new communication sense and sensitivity to its readers as well. For most Chinese students, the latest information technology is the second-most favored area for Internet visits. Comparatively, cyber games and music had to give way to news and technology as the third and fourth categories for their information consumption. Considering the fierce professional competition in the local, national, and global market, the students preferred to be better informed than better entertained.

Cultural Specificity

In response to the need to control Internet contents, most Chinese students opted for the choice of depending on the situation. Many others simply chose "No." Since the Chinese government still makes tremendous efforts to monitor Internet activities, the younger generation is obviously more liberal-minded and is looking forward to the free information flow in the democratized space.

At Tsinghua University, one-third of Chinese students used the Internet to communicate with people in other countries, although the latter were not necessarily Westerners. Many students kept in touch with friends studying or working overseas. The most frequently visited countries, in order, were the United States, Japan, Canada, Australia, and France. Regardless of ideological and cultural differences, the students demonstrated a distinctive communication objective in pursuit of new information from those media-rich countries.

It is worth mentioning that the dominant cyber-language used by Chinese students was English, which is the lingua franca of both conventional and new telematic media in global communication. Chinese was only listed as the second most popular language, with which they visited Chinese websites in the mainland, Taiwan, and Singapore. Since many Chinese graduate programs require competency in a second foreign language, it was not surprising that some Chinese graduate students also used French or German as their alternative cyber-language for their Internet communication.

Cybersex is a sensitive issue in Chinese online communication. Many Chinese students adopted a traditional stance against it. They believed that it was "bad," "chaotic" on the net and "should be controlled in some way" or even "prohibited." However, many other respondents took a neutral stand. Some argued that it was "just visual [images]," and that it may have no "bad effects on somebody." A few others attempted to legitimize its online existence by stating, "On the Internet, sex is not an important issue; the Internet only supplies a place to communicate ideas." In view of the heated debates on this formerly taboo issue, the polysemic reading of cybersex among the top Chinese students created an open forum for diverse and oppositional views, which can scarcely be found in the official media.

Cyberpractice is culture-specific and time-bound. The response to the inquiry about hate speech is typical of the students' interpretations in their local context. In early 1999, most Chinese students associated hate speech with the angry and at times radical responses against the U.S. bombing of the Chinese embassy in Yugoslavia. One science student argued "that is a way for people to express their feelings." Yet, they had very little knowledge of the online extremist discourses disseminated by various white separatist groups in the United States and Europe, not to mention the pseudoscholarly arguments of the Holocaust deniers.

As a general principle of online practice, the majority of Chinese students did not buttress the bigotry deriving from hate speech. However, one-fourth of the students remained neutral, for they believed some hate speeches "can be understood" because "the Internet is a free place and the hate speech can only be published there." For those students, the Internet could be used as an outlet to release their indignation and frustration under particular circumstances. Therefore, hate speech was justified as a "reasonable" reaction to the incident or as a different voice from that reporting in the Western media. This finding proves that online communication at times can be construed as a "local semantic move," which carries the local level of meaning in the discourse with the two communication strategies of "positive self-presentation and negative other-presentation" (van Dijk, 1995, p. 8).

Cyber Impact

Unlike most American students who take Internet communication as part of their life, only 50 percent of Chinese students in the study held the same view. In terms of the direct impact of cyberpractice on personal communication and daily life, most Chinese students took the Internet as the channel to seek new information and learn of the outside world. Some conceive it as a convenient and gratifying means of learning for their social needs, such as making friends online. Some others used it as a specific information source to pursue academic or career success. However, due to the access cost and their limited online time in 1999, the Internet then served primarily as an additional source of information rather than a source of solutions.

The Tsinghua case is only an exemplary case in China's computer-mediated communication. The research findings indicate that generally, Chinese students use the Internet as an *exogenous* media source, from which they can receive the latest information about the world. In China, online information may differ from that found on the other domestic media, particularly from that of official media. Not coincidentally, 68.9 percent of Chinese netizens stated that information gathering was their primary reason for accessing the Internet (CNNIC, 2001).

DISCUSSION

Civic, Alternative Medium

The research findings from Tsinghua University echo the latest national investigation by the China Internet Network Information Center that Internet practice constitutes a fast-growing public domain in Chinese communication. The college students, who will come to constitute the ranks of urban intellectuals, office workers in joint ventures, and the next generation of government officials, have already constituted a dedicated driving force for Chinese Internet communication. With advanced online technologies and diverse information sources ever available in the country, the Internet is indeed becoming a new form of depoliticization and domination. As Nguyen and Alexander (1996) pointed out, "In cyberspacetime, the social realm is engulfing and overwhelming the political realm. The 'social' is decomposing the body politic" (p. 109). When individually based communication alienates official political discourses, it actually increases its civic presence in the "colonization of the life world" (Habermas, 1987, pp. 362-363).

The Tsinghua case indicates that the Chinese students and the bulging urban middle class embraced the emerging online technologies as a civic communication means. Their diverse cyberpractices celebrate the Internet as a secularized communication means, for cyberspacetime promises people liberation from the constraints of space, time, and materiality (Nguyen & Alexander, 1996, p. 117). In Chinese communication, the online practice embodies a popular communication move that facilitates the information explosion and the cyber-meaning implosion, and computer-mediated communication has established itself as an alternative medium in the public sphere. From the Foucauldian perspective, the new human-machine interface "alters the old relationship between knowledge and power" (Nguyen & Alexander, 1996, p. 99).

The Tsinghua investigation implies that Internet communication symbolizes both convergence and fragmentation in Chinese communication culture. As the student demographics indicate, online communication draws together individuals of different professional backgrounds; it facilitates the inter-connectivity between local and global communities. Meanwhile, it diversifies online services, contents, and audiences based upon information categories or cultural interests. To a great extent, it blurs the temporal-spatial boundary between the politically taboo and civic free speech, and between the national and the international terrains.

For the majority of Chinese people, the use of the civic medium also symbolizes personal status in the current sociocultural context. A Tsinghua student surfing the net signifies his or her decent education, technophile mentality, and openness to the transnational culture. Following McLuhan's dictum that the new electronic interdependence recreates the world in the image of a global village (1962), the Internet creates an extended personal space in the overcrowded Chinese urban setting. Thus, the popular Internet café is merely a microcosm of the neocapitalistic, urbanized media culture, in which the net surfing is reified as the playful representation of the netizens' individuality and interconnectivity.

The Chinese Internet network has created its own virtual communities. Government departments, research institutes, private business organizations, and dissident groups utilize their websites for their organizational communi-cation. In terms of users' online preferences, their Internet practice often signifies their self-identity, possibly gender identity, group identity, and even national identity, as in the case of hate speech. Invariably, group online practices not only produce the virtual reality of their small group communi-cation but also solidify the interactive medium as an effective channel to disseminate collective ideas and values.

New Interpretive Paradigm

The Tsinghua case shows that Chinese Internet practitioners are preoccu-pied with seeking their understanding from other media perspectives and cultures. Via the alternative medium they attempt to find new interpretive schemata by reaching, perceiving, and interpreting the outside world. Accord-ing to Weber, understanding (*Verstehen*) becomes the premise of explanation (Polkinghorne, 1983, p. 49). Chinese computer-mediated communication reflects a new epistemic move to incorporate transborder interpretive practice in the Chinese media environment.

For most Chinese college students and other Internet users, Internet com-munication serves as an instrument of truth claiming and personal empower-ment. As the online information logic alters the traditional media power relationship between the central gatekeepers and peripheral media practition-ers, millions of individuals around the country "have been empowered to act, communicate, or participate in the broader society and political process" (Pavlik, 1998, p. 319). Accordingly, Chinese netizens post on the net their spontaneous feedback to some reform issues, which includes the resistance discourse against official policy and the alienated discourse against popular opinion. While the government policing is weakened in the interplay of online communication with various social reform forces, Chinese netizens are now able to read various sensitive cyber texts and air their critical viewpoints to a varying degree. In so doing, they may not follow the "preferred reading" of the dominant channel, for "the Internet provides increasingly direct access to a variety of information sources" (Pavlik, 1998, p. 320).

The Tsinghua case also illustrates that communicative meaning, as Stuart Hall (1982) explicated, is always the result of an act of "articulation," an act of active production in use; its expression connected to, and conditioned by, a specific historical context (Dyson, 1996, p. 7). Internet communication in the current Chinese context is a cultural practice that articulates the urgent need for continued cultural and political reform. Since so many Chinese netizens seek information from Western websites, their communicative act virtually cements the intercultural relationship between the Self and the Other, and their cyber vision reflects a new world outlook (the Gestalt) as they strategically consume online news and technology from the latter.

CHALLENGES AND OPPORTUNITIES

Online Control

Since Internet communication is a vehicle for circumventing the traditional Chinese censorship system, it indeed caused hypersensitive concern among the top Chinese leadership. In order to tighten online control while preventing hacker attacks and cyberporn, the Chinese government built its special Internet police at the national and provincial levels in 2000. By implementing a five-step security system, this contingent of 300,000 computer specialists is expected to purge "detrimental information" from the Chinese Internet (China Press, 2000). In his interview with Mike Wallace, the senior TV host of the CBS News show "60 Minutes," Chinese president Jiang Zemin clearly indicated his support for the close monitoring and censorship of the Internet (Greenberg, 2000, pp. 1-2).

However, "the Internet is the first medium that allows the democratic principles of free speech and self-governance to play themselves out unhindered" (Pavlik, 1998, p. 297). As Greenberg (2000) noted, "Already, the Internet has been a very effective agent of change in the largest, and one of the last, Communist nations in the world," and "nearly 20 million Chinese citizens are now able to communicate faster, cheaper, and more anonymously than ever before." Even the government officials understand that technically it is impossible to control the Internet to their desired degree.

Interestingly, the social meaning of the Internet challenges to the dominant censorship system resembles the sociolinguistic meaning of the Chinese term

Weiji, which means both risks and opportunities at a historical moment. If the Chinese government imposes too rigorous control, it will run the risk of impeding the further development of the information superhighway. This obviously is not a consequence that the Chinese leaders want to face, for they recognize that the free flow of information is absolutely essential to a competitive, efficient market economy (Greenberg, 2000, p. 3).

In fact, due to the extreme difficulty of controlling the tide of information flooding into and out of the country, the government may eventually loosen online control. Those subtle changes occurred recurrently with the ups and downs of reform in the last decade. Despite the release of the latest Internet administration regulation in November 2000, the government has to struggle painfully in the conflict between further development and futile control, particularly in view of the palpable and potential opportunities the Internet brings to the national economy and the transitional society.

Policy Change

China is to enter the World Trade Organization (WTO) in the new century. When China joins the world community, it will have to change its media policy, particularly that for the Internet development. For once the Chinese media are faced with the massive invasion of powerful international media, plus market competition in the internal market, the government will have to make a cruel choice between reform and demise (Chen, 1999, p. 14). According to Zhao Bo of the Chinese Ministry of Information Industry, "The government really wants to develop the Internet. The advantages outweigh the disadvantages" (CND, 2000).

The recent pro-tech regulations in China signify a quiet policy change by both the central and local governments. While the number of telephone users in 1998 reached 110 million, about one telephone for every ten Chinese, the monthly charge for leased lines by Internet service providers (ISPs) was reduced from time to time (CND, 2000). In order to attract more overseas venture capital and promote the development of local high-tech businesses, the Shenzhen municipal government will allow overseas venture capital enterprises to exchange their profits from Chinese currency into foreign currencies (Anonymous, 2000).

Formerly, no foreign company was allowed to own telecommunications enterprises, including investment in ISPs. But in actuality, international companies control that market as major financial supporters (*Xinhua*, 1999). With the new Internet regulations issued in 2000, the Ministry of Information Industry is expected to further open up the growing Internet market.

Currently, the government is seeking a delicate equilibrium in Internet development. In early 2000, China Liang Tong put an end to the monopoly by the state-run company in Internet communication. When China becomes a member of the WTO in the new century, international media corporations may have up to a 50 percent share of Chinese Internet businesses. Greater changes in Internet policies can well be expected.

Global Influence

Since the inception of Chinese Internet communication, the influx of Western information and new technologies has exerted tremendous influence on the Chinese Internet market, Internet users, and the cyberculture.

In March 1999, Bill Gates's Venus Project promised 320 million Chinese television viewers access to the Internet at a cost ranging from 1,500 to 2,000 Chinese yuan. Later that year, IBM received approval from the Chinese government to set up the first computer-leasing company in China (CND, 1999; *Xinhua*, 1999). Yahoo launched a China-based website with a Beijing company, defying concern about a ban on foreign investment in China's Internet companies (CND, 1999). At the same time, AOL provided its first Chinese language service in Hong Kong, one that can be used for data communication into Mainland China. These multinational media corporations pushed China to be more open to the world before its entry into WTO. When the world's information technology chiefs met at the Fortune Global Forum in Shanghai in September 1999, they called for further Internet development.

As indicated on the Tsinghua campus, international influence from the Internet promotes the critical sense of the spatial and temporal democratization among the younger generation in China. Getting immersed in the online information flow, they rediscover their international being, and their Self has become part of intercultural communication with the Other.

CONCLUSION

The foregoing analysis of the Chinese Internet demonstrates that computer-mediated communication in China is still in the early stage of development. Further online growth depends largely on sustained investment in the information infrastructure, more expedient interface with the global network, and ultimately, continued reform of the political and media system. When China endeavors to speed up its modernization process in the new century, it must cross the hurdle of stringent media regulations to facilitate the information flow on the Internet. As Chen (1999) observed: "The [current] reform of the Chinese media system is a limited reform, but it is also an interest-oriented irreversible reform. Perhaps the external influence is the driving force to promote further reform for the huge market incentives will inevitably lead to new institutional innovations" (p. 13).

The Tsinghua investigation supports the research findings that the Internet is indeed used as an alternative medium by millions of Chinese netizens. Their

Internet fantasy along with various online communication practices creates a variety of new perspectives in interpersonal and intercultural communication. Further research may focus on the ramifications of Chinese online communication in the global media culture, particularly after China's entry into the WTO.

At the turn of the new millennium, cyberspace has opened up an entirely new public sphere for Chinese communication. Both internal and external online information helps improve people's interpretive understanding of the kaleidoscopic cyberculture. For instance, recent online discussions regarding the different standards of the Chinese domain-name system enabled many Chinese netizens to see the significance of Internet communication in a global context. With online interrogation of the standard by the leading Internet organizations in the world, Chinese netizens learned different perspectives on the international issue. In their online discussion after the Mainland Chinese and Taiwanese authorities tried to reach a consensus on the domain system, they also envisaged a possible collaboration in the greater China areas.

The Chinese Internet communication provides a fine public forum for political reform, for the alternative medium has already created an epistemic liberation among the netizen class. People love to see that the influx of information via the Internet bridges the gap between the Self and the Other and creates a new communication ritual in "sharing, participation, association, fellowship and the possession of a common faith" (Carey, 1988, p. 18). As they become more international, the Internet will be taken as an indispensable conduit to the exogenous source of information.

To the extent that Chinese computer-mediated communication can yet explicate greater sociocultural meanings, online communication will be construed as what Raymond Williams called "a whole way of life" in Chinese urban society (1976, p. 16). As a democratic-participant approach to promote media reform and intercultural communication between China and the rest of the world, the Internet has solidified its unique position in Chinese communication. Although the Internet may not cause an overnight change in the Chinese political system, it has changed the concept of mediation in Chinese communication. When the world is looking at the rise of China in the new century, the Chinese netizens, including millions of college students and the growing middle class, will seize every opportunity to reshape the Chinese Internet culture and reinvent its discursive meanings. In essence, "The Internet is the leading edge" (Nguyen & Alexander, 1996, p. 120) in our cultural innovations.

NOTE

1. Before the 1998 survey Gallup conducted two nationwide surveys in China in 1994 and 1997. For the details, see *Fortune Magazine,* October 11, 1999.

REFERENCES

Anonymous. (2000, December). Another cut of Internet access fee: Only 1 dollar per hour. Retrieved December 4, 2,000 from http://cndaily.sina.com/headline/tech-Headline/2000/1204/2334597.html.

Anonymous. (2000, December). To entice foreign investment, Shenzhen allows remittance of profits from venture capital. Retrieved December 4, 2000, from http://english.sina.com/news/tech/2000/1201/tech_1.html.

Anonymous. (2000, December). Tom.com subsidiary launches mainland's first voice-operated Web portal. Retrieved December 4, 2000, from http://english.sina.com/news/tech/2000/1201/tech_1.html.

Anonymous. (2000, December 1). To be world's No. 1 in five years' time: Chinese Internet network is expected to supersede the American network. *The China Press,* A5.

Carey, J. (1988). *Communication as culture.* Boston: Unwin Hyman.

Chen, H. (1999). Institutional changes of Chinese mass media in the nineties. *Twenty-First Century, 53,* 4-14.

CNNIC. (2000, July). Semiannual survey report on the development of China's Internet (2000.7). Retrieved October 17, 2000, from China Internet Network Information Center on the World Wide Web: http://www.cnnic.cn/develst/e-cnnic200007.shtml.

CNNIC. (2001, January). Semiannual survey report on the development of China's Internet (2001.1). Retrieved March 4, 2001, from China Internet Network Information Center on the World Wide Web: http://www.cnnic.cn/develst/e-cnnic200101.shtml.

CND. (1998-2000). *Chinese News Digest.* Retrieved 1988-2000 from http://www.cnd.org.

Dyson, K. (1996). Revisiting culture and anarchy: Media studies, the cultural industries and the issue of quality. In K. Dyson & W. Homolka (Eds.) *Culture first: Promoting standards in the new media age* (pp. 1-23). London: Cassell.

Greenberg, J. (June 23, 2000). Newest web surfers in China are younger, less educated. Retrieved October 17, 2000, from www.virtualchina.com.

Guattari, F. (1992, November 6). Pour une ethique des medias. *Le Monde,* p. A2.

Hall, S. (1982). The rediscovery of ideology: The return of the repressed. In M. Gurevitch et al. (Eds.), *Culture, society and the media.* London: Methuen.

Habermas, J. (1987). *The theory of communicative action* (Vol. 2). Boston: Beacon.

Hao, X., Zhang, K., & Huang, Y. (1996). The Internet and information control: The case of China. *The Public, 3,* 117-130.

He, Z. (1998). A history of telecommunications in China: Development and policy implications. In P. S. N. Lee (Ed.), *Telecommunications and development in China* (pp. 55-87). Cresskill, NJ: Hampton Press.

Lewis, T. (Spring 1999). Research in technology education—some areas of need. *Journal of Technology Education, 10* (2), 1-16.

Li, X, et al. (1996, July). China's education and research network. *CINET-L Newsletter.* Retrieved July 22, 1996 from http://info.isoc.org/isoc/events/inet/96/proceedings/c6/c6_2.htm.

Lu, Q. (1997, July). National information industry policy and prospects for commercial ISP. Retrieved December 1, 2000, from http://china-window.com/magazine/97/9/luq.htm.

McIntyre, B. T. (1998). China's use of the Internet: A revolution on hold. In P. S. N. Lee (Ed.), *Telecommunications and development in China* (pp. 149-169). Cresskill, NJ: Hampton Press.

McLuhan, M. (1962). *The Gutenberg galaxy.* Toronto: Toronto University Press.

McQuail, D. (2000). *McQuail's mass communication theory* (4th ed.). Beverly Hills, CA: Sage.

Mueller, M., & Tan, Z. (1997). *China in the information age: Telecommunications and the dilemmas of reform.* Westport, CT: Praeger.

Nguyen, D., & Alexander, J. (1996). In R. Shields (Ed.), *Cultures of Internet: Virtual spaces, real histories, living bodies* (pp. 99-124). London: Sage.

Pavlik, J. V. (1998). *New media technology: Cultural and commercial perspectives* (2nd ed.). Boston: Allyn and Bacon.

Polkinghorne, D. (1983). *Methodology for the human sciences: Systems of inquiry.* Albany: State University of New York Press.

Rogers, E. (1983). *Diffusion of innovations.* New York: The Free Press.

van Dijk, T. A. (1995). Elite discourse and the reproduction of racism. In R. K. Whillock & D. Slayden (Eds.), *Hate speech* (pp. 1-27). London: Sage.

Williams, R. (1976). *Keywords.* London: Fontana.

Xinhua. (1999, March 3). Over 40 [Chinese] government departments got on the net for public opinions. *World Journal,* p. A8.

Xinhua. (1999, June 9). Booming Internet Cafés in China. *World Journal,* p. A7.

Xinhua. (1999, November 29). "The fourth medium" forces China to face news reform challenges. *World Journal,* p. A2.

Xu, R., Liu, B., & Zheng, P. (1997, July). Internet development in China. Retrieved December 15, 2000, from http://china-window.com/magazine/97/1/xurs1.htm.

Zhao, Y. (2000). Caught in the Web: The public interest and the battle for control of China's information superhighway, *Info, 2,* 41-66.

15

The Essential Role of Chinese as the World's Leading Logographic Writing System in Global Communication

Virginia Mansfield-Richardson

We do not understand the relationship between language and thought. Can we have thoughts that cannot be expressed in words? Can everything that can be expressed in one language be expressed in any other language as well?

—Charles M. Vest, president of the Massachusetts Institute of
Technology, in his annual report to the university, 1995
(Vest, 1995, B5)

This chapter begins with the premise that logographic writing systems may possibly face near elimination within the 21st century and that preservation of these character-based scripts should be a priority for any person or institution concerned with future cross-cultural communication. In 1997, the *World Press Review* ran a series of articles from newspapers and magazines throughout the world discussing the growing dominance of English, beginning with the lead article's headline, "Winning the Language Wars: The World Speaks English" (Drohan & Freeman, 1997, pp. 6-8). The world dominance of English-language media corporations is only one problem in the labyrinth. The lack of a design for a computer that is truly compatible with character-based writing may be an even larger threat to logographic writing (Lee, 2001). Finally, the serious absence of interest in the cognitive differences between logographs and alphabets among most Western scholars presents a threat to the future of character-based writing systems.

As communication technology advances at exponential rates, so too does the possibility that China, Taiwan, and Japan (*Kanji* portion of the language) will go the way of Thailand, Vietnam, and South Korea (although some characters are still used) within this century by converting to a "convenient" alphabetized version of their language that will make it much easier to converse globally via computer and to create words for the explosion of new scientific terms that can better suit the needs of English-speaking scientific communities. This study further argues that as the world continues to lose logographic writing systems to alphabetized counterfeit versions of the languages, it also loses a cognitive process, eliminating creative approaches to problem solving and other forms of thinking that scholars have yet to unfold.

As Western entertainment conglomerates continue to penetrate markets in more countries, communication theory must also expand to examine whether these are Western communication approaches masquerading as international approaches and whether different cultural and cognitive processes can be incorporated into a truly catholic system of multicultural communication. If language does shape the neurophysiological pathways of the brain, how then should this research be applied to communication between peoples of logographic languages and peoples of alphabetic languages?

Character-based languages historically prevailed over most of Southeast Asia, including what is now Vietnam and Thailand. The most widely spoken of those languages, Chinese, is one of two or three independent full scripts in human history (Mote, 1971, p. 4). Thai was alphabetized in the latter part of the nineteenth century; however, the trend toward alphabetizing character-based languages sped up considerably in the last century. Within the twentieth century, Vietnamese and Korean were alphabetized, as was the *Kana* portion of Japanese. As the world bears down on China and its lucrative market potential, so too do those who want Chinese to be formally alphabetized to make it easier for non-native speakers to learn the language. However, linguists have learned it is easier for a native English speaker to learn to read and write Chinese than it is for a native Chinese speaker to learn to read and write English. Therein lies one of the many arguments for increasing Chinese and other logographic languages in global communication. Modern stages of Chinese language development relate directly to Westernization of the language; alphabetized romanization methods for learning the language have been around since the Wade-Giles method was introduced in China in the 1920s, followed by other romanization methods including Yale, Gwoyeu Romatzyh (created by Chinese scholars), a Soviet system called Latin *hua,* and *pinyin*, which has been the official romanization system in China since 1958 (Newnham, 1980, pp. 173-174).

BRAIN HEMISPHERICITY AND ETHNOCOGNITIVISM

Ethnocognitivism refers to dominant thought patterns within a culture (Porter & Samovar, 1991, p. 231). It is an area of communication theory based on the study of ethnolinguistics, meaning that a person's thought processes are directly related to that person's native language. T. Wilhem von Humboldt, a German linguist, believed that poetry could not be separated from music and that the language poetry was written in was insignificant to the process, but that how the mind processes prose depends solely on the language it is in and that it is dominated by thought. Prior to 1949 in China, and up until as recently as the 1970s in Hong Kong and Taiwan, newspapers published in traditional Chinese characters had headlines written in poems of often lilting rhyme and with equal numbers of characters per line. These artistic headlines were similar to traditional Chinese poetry and represented culturally a purely Chinese approach to headline writing. By the 1990s this tradition of poetic headlines was all but dead and occurred only when an older editor at a Hong Kong or Taiwanese newspaper decided to write a headline "the old way." It is an excellent example of ethnocognitivism.

Benjamin L. Whorf was one of the first scholars to conceptualize the idea of ethnocognitivism (Whorf, 1956). In all of his research, around the 1930s and 1940s, there were two underlying themes: (1) an individual's perception of the world via abstraction, rationalization, and categorization processes is intimately tied to his or her native language; (2) languages differ from each other, which suggests that the people who speak those languages differ as a group in their psychological potential (Whorf , 1956).

Brain hemisphericity refers to studies in the functions of the brain's left and right hemispheres based on the premise that individuals rely more on one hemisphere than the other in language cognition and in other brain functions. Researchers Sally Springer and Georg Deutsch contend that different languages result in different hemispheric dominance in the brain (Springer & Deutch, 1985, p. 3). Specifically, the cognitive process required to learn an alphabetic/phonologic language such as English, French, or German occurs in the brain's left hemisphere. Conversely, a portion of the cognitive process required to learn an ideographic/morphologic language such as Chinese or Japanese *(Kanji)* occurs partially in the brain's right hemisphere according to several studies, but this research is still much debated among neurolinguists.

Ethnocognitivism and brain hemisphericity can be logically linked to ask whether a culture causes its individuals to have dominant left or right hemisphericity. The cross-cultural and international communication implications of this theory are numerous. In 1978, the controversial Japanese scholar Tadanobu Tsunoda wrote the book *The Japanese Brain: Brain Function and East-West Culture*, which became a best-seller in Japan. In it, Tsunoda hypothesized that an individual's native language develops that person's cognitive processes and the way the brain's two halves process language (Porter & Samovar, 1991, p. 233; Tsunoda, 1985, p. 29). Tsunoda says the brain of a person whose native language is Japanese actually functions differently from the brain of a person whose native language was acquired in a Western culture. This was in no way racist, since test subjects who were Caucasian but raised with Japanese as their native language showed the same results. It is specifically the characters used in written Japanese that created the difference (Porter & Samovar, 1991, p. 233). This research can be applied to Chinese and other character-based languages that rely on logographs for writing.

Aleksandr R. Lauria conducted similar research on Japanese patients with and without aphasia who had lost the ability to understand and express ideas because of brain damage. His research states that it is the Chinese character component of Japanese (called *Kanji*) and the syllabary or hiragana (called *Kana*) parts of the Japanese language that are actually processed differently in the brain's neural mechanism (Feitelson, 1979, p. 170). Researcher C. K. Leong explains that Luria's studies indicate that "the Kana transcription seems to relate to the 'phonological processor' in the brain while the Kanji transcription could bypass such processing" (p. 170). This could indicate that auditory short-term storage, which is very important in learning and processing English language, is not as important or as needed in learning and processing Chinese or Japanese.

Some of the most exhaustive studies in the area have been conducted by researchers Hoosain, Tzeng, Chen, and Ho, to name a few (Chen, 1986; Chen & Chen 1988; Chen & Juola, 1982; Hoosain, 1984, 1986, 1991; Hoosain & Shiu, 1989; Ho & Hoosain, 1984, 1989). Looking at their studies collectively indicates numerous unique qualities in the processing of logographs, including studies that single-character words are often processed in the brain's right hemisphere. This is one of the more controversial and fascinating realms of ongoing research dealing with cognitive processing of logographs.

In the March 1992 issue of the *Journal of Chinese Philosophy*, a discussion of Whorf's theories references some common theories about ethnocognitivism as it relates to Chinese:

> Graham's position that Chinese thinking accepts correlative thinking whereas Western thinking seeks to eliminate it in favor of a purely analytic mode of thinking deserves careful exposition, in connection with his view that Chinese language/thought "provides the ideal test case for Whorf's hypothesis that the thought of culture is guided and constrained by the structure of its language." (Fleming, 1992, p. 109)

Research in hemisphericity and ethnocognitivism certainly helps support the importance of logographic-based writing systems thriving as global languages rather than withering away, as has happened in the twentieth century.

LOGOGRAPHS' STRENGTH IN MEMORY AND READING

Much of the research indicating that Chinese speakers have greater language memory skills compared to native English speakers has been done with children in China, Hong Kong, and Taiwan. Similar to English language instruction in the United States, children in China begin language instruction upon entering primary school roughly at the age of five or six (Feitelson, 1979). Character learning goes hand-in-hand with the learning of *pinyin*. By the end of the sixth grade, students are expected to know approximately 3,000 characters (Feitelson, 1979, p. 153). According to research by psychologists Liu Fan and Tong Le-quan there is a strong psychological backing that justifies this new way of teaching written language in the People's Republic of China (National Academy of Sciences et al., 1983). This research shows that there are six ways to construct Chinese characters: (1) pictographs, (2) pictophonetics, (3) self-explanatories, (4) associate compounds, (5) phonetic loans, and (6) synonyms. Among these variations, 80 percent of all Chinese characters are pictographs, which usually have two parts: one that indicates the meaning, the other that relates to pronunciation or phonetics (National Academy of Sciences et al., 1984).

Researchers first examined what causes Chinese children to recognize characters, and whether they learn faster by learning the rules of character construction (i.e., stroke order, radicals). Research indicates that young children learn best when they first are introduced to characters that combine pronunciation, meaning, and the form of the character. This method stresses the rules of pictophonetics (National Academy of Sciences et al., 1984). It puts together characters that have the same pronunciations so that children can draw inferences about other meanings from one instance. This means that often the first characters learned are complex, not the simplest characters. In the traditional Confucian instruction of Chinese, the simplest characters (those with the fewest strokes) were taught first, along with the most commonly used characters. The traditional method of teaching new characters was also to introduce them by adding them in sentences.

Characters that are strictly pictographs are not as easy for children to learn because they do not have enough life experience to draw associations to the pictographs (National Academy of Sciences et al., 1984, p. 203). For example, as they might not yet know what a reptile is, a pictograph depicting a reptile is useless to them from a learning standpoint. Research also indicates that very young children cannot analyze characters until they have learned how to properly draw strokes, as well as stroke order. At that point children can recognize characters by their structure. Once children have learned anywhere from 200 to 300 characters, they recognize that characters are often made up of two or three parts (often radicals). Experiments conducted by Le-quan in 1979 show that in writing characters, simple characters are easier than complex characters for children (National Academy of Sciences et al., 1984, p. 205). However, in reading characters there is no difference in difficulty for the same children between simple and complex characters. The experiments indicated the importance of vision-motion in learning to write characters. This trait is not so important in learning to write English.

There have also been several linguistic-based studies in Chinese that relate to its logographic-morpheme qualities. One of the most interesting studies relating to the Chinese language examines the different numbers of words it takes to describe complex thoughts in English, as compared to Chinese. It indicates that morphological change in Chinese is less developed than in English and that the dependency on word order is greater in Chinese than in English (National Academy of Sciences et al., 1984, p. 205). Both languages have sentence structure that is dependent on word order, but Chinese is more strict in word order. This has led to other studies on sentence comprehension with Chinese students.

One study looked at expectancy in reading (National Academy of Sciences et al., 1984, p. 207). About 26 children in the second and fourth grades were shown 24 short sentences in Chinese. Half of the sentences expressed ideas that corresponded more to the expectations of children. The other sentences expressed thoughts that were considered unexpected, but rational. The students had one-fifth of a second to read each sentence, and they were asked to repeat aloud what they thought each sentence said. The children fared much better with the first category of sentences. This research supports the need for a closer look at semantic content in Chinese sentence structure and how it relates to comprehension of written communication.

Other studies in Chinese reading comprehension show that one advantage of the language is that reading a character is directly tied to meaning (Wang, 1974, p. 88). For example, comprehension occurs in two stages: (1) visual and (2) comprehension (cognition), whereas in English there is a third stage of tying meaning to sound, called subvocalizing. Even though the word is not read aloud, the reader: (1) sees the graphic image, (2) subvocalizes the sound of the word, then (3) processes it into meaning (cognition) (Wang, 1974, p. 89). In reading Chinese this second stage does not occur (Wang, 1974, p. 90). This may affect how Chinese-speaking persons interpret information they read in newspapers or documents as compared to the English language news and information comprehension of English-speaking persons.

LOGOGRAPHS AND COMPUTERS

There is a serious problem with the types of computers available to people who communicate in Chinese and Japanese. Based on a Western approach to computers. they are nearly all based on romanization keyboards, including most of the research being conducted in Singapore, Japan, Korea, Taiwan, and China.

Computer experts who are attempting to develop a quick and efficient way to electronically communicate in logographic languages have lost one of the most essential ingredients of scientific research: creativity. In 1997, George Wang, director of IBM's Beijing lab, explained that with all the technological advance made in the computer industry, design engineers have not been able to come up with a successful system to serve the language spoken by the most people in the world—Chinese—even though the number of Chinese speakers represents more than double the number of people who speak English (Maney, 1997, B1).

"Solve the input-output problem and the Chinese computer industry takes off," Wang explained (Maney, 1997, B1). Unfortunately, that problem has not been solved, which makes the idea of alphabetizing Chinese characters all the more tempting, but wrong. The 1997 *USA Today* article begins by saying, "The Chinese language and computers are, as they might say in Silicon Valley, not compatible" (Maney, 1997, B1). According to a February 2001 article in the *New York Times,* the problem is still not solved, and native Chinese speakers who use computers are fast losing their memory of how to stroke characters when writing Chinese since most computer systems for Chinese require *pinyin* to be typed in order to retrieve a character (Lee, 2001, B1). One Microsoft researcher is working on computer software that would even eliminate the need to bring up characters via typing *pinyin*; instead, the computer would be able to "convert entire sentences from phonetics into characters using the context" (Lee, 2001, B1). Since 97 percent of computer users in China type by phonetically spelling out character sounds, they are not required to construct the characters using the important radicals as well as the needed stroking order necessary for memory and recall of the characters (Lee, 2001, B1). Ovid Tzeng, a leading cognitive neurolinguist and Taiwan's Minister of Education, says little research has been conducted on the effect of computer use on written language (Lee, 2001, B1). Clearly, when it comes to Chinese, there is an urgent need for more research on the effects of computer use on users' ability to recall and write Chinese logographs.

Part of the problem may come from approaching computing from a left-brain, alphabetic-based language way of thinking. Where is it written that a keyboard is needed to operate a computer? Is typing really the most efficient way to manipulate a computer in all languages? With all the bravado of computer companies, which claim bigger and better storage capacities in smaller and smaller units, why do designers throw up their hands in frustration when storage and easy retrieval of a language with 50,000 characters (Chinese) is discussed?

Most of these questions have the same answer: The majority of computer research and development is being conducted by people who are either native

English speakers or who are fluent in English as a second language and being encouraged to think like the gurus in Silicon Valley. Nearly all international conferences on computer technology are conducted in English, and the subsequent research presented at those conferences are written in English. Most computer programs are in English, and those that sell in "foreign" markets have been translated into other languages.

This last point may seem insignificant if the conventional argument is accepted that goes: As long as a program is translated into other languages, it is serving the needs of the international community. If the Sapir-Whorf hypothesis is correct, the very nature of a language determines how people think and how they communicate. Therefore, the language that computer hardware and software are designed for affects how that computer will suit the needs of users from different cultures who speak different languages.

A good example is the IBM Chinese-language program called "Brushwriter." It offers the user four choices for inputting information, including typing in a romanized version of Chinese called *pinyin* that uses the English alphabet or typing in parts of characters to receive a set of characters from which to choose the desired character. But in most cases, the word is typed in with the appropriate tone (there are four tones in Chinese), and the user is given a choice of several characters that meet that criteria. With the word "*shi*" in the second tone, the user must select from over 36 different characters that meet the criteria. It would be as if each time the word "and" was typed in an English-language software package, the user had to look through 36 different spellings to find the appropriate word. In short, this is ridiculously time consuming, yet it is one of the most popular approaches to computing in Chinese.

Some people say that to efficiently keep pace with the explosive developments in international telecommunications, computers must be an interactive technology that is easily transferable to all languages. It is also argued that to bring the entire world community into efficient telecommunication, all languages must be brought online. These are the ideological approaches to the problem of telecommunication technology growing much faster than policy and standardization is formed to regulate it.

In reality, the language of computing is dictated by the countries with the most research and development, marketing, political power, and/or need for computers. This is why there are very few computers designed for people who live in less developed countries such as Kenya, because they have a restrictive government and not much technological infrastructure to handle a lucrative computer market. Also, Kenya and other sub-Saharan African countries are not politically powerful in the global arena. However, many programs have been converted to Russian, not because there is a lot of computer research and development going on in the countries of the former Soviet Union, nor because high volumes of computers are being built in those countries. Russian is much more a language of political and economic power than, say, a language like Swahili, and this is reflected in computer programs made available in these languages.

It seems obvious, but necessary, to mention why it is essential to develop computers that best interact with the language of a particular culture. The more compatible a computer is, the more it is used. The more computers are used, the more people will hook up to services such as electronic mail, computerized news services, and the numerous other possibilities for using computers to further the advancement of education, medicine, international communication, and positive humanitarian efforts worldwide.

Most computers are designed to mimic a phonetic-based language. Computers are all based on the binary system, but that is translated into a keyboard based on the typewriter for an alphabetic language. Most computer systems for Chinese have some form of *pinyin* application using an alphabetic keyboard. For example, if a user selects the *pinyin* application for IBM's Brushwriter software, the word is typed in *pinyin*, then a 1, 2, 3, or 4 is typed to indicate what tone is required for the word, and a series of characters appears on the computer screen if there is more than one character for that word/tone combination. The user then selects the desired character. However, this process can be cumbersome and time-consuming, causing many Chinese speakers to use the computer system only if absolutely necessary.

Herein lies one of the biggest problems with computer applications for logograph-based languages. They are slow. Anyone who is a fast typist prefers to type something in English rather than write it out in longhand, simply because it is faster. Computers, with their ability to erase and write over errors, have made that word processing function even faster and easier for those writing in an alphabet-based language.

The newer versions of Chinese computer systems still use keyboards but also have strokes on the keys. The typist begins stroking the character and often before he or she is finished with all the strokes the character appears on the screen. This is a strong improvement over the *pinyin*-to-character method, but users are still having problems with forgetting how to stroke a character if they lean too much on computers for their writing needs. The largest chain of Chinese-language newspapers, *Sing Tao Daily*, as recently as 1997 installed a new computer system that still operates in this manner and requires trained typists to enter the handwritten notes of their reporters. Even the senior editors of the *Sing Tao* publishing empire recognize the absurdity that their reporters must submit handwritten notes to typists before a story can be typeset to the composing room. Newspapers published in English and other alphabetic languages require reporters to type their stories directly into computers, often laptops in the field, and then transmit the copy to editors, where final-edited copy is eventually typeset to the composing room or directly to a laser computerized printing process. It doesn't take a genius to figure out which system is faster (speed being a crucial element in news gathering). Clearly it is time to start being more creative in designing logographic-based computer systems.

Learning Three Languages

To fully use a computer program such as Brushwriter, the user is forced to learn the equivalent of three languages. The first two languages are Chinese characters and *pinyin*, which is not the fault of the computer designers. The debate over whether *pinyin* is Westernizing Chinese will be reserved for another study. But, with Brushwriter, as well as less than a handful of other widely available Chinese-language software packages, there is another amazing feature that is used by people such as teletype operators in China. The entire language, or at least the most commonly used words, has a conversion translation to numbers. A user need only memorize approximately 75 pages of numeric conversions of the language to successfully write the most commonly used Chinese characters on the calculator portion of the keyboard. Imagine a computer company that devised a program where the user had to memorize a unique numeric equivalent for each word in English in order to use the program. The company would not only be laughed out of business, but the program would not sell. Yet, computer designers actually offer this as an option for transcribing Chinese into a Western-style keyboard setup. This is insulting to the people who speak the most widely spoken language in the world.

The Two-Step Process

There certainly have been some attempts to create more user-friendly and less complex Chinese software packages. One reason for this lack of design again goes back to economics. If a keyboard fits only a logographic-based language structure, it would not be marketable in the vast English/alphabetic-based language market of computers. Even Japanese computers have alphabetic keyboards. However, it was the invention of the laptop computer that helped speed up the conversion process from the character component of Japanese to the phonetic component of the language. Most Japanese computers are now laptops that can be flipped, by hitting a command key, from a keyboard for displaying characters on the screen, typed in a romanization system to the same keyboard that types out the alphabetic portion of the language on the screen.

Another method for typing Chinese characters in some computer programs comes about by typing in portions of a character. Chinese consists of 214 characters called radicals. These radicals can be words in themselves and are also parts of other characters. There have been keyboards with as many as 350 keys designed to make room for the radicals and other commonly used characters, but these are cumbersome and complex to use.

Most programs that deal with typing portions of a character place several characters in a grouping under a function key. Through a two- to three-step process the user goes into the character segment and searches out the exact character he or she desires to appear in the screen text. The character groupings, also used in some Japanese software packages, are sometimes based on the radicals, but often based on word groupings. Much of the research being done for strictly Chinese language keyboards relates back to this categorization structure, sometimes with as many as seven characters displayed on each key to log into different categories in the language.

Even researchers who are trying to make the typing process easier for untrained typists in Chinese use this categorization process. Four researchers at the National University of Singapore—Chan Sing Chai, Low Hwee Boon, Yu Wellington Chia-peir, and Chang Ifay—discussed this problem in their paper entitled "Conceptual Framework and the Implementation of Intelligent Chinese Input," which was presented at the 1986 International Computer Symposium held at National Cheng Kung University in Tainan, Taiwan. They explained that many input methods are available to the Chinese computer users, but that "many methods relied on the assumption that the users possessed certain previous knowledge. . . . However, for a first time user or the infrequent users, the input methods provided so far do not have the same [appeal] as the English keyboard input" (Chai et al., 1986, p. 487).

They go on to explain, "The English keyboard is 'obvious' to any user whereby a person without any typing training can still use it to enter the English text slowly even with one finger or one hand" (Chai et al., 1986, p. 487). They explain that *pinyin* and stroke-order computer systems require the user to know the exact *pinyin* spellings and tones (many Chinese do not know *pinyin*) and that stroke order requires the user to know exactly how a character is stroked. This is similar to requiring English script writers to know an exact, standardized set of rules for writing longhand.

After examining the more than 400 Chinese input schemes available for computers, Chai, Boon, Chia-peir, and Ifay concluded that the two-step process was the most efficient (Chai et al., 1986, p. 491). However, this process still uses an alphabetized keyboard and requires typing two letters, such as A and B, to call up any single Chinese character. Again, this requires a great deal of training. These researchers conclude that "an easy to use and easy to learn Chinese input system can be built on a low cost standard English keyboard with a mouse device" (Chai et al., 1986, p. 1493).

Like much ongoing research, this idea is based on using existing English keyboards for processing Chinese characters. In this chapter I argue that this is not only a backhanded approach to word processing in logographic languages, it is also like comparing apples and oranges in the research laboratory. In essence, as long as research and development are based on alphabetic-language keyboards and computer concepts, a creative approach will never be arrived at for computing in ideographs.

The Calligraphy Approach

Some of the best research that has been done in the area of Chinese computer programs uses a method of computerized Chinese calligraphy. This successfully combines the fields of ethnocognitivism and hemisphericity because it considers the cultural and historical importance of calligraphy in China and Japan, and it is the only application, other than voice-activated processes, that does not use a Western-style keyboard.

Recent research has Chinese and Japanese educators very concerned. It indicates that people who use computers for even a short period of time begin to lose their knowledge of how to stroke a character. Since this does not occur in alphabetic languages, it directly relates to the difference between the two types of language structures. When typing an alphabetized word, the typist is still spelling out the word and sounding out the word phonetically—the identical process that occurs when writing in script.

However, when a person who normally strokes a character uses a computer, he or she is not stroking the character but instead going through a *pinyin*-to-character process, or radical base-to-character process. In no portion of the process does the user stroke the character. This is why the research conducted by Yoshinao Aoki and Chong-ming Shi in computers that generate calligraphic characters is so relevant. Aoki and Shi are faculty members in the Division of Information Engineering at Hokkaido University in Japan. They have devised a computer, with a keyboard for basic commands (and an alphabet for switching to romanization), that has as one component a large, mechanized arm that strokes calligraphy on a computer tablet (Aoki & Shi, 1986, p. 496).

They contend that the most useful application for this research is in generating signs and artistic word processing. However, they presented their initial research in 1986, before psychologists had discovered the effects of using computers on loss of stroke order memory. It is clear that Aoki and Shi's research should now be considered in new designs for ideographic software as a more efficient approach to word processing in Chinese and Japanese.

Voice Application

In recent years a great deal of research has been conducted in voice application to computers. Many people who work in the international arena are anxiously awaiting the perfection of technology that allows people to speak into a computerized telephone that will automatically translate one language into another language. Parts of this same technology are being applied to the creation of large, multilanguage computer dictionaries.

Electrical engineers Soo-Chang Pei and Twei-Ying Wang of National Taiwan University have conducted extensive research in the area of Chinese speech processing as a means of inputting information into computers. In fact, this research may be more applicable to Chinese, since it is a language of crucial intonation, than to other languages that do not infer word meaning from tones. Finally, there is a major difference between printing Chinese or Japanese characters and printing written alphabetic scripts. In essence, an ideographic character packs many more intricate lines and images into the same area than does a printed letter. Literally, it takes a much finer quality printer to print an ideographic character than is required to print a romanized writing system. Also, logographs often require that a radical be printed in varying sizes to fit the number of strokes in a character. For instance, the radical for "heart" (three strokes) would appear much larger on its own than if it were only part of another character that might have up to fifteen strokes. It is a challenge to program a printer to understand this difference in character size.

The technology has been perfected, but only recently, and it is an ongoing process. Hewlett Packard was the first major company to create a Japanese-language printer, the DeskJet 500J, that was the first of several Asian-language inkjet products that Hewlett Packard's Asia Peripherals Division (APD) in Singapore continues to introduce into the market. This printer is capable of printing in *Kanji* (characters) and Roman Latin. A similar printer is available for Chinese. There are now several laser printers available through most of the leading corporations manufacturing computer equipment that print characters with a fair amount of clarity, but many are still flawed in offering finepoint printing of characters in font sizes of 10 points or less.

The key question here is: Why has it taken this long to perfect a printer that duplicates the most commonly written language in the world? It is because computerized printer technology began in alphabetized languages, and engineers are only now beginning to perfect similar technologies for ideographic-based languages.

CONCLUSION

We have seen that historically logographic writing systems have been alphabetized at a faster pace in this century than in the last century. One must ask if that trend will continue to speed up in this century. We have also seen that the way in which the brain processes portions of character-based languages are dramatically different from the left-brain cognition of alphabetized languages. To eliminate this thought process would be to eliminate an entire approach to thinking. Who knows what thoughts and creative ideas or approaches to problems are eliminated each time a logographic-based language is alphabetized? We have also seen that character-based languages improve areas of memory skills. There are also numerous economic, political, and cultural arguments for maintaining logographic-based languages and using them more in global communication that have not been addressed in this chapter. In aggregate terms it seems clear that a language such as Chinese should eventually become the second global language in this century, taking its rightful spot next to English. If more persons were able to take the time to learn a logograph-based language, entirely new venues to true global—as well as true cross-cultural and intercultural—communication would also arise.

Should the future world be one of several cultures and languages or one of a handful of languages reflecting the world's most influential political systems? We also need to consider seriously not only the cultural implications of global communication in a few languages but also the cognitive and neurological implications of this trend. These are crucial questions to ponder now that we are in a new century of defining what culture is and how to effectively communicate between cultures while at the same time preserving cultures.

> *We do not know how we learn and remember, or how we think and communicate. We do not yet know the chemical or physical nature of storage of information in the brain. We do not know where in the brain information is stored, how we retrieve it, or whether there are limits to the amount we can store.*
> —Charles M. Vest, president of the Massachusetts Institute of Technology, in his annual report to the university, 1995
> (Vest, 1995, B5).

REFERENCES

Aoki, Y., & Shi, C. M. (1986). A calligraphic character generating and brush writng system. *Proceedings of international computer symposium 1986, 3*, 596-1501.

Besner, D., & Coltheart, M. (1979). Idographic and alphabetic processing in skilled reading of English. *Neuropsychologia, 17*, 467-472.

Besner, D.S., Daniels, C. E., & Slade, C. (1982). Ideogram reading and right hemisphere language. *British Journal of Psychology, 73*, 21-28.

Biederman, I., & Tsao, I. C. (1979). On processing Chinese ideographs and English words: Some implications from Stroop test results. *Cognitive Psychology,11* (2), 125-132.

Chai, C. S., Boon, L. H., Chai-peir, Y. W., & Ifay, C. (1986). Conceptual framework and the implementation of intelligent Chinese input. *Proceedings of international computer symposium 1986, 3*, 1487-1495.

Chen, H. C. (1986). Component detection in reading Chinese characters. In H. S. R. Kao & R. Hoosain, (Eds.), *Linguistics, psychology, and the Chinese language* (pp. 1-10). Hong Kong: University of Hong Kong Centre of Asian Studies.

Chen, H. C., & Chen, M. J. (1988). Directional scanning in Chinese reading. In I. M. Liu, H. C. Chen & M. J. Chen (Eds.), *Cognitive aspects of the Chinese language* (pp. 15-26). Hong Kong: Asian Research Service.

Chen, H. C. & Juola, J. F. (1982). Dimensions of lexical coding in Chinese and English. *Memory and Cognition, 19*, 216-224.

Chen, L. K., & Carr, H. A. (1926). The ability of Chinese students to read in vertical and horizontal directions. *Journal of Experimental Psychology, 9*, 110-117.

Chen, M. J. (1981). Direction scanning of visual displays: A study of Chinese subjects. *Journal of Cross-Cultural Psychology, 12*, 252-271.

Chen, M. J., Yung, Y. F., & Ng, T. W. (1988). The effect of content on the perception of Chinese characters. In I. M. Liu, C. Chen, & M. J. Chen (Eds.), *Cognitive aspects of the Chinese language* (pp. 27-39). Hong Kong: Asian Research Service.

Drohan, M., & Freeman, A. (1997). Winning the language wars. The world speaks English. *World Press Review, 44*, 6-8.

Feitelson, D. (Ed.). (1978). *Cross-cultural perspectives on reading and reading comprehension.* Newark, DE: International Reading Association.

Feitelson, D. (Ed.). (1979). *Mother tongue or second language? On the teaching of reading in multilingual societies.* Newark, DE: International Reading Association.

Fleming, J. (1992). Structure of (Chinese) mind. *Journal of Chinese Philosophy, 19*, 109-115.

Ho, S. K., & Hoosain, R. (1984). Hemisphere differences in the perception of opposites. In H. S. R. Kao & R. Hoosain (Eds.), *Psychological studies of the Chinese language* (pp. 11-22). Hong Kong: The Chinese Language Society of Hong Kong.

Ho, S. K., & Hoosain, R. (1989). Right hemisphericity advantage in lexical decision with two-character words. *Brain and Language, 37*, 606-615.

Hoosain, R. (1984). Experiments on digit spans in the Chinese and English languages. In H. S. R. Kao & R. Hoosain (Eds.), *Psychological studies of the Chinese language* (pp. 23-38). Hong Kong: The Chinese Language Society of Hong Kong.

Hoosain, R. (1984). Lateralization of bilingual digit span functions. *Perception and Motor Skills, 58*, 21-22.

Hoosain, R. (1986). Language, orthography, and cognitive processes: Chinese perspectives for the Sapir-Whorf hypothesis. *International Journal of Behavioral Development, 9*, 507-525.

Hoosain, R., & Osgood, C. E. (1983). Information processing times for English and Chinese words. *Perception and Psychophysics, 34*, 573-577.

Hoosain, R., & Shiu, L. P. (1989). Cerebral lateralization of Chinese-English bilingual functions. *Neuropsychologia, 27*, 705-712.

Hoosain, R. (1991). *Psycholinguistic implications for linguistic relativity, a case study of Chinese.* Hillsdale, NJ: Lawrence Erlbaum Associates.

Issues in cognition: Proceedings of a joint conference in psychology. Washington: National Academy of Sciences, American Psychological Association, Chinese Academy of Sciences.

Mair, V. H., & Liu, Y. (Eds.). (1991). *Characters and computers.* Amsterdam: ISO Press.

Maney, K. (1997). Computers link with Chinese language. *USA Today*, B1 (Nov. 6).

Mathias, J., & Kennedy, T. L. (Eds.). (1980). *Computers, language reform, and lexicography in China.* Pullman: Washington State University Press.

Mote, F. W. (1971). *Intellectual foundations of China.* New York: Alfred A. Knopf, Inc.

Newnham, R. (1980*). About Chinese.* Middlesex, England: Penguin Books.

Porter, R., & Samovar, L. (1991). *Intercultural communication.* Belmont, CA: Wadsworth .

Springer, S. P., & Deutsch, G. (1985). *Left brain, right brain.* New York: W.H. Freeman and Company.

Tsunoda, T. (1985). *The Japanese brain.* Tokyo: Taishukan.

Tzeng, O. J. L., & Hung, D. L. (1981). Linguistic determinism: A written language perpsective. In O. J. L. Tzeng & H. Singer (Eds.), *Perception of print: Reading research in experimental psychology* (pp. 237-255). Hillsdale, NJ: Lawrence Erlbaum Associates.

Tzeng, O. J. L., Hung, D. L., Cotton, B., & Wang, W. S. Y. (1979). Visual lateralization effect in reading Chinese characters. *Nature, 282,* 499-501.

Vest, C. M. (1995). The pursuit of the truly unknown. *The Chronicle of Higher Education,* Dec. 15, B5.

Wang, W. (1982). *Human communication: Language and its psychobiological bases.* San Francisco: W.H. Freeman.

Whorf, B. L. (1956). *Language, thought, and reality: Selected writings of Benjamin Lee Whorf.* Cambridge, MA: MIT Press.

16

Problems and Prospects of Chinese Communication Study

Guo-Ming Chen

Although the study of communication in the West can be traced back to Aristotle's *Rhetoric*, it had to wait until the twentieth century for communication study to become an independent discipline. According to Delia (1987), three major social trends in the nineteenth century fostered the systematic study of human communication at the beginning of the twentieth century. First, industrialization brought about the speed and quality of printing; second, urbanization led to the clustering of population; and third, the widespread nature of education increased the quantity of media. These trends transformed the Western world, especially the United States, from an agricultural into an industrial or modern society. With the rapid development of the communication industry, the study of communication as well began to burgeon. A century later, the collective efforts of scholars have advanced the study of communication into a highly inclusive and well-identified discipline (Infante, Rancer, & Womack, 1996; Littlejohn, 1982, 1998; Zarefsky, 1995).

To succinctly summarize the discipline of communication study, ontologically, communication scholars, influenced by mechanism, actionalism, and constructivism, agree that communication is a holistic phenomenon, a social reality, and a developmental and orderly process. Epistemologically, in order to determine what are the most appropriate methods for studying communication, scholars in the communication discipline approach the question from six epistemological perspectives, including rationalism, rational empiricism, mechanistic empiricism, logical positivism, constructivism, and general systems theory. Metatheoretically, communication scholars continue to employ laws, rules, and systems approaches to guide the theoretical explanations of communication behaviors. Finally, in terms of methodology, communication study has gradually moved from functional and interpretive paradigms to integrate scientific and humanistic approaches by employing triangular methods and multivariate analyses (Chen, 1999a; Smith, 1988).

Based on these paradigmatic assumptions, the discipline of communication study has grown to a fully blossoming tree that embraces branches from intrapersonal, interpersonal, small group, organizational, public, mass, and intercultural/international communication. This communication tree shows a strong integration of knowledge and principles of other disciplines such as anthropology, business, English, psychology, sociology, and philosophy (Chen, 1999b; Littlejohn, 1982). The feature of inclusiveness and diversity is clearly reflected in the topical areas of communication education. For example, according to a report from the National Communication Association (Chesebro, 1989), communication majors in the United States may focus on any one of the following areas that are attached to branches of the communication tree: advertisement, argumentation, debate, communication education and development, forensics, interpretation and performance, journalism, language science, media, political communication, public relations, public speaking, and technology and information science.

The picture of communication study in the United States just described serves as a nice model for contrasting the development of the discipline in other areas of the world. This chapter examines the development of communication study as a discipline in Chinese societies. Problems of Chinese communication study and solutions from the perspective of globalization are discussed.

COMMUNICATION STUDIES IN CHINESE SOCIETIES

As a daily phenomenon of human societies in general, the practice of communication shows its diversity and variations as well in Chinese societies. The concept of communication emerged in China more than two thousand years ago. Although the meaning of communication in traditional China, which emphasized verbal exchange or delivery, is not identical with the modern perception of the concept, it is found that the following terminologies were used to represent communication activities (Huang, 1997):

1. *Chuan* means "to turn, to revolve," referring to delivering or forwarding a message, teaching knowledge and skills, recording a person's life, and orally distributing information.

2. *Bo* means "to sow seed," referring to spreading or disseminating messages.
3. *Yang* means "to rise up and flutter (as a flag), to flourish, to manifest," referring to consciously making a message or person flourish or manifest in public.
4. *Liu* means "to flow (like water)," referring to a process in which one's reputation or virtuous message is disseminated naturally and unintentionally.
5. *Bu* means "the woven cloth," referring to the downward process of announcing or disseminating organized information or government order to the public.
6. *Xuan* means "the emperor's room or the imperial decree or edict," referring to the dignified declaration or proclamation of the emperor's order.
7. *Tong* means "unobstructed," referring to the free flow of oral communication.
8. *Di* means "to deliver or exchange," referring to the exchange or delivery of materials via, for example, the courier system.

These extended meanings relating to the concept of communication in traditional China were found in settings of both formal and informal communication. Formal communication, usually between the emperor and government officials or common people, was conducted through nine common channels in traditional Chinese society: *zhao, chi, cheng, zou, biao, yi, jian, shu,* and *xi.*

Both *zhao* and *chi* are imperial decrees, mandates, or edicts by which the emperor conveyed an order, proclamation, or benevolence to government officials or citizens. If the message targeted an individual, it would be read openly to the person. If the message aimed to reach the public, it would be posted prominently in the town.

Cheng is an appeal letter written by an official to the emperor. The purpose of *cheng* is to express a subordinate's appreciation for the reward, grant, or benevolence. *Zou* is an impeachment report, issued by lower-rank government officials to the emperor to report the disloyalty of another official. Provocative language usually was used in *zou* to describe the disloyal behaviors of an official and how to impeach him or her. *Biao* is a formal statement that states one's situation in order to let the emperor understand, for example, why the subordinate cannot carry out the obligation or accept the order. The message in *biao* is usually highly emotion-laden.

Yi is an argumentative statement used by government officials to express their disagreement or different opinions to the emperor when *jian* (the oral admonition) is not available. Although using *yi* or *jian* to admonish the emperor often put the presenters in a situation that risked execution, it was a common way for the Chinese literate elite, as government officials, to try to persuade the emperor to do a good deed. The language in *yi* or *jian* tends to be acute and sharpened. *Shu* is a petition letter, in which a grievance or suggestion is expressed, used in upward communication. Finally, *xi* is a summons to arms, which lists the crimes of a tyrant and is usually issued by an emperor or a challenger to seek the support or acquiescence of the population in a given region (Wright, 1979).

In addition to formal written channels of Chinese communication, messages exchanged through oral communication have long been elaborated by Chinese, especially in the practice of informal communication among common people. For example, Han Fei, born around 280 B.C., pointed out twelve kinds of obstacles and twelve kinds of taboos used in the process of oral communication (Han, 1978). In informal communication, in addition to channels, such as *shuo* (to say), *tan* (to talk), *jiang* (to speak), and *lun* (to comment), used for the daily oral interaction and channels, such as *song* (to intone), *yin* (to chant), *yong* (to hum), and *chang* (to sing), used for literary exchanges, *shui fu* (persuasion) was the most common practice, which was used in both formal and informal communication (Wu, 1991). Chinese not only considered *shui fu* as a skill, but also developed a systematic theory to explain it; thus one must go through a rigid learning and training process in order to fully acquire the ability of *shui fu*. Although the Confucian tradition did not emphasize this line of oral communication, abundant writings and anecdotes on persuasion exist in Chinese literary history (Chen, 1995; Chen & Starosta, 1997-98; Chen & Zhong, 2000). The tradition continues today and scholars have begun to systematically study Chinese persuasive communication (Fong, 1975; Heisey, 2000; Lu, 1998; Oliver, 1971). However, the study of persuasive communication represents only a small portion of the field of human communication. Research on other areas of communication study is still scarce in Chinese societies.

PROBLEMS OF COMMUNICATION STUDY IN CHINESE SOCIETIES

Although communication education and research in Chinese societies have begun to burgeon in recent decades, a close observation of the field in China, Hong Kong, and Taiwan found that the emphasis of the field is fragmented and unbalanced (Chen, 2000, 2001; Chen, 1993; Liu, 1993; Sun, 1993; Wong & Zang, 1993). Despite the recent establishment of the first speech communication department at Shi Xin University in Taiwan and the department of communication studies at Hong Kong Baptist University, China is still behind the trend. Having the largest Chinese population, China is slow in instituting a more systematic study in the field of communication. Sparse studies and courses on the subject of communication continue to be operated, especially in the discipline of English and linguistics. Compared to the West, the development of the communication discipline in Chinese societies shows a picture of fragmentation and incompleteness (Chen, 1999a). More specifically, the discipline of communication study in Chinese societies suffers from four common problems: incomplete landscape, skill orientation, lack of collaboration, and Westernization.

Incomplete Landscape

Chen (1988) criticized communication study in Taiwan as mainly being embedded in the discipline of journalism and limited to the content of mass communication. In other words, the department of journalism is the field in which we see the subjects of communication study being taught, and the term "communication" refers only to the study of printed and telecommunication media. Other communication subjects either do not exist or are partially situated in other disciplines. For example, rhetoric is studied in the English department, focusing on writing and speaking skills only, and small-group and organizational behaviors are studied in sociology, with an emphasis on the group level of communication. As previously indicated, although the department of (speech) communication has been established in the 1990s and more human communication courses are offered in traditional journalism or mass communication departments, the emphasis on journalism and media continues to dominate in higher education in China, Hong Kong, and Taiwan. This orientation results in an incomplete landscape for the discipline of communication study in Chinese societies.

Skill Orientation

With the influence of journalism, which traditionally orients to basic education and career training, theory building becomes a victim in the process of developing the communication discipline. Except for adopting theories developed by Western communication scholars and borrowing a few other theories from social science disciplines for the purpose of instruction in the classroom, communication study and education in Chinese societies are clearly slanted toward the acquisition of practical skills. Although the overemphasis on skill acquisition is an inherent problem of the communication discipline everywhere and although it is understandable that one goal of college education is to equip students with appropriate skills for a successful career, the problem becomes more severe if the practical orientation is extended to the education in the graduate level. For students, a focus on the study of practical areas, such as public relations, advertising, broadcasting, oral communication, debate, persuasion, and building interpersonal relationships, is advantageous in searching for a job; the disadvantage is that most communication graduates tend to receive lower-paid jobs with this practically oriented college education. Another disadvantage is that the lack of theory courses often leads communication graduates to a less competitive situation, compared to graduates from other disciplines, because creativity and critical thinking are limited. Thus, in the short term, it may be easier for communication graduates to find a job, but in the long run, their weakness of being less competitive will prevent them from achieving full development in their careers (Chen, 1998).

Lack of Collaboration

The incomplete landscape and the skill orientation of communication study in Chinese societies also cause the problem of sharing existing resources among different colleges. This is clearly reflected in the curriculum design and in the process of developing a new program of communication study. For example, especially in Taiwan because of the rapid development of communication education in recent years, in order to attract students for enrollment, program development and curriculum design are directed to the practical or skills direction of communication study. Scholars' research, in order to compete for funding or grants, also tends to orient to practical subjects and personal interests. Worse still, competition among colleges and scholars leads to a lack of collaboration and idea exchange. This results in several negative effects, including program overlapping, wasting resources, and identity problems (Chen, 1999b).

Westernization

The trend of Westernization mirrors the history of modern China. From the late nineteenth century science and democracy movements flourished and affected every aspect of Chinese life. There was no exception to this trend in the educational system and academic scholarship, including new disciplines such as communication study. In the process of Westernization the traditional cultural identity began to thin out and a new identity was not yet established. For example, in the communication discipline, most instructors in Chinese societies are trained in the West, curricula are designed following the Western model, textbooks adopted in the class are either written by Western scholars or translated from their work, and communication theories lack Chinese cultural components. Transplanting Western communication models into Chinese societies without going through a critical evaluation process will soon be challenged. In other words, the trend of Westernization in the communication discipline will soon run into a difficult situation because of the demand for cultural identity inherent in the trend of globalization.

PROSPECT OF COMMUNICATION STUDY IN CHINESE SOCIETIES

The advent of a new era of telecommunications and human interconnection has introduced a globalizing trend in human society in which people are forced to redefine the meaning of identity, community, and citizenship, and communication educators and scholars everywhere are required to face this impact of globalization. According to Chen (1998) and Chen and Starosta (1996, 1998, 2000), four issues that emerged from the trend of globalization will constantly challenge the communication discipline, including how to build a new sense of community, how to balance the dialectical relationship between cultural identity and cultural diversity, how to deal with the impact of global media, and how to foster citizenship in the global civic society.

A close examination of these potential effects of globalization reveals that the center of problems faced by human beings in the future actually surrounds the movement and counter-movement between two dialectical forces, that is, globalization versus localization, or between cultural diversity and cultural identity. In other words, it is assumed that the success of communication study in Chinese societies in the twenty-first century is dependent on the ability to balance the pulling and pushing forces between globalization and localization. All the problems of communication study Chinese societies face now, including incomplete landscape, skill orientation, lack of collaboration, and Westernization, should be improved and resolved under the umbrella of this assumption.

Globalization versus Localization

Globalization refers to a process of reducing barriers between countries and encouraging a closer interaction in different aspects of human society. The process dissolves the limit of space and time through widespread connectivity and integrates human societies into a global community. It challenges human beings to understand the magnitude and implications of such a powerful and complicated transformation and to learn how to collaboratively take part in shaping a better future world. That is, instead of being an isolated island, people will live in a global network characterized by global connectivity in all levels of our life (Chen & Starosta, 2000).

However, according to Chuang (2000), the process of globalization also reflects a dilemma of a pulling and pushing between local diversity and global identity or between heterogenized local cultures and a homogenized world culture. The dilemma was called "global paradox," indicating that the more globalized the world is, the more powerful its smallest players will be (Naisbitt, 1994). In other words, "globalization not only demands an integration of cultural diversity in the global community, but at the same time also reflects people's needs to develop a strong self or cultural identity(ies)" (Chen & Starosta, 2000, p. 5). How people learn to integrate, negotiate, and co-create diverse cultural identities through communication in order to establish a new global civic community will be the key issue of human education in the future (Boulding, 1988; Collier & Thomas, 1988). In sum, globalization has broken through the boundaries of space, time, and cultural assumptions and the scope, structure, and function of human society. It demands new ways of thinking and organization and opens up new imperatives for investigating every aspect of human life, including the design and content of academic and scholarly activities. The communication discipline in Chinese societies cannot exempt itself from the impact of this demand.

Prospects of Chinese Communication Study

Applying the impact of globalization to communication study in Chinese societies, we see the problems of incomplete landscape, lack of collaboration, and Westernization are typically caused by an inability to balance the dialectical relationship between globalization and localization. These problems lie at the root of misunderstanding the communication discipline in a global level or at the root of protecting personal or group interests in the local market. In other words, in the process of program establishment and curriculum design communication, educators and scholars in Chinese societies only accept the resources and adopt the policies that fit their own perspective. This orientation not only shows the narrow-mindedness and blindness of communication study and education in Chinese societies but also creates a barrier for developing a locally distinctive and a globally ingrained communication program. As to the problem of skill orientation, the neglect of knowledge and theories about the nature, structure, and impact of globalization and localization can only lead communication majors not equipped with a clear perspective on the demands of the new millennium to live and work in a limited space in the society.

To foster the ability to balance the dialectical relationship between globalization and localization, Chinese societies must cultivate a global mindset that demands members of the communication discipline to think globally and act locally. That is, communication study, including education and research, needs to be grounded in the soil of Chinese culture, while its voices are projected to the global context. To achieve this balance a clear goal must be made, that is, connection and cooperation.

More specifically, in order to develop a global mindset, the Chinese communication community must first build connection and cooperation among themselves and then endeavor to harmoniously balance contradictions inherent in the differences and competition between themselves and the world through the process of learning, negotiation, and strategic alliances. Taken together, the prospect of communication study in Chinese societies is founded on the fulfillment of the following four fundamental imperatives through the means of connection and cooperation.

First, the Chinese communication community needs to expand its perspective to a global picture. The Chinese communication community must equip its program, its curriculum design, and its members with a mental ability to scan the world in a broad perspective and always consciously expect new trends and opportunities so that personal, social, and organizational objectives can be achieved in a harmonious way (Gupta & Govindarajan, 1997; Rhinesmith, 1992, 1996). Through the process of observation, competition, cooperation, and exchange with other communication communities in different cultures, the research, education, and policy of communication study in Chinese societies must move like a running river in which the elements of global perspective are its evolving forces. It reflects as well the global trend shared by communities all over the world.

In a nutshell, the internal drive for a broad perspective is the foundation of globalizing Chinese communication study. This demand for globalizing necessarily involves integration of the three dimensions of human ability: affective, cognitive, and behavioral. It begins with a feeling of relatedness to others in the global communication community and then continues with a motivation to broaden our understanding of global phenomena in the communication discipline. It culminates in the construction of working models of relationships on the behavioral level, which leads to the formation of new institutional patterns, including curriculum, program, and policy designs (Boulding, 1988). Moreover, this is a process of molding members in the Chinese communication community into multicultural persons to share a common global space, resources, and opportunities in order to build interdependence with "strangers" who constitute the population of the global communication societies.

Second, the Chinese communication community needs to be knowledgeable enough to balance the contradictions of globalization. The main contradiction of the globalizing process is caused by the pulling force of localization. Localization demands that the Chinese communication community has its roots grounded in the soil of Chinese culture. It is a process for Chinese communication study to define, redefine, invent, and reinvent its own cultural components in a historical sense that forms the identity and characteristics of "Chinese communication study." This especially refers to curriculum design and the building of communication theories from the Chinese cultural perspective. For instance, in addition to communication theories embedded in Western cultural milieu, which components of Chinese culture can be extracted to form a set of explanations regarding the issues, such as the impact of global communication and transportation technology, multiculturalism, and postmodern fragmentation and inconsistency, faced by the global society? Thus, knowing cultural, social, and other similarities and differences not only ensures sound action in localizing Chinese communication study, but also helps to transform members into multicultural persons and maintain a multicultural coexistence in order to develop a global civic culture (P. Adler, 1982; Boulding, 1988; Chen & Starosta, 1997, 1999). This is the level of "glocalization" depicted by Robertson (1995), which describes the dynamics of the local in the global and the global in the local.

Third, the Chinese communication community needs to be flexible enough to flow with and manage changes on the personal and professional levels that are due to the impact of globalization. In addition to cultivating a mindset for global perspective and knowledge for balancing the inherent contradictions between globalization and localization, the abilities for dealing with the impact of globalization need to be nourished. Among them, the ability of cognitive, affective, and behavioral flexibility to ride the wave of globalization on the personal and institutional levels is the cardinal one. In other words, the trend of globalization brings about a dynamic change by breaking through the boundaries of space, time, and human societies. How to educate members of the Chinese communication community, including faculty, staff, and students, to be flexible enough to integrate different cultural identities and interests and to negotiate and co-create cultural identity through communication becomes a critical issue that Chinese communication study must face. Flexibility mirrors a high degree of cognitive complexity, acknowledgment of and respect for cultural differences, and the ability to manage interaction that moves beyond the goals that traditional communication study aimed to achieve. Without the complement of flexibility to flow with the wave and manage changes of globalization, practical communication will prove to be insufficient for members of the Chinese communication community to survive in the globalizing society.

Finally, the Chinese communication community needs to be sensitive and open enough to value diversity for continuous improvement. Engaging in a perpetual learning and improving process to foster sensitivity and openness toward cultural diversity is another ability that members of the Chinese communication community should have. Because globalization brings people of different cultures together in every aspect of communication and life, cross-cultural sensitivity becomes a significant ability for citizens of the Chinese communication community to communicate constructively among one another within their own community and among different communities. The ability not only helps members assert their own identity but also confirm others' identities.

As a prerequisite component for having cross-cultural sensitivity, openness allows members of the Chinese communication community to seek continuous improvements in the constantly changing environment that characterizes the process of globalization. Openness as well provides a strong motivation for continuous learning to deal with cultural differences. It represents the decrease or absence of ethnocentrism and parochialism. Adler (1996, 1997) pointed out that ethnocentric and parochial people are incapable of appreciating cultural diversity, because they are often blinded by their own practice and unable to detect the changes and complexity of globalization trends.

Through the willingness of cooperation, sensitivity and openness function as key abilities in improving the problem of incomplete landscape faced by Chinese communication study. The cooperation and idea exchange among three recently founded Chinese communication associations, The Chinese Communication Association, The Association for Chinese Communication Studies, and The Chinese Communication Society, is a good example. Although the three associations are situated in different geographical areas, their collaboration disintegrates the limit of time and space by drawing, on the one hand, a dynamic picture of demanding independence and self-rule for the study of Chinese communication and, and on the other hand, developing a sound and solid foundation of riding on the wave of globalization. It provides a great opportunity for scholars and practitioners in the global Chinese communication community to prepare and equip their members with necessary knowledge and abilities for a successful and productive participation in the upcoming global society.

To summarize, the future of Chinese communication study must aim to educate its members to become competent citizens in both global and local levels, and the problems faced by Chinese communication study should as well be solved under this framework. By first developing a global mindset, members of the Chinese communication community are enabled to envision the change of world trends and to engage in the process of regulating the change through the abilities of motivating themselves to respect diversity, expecting themselves to reconcile conflict, propelling themselves to regulate change, and orienting themselves to the globalizing process.

Based on this global mindset, the Chinese communication community must equip its members with knowledge or cognitive awareness of its own traditional study or practice of human communication and those from other cultural perspectives in order to integrate them into the flux of globalization. This integrating knowledge in turn will function as the basis for the Chinese communication community to help its members unfold their potentiality by fostering a set of communication abilities, including flexibility, sensitivity, and openness, to manage changes and balance contradictions caused by the dialectical relationship between globalization and localization, and to further become constructive communicators who are able to recognize and assert their own and others' multiple identities on the personal, departmental, community, national, regional, and global levels. Through this effort problems of incomplete landscape, skill orientation, lack of collaboration, and Westernization faced by Chinese communication study and education will be solved with a hope of moving into the new millennium.

CONCLUSION

Using the impact of globalization on human society to examine the problems and prospect of communication study and education in Chinese societies, this chapter starts with the discussion of communication practice in the West and then explicates the traditional Chinese communication study and practice. Through comparisons and observation of Chinese communication study and education in China, Hong Kong, and Taiwan, the author points out four problems faced by the Chinese communication community: incomplete landscape, skill orientation, lack of collaboration, and Westernization. In order to cope with these problems, the author argues that they must be put under the framework of riding on the wave of globalization by leading Chinese communication study and education to accomplish four goals: (1) to establish a global perspective, (2) to cultivate cognitive awareness to balance contradictions caused by the dialectical relationship between globalization and localization, (3) to equip the ability of flexibility to flow with and manage changes due to the impact of globalization, and (4) to foster communication abilities of sensitivity and openness to value diversity for continuous improvement.

REFERENCES

Adler, N. J. (1996). Organizational development in a multicultural environment. *Journal of Applied Behavioral Science, 19,* 349-365.

Adler, N. J. (1997). *International dimensions of organizational behaviors.* Cincinnati: South-Western College.

Adler, P. S. (1982). Beyond cultural identity: Reflections on cultural and multicultural man. In L. A. Samovar and R. E. Porter (Eds.), *Intercultural communication: A reader* (pp. 389-405). Belmont, CA: Wadsworth.

Boulding, E. (1988). *Building a global civic culture.* New York: Teachers College.

Chen, G. M. (1995, November). *A classification of Chinese persuasive communication strategies.* Paper presented at the annual convention of the Speech Communication Association, San Antonio.

Chen, G. M. (1998). Intercultural communication via e-mail debate. *The Edge: The E-Journal of Intercultural Relations, 1(4).* Retrieved November 15, 1998, from the World Wide Web: http://kumo.swcp.com/biz/ theedge/chen.htm.

Chen, G. M. (1999a). An overview of communication theory and research. *Mass Communication Research, 58,* 257-268.

Chen, G. M. (1999b). The prospect of communication education in Chinese societies. *Mass Communication Research, 59,* 179-181.

Chen, G. M., & Starosta, W. J. (1996). Intercultural communication competence: A synthesis. In B. R. Burleson (Ed.), *Communication Yearbook, 19,* 353-384.

Chen, G. M., & Starosta, W. J. (1997). A review of the concept of intercultural sensitivity. *Human Communication, 1,* 1-16.

Chen, G. M., & Starosta, W. J. (1997-8). Chinese conflict management and resolution: Overview and implications. *Intercultural Communication Studies, 7,* 1-16.

Chen, G. M., & Starosta, W. J. (1998). *Foundations of intercultural communication.* Boston: Allyn & Bacon.

Chen, G. M., & Starosta, W. J. (1999). A review of the concept of intercultural awareness. *Human Communication, 2,* 27-54.

Chen, G. M., & Starosta, W. J. (2000). Communication and global society: An introduction. In G. M. Chen and W. J. Starosta (Eds.), *Communication and global society* (pp. 1-17). New York: Peter Lang.

Chen, G. M., & Zhong, M. (2000). Dimensions of Chinese compliance-gaining strategies. *Human Communication, 3,* 97-109.

Chen, S. (2000). Reflections on the first course in communication studies. *Mass Communication Research, 65*, 1-18 .

Chen, S. (2001). An analysis of communication publications in Taiwan over the past 50 years. *Mass Communication Research, 67*, 1-24 .

Chen, T. (1993, June). *An overview and prospect of communication research in Hong Kong.* Paper presented at the conference of Chinese Communication Research and Education. Taipei.

Chesebro, J. (1989). *Pathways to careers in communication.* Annandale, VA: Speech Communication Association.

Chuang, R. (2000). Dialectics of globalization and localization. In G. M. Chen and W. J. Starosta (Eds.), *Communication and global society* (pp. 19-33). New York: Peter Lang.

Collier, M. J., & Thomas, M. (1988). Cultural identity: An interpretive perspective. In Y. Y. Kim & W. B. Gudykunst (Eds.), *Theories in intercultural communication* (pp. 99-120). Newbury Park, CA: Sage.

Delia, J. G. (1987). Communication research: A history. In C. R. Berger & S. H. Chaffee (Eds.), *Handbook of communication science* (pp. 20-98). Beverly Hills, CA: Sage.

Fong, P. C. (1975). *The persuasion study of pre-Chin's he zong and lian heng.* Taipei: Shan Wu.

Gupta, A. K., & Govindarajan, V. (1997). *Quest for global dominance: Building global presence* [on line]. Available: http//www.bmgt.umd.edu/cib/wplist.htm/.

Han, F. (1978). *Essays of Han Fei Tze.* Taipei: Pu Tian.

Heisey, D. R. (Ed.). (2000). *Chinese perspectives in rhetoric and communication.* Stamford, CT: Ablex.

Huang, J. K. (1997). Communication concepts in the ancient Chinese culture. In X. P. Sun (Ed.), *Essays on Chinese communication* (pp. 21-32). Beijing: People's Press.

Infante, D. A, Rancer, A. S., & Womack, E. F. (1996). *Building communication theory.* Prospect Heights, IL: Waveland.

Littlejohn, S. W. (1982). An overview of contributions to human communication theory from other disciplines. In F. E. X. Dance (Ed.), *Human communication theory* (pp. 243-285). New York: Harper & Row.

Littlejohn, S. W. (1998). *Theories of human communication.* Belmont, CA: Wadsworth.

Liu, H. K. (1993, June). *An overview and prospect of communication research in Mainland China.* Paper presented at the conference of Chinese Communication Research and Education. Taipei.

Lu, X. (1998). *Rhetoric in ancient China, fifth to third century B.X.E.: A comparison with classical Greek rhetoric.* Columbia: University of South Carolina Press.

Naisbitt, J. (1994). *Global paradox.* New York: Aven.

Oliver, R. (1971). *Communication and culture in ancient India and China.* New York: Syracuse University.

Rhinesmith, S. H. (1992). Global mindsets for global managers. *Training & Development*, October, 63-68.

Rhinesmith, S. H. (1996). *A manager's guide to globalization.* Irwin, IL:University of Chicago.

Robertson, R. (1995). Glocalization: Time-space and homogeneity-heterogeneity. In M. Featherstone, S. Lash, and R. Robertson (Eds.), *Global modernities* (pp. 25-44). Thousand Oaks, CA: Sage.

Smith, M. J. (1988). *Contemporary communication research methods.* Belmont, CA: Wadsworth.

Sun, S. P. (1993, June). *An overview and prospect of communication research in Mainland China.* Paper presented at the conference of Chinese Communication Research and Education. Taipei.

Wong, C., & Zang, G. (1993, June). *An overview and prospect of communication research in Taiwan.* Paper presented at the conference of Chinese Communication Research and Education. Taipei.

Wright, A. F. (1979). Chinese civilization. In H. D. Lasswell, D. Lerner, & H. Speier (Eds.), *Propaganda and communication in world history.* Honolulu: The University of Hawaii.

Wu, D. C. (1991). *Oral communication in the pre-Chin period.* Taipei: The Cultural Committee of Administration Yuan.

Zarefsky, D. (1995). On defining the communication discipline. In J. T. Wood and R. B. Gregg (Eds.), *Toward the twenty-first century: The future of speech communication.* Cresskill, NJ: Hampton.

Index

About the Editors and Contributors

WENSHAN JIA is an assistant professor of communication in the Department of Communication and Media, State University of New York at New Paltz. His is the author of *The Remaking of the Chinese Character and Identity in the 21st Century: The Chinese Face Practices* (Ablex, 2001) and several articles/book chapters on communication and culture. During his graduate studies, he was selected as a member of the National Communication Association's Doctoral Honors Seminar (1998) and chosen as a top-paper presenter at the 1995 NCA Annual Convention. He is a member of the Editorial Board of *The American Review of China Studies*. His primary research interest is (inter)cultural communication theory grounded in the East and West context.

XING LU is an associate professor in the Department of Communication of DePaul University. Her academic interests include Chinese rhetoric, intercultural communication, language and culture, and Asian-American communication. She has published articles in *The Western Journal of Communication*, *The Howard Journal of Communication, Discourse and Society,* and *Intercultural Communication Studies*. Her book *Rhetoric in Ancient China, Fifth to Third Century B.C.E.: A Comparison with Classical Greek Rhetoric* (1998) won the Winans-Wichelns Memorial Award for Distinguished Scholarship in Rhetoric and Public Address from the National Communication Association.

D. RAY HEISEY is a professor and director emeritus of the School of Communication Studies, Kent State University. He taught rhetorical criticism and intercultural communication at Kent State University from 1966 until his retirement in 1996. He served as president, Damavand College, Tehran, Iran, from 1975 to 1978 and as visiting professor of international communication at universities in Belgium, Sweden, and twice in China at Peking University (1996 and 2000). He has published in the *Quarterly Journal of Speech, Communication Monographs, Southern Communication Journal, World Communication*, and *The Journal of Communication and Religion*. He co-edited, with Wenxiang Gong, *Communication and Culture: China and the World Entering the 21st Century* (1998) and edited *Chinese Perspectives in Rhetoric and Communication* (2000).

DEBORAH A. CAI is an associate professor in the Department of Communication at the University of Maryland at College Park. As an international researcher with ties to China, her scholarly interests center on intercultural communication, negotiation, and conflict management. Her past works examine cultural differences in negotiation plans, enactment of face-management strategies, and the mediating effects of role on culture in business negotiation. Her research has been presented at national and international conferences and is published in places such as *Communication Monographs, Communication Yearbook, Human Communication Research, Journal of Applied Communication*, and *Asian Journal of Communication*.

GUO-MING CHEN is a professor of communication studies at the University of Rhode Island. Chen is the recipient of the NCA-IICD 1987 Outstanding Dissertation Award and the founding president of the Association for Chinese Communication Studies and the recipient of the Outstanding Research Award from the University of Rhode Island. His primary research interest is intercultural/global communication. He has presented more than 60 papers and published numerous journal articles, books, book chapters, and essays.

YANRU CHEN currently teaches in China's first-ever communications department at Xiamen University. Her main research interests are development communication, Chinese communication, intercultural communication, and women's image and social problems in the media. In addition to several book chapters, she has published in *Journal of International Communication, Intercultural Communication Studies, Journal of Development of Communication, Asian Journal of Communication, Media Asia, Journal of Popular Film & Television*, and *Journal of the Northwest Communication Association*.

RUEYLING CHUANG is an assistant professor in the Department of Speech Communication, California State University, San Bernadino. Her work appears in *The Southern Journal of Communication, Free Speech Yearbook,*

Gazette: The International Journal for Communication Studies, and other publications. Her major areas of interest include intercultural communication, interpersonal communication, organizational communication, language and culture, conflict resolution, and Chinese communication.

GE GAO is an associate professor in the Department of Communication Studies at San Jose State University, California. Her recent work includes *Communicating Effectively with the Chinese* (with Stella Ting-Toomey; Sage, 1998) and "An initial analysis of the effects of face and concern for 'other' in Chinese interpersonal communication" in *International Journal of Intercultural Relations* (1998).

ZHIHONG GAO is a Ph.D. candidate at the Institute of Communication Research, University of Illinois at Urbana-Champaign. His major research interest is Chinese advertising.

CLAUDIA L. HALE is a professor of communication with the School of Interpersonal Communication, Ohio University. Her research interests center on the relationship between social cognition and communication competence, particularly in situations involving conflict, negotiation, and/or dispute mediation. Her work has been published in *Communication Monographs*, *Discourse and Society*, *Health Communication*, and *Mediation Quarterly*, among others.

JOHN C. HWANG is a professor of communication in the Department of Communication Studies, California State University, Sacramento. He has published *Bookman's Concise Handbook of Rhetoric and Language* (first author) and *Oral Communication: Theory and Practice of Public Speaking*. His research interests are ethnic studies and Chinese communication studies.

RINGO MA is a professor of communication at the State University of New York, Fredonia. He is currently an associate editor of the *Quarterly Journal of Speech, and* his major research area is communication and culture in East Asia and North America. He has contributed articles to *International and Intercultural Communication Annual, Communication Quarterly, Southern Communication Journal, World Communication, Journal of Pragmatics, New Jersey Journal of Communication*, and *Journal of Asian and African Studies*.

VIRGINIA MANSFIELD-RICHARDSON is associate dean of the Roy H. Park School of Communication at Ithaca College in New York. Her research interests are logographic language cognition, media coverage of Asian Americans, and the Asian language media in the United States. She speaks and writes Chinese at an intermediate level and has conducted other research on Asian media. She has published *Asian Americans and the Mass Media* (Garland, 2000) and is currently working on two books on the history of media coverage of Asian Americans for Greenwood. She is also the author of an entry on Asian-American media in *History of the Mass Media in the United States: An Encyclopedia*, and she wrote the chapter on Asian Americans in *News Coverage of Racial Minorities: A Sourcebook, 1934-Present*. Dr. Mansfield-Richardson has presented numerous scholarly papers on Asian-American issues, the Chinese language, and the early press in China.

JOHN H. POWERS is an associate professor in the Department of Communication Studies, Hong Kong Baptist University. He has published in *Intercultural Communication Studies* and *Communication Education*. He published *Civic Discourse, Civil Society and Chinese Communities* (co-edited with Randy Kluver, 1999). His major areas of research are communication theory, Chinese communication, and Western rhetoric.

JAMES JINGUO SHEN is an assistant professor of communication and the coordinator of the Communication Program at the Richard Stockton College of New Jersey. His research interest includes international/intercultural communication, telecommunications, and critical cultural studies. His major publications include "Dual Cultural Reading and Televisual Experience of Chinese Students in the United States" in *Communication Studies in Mainland China* (Taipei, National Chengchi University Press, 1995), and "The Rise and Fall of *The World Economic Herald*, 1980-1989" in *Journalism and Mass Communication Quarterly*.

ZHENBIN SUN is an assistant professor of communication at the Fairleigh Dickinson University School of Communication Arts. He is primarily interested in Chinese and Western theories of language and has published papers in this area. Currently he is working on Nietzsche's philosophy of language.

LEAH WAKS is a lecturer and director of undergraduate studies in the Department of Communication at the University of Maryland at College Park. She combines communication education, mediation, and conflict management training in organizations. Her primary interest is studying how social cognitions interact with affect in communication behavior and how they impact individuals' quality of life and organizational culture.

JIANGLONG WANG is a professor of communication in the Department of Communication, Western Washington University, where he teaches courses in intercultural communication, interpersonal communication, and communication campaigns. His research interests focus on intercultural/international communication, Chinese culture and communication, Chinese communication campaigns, and teaching and learning as non-native speakers in North America. Wang's recent research has appeared in *Intercultural*

Communication Studies, Howard Journal of Communication, and *World Communication,* among others.

MEI-LING WANG is an associate professor of communication at the University of the Sciences in Philadelphia. She has published *The Dust That Never Settles: The Taiwan Independence Movement and U.S.–China Relations.* She has also published in *Asian Journal of Communication.* Her current research areas focus on health, development, culture, and communication.

XIAOSUI XIAO is an assistant professor in the Department of Communication Studies, Hong Kong Baptist University, where he teaches courses in rhetoric and media criticism. He has published in the *Quarterly Journal of Speech, Rhetoric Society Quarterly,* and *Communication and Culture.* His research areas include intercultural rhetoric, political communication, and media discourse.

DATE DUE			